Reluctant Refuge

RELUCTANT REFUGE

UNACCOMPANIED REFUGEE AND
EVACUEE CHILDREN IN AUSTRALIA
1933-45

GLEN PALMER

Kangaroo Press

ABBREVIATIONS

AA Australian Archives; AIF Australian Imperial Force; AJCP Australian Joint Copying Project; AJWS Australian Jewish Welfare Society; AMF Australian Military Force; BOAS British Orphans Adoption Society; CAC Civil Alien Corps; CBF Central British Fund (for World Jewish Relief); CGJ Council for German Jewry; CORB Children's Overseas Reception Board; CPA Comprehensive Plan of Action; GEFC German Emergency Fellowship Committee; JDC Joint Distribution Committee; ORT Organisation and Rehabilitation through Training; OSE Abbreviation of a Russian term meaning Jewish Health Society; PJRF Polish Jewish Relief Fund; PRO Public Record Office; RAAF Royal Australian Air Force; SCF Save the Children Fund; UNRRA United Nations Relief and Rehabilitation Administration; VAD Voluntary Aid Detachment; WIZO Women's International Zionist Organisation; YMCA Young Men's Christian Association

NOTE ON NAMES

The names of European child refugees were regularly Anglicised on arrival in Australia. As these names were often adopted permanently, they have been used throughout the book.

The maiden names of female child evacuees and refugees have also been retained throughout.

COVER PHOTOS

Jewish refugee children en route to Australia, 1939. For names see page 53.

Travel documents of Ellen Shafer (née Rothschild), issued in Germany with a visa for Australia attached. The date stamps tell the story: Ellen's mother organised Ellen's passport before the November pogrom, Kristallnacht, and long before the Australian government agreed to admit a quota of German Jewish children. The passport was issued in Kassel on 4 August 1938. Ellen's landing permit for Australia was approved by Canberra on 21 April 1939.

© **Glen Palmer 1997**

First published in 1997 by Kangaroo Press
an imprint of Simon & Schuster Australia
20 Barcoo Street (P.O. Box 507)
East Roseville NSW 2069 Australia
Printed by South Wind Production, Singapore

ISBN 0 86417 858 1

Contents

Acknowledgments **6**
Introduction **7**

1. Who Will Take My Child? **12**
2. Unwanted Gifts **29**
3. Children from Germany **41**
4. The Lottery of Life **55**
5. Room, and Welcome **71**
6. Rescue Attempts **95**
7. Larino **103**
8. Borrowed Families **129**
9. No Time for Childhood **148**
10. Going Home **164**

Conclusion **182**
Appendices **199**
Notes **211**
Bibliography **226**
Index **236**

Acknowledgments

So many people contributed to this book. My foremost debt is to the many now-adult child refugees and evacuees who recounted their pasts and gave me access to photographs, diaries, letters and other artefacts from that period. I also wish to acknowledge those who were involved with child refugees and evacuees, as matrons, escorts and in other capacities, and who also generously shared their memories and artefacts.

My interest in this story began over a decade ago. While working for the Kindergarten Union of South Australia, I became intrigued with the story of former employee, Doris Beeston, who escorted British evacuee children to Australia in 1940, and who died on the return journey to England. After investigating her story, and that of British children evacuated to Australia during World War Two, I felt impelled to search further. What about non-British children? What about Jewish children who needed refuge in that period? How did Australia respond to them?

My investigations into these and other questions were assisted by numerous individuals and organisations. Some of those contacts unwittingly charted the research into new waters; for example, Sophie Caplan who directed me to Jonas Pushett, my threshold for the story of the Polish Jewish youths who came to Australia in 1939; Helen Bersten of the Australian Jewish Historical Society, Sydney who helped me find initial clues to the Larino story. Others who provided advice, encouragement and information at various stages of the research included Anne Andgel, Paul Bartrop, Beryl Daley, Richard Dreyfus, Paul Farquharson, Hedi Fixel, Tony Hamilton-Smith, Dorothy Hughes, Aleck Katz, Isabella Lupton, Ursula Meyerstein, Suzanne Rutland, Ellen Shafer and Joyce Turnbull.

The cooperation of people in a wide range of archives, libraries, and organisations in Australia, England and Israel is also acknowledged: they include Moira Smythe, Australian Archives, Canberra; Dan Midalia, Australian Archives, Perth; Beverley Davis, Australian Jewish Historical Society, Melbourne; Marianne Dacey, Archive of Australian Judaica; Yehuda Dayag, Jerusalem office of the Zionist Federation of Australia; Steve Denenberg, Australian Jewish Welfare Society, Sydney; Laurence Joseph, Australian Jewish Welfare Society, Melbourne; Flora Rich, Australian Jewish Welfare Society, Perth; Brian McLure, State Library of Victoria; Rodney Breen, Save the Children, London; Josef Keith, Library of the Religious Society of Friends, London; Yossel Birstein, Givat Ram University, Jerusalem; Shlomo Mayer, Leo Baeck Institute, Jerusalem; Hadassah Modlinger, Yad Vashem Archives, Jerusalem. I wish also to acknowledge those who gave me special access to material: Andrew Duguid, child welfare records in South Australia; Michael John, Children's Overseas Reception Board files for Victoria; Ruth Haig, records of the Religious Society of Friends, Sydney; Margaret Gutman, records of the Jewish Board of Deputies; Jeremy Jones, records of the Executive Council of Australian Jewry; Film Australia, interview notes of Avivah Ziegler; David Massel, records of the Board of Deputies of British Jews, London.

This book began as a doctoral thesis under the supervision of Australian historian, Bill Gammage. My thanks to Bill for his support and encouragement. Thanks also to Margarita Luka and Lois Zweck for the many translations from German to English, and to Julianne Cleworth and Gabrielle Matthews for help in transcribing the interviews.

My partner, Bob Anderson, helped in countless ways, sharing some of the interviews and the ongoing relationships they have forged. I would particularly like to mention Bob's assistance with photography and with the onerous task of indexing this volume.

Research of this nature is costly. Grants from the Australian War Memorial and the University of South Australia were of immense support. Thankyou to those institutions and to my publisher, Kangaroo Press, for believing in the project, and for their contribution to recording this story for posterity.

INTRODUCTION

Children have always been the innocent victims of adult wars. As Eglantyne Jebb observed in the aftermath of the First World War, 'Every war is a war against the child'. The suffering of children throughout famine and war-stricken Europe prompted this educated English woman to campaign for global responsibility for children. 'If children of any country are physically or morally abandoned, the whole world loses by it. And the whole world gains if children grow up healthy, capable and ready to work for the good of their neighbour.'[1] In 1919 Eglantyne Jebb established Save the Children Fund, the first of the modern development agencies. Committees quickly spread throughout the world, united by an international body in Geneva. In 1924, through the efforts of Eglantyne Jebb and Save the Children Fund International Union, the League of Nations endorsed the first international treaty on the rights of the child:

> By the present Declaration of the Rights of the Child, commonly known as the Declaration of Geneva, men and women of all nations, recognising that mankind owes to the child the best that it has to give, declare and accept it as their duty that, beyond and above all considerations of race, nationality or creed:
>
> 1. The child should be given the means needed for its normal development, both materially and spiritually.
> 2. The child that is hungry should be fed; the child that is sick should be nursed; the child that is backward should be helped; the erring child should be reclaimed; and the orphan and the waif should be sheltered and succoured.
> 3. The child should be the first to receive relief in times of distress.
> 4. The child should be put in a position to earn a livelihood and should be protected against every form of exploitation.
> 5. The child should be brought up in the consciousness that its talents are to be used in the service of its fellow men.

At meetings held around the world, large numbers of people signed the declaration. In 1930, at the Imperial Conference in London, prime ministers of several dominions appended their signatures to a copy of the document, among them James Scullin of Australia. As a signatory, Scullin agreed to the relief and protection of all children under sixteen 'in times of distress [regardless of] race, nationality or creed'. That agreement was sorely tested in the following decade and during the Second World War.

★ ★ ★

Millions of children died during that war, victims of both the war and related atrocities. Countless others were physically maimed or psychologically scarred. For many the suffering began long before September 1939, at a time when the global community could have offered considerable relief and protection. Australia was one of many countries called upon in those years, and during the war, to offer refuge to children, especially European children. This book is about those children and Australia's response to them. It is confined to those under sixteen, that being the definition of 'child' used in the 1924 Declaration of Geneva

The story begins in Germany in 1933 with the accession to government of Adolf Hitler and the National Socialist Party. This was the event which ultimately created the need for overseas refuge for children from both the Continent and Britain. As doors closed on families wanting to emigrate, parents grasped at opportunities to remove their children, including by 1938, young children.

By 1938 Australia was well placed to admit child and youth refugees. Immigration had resumed and, with it, a renewed interest in child migration. While the refugee crisis was being played out in the late 1930s, numerous British child and youth migrants arrived in Australia. Yet the doors closed on foreign children needing refuge. Small concessions were made, but the response lacked any sense of urgency or any commitment to rescue. The number of unaccompanied refugee children and youth admitted to Australia through group schemes was pitifully small — less than fifty under sixteen years of age.

Pressure to help children did not cease with the outbreak of war, although opportunities to remove children from Continental Europe diminished greatly. Australia was involved in a number of aborted ventures during the war. These reveal little change in the official attitude to foreign children, even after knowledge of atrocities in Europe became public. Unaccompanied children who arrived in Australia during the war came mainly from Britain, with a small number from Asian and Pacific countries involved in the war with Japan. The Australian government adopted a more flexible approach when dealing with the crisis in the Pacific. Nevertheless, children admitted to Australia from neighbouring countries were mostly British and most came with their mothers. There was no organised scheme to move them to Australia alone. Those who arrived unaccompanied came through private arrangements or left in the scramble that occurred as the Japanese advanced.

From the first rumblings of war, various dominions, including Australia, put forward schemes for transferring British children overseas. The Australian government saw the war as an opportunity to revitalise British child migration and, with an invasion seemingly imminent, the British government approved a children's overseas evacuation scheme in June 1940. This was despite Churchill's aversion to evacuation, which he described as running away 'like rats from a sinking ship'. The Australian government was elated with the news. Although the scheme planned was for evacuation for the duration of the war, overtones of migration pervaded announcements and correspondence relating to it. Fearing the worst, British parents flocked to register their children for overseas evacuation, just as parents on the Continent had earlier grasped at opportunities to remove their children to safety. Although the Dominions Office initially held the position that alien children then in England would have priority, intervention by Prime Minister Menzies ensured that foreign children were not included among evacuees to Australia.

This book inevitably raises many questions about the separation and care of children. Recent publicity on British child migration has tended to taint all long-term separation and to foreclose debate on the topic. The stories of these children, whose parents voluntarily sent them away under emergency conditions, throw another perspective on separation. Their experiences and the effects of their separation and substitute care varied greatly; they provide valuable information on the needs of separated children and on factors which determine children's ability to cope with separation. At the same time, their stories reinforce the importance of family to children's well-being and reveal that many separated children, although spared the horrors of war, endured considerable emotional suffering and stress as a result of separation and inadequate substitute care. For Jewish children this acknowledgment is particularly important as, in the aftermath of the Holocaust, little attention was paid to the experiences of children who escaped overseas before the war. Because they were neither in concentration camps nor in hiding, their experiences were generally overlooked. As one informant commented, when she is with concentration camp survivors she sums up her history in a few words — 'Germany, Australia, America and then I came here [Israel]'. Only in recent years have the stories of these children begun to unfold. Studies have emerged of children who went to Britain and the United States before or during the war, but Australia's response to refugee children, and the experiences of those who came to Australia, have not previously been recorded.

By focusing on children, this book makes an important contribution to the literature on Australia and refugees between 1933 and 1945. Children are noticeably absent from the general histories of war, yet their experiences contribute another dimension to the overall picture. Not only do they highlight the negative impact and futility of war, their stories also convey much about the human condition. Martin Gilbert, whose writings are fine examples of the integration of the human story into the narrative of war, claimed that 'Every historian can, if he wishes, tell the human story of mankind, to find examples that can touch the soul of every person as well as illuminate an argument or theory'.[2] Children's stories add that human dimension.

There is value in telling the stories separately, but the integration of the stories of evacuee and refugee children adds immensely to both the individual stories and to the collective story of Australia and unaccompanied children. The value of this approach became increasingly obvious during the interviews. Few of the participants knew about other unaccompanied children who came to Australia. The collective story will allow them to see their personal experience within a broader context.

Using the testimonies of adults for information on their childhood raises a number of issues. What is remembered is not just affected by the passage of time, but can be skewed by the age and intellectual development of the child at the time of the event. Since effective retrieval depends largely on successful storage in the first place, young children's limited ability to use memory strategies and to understand abstract ideas inevitably affects the nature of the memory that is retained. These factors explain the limited recall of events experienced in early childhood. However, they do not explain the rich cameos of early childhood experience which often survive in memory despite a general haze. What enables even very young children to store these memories and how reliable are the memories?

Paul Thompson, who has focused on the social context of memory, suggests that material is more likely to be stored and recalled if it meets a social interest and need, if it concerns people and has been periodically recalled. Highly emotional, novel or meaningful experiences are also more likely to be committed to memory.[3] Given its social context, memory is rarely static. The reconstruction of a personal experience often includes details gleaned from hearsay, assumption, speculation, reading and discussion with others who shared the experience. This phenomenon is not peculiar to memories of childhood, but can be expected from informants giving evidence on any event about which their personal knowledge is limited. George Dreyfus, who left Germany for Australia at age ten, commented astutely on this factor: 'I fantasise and romanticise a lot because people ask me for stories ... then you start making them up. It's not a matter of forgetting the truth. You don't know the truth.' People reconstruct and retell their pasts in styles as varied as writers. George's romantic style matched his rather maverick personality.

Others were meticulous about trying to separate what they know now from what they actually experienced.

Traumatic, highly emotional experiences can leave eidetic images on the mind, regardless of age. The reverse effect, total repression, can also occur. Italian Holocaust survivor Primo Levi wrote in *Moments of Reprieve*:

> It has been noted by psychologists that the survivors of traumatic events are divided into two well-defined groups: those who repress their past *en bloc,* and those whose memory of the offence persists, as though carved in stone, prevailing over all previous or subsequent experiences ... Not by choice but by nature I belong to the second group. Of my two years of life outside the law I have not forgotten a single thing. Without any deliberate effort, memory continues to restore to me events, faces, words, sensations, as if at that time my mind had gone through a period of exalted receptivity, during which not a detail was lost.

Children experienced a similar phenomenon. Informants described extraordinarily vivid images — a parent's face and behaviour at the time of departure, fearful experiences when their homes or families were attacked — and events which, perhaps not significant to adults, were exceptionally meaningful or painful to them as children — a treasured gift being taken away, mean or unfair treatment which was incomprehensible at the time.

What is remembered, emphasised and suppressed in a testimony of childhood experiences provides a window on the experiences which deeply affected the informant. Patterns which emerged from interviews for this book provided information that could not otherwise have been gathered. A number of interviewees reflected on the apparent distortion in their memories. Ken Gregory, a British evacuee, commented, 'You can take the unhappy part of it and magnify it and convince yourself later on that you were always unhappy, but you weren't necessarily.'

Margot Goldstein's (now Herschenbaum) letters to her family in Germany suggest she missed her family greatly but was relatively settled in the home in Melbourne: 'I am well and everything is fine with me.' The matrons added comments to her letters. Reading these, Margot reflected, 'I must have been very cheerful because all these letters say "She is very cheerful and she makes everybody laugh" ... I think I was. I don't think I was unhappy all the time.' Yet the pervasive memory for Margot is one of deep unhappiness. 'When I look back on it I don't remember being happy. I don't have happy recollections of any particular incident in Australia.' The preoccupation of an adult with lost families and opportunities may obscure happier times, but in doing so it becomes a powerful statement about the impact of the loss on the child and the persistent effects of that loss throughout life.

Oral history is thus an invaluable source for information on childhood experiences. Its potential for misinterpretation is probably no greater than for any other source, nor for many statistical methods of data gathering. It remains for the historian to apply to it the usual rigours of research.

Oral evidence was by no means the only source used for this book, nor was it always the most appropriate. Sometimes oral history played a very subordinate role to other sources. For information on requests for Australia to help refugee children, and on Australia's response, government and non-government records were major sources. A wide variety of archival records in Australia, England and Israel were used for this purpose. Information on Nazi Europe and wartime Britain also came largely from original documents and from published sources. Archived oral testimonies of children were occasionally used, although generally citations of children's experiences came from first-hand accounts collected through interviews and written testimony. A notable exception was data on some British evacuees gained through special access to child welfare records in various Australian states. These were an invaluable primary source, supplementing information gathered through interviews and other government records. Under the terms of access, the identities of evacuees whose records I viewed have not been disclosed, unless permission was given by the individual concerned.

Informants contributed an amazing array of documents, photographs and other original records, including letters and diaries. Many of these were written originally in German, some in Yiddish. The letters are particularly noteworthy as they convey an immediacy that transports the reader to another time and place. They also provide a unique glimpse of children's families and parent–child relationships, and the emotional trauma for parents in sending away their children. While a number of informants had saved letters from parents, the recovery of children's letters to parents was more extraordinary. For this to happen in Nazi Europe other people had to be involved. Margot Goldstein is not sure how her letters survived, but after the war a cousin recovered them from a gentile neighbour. 'My cousin found this box with all kinds of letters and a few photos.' A few weeks before meeting me in London, Freda Morgan (now Welsh) also recovered family letters. They were discovered in a farm shed in Australia by the foster family with whom she had lived for five years.

It has been gratifying while conducting this research to have been able to return pieces of the past to those searching and researching their history. It has emphasised the two-way process of oral history. The collective history woven from the threads of oral evidence and documented sources acknowledges individual experience and uses their evidence to illustrate the story of Australia's involvement with unaccompanied children between 1933 and 1945. Paul Thompson wrote that 'one of the deepest lessons of oral history is the uniqueness, as well as representativeness, of every life story.'[4] In that respect, these children speak for all children, both in the past and the present, who are victims of war, persecution and inhumanity, and of government indifference to their rights.

1

Who will take my child?

17 June 1939: Tilbury Docks, London

From dawn they gathered in the dockland shelter, waiting to board the ship. Sounds of Polish, Czech, German and Yiddish filled the air, reassuring those still arriving. The sight overwhelmed Harry Hurwitz, their interpreter. 'I shall never forget my first sight of them,' he wrote, 'standing there forlornly in the misty morning light. For the first time I realised the poignant tragedy of the refugees' plight. Here, surrounded by all they possessed in the world, were the victims of dictator politics.'

In a nearby dock the Orama was being prepared for a late morning departure. It had travelled the 12 000 miles to Australia many times, returning always for another human cargo. But for the two hundred or so refugees gathered in the shelter there was no thought of return. Australia offered them a new beginning, far removed from the oppression which had destroyed their former lives.

They were all ages — men, women and children. A ninety-two-year-old from Danzig defied all stereotypes. She was preparing to start life afresh with a son she had not seen for forty years. There were many adolescents, including a group of sixteen Austrians and Germans being farewelled by the Society of Friends. A party of seventeen young Jewish children had also gathered. Several days earlier they had left their families in Germany, part of a wave of children being sent to safety by distraught parents. The offer of refuge in Australia had given the parents of these seventeen a ray of hope, one they snatched in relief and anguish. They farewelled their children with promises of speedy reunions, neither they nor their children realising the enormity of the separation which then began. The children would pay heavily for the privilege of being rescued. One child refugee later commented, 'Their share of the Jewish fate had not been left behind but was the refugee life facing them.'[1] *Now, as they waited to board the Orama, the sadness of parting was tinged with the excitement of the moment, and thoughts of the journey ahead.*

* * *

The familiar world began disintegrating for these children, their parents and millions like them on 30 January 1933 when Adolf Hitler was appointed Chancellor of Germany. Anti-Jewish ideas, central to Hitler's vision of a greater Germany, were now sanctioned and began permeating every aspect of life. As Hitler consolidated his position in the following months, acts of violence against Jews and political opponents became rampant. Nevertheless, Hitler preferred controlled violence to wanton thuggery:

> I always go as far as I dare and never further. It is vital to have a sixth sense which tells you broadly what you can and cannot do (hearty laughter and applause). Even in a struggle with an adversary it is not my way to issue a direct challenge to a trial of strength. I do not say, 'Come and fight because I want a fight'; instead I shout at him, and I shout louder and louder, 'I mean to destroy you'. Then I use my intelligence to help me to manoeuvre him into a tight corner so that he cannot strike back, and then I deliver the fatal blow. That is how it is (shouts of Bravo).[2]

In Germany he delivered escalating blows in calculated measures over a number of years. In annexed and occupied territories the blows were usually dealt in swift succession, but always with the same intent — to remove the Jews, and other undesirables, one way or another.

Within weeks of the victorious March 1933 election, Hitler made his first tactical move against Jews and political opponents, passing legislation dismissing non-Aryan civil servants, both clerical and professional. According to the legislation, 'A person is to be considered non-Aryan if he is descended from non-Aryan, and especially from Jewish parents or grandparents. It is sufficient if one parent or grandparent is non-Aryan. This is to be assumed in particular where one parent or grandparent was of the Jewish religion.' Dismissals also applied to those suspected of political deviancy: 'Civil servants whose previous political activities afford no assurance that they will at all times give their fullest support to the national State, can be dismissed from the service'.[3]

Therefore, while Jews in particular were marked for persecution under the National Socialist regime others also were victimised. From the beginning, political opponents figured prominently among these, but over time a range of those considered 'Aryan', but vagrants or anti-social, were also included — gypsies, homosexuals, prostitutes and the disabled. Exempted from dismissal at this stage were those who had been in office on 1 August 1914, who had fought at the front during World War I, or whose fathers or sons had been killed in the war.

Legislation aimed specifically at children was also introduced in 1933. It limited the non-Aryan enrolment in secondary schools and places of higher education to 1.5 per cent of the total intake. Again, a war clause was included for those whose fathers had fought at the front. These exemptions were removed in 1935.

While this legislation appeased many Germans, restraining party terror at the local level was extremely difficult. Local authorities often initiated boycotts and discriminatory practices and either induced or ignored outbreaks of mob terror. A frenzy of hate and violence erupted in March 1935, following which Jews throughout Germany were barred from many public places — theatres, swimming pools, cinemas, resorts — and numerous businesses were boycotted and violated. Hitler responded by giving the hard core of the party the legislation they had long been seeking — laws connecting blood and race to citizenship.

The first of these laws, the Law for the Protection of German Blood and German Honour, promulgated in Nuremberg in September 1935, forbad sexual relations and marriage between Jews and 'subjects of German or kindred blood'. Included in this law was a restriction on German women under forty-five being employed in Jewish households. Ideas regarding the purification of the German race, and its supremacy, were as central to Nazi dogma, and as ingrained in the German psyche, as anti-semitism. The laws were generally accepted with indifference, occasionally with eagerness, by the majority of Germans.

The second Nuremberg Law, the Reich Citizenship Law, provided the legal link between racial purity and citizenship: 'A Jew cannot be a Reich citizen. He is not entitled to the right to vote on political matters; he cannot hold public office.' Definitions of Jews were further refined within this legislation, thereby creating another category of citizen, the Mischling, or person of hybrid race. The Mischling was to remain in a precarious position throughout the Third Reich, though ultimately being a Mischling of the second degree (one Jewish grandparent) meant the difference between life and death. Civil rights were also removed from anyone unable to prove 'he was willing and able loyally to serve the German people and the Reich'.

With the passing of the Nuremberg Laws the German Jewish community became a ghetto without walls, 'cut off from economic as well as from social and intellectual contact with the general community.'[4] Social contact with Germans was now illegal and removal to concentration camp became a common

German identity card issued by the Third Reich when a child turned seven. The large 'J' indicates the bearer of the card, Lothar Siegesmund Israel Badrian, is Jewish. The writing above the Nazi stamp states that Lothar's mother is his guardian. Above that, to the right, are two boxes for fingerprints. The handwritten note states that these are not required because of his age. (Laurie [formerly Lothar] Badrian)

punishment for those caught breaching the rules. The 1935 legislation also accelerated the economic destruction of German Jewry. While many Jewish traders continued in business, boycotts and violation of their property forced the majority to liquidate their businesses or sell to Aryans. In 1938 expropriation became compulsory, and the final expulsion of Jews from economic life began.

In the face of Nazi oppression, the Jewish community responded with organisational solidarity. In 1933 it set up the Reichsvertretung der Juden in Deutschland (the National Organisation of German Jews), with Leo Baeck as its head, to coordinate Jewish communities and organisations in Germany. With the impoverishment of the Jewish community, the Reichsvertretung relied heavily on the philanthropy of American and British Jews — the Joint Distribution Committee in America and the Central British Fund in England. Even with this injection of funds, meeting the spiralling welfare needs was impossible. In 1937 its welfare arm, the Zentralausschuss (the Central Committee for Relief and Reconstruction), highlighted its inability 'to meet even extremely urgent requests' in provincial towns. Many of the new applicants had 'hitherto been able to earn their living with a pedlar's licence [but] were now deprived of this because they were unable to renew the licence'.[5] The demand for relief was exacerbated by the need to 'embrace all those within the Reich who are Jews within the meaning of the Reich Citizenship Law.'[6]

Families fled in droves from provincial towns, searching for the greater security, opportunities and services offered in the cities. Abraham Margaliot wrote of the massive internal movement of Jews in Germany in those years. In 1936, 10 000 moved from smaller settlements to large cities where 'it was easier to obtain work, and where they could find moral support within the large Jewish communities.'[7] 'As the largest Jewish community with the greatest number of welfare offices and social institutions of all kinds, Berlin [was] an especially attractive goal.'[8] In Berlin people also had better opportunities for organising emigration.

These were years of overwhelming insecurity for Jewish children — seeing, hearing, experiencing the injustice and hatred, but not comprehending it.

> I was too young to understand what it was all about, but I knew that something bad had happened. Then I began to experience the first anti-semitic utterings. A fellow pupil in the small private school which I attended would snatch the sponge from me as I was about to wipe the blackboard, and say: 'Don't let the Jew have the sponge'. Or children would spit at me in the street and call me a 'dirty Jew'. Since there had been so little accent on our Jewishness at home, I found all this very bewildering and was full of envy of people who did not have this mysterious stigma.[9]

Childhood memories reveal how racism gnawed away at children's self-confidence and self-esteem long before gross physical violence or separation from families overcame them. Friends turned against them. 'I had a lovely girl friend at school,' recalled Ingrid Ehrlich (now Naumberger). 'Real Aryan-looking blonde girl, long plaits. We were very good friends and one day she came and said, "I can't play with you any more. My brother has joined the SS".' Even preschoolers at the time remember the signs, 'Jews not allowed', and the park benches: 'You had to sit on separate benches in the park — yellow benches with a big J on them,' commented Edna Lehmann (now Samson). Then there were the shopping restrictions. 'Grocery stores which we'd been patronising for years wouldn't serve us any more — unless we came late at night when nobody else was around. Then the proprietor would slip my mother a loaf of bread.' Ellen Rothschild (now Shafer) remembered her mother telling her, 'I can't go into that shop. They know I'm Jewish. You go in and get the bread'.' The young child's penchant for imitation was another daily hazard. 'My mother had a country woman help her in the house. She'd say, 'These stupid idiots! Nazi idiots!' and my brother would repeat that. If you said that too loudly they would take you straight away.'[10]

School-age children experienced the full brunt of Nazism, being victims of legislation aimed specifically at them. Although children in the compulsory years of schooling were not directly affected by the quotas imposed in 1933, indirectly these affected the educational and career prospects of all Jewish children. State schooling beyond fourteen years of age was now only remotely possible. Even being included in the 1.5 per cent quota was a doubtful privilege. These children were often alone in an extremely hostile environment.

> There were no other Jewish boys there and it got very uncomfortable ... I was top of the class one season, but you couldn't have a Jewish boy do well, so the teachers made sure I was at the bottom the next season ... I finished off sitting on my own down the back ... After that my father took me out of school and I worked for a Jewish plumber. His business was going down too — working only for Jewish people.[11]

Another teenager commented:

> I was allowed to stay at high school because my father had the blasted Iron Cross First Class. But I had to sit at the back of the classroom ... sat on the last seat. I am extremely short-sighted and I couldn't see a dashed thing ... The Maths teacher would be goose-stepping around, wouldn't touch my books to correct anything. They weren't all like that, mind you. The whole teaching changed. They changed the books. Suddenly the First World War had a different slant. I know nothing sensible about the First World War.[12]

Career and employment prospects were negligible for non-Aryan children.

> All forms of public employment, all aesthetic pursuits, all apprenticeships to an Aryan firm are closed to non-Aryans. They are debarred from sitting for state examinations ... and since the examination is sacrosanct in Germany ... all avenues to advancement and honour are effectively closed. The regulation which forbids any non-Aryan child to be a member of the Hitler Youth movement closes the last gap in the invisible but deadly circle in which these children are imprisoned ... an Aryan employer must always give preference to a member of the Hitler Youth.[13]

Segregation occurred in many schools from 1933. In July of that year a visitor from London noted:

> In numerous schools Jewish children are segregated from the non-Jewish, they are excluded from participating in school sports and other entertainments. In the playgrounds they are shunned by their schoolmates, and teachers have even gone the length of refusing to accept from Jewish children, charitable gifts of rolls and sandwiches, brought by them for distribution to poor and destitute children of the other schools.[14]

In 1936 ostracism of Jewish children became law. They were forbidden to mix with Aryan children and were relegated to benches at the back of classrooms, or to separate classrooms. Amongst them were children for whom being Jewish was a bewildering new identity, bestowed on them through having the 'wrong' grandparents.

The school environment was presided over by teachers generally supportive of the Nazi cause. Jewish teachers, and others recalcitrant to that cause, had been dismissed in 1933, with further weeding out of undesirables a continuing process. Teachers were investigated openly and privately, with students being encouraged by Nazi inspectors to denounce teachers who seemed to oppose the new ideology. Thousands of teachers were dismissed from both schools and universities, many being sent to concentration camps. While many universities closed as a result, school teachers were replaced by approved Nazis who imbued every subject in the curriculum with the new Weltanschauung — the world-outlook of the master race. Jewish children were thus subjected to lessons in which Aryan children were shown how to recognise a Jew by head shape or other physical features; they heard and read stories and fairy tales in which the Jew was always the villain and the hero or rescuing knight a good Nazi; they were obliged to listen to, if not sing, patriotic Nazi songs:

> Our music teacher taught us Nazi songs, one of which had the refrain: Wenn's Judenblut vom Messer spritzt, dann geht's nochmal so gut. (When Jewish blood gushes forth from your knife, you can work much better.) The teacher would kindly tell us Jewish boys that we did not have to join in the refrain. We had special lessons, called National Politics ... The teacher explained that my skull was several inches shorter than that of others, which meant that I was inferior ... Such lessons served a double purpose: they gave a sense of superiority to the majority, and at the same time inculcated a sense of inferiority in Jewish children. This feeling began to develop within me, and when the boys played games in the playground I asked meekly whether I was allowed to participate. More often than not I was told, 'Jews may not join.' I accepted this as normal and on a few occasions when no objection was raised, I was only given minor roles in the game. However, I was pleased, and accepted this minor role as normal. I regretted being Jewish and thus inferior, and secretly wished I was 'Aryan' like my peers.[15]

Hitler's ideas on education and youth had been clearly outlined in *Mein Kampf*. On numerous occasions he publicly articulated his vision of youth: 'In my Ordensburgen a youth

From birth German children were bombarded with racist messages and images of the 'good' Nazi. Page from a children's picture book. (Weiner Library, London)

Nazi propaganda on a school yard wall in Germany (Still from an Australian film, *March of Time: the Refugees of Today and Tomorrow*, reprinted in *Pix*, 4 March 1939, p. 19)

will grow up before which the world will shrink back. A violently active, dominating, intrepid, brutal youth — that is what I am after. There must be no weakness or tenderness in it. I want to see once more in its eyes the gleam of pride and independence of the beast of prey.'[16] Youth was perceived as the lifeblood and future of Germany and, to this end, the primary educational task was to instil in every child a racial consciousness. A directive issued by the Minister of Education stated the case simply: 'The whole function of all education is to create a Nazi.[17] In line with this thinking, teachers were required to take an oath: 'Adolf Hitler, we swear that we will train the youth of Germany that they will grow up in your ideology, for your aims and purposes, in the direction set by your will. This is pledged to you by the whole German system of education from the primary school to the university.'[18]

Escaping this dragnet was almost impossible. While some teachers might have objected silently to the priority now given physical prowess over intellectual pursuit, few, if any, teachers sympathetic to Jews remained in the classroom by 1938. This had a double sting for Jewish children still in the system — the lack of caring adults to whom they could turn for support, and the presence of adults who instilled in the other children the venom of racial supremacy.

Many Jewish children were spared this oppression by being removed to Jewish schools. However, even with the expansion in Jewish education which occurred after 1933, there were never enough schools to meet the demand. Jewish children in small communities were most at risk, but the Reichsvertretung had insufficient funds either to build or maintain children in district schools. A report for 1937 shows the welfare department having to refuse numerous urgent applications, the result being that in 1937, 39 per cent (15 230) of Jewish children continued to attend general schools, and suffer daily humiliation and harassment.

The oppressive atmosphere in state schools was enhanced by the Hitler Youth Movement, which was intended to supplement the educational function of the school in the realms of both ideological and physical training. In its pre-1933 days, the movement probably held all the appeal of any youth group, of which Germany had many — friendship, hiking, songs around the camp fire, marching drill ... With the Nazis in power, its function as an expression of youth culture ceased. It became instead an arm of the government, regimented by rules and regulations and following set patterns of training.

From their pre-school years children imbibed Nazi ideology and were prepared for the Hitler Youth. Adulation of Hitler was part of this. According to a former teacher, kindergarten children performed a daily ritual, being told, 'fold you hands and bow your head and think of Adolf Hitler'.[19] By ten, the age of entry to Hitler Youth, most were ready and eager to pledge themselves to Hitler. Their motto, 'Fuhrer, command — we follow!' and slogans such as 'We are born to die for Germany' epitomised the Hitler Youth ethos. Richard Grunberger claims that from age ten children also learnt to handle lethal weapons on a scale unprecedented in history.[20] They also participated in feats of physical endurance for which derision from peers was the price of failure; there was no room for weaklings in this society. At fourteen, those boys who had proved their worth became full members of the Hitler Youth, entitled to wear a red swastika armband like that worn by stormtroopers. Girls entered the League of German Girls.

Not all children revelled in the lifestyle. It was a spawning ground for abuse and brutality:

> Twelve-year-old horde leaders bawling out ten-year-old cubs and driving them all over the school playground and meadows ... The slightest signs of recalcitrance, the slightest faults with our uniforms, the slightest lateness on parade were punished with extra drill —

powerless subleaders projected their rage onto us. But there was method in the madness: from childhood onwards we were drilled in toughness and blind obedience. At the command 'down', we had to throw ourselves with bare knees onto the gravel; when we were doing pressups our noses were pushed in the sand; anyone who got a stitch cross-country running was ridiculed as a weakling ... 'Youth must be led by youth' was the motto. In practice that meant that those on top could put the boot in.[21]

Even those not captivated by the euphoria and lifestyle of the Hitler Youth movement were victims of gross indoctrination, instilled with hate and a blind obedience to authority. Kiryl Sosnowski attributes much of the moral degeneration witnessed during the war to the moral deformation of German youth. He claims German youth were outstandingly active participants in the atrocities and that Hitler Youth members often grew into the most fanatical elements of the party. It was they, for example, who were entrusted with the abduction and deportation of children from the occupied territories.

For some families the situation must have been devastating. Parents watched powerlessly as their children became cogs in the Nazi machine. Those who opposed their children's ideals risked being denounced by their offspring, an action which frequently led to internment in a concentration or labour camp. A foreign writer reported from Austria in 1939: 'The silent dictatorship exercised by the child over his parents within the family home must be regarded as one of the characteristic features of the regime, which does not allow for any emotional life outside itself.'[22] Children could be removed from parents whose political or religious convictions were nonconformist. When membership in the Hitler Youth became compulsory, refusal to enrol a child in it could be punished by 'judicial kidnapping'. Friendship with Jews could also elicit legal removal of children from their families. Although some non-Jewish children remained outside the Hitler Youth, their emigration from Germany became increasingly difficult. From April 1939 any child who had not joined the Hitler Youth was refused documents to travel outside Germany for even a day.

Contradictions within Nazi policies complicated efforts by Jews to emigrate. While one government office encouraged emigration, another stripped the Jews of the capital needed for entry and settlement in another country. The Havaara Agreement provided the only possibility of transferring capital abroad. Under this agreement Jews granted entry permits to Palestine could export a certain quantity of German goods. The agreement was cancelled in 1938 under protest that 'through the influx of German capital in Jewish hands into Palestine the creation of a Jewish State is only furthered, which is certainly not in the interest of Germany'.[23]

Thirty per cent of Jews left Germany between January 1933 and November 1938. Numerous factors weighed against the emigration of the remainder. Foremost was the scarcity of visas. Strict quotas operated in all countries, including Palestine. Chaim Weizmann, a leading Zionist, described the situation throughout Europe in 1936: 'For six million Jews in Eastern and Central Europe the world is divided between states in which it is not possible for Jews to live, and others which prevent them from entering their boundaries.'[24] A visiting London Zionist described German Jews as 'rats in a trap' — those countries open to immigration required substantial sums of money and skill in particular trades, neither of which most potential emigrants had.

Before 1935 Jewish organisations in Germany did not advocate wide-scale emigration. Periods of hostility alternated with times when the pressure was relaxed, encouraging many people to believe they could tolerate life under Nazi rule. Persecution also had the initial effect of reviving Judaism, thereby giving people the courage to withstand the hostility. Ties to their homeland or to family too old to move, lack of means, and a host of personal and social factors deterred other adults from emigrating.[25]

Unlike their elders, Jewish youth had few reasons for staying in Germany. The 1933 laws had destroyed their education and career prospects, and the quality of their lives deteriorated constantly. In 1934, Leo Baeck declared, 'The only thing to do is to get them out'. Zionist youth organisations worked towards this goal, training young people for emigration to Palestine. Between 1934 and 1936 Youth Aliyah sent 1600 children between the ages of fourteen and seventeen to Palestine.[26] The enactment of the Nuremberg Laws in 1935 reaffirmed the 'hopeless' position of Jewish youth in Germany,[27] and prompted a rapid expansion in vocational and agricultural training centres. Among them were some, such as a farm school in Gross-Breesen, which were openly anti-Zionist, and trained youth for group emigration to countries other than Palestine. From 1935, the Reichsvertretung gave priority to youth emigration overseas as well as to Palestine. It was supported in this move by the establishment in 1936 of the Council for German Jewry, comprising leaders of British, American and Continental Jewry. The Council immediately launched a worldwide appeal for three million pounds to resettle 100 000 young German Jews in Palestine, overseas, and, to a lesser extent, in Europe.

Parents with connections and money frequently made private arrangements for their children with schools and families outside Germany. Clearing scheme arrangements with England allowed parents to contribute German marks to the Reichsvertretung or to British-funded programs in Germany, with the equivalent amount of sterling being released in England for school fees and maintenance.[28] In March 1936 the first organisational effort to remove young children emerged in Britain. The Jewish Refugees Committee approached Save the Children Fund about coordinating a committee which would find school and family placements for German children. The resulting Children's Inter-Aid Committee amalgamated work previously done for German children by Save the Children Fund, the Jewish Refugees' Committee and the Society of Friends. Throughout its operation this non-denominational committee maintained a ratio of 45 per cent Christian to 55 per cent Jewish. Funding was never in that proportion, with most of the funds coming from Jewish sources. In 1935 the High Commissioner for Refugees spoke out about the failure of the Christian world to provide adequate funds for non-Jewish emigration from Germany. In 1938 the Bishop of Chichester expressed a similar concern. A Catholic refugee committee formed later that year raised very little money; its only contribution to the Inter-Aid Committee was the placement of a few children in Catholic schools. In January 1938 the Inter-Aid Committee was maintaining 130 German children in English schools and, with that, was stretched to its limits. It was certainly not equipped to handle the crisis which erupted in March 1938.

When the Reich army entered Austria on 12 March 1938 it unleashed overnight on Austrian Jews and political opponents all the violations perpetrated in Germany since 1933.

> Austrian Nazis went on the rampage through the streets of Vienna, in an outburst that lasted for days ... Anyone who looked remotely Jewish was attacked and beaten. Jewish shops were pillaged, windows smashed, goods stolen ... No Jew was safe, however exalted. The Chief Rabbi of Vienna was dragged into the streets and forced to scrub pavements ... Hundreds of Jews committed suicide, unable or unwilling

to face the horrors of mob rule. Thousands more fled from the city and the country into neighbouring states. Those who could headed further afield, to France, Britain or the United States.[29]

Seven-year-old Alfred Stricker was in bed with whooping cough when the annexation occurred. He remembered hearing the abdication speech of the Chancellor of Austria: 'I was in bed and the radio was on and I heard him say, "God protect you Austria". The old Austrian national anthem was played and then straight after they played the German national anthem. That was the turnover.' In more ways than one, the world turned round for Alfred during his illness. 'When I went to bed all traffic was on the left hand side and when I got up after six weeks all traffic was on the right hand side ... that made a big impression on me ... I thought, "What's happening? Everything's the wrong way round."' Keith Muenz also recalled the fiasco caused by the traffic turn-around: 'I was right in the centre of town observing what was going on. Blooming copper didn't know if he was Arthur or Martha.'

The Anschluss provided little other comic relief for Alfred or Keith, or for the other approximately 200 000 Jews and half million non-Aryans in Austria. The racial legislation of the Reich was imposed immediately, introducing appalling destitution. Provincial Jewish communities ceased to exist in Austria and, as people flocked to Vienna, the Israelitische Kultusgemeinde became the only Jewish organisation remaining to help. The Friends Centre, soon operating as the German Emergency Committee, was one of several organisations which helped 'baptised Jews and other non-Aryans', as well as political dissidents. Authorities refused to allow the Friends to set up feeding centres. Their most urgent task therefore became getting people out of the country.

Emigration was ruthlessly enforced by Adolf Eichmann, in charge of a special emigration office in Vienna. Even so, provocation occurred at every opportunity.

While threats of dire consequences for failure to leave Austria were heaped on the unfortunate non-Aryan, every obstacle to his fulfilling all the conditions necessary for the receipt of the exit permit required was put in his way and there was no limit to the humiliations to which he had to submit in the process. Even when all seemed accomplished it was often necessary to give enormous bribes to the officials responsible for handing out the final document.[30]

Keith Muenz was among the thousands who besieged the premises of the Friends in 1938:

To emigrate you had to have a passport, tax clearance, visas ... There were queues. You had to stand for hours. Of course, you got picked on even while you were in those queues. I saw one nasty incident where a jeep of SS deliberately ploughed into the queue. People paid money to hold a place in the queue. I was doing that.

Efforts to remove young children, as well as adolescents, became urgent. Letters poured into the Children's Inter-Aid Committee in London. 'All the cases dealt with were extremely tragic, but the most urgent seemed to be those of children whose parents were in concentration camps or had committed suicide'.[31]

The Austrian crisis finally galvanised the world into action. In July 1938 a conference of representatives of nations and organisations around the world was held at Evian in France to consider ways of facilitating the migration of German and Austrian refugees. The failure of that gathering to provide a solution to the refugee problem is well documented. In the following months Britain issued more stringent entry requirements, and further restricted entry to Palestine in the face of a tidal wave of new applications.

The Anschluss, and the indifference of the

world to the Jews as expressed at the Evian conference, gave Hitler and his party the impetus they needed to enter another stage of their war against the Jews. By now they had the military might to ignore world opinion on their policies. 'Because it is necessary, because we no longer hear the world's screaming, and finally because no power in the world can stop us, we shall therefore now take the Jewish Question towards its total solution. The program is clear. It is: total elimination, complete separation.'[32] In another speech Hitler mercilessly berated the democracies of the world for their 'oozing sympathy for the poor tormented Jewish people', but their 'hard-hearted and obdurate' response when it came to helping them.[33] 1938 became a watershed year for the National Socialist Party and the Jews alike. Various new decrees were issued, including one relating to identification. Henceforth Jews had to adopt the additional names, Israel or Sarah. Fired by the success of Eichmann's harsh expulsion methods in Austria, tactics to force Jews to leave Germany were brutally enacted. In June 1938, Goebbels declared that 'In the coming half year, the Jews must be forced to leave Berlin'.[34] House-to-house searches and arrests of Jews became common. Thousands ended up in concentration camps where brutality and hard labour were regular fare.

Since 1936 the Polish government had also been trying to enforce Jewish emigration. In 1938 it instructed its consulates throughout Germany to confiscate the passports of Jewish Polish nationals who had been absent for a period of five years. Hearing of this, the German government retaliated. On 27 October, several weeks after the annexation of the Sudetenland, the German government rounded up and deported 16 000 Jewish men, women and children of Polish nationality. The Polish government refused at first to accept the deportees, leaving many stranded in pitiful circumstances in the border town of Zbonszyn.

A further 26 000 Polish Jewish inhabitants in Germany 'were put in concentration camps after notices of deportation were served upon them'.[35] In several cities, including Berlin, women and children were excluded from the original deportation. In February 1939 they received orders to leave immediately.[36]

His parents' deportation was the breaking point for one seventeen-year-old Jewish boy living in Paris. On 7 November 1938, Herschel Grynszpan walked into the German Embassy in Paris and shot dead the Third Secretary, Ernst vom Rath. His action provided the Nazis with the excuse they needed to mobilise their forces against the Jews. Throughout Germany, including Austria and the Sudetenland, the order went out to avenge the diplomat's killing. Instructions were that the pogrom be seen as a spontaneous act by the German people, not instigated by the party. The orgy of destruction and violence that took place over the night of 9–10 November had no equal. Kristallnacht, the euphemistic name given to that night, belittles the magnitude of the terrible events that occurred.

Kristallnacht and its aftermath monopolise the prewar memories of most Jewish child refugees from Germany and Austria. Memories have been etched in their minds of events witnessed and terror experienced. Protecting children from these things was almost impossible. They experienced, along with adults, the destruction of family businesses, the burning of synagogues and Jewish schools; they were there when storm troopers attacked their homes, destroying and confiscating their possessions; they saw their adults brutalised and humiliated, if not killed; and some watched as those adults, plummeted into the depths of despair, took their own lives. 'My grandmother was about eighty,' recalled Ellen Rothschild. 'She threw herself off the balcony when she saw them downstairs, coming to arrest the men.' Nine-year-old Ellen had already lost her father to suicide earlier that year. 'My father lost a leg in the First World War, and he could not come to terms with the fact that the country in which he had grown up could treat the Jews that way.'

Hermann Levy recalled how his family was terrorised. At 6 a.m. on 8 November the family was awakened by the Gestapo and police who demanded to search the flat, supposedly for firearms. The next morning they returned for Hermann's father.

> Mother hurriedly prepared two sandwiches which she stuffed into my father's overcoat pocket. Trembling I looked on. 'Better you shoot me on the spot that I need not be subjected to this humiliation', said my father. These words, this situation I've never forgotten. For how could I as a boy of nine understand the meaning of what had happened.

His fear intensified the following morning:

> Eight a.m. The door bell rings. Mother hesitated to open it ... Our fears increased as the opaque, partly glass door was shattered by a strong kick. Three men in long overcoats with upturned collars broke into our flat. Each man held a tomahawk hidden beneath his coat. They ordered us out and set about systematically destroying. Through the broken door we witnessed the destruction. Chairs, books, kitchen utensils and whatever else they laid their hands on were tossed through the windows into the street where curious bystanders waited for the continuation of the spectacle.

Children in institutions were also targeted during Kristallnacht. Ursula Kaye (now Meyerstein) was working as a cook in a boarding school near Potsdam:

> At 7.30 or 8 a.m. we came into the kitchen and started to make breakfast. Then the Nazis came and started to break all the windows. They told us, 'Get out!' and with that we walked out, some 200 kids and grown-ups. We just walked out and went into the forest. We walked on and on and on. They broke everything. We heard the glass breaking behind us. There were some children who were not well. The Nazis said, 'Take them all ... either you take them or they die here'. So we took them and went to a convent. The convent took in the children who were so ill they couldn't walk on.

After walking all day, Ursula broke away from the main party with one little boy of eight.

> I could see the road and everything was quiet down there, so I said, 'Let's go on the road'. By about 6 o'clock we came to the railway station. I had money on me and we bought a ticket ... Before we changed trains I rang home. It was engaged and I thought I would go crazy. I thought they had taken my parents away already. So I rang a neighbour ... she ran and called my mother ... I told her about the little boy. I said, 'He can't walk anymore'. So my brother came to the station and carried him home. The little boy thought it was marvellous ... I rang his mother and explained that I had her little boy and asked what she wanted me to do. She said, 'They just took my husband away, so can you keep him?' And she didn't even worry, me being a stranger. He stayed with us a fortnight and then we sent him home.

During Kristallnacht, a further 60 000 Jewish men and boys in Germany were arrested and sent to Buchenwald, Dachau and Sachsenhausen concentration camps where they were subjected to gross humiliation and sadistic cruelty. Charlie Trainor, sixteen at the time, recalled a barrack at Sachsenhausen where boys as young as twelve were held. In Austria whole families were sometimes arrested. Thirteen-year-old Hans Eisler was arrested in Vienna with his parents and older brother. Until then his parents had believed themselves immune from Nazi persecution.

> My father and brother had both served in the Austrian army in the First World War. When

Hitler arrived in March 1938 my parents thought, as they were good Austrians, well-liked, respected business people, they would be safe. Fearful it was, but then it was the Jews on the other side [eastern Jews] who would suffer, not us. As the pogroms and the beatings and the restrictions increased through March to September — the annexation of part of Czechoslovakia — my parents realised that the Nazis meant business. But still they were convinced that they would be unscathed because they were respected. Not so on Kristallnacht. The morning of 10 November 1938 there was a knock at the door at 5 or 6 o'clock in the morning. SS entered the unit, beat up my brother whom they accused of having slept with a non-Jewish woman, forced my father to go to the shop and declare all his money and possessions, beat me on the head with a revolver, and took us all away to the Hotel Metropole on the shores of the Danube canal. There we were locked up separately ... I spent two nights there with other Jewish boys, then I was released. My parents were released about a week afterwards, but my brother was sent to Dachau.

Men used various strategies for avoiding detention. 'My father got a tip-off,' commented George Dreyfus. 'He just stayed on the trains. He lived on the trains for three days. After three days the wave of arrests was over.' At great risk to themselves, some non-Jews helped their Jewish friends and neighbours. William Kahle described how his family was persecuted after he and his mother were caught helping the Jewish owner of a haberdashery shop clean up the mess left by the Gestapo.

> Any contact with Jews at that time, and worse, to help them, was considered 'an act of treason against the German people'. The steps taken by the Gestapo against our family were systematically designed to destroy us. My father, a well-known linguist, lost his post as professor at the university. I, the eldest son, was expelled from the university and was not allowed to study at any institution in the German Reich. My mother, recognised as being the main spirit of the opposition against the ideology of the Nazis, had to bear the brunt of the offensive. She was condemned by the secret Nazi Court to suffer to breaking point, so that she be forced to end her own life. She and myself, the two who were caught in the Jewish shop, had to disappear before anything could be done for my father and brothers ... Our only hope was to flee to England, but it was even dangerous to prepare for emigration.

Men could buy their release from the camps by giving proof of intent to emigrate immediately and by signing over all their assets to the Reich. Visas gained under such pressure generally did not include other family members. A father or teenage boy would thus be forced to emigrate alone, with the hope the rest of the family would follow. In their desperation, people explored all avenues of escape, frequently applying for visas to various countries, but ready to accept whichever came first. In this way, many families became dispersed over several countries, with some members invariably remaining in Germany or Austria.

Even families that remained intact after Kristallnacht could often no longer protect and nurture their children. Jewish children were now banned from state schools. Violence on the streets meant that many were virtually under house arrest. Even their homes were no longer a sanctuary. With so many men disappearing through incarceration, hiding or emigration, few Jewish families did in fact remain intact. Children of mixed marriages suffered the same abuses and deprivations. Many were also the victims of divorce, often brought about through necessity — so the Aryan partner could earn a living or the non-Aryan could emigrate. Custody of the children always went to the Aryan partner; where this was the father, abandonment of children was not uncommon, men being called away for military service or work. A representative from the German Emergency Committee in London commented after a visit to Berlin in January 1939: 'The break-up of family life is universal amongst the Jews and the non-Aryans and one wonders what the ultimate effect is going to be'.[37]

In Vienna the plight of non-Aryan children was very severe. A series of letters from a young Jewish girl in Vienna tells the story. The writer, Leni, was an orphan by 1939. Leni lived with her aunt Martha until Martha was taken away for speaking out against the Nazis, who had confiscated her possessions. After that Leni was responsible for Martha's eighteen-month-old baby, Hansi. Leni wrote the letters to an unknown relative in Amsterdam, someone she called 'aunt'. In her last letter Leni explained what had happened to her family:

> Vienna, June 1939
>
> My sister is seven years old and has been in London since December. My brother Julius was eighteen years old and died in Buchenwald. I turned twelve on 2 June, and I am still alive for the time being. My good Papi was fifty-three years old and died in October. What he died of Aunt Martha won't tell me. He was a police inspector until March 1938. My dear little mother was sickly for seven years, and the death of my father was too much for her. She was also fifty-three years old.

Earlier letters were filled with the cynicism and bitterness of a child old beyond her years:

> Vienna, April 1939
>
> Dear aunt, you write that we should have trust in God. I don't believe in God. Why has he punished us so? I can't describe to you what we have suffered. God has taken my beloved parents away from me. My brother was in the same rehabilitation home with your brother last year, and he died there. That's the same home where my aunt is now.
>
> The most dreadful thing was that thieves were here and have stolen everything. We hid in the cellar for three days then and didn't dare to come out. Can one still trust in God after that?
>
> Look, dear auntie ... I am not allowed to go to the cinema, to the theatre, I'm not allowed to go into the park, some days I'm not allowed to show my face on the street. Isn't that enough? I am not yet twelve years old, but sometimes I believe that I am already one hundred years old.

> Vienna, May 1939
>
> Dear dear Auntie,
>
> I received your letter and read it with great joy. I am always happy when you write. As far as the subject of God is concerned, I would like to ask you what you really understand by that term. You will reply that God is an invisible power, but one must believe in him all the same. Now I will give you a small example. If I write to you that I am sending you one thousand marks, but you will never receive it, the money will remain invisible, would you believe that? You will reply that you will believe it when you see it. And I say the same. I believe only what I see. You write that you could tell me about cases you have seen. Dear Auntie, what I have seen you certainly have never seen ... I'm sending you a picture of me. I'm wearing everything you sent me. You will laugh at me because I had my photo taken with the doll. I still like to play sometimes. Please don't laugh at me.

In her June letter, Leni vented her disgust with the Jewish community:

> I have already turned to the Jewish Welfare three times on behalf of my aunt, asking for support, and they didn't reply. They always say they don't have any money. Do you really believe that the Jewish community cares for its people? One could die like a dog and they don't care. When I am fourteen years old I

will leave the religion completely ... I fetch meals for Hansi and myself from the Jewish kitchen ... the food is very bad. Not even the pigs would eat it. That's the way the Jewish community takes care of its people.[38]

By June 1939 Leni was one of 8000 Jewish children still in Vienna. Of these, 1600 depended on the Kultusgemeinde for meals, but the demands on the organisation were so great it could offer children only one meal a day. While emigration remained the priority for children, in June the Kultusgemeinde appealed to the Council for German Jewry in England for a larger grant for children's work in Austria.[39]

Numerous children had left Austria and Germany by then, through private arrangements as well as through group schemes. In desperation parents made courageous decisions and took enormous risks in sending their children away alone. When fourteen-year-old Hans Eisler's parents returned from detention in Vienna they immediately organised his departure.

> I was put on a rickety old plane and landed in England on 16 December 1938 ... You can imagine the good-byes. To me it was adventure, to my parents it was ... they knew they wouldn't see me again ... Some fellow by the name of Mr Myer met me. It was his job to give refuge to people as they arrived in England. When I arrived at the airport he took my hat and I believe he took something out of my hat.
>
> I felt free immediately. I loved football, so I immediately went to see a game of football. I played pinball machines in the centre of London. I was free. I could do whatever I liked. Lost the little money I had — about five pound — on pin-ball machines. Mr Myer threw me out on some pretext about a week or so after ... the police picked me up in Trafalgar Square. It was midnight and I had nowhere to go and I couldn't speak English. They looked after me particularly well.

In November 1938 the Netherlands government set a precedent by agreeing to admit temporarily any number of German and Austrian children, provided the Dutch Refugees Committee could support them. Proposals for other group schemes followed. The Jewish Agency for Palestine appealed to the British government to admit 10 000 children to Palestine. The British government refused the request, stating that additional migration to Palestine would prejudice forthcoming discussions with the Arabs. In making this decision, Malcolm MacDonald, Secretary of State for the Colonies and Dominion Affairs, claimed the refusal was not necessarily permanent. In the meantime the children were to be allowed into England as long as the refugee organisations could guarantee their maintenance.[40]

In this way the proposal was married with another, initiated by Norman Bentwich and his wife, Mami,[41] for the admission of large numbers of children to Britain. In November the British government agreed to admit all children up to the age of seventeen 'whose maintenance could be guaranteed either by the funds of the voluntary organisations themselves or by the generosity of individuals'.[42] This gave birth to the Movement for the Care of Children from Germany, afterwards renamed the Refugee Children's Movement. The Movement decided on 10 000 as the maximum number of children that could be supported voluntarily at any one time, and immediately set out to achieve that goal. In offering this guarantee the Movement undertook responsibility 'that the children should not become a public charge, and that they should be re-emigrated before they reached the age of eighteen or when their training in this country was completed'.[43] The Children's Inter-Aid Committee merged with the new organisation, which retained a non-denominational character and had representation from a wide range of voluntary organisations. The Society of Friends, one of those voluntary organisations, continued to play a pivotal role, being responsible for selecting Christian non-Aryan children from Vienna. An early report on the operation in Vienna included the comment, 'mothers leapt unanimously at the chance and without exception put their children's names down. (the fathers could generally not be consulted)'.[44]

The Refugee Children's Movement gave priority to the most urgent cases, firstly, to children who 'had no home, or no parents, or no means; and secondly, as a group, the big boys who were held to be in special danger of arrest and ill-treatment'.[45] Many of these boys were already in concentration camps and were released when parents secured them a place on a children's transport, commonly known as a kindertransport. Some had British guarantors, but many were unguaranteed and were cared for at the expense of the Refugee Children's Movement. This system of bringing over only the most urgent cases became untenable, as did the Movement's ability to maintain more than 300 unguaranteed children at any one time. From January 1939 the Movement began accepting any child whose maintenance was guaranteed by a British resident. In April the government introduced a requirement that guarantors deposit £50 to cover re-emigration of all children over twelve.

Although selections were made in Berlin and Vienna, thousands of parents wrote directly to the Refugee Children's Movement in London searching for guarantors. Others advertised in British newspapers:

Would family temporarily ACCEPT VIENNESE BOY (13) very gifted, well-mannered, excellent violinist.[46]

Very nice healthy boy, 13 years, speaking English, half Jewish, of best Roman Catholic family, would like to find a HOME in ENGLAND. Vienna.[47]

English family is requested by Czechoslovak parents (surgeon) to find a temporary home for their two children (even only one), aged 14 and 16, well educated and extremely gifted for languages and music. Best references.[48]

Will someone offer home to Czech girl, 7, and boy, 12 years, wishing to come to England together or separately?[49]

A report to the Council for German Jewry from the Jewish community in Frankfurt showed parents by November 1938 indifferent to the type of care provided their children: 'There is a fervent desire among Jewish parents at least to see their children moved quickly; it is immaterial whether they are offered individual hospitality or accommodation in camps, so long as they are removed from Germany'. The director of an orphanage in Frankfurt pleaded with the Council for German Jewry for help: 'Continually, almost hourly there are requests for new cases; refugees are on the brink of despair ... You have no idea what responsibility rests on us.' Groups of children under fourteen were leaving the orphanage daily for Holland, France, Switzerland and Belgium, but the situation for those who had turned fourteen was desperate.

I beg you most urgently to grant permission for these young people to come over immediately if possible, to be trained for a trade somewhere until they can be distributed and sent to some place ... the point is to give these young people who are no longer children and not yet grown up some new hope and courage, as they have lost every courage and hope and every prospect of work.[50]

Committed people worked tirelessly to organise the movement of children. Between December 1938 and September 1939 the Refugee Children's Movement removed to Britain 9354 German and Austrian children, 7482 of whom were Jewish, 1123 Christian and 749 undenominational.[51] Six thousand of the children were guaranteed. Small numbers of children from Czechoslovakia[52] and Poland[53] were rescued by other committees and individuals in Britain. No other country followed Britain's example. In the United States, the Wagner–Rogers Bill to admit 20 000 children outside the refugee quota was widely debated, but defeated. Only 590 unaccompanied German refugee children entered the United States before the war, although overall about one thousand entered by 1945.[54] Other children found refuge throughout Europe, some experiencing only a brief reprieve before those countries also were under German occupation. For many children there was nowhere to go. Although not all parents were willing to send their children away, the majority probably were. Both Nicholas Winton and Norbert Wollheim, involved in the organisation of kindertransports, believe parents 'would have sent their children anywhere to save their lives'.[55] A report on a visit to Breslau in June 1939 by members of the Central British Fund supports this belief:

> We were run after in the street by people simply begging us to take their children away, and the leaders of the community there implored us to do all we possibly could to get their children out. The children of the Staatenlos [stateless] were being arrested daily in the streets and boys of thirteen and fourteen being sent over the frontier. I cannot describe the terror in the people's faces and their absolute despair not knowing where to go and to whom to turn.

Norbert Wollheim commented: 'There is no doubt in my mind that parents tried desperately to give their children a chance to escape persecution by the Nazis, but the gates of most countries were closed and only England was the shining exception.'[56]

In Australia the cry for help went largely unheeded. The seventeen children who sailed on the *Orama* that June morning in 1939 were the only young unaccompanied children from the Continent to find refuge in Australia. A small number of fourteen- and fifteen-year-olds, and some adolescents over sixteen, also arrived before the war. This meagre response came from a country with a long history in child migration and during a time of intense activity in British child and youth migration. Most ships travelling to Australia in 1938 and 1939 carried groups of young British migrants amongst the passengers. The *Orama* was no exception. On board were twenty-three children, aged five to twelve, bound for the Fairbridge, and the affiliated Northcote, children's homes. Five other parties of Fairbridge children travelled to Australia in 1939,[57] as did numerous British children and youth for other institutions.

2

UNWANTED GIFTS

Kingsley Fairbridge had a vision when he opened a farm training school at Pinjarra, Western Australia, in 1912. He envisaged offering a future to Britain's numerous destitute and vagrant children; he saw the children in turn as building blocks for the British Empire.

> Every day I saw a street in the East End of London ... crowded with children — dirty children ... no decent air, not enough food. The waste of it all! Children's lives wasting away, while the Empire cries aloud for men ... I saw great colleges of agriculture springing up in every man-hungry corner of the Empire. I saw little children shedding their bondage of bitter circumstances and stretching their legs and their minds. I saw waste turned to providence, the waste of unneeded humanity converted to the husbandry of unpeopled areas.[1]

This vision of child migrants populating the empty lands of the Empire was enhanced and diversified after the First World War. The Governor of South Australia, Lord Weigall, made the role quite explicit in 1921 when he addressed the first group of children headed for the Barnado Home in New South Wales: 'You are going to live in the country as God made it ... you must remember the 61 000 men who gave their lives for Australia in the late war. You will help replace them and I am perfectly sure you realise what your duty to Australia is ... Don't swank!'[2]

The children chosen for this dubious honour were sometimes orphans, although many had families who simply could not afford to support them. In those times of little or no government assistance, when an illegitimate birth was equated with vagrancy, it was not unusual for parents or guardians to place children in an orphanage, either temporarily or permanently. The situation of the five Boucher children, who sailed on the *Orama* in June 1939, was perhaps typical of the circumstances that caused many children to become child migrants. Their mother had died of pneumonia when the youngest was a baby, and the eldest six years old. Grandparents had tried to keep the children but, without support, found this impossible. When their father was imprisoned, the children were placed in an orphanage. Two years later they were selected for emigration to the Fairbridge Farm in Australia.[3] The extent to which parents and guardians were consulted or informed of their children's emigration is debateable. Barry Coldrey contends that gaining the consent of parents was a high priority for the Catholic Church, especially in the 1930s, although often parents could not be found.[4] Fairbridge records show a similar practice.[5] Nevertheless, testimonies collected by Margaret Humphreys indicate numerous parents and guardians had no knowledge of their children's emigration.[6]

The 1922 Empire Settlement Act ensured the development and prosperity of child migration. Under this agreement the British and Commonwealth governments jointly paid the passages of children selected for approved institutions in Australia. In addition, the British government paid the institutions five shillings a week and the Commonwealth and state governments each paid three and sixpence. Every child thus attracted twelve shillings a week to age fourteen. Assisted passages were

> **AUSTRALIA** OFFERS OPPORTUNITIES TO
>
> **BOYS** (15-18 YEARS) FOR FARM WORK
>
> AND
>
> **YOUNG WOMEN** FOR HOUSEHOLD EMPLOYMENT.
>
> **EMPLOYMENT GUARANTEED.**
>
> **GREATLY REDUCED FARES.**
>
> REDUCED FARES ALSO AVAILABLE TO
>
> PERSONS **NOMINATED** BY FRIENDS OR RELATIVES IN AUSTRALIA
>
> For Further Particulars — — APPLY WITHIN
>
> Authorised by The Official Secretary, Australia House, London.

Poster issued in 1938 by the Australian High Commissioner's Office, London, encouraging the migration of British youth to Australia. During 1938 and 1939, the peak of the prewar refugee crisis in Europe, the Australian and British governments jointly subsidised numerous voluntary organisations for the migration of British children and youth to Australia. The organisations had difficulty finding sufficient British children to fill their quotas, yet ignored the plight of non-British children then desperately seeking refuge. (AA445/1 124/1/47)

also provided for British youth admitted under approved schemes, thereby promoting the development of new schemes and the expansion of existing ones, for example Dreadnought, Big Brother, Barwell. Together these schemes involved thousands of British children and youth before the outbreak of the Second World War. Through them, the migration of unaccompanied children and youth became an accepted practice in Australia, and British child and youth migration became a vital part of Australian immigration.

With the onset of the Depression, assisted migration ground to a halt, except for Fairbridge Farm children, and families of British immigrants who had come to Australia before 1 January 1930. Regular immigration was also strictly controlled. Entry depended on a nomination from close relatives settled in Australia and possession of £500 landing money. The effect of these measures in the early 1930s was a negative growth in British population — more departed than arrived — and a small increase in non-British immigrants. In a world of growing unrest, this pressured the Australian government into searching for new ways to stimulate the flow of migration. An Inter-Departmental Committee on Migration Policy was set up in London in 1934, but offered few ideas. Nevertheless, there was general agreement that Fairbridge-type operations had been among the most successful of all migration schemes and should be resumed and expanded as soon as possible.

Although the Fairbridge operation was then quite small — one farm, accommodating around 350 children at any one time — it had particular appeal. Part of the attraction was the age of the children; they posed no threat to unemployed Australians. Equally important was the belief that young children with country training would become assimilated to farm and country life and would stay on the land throughout their lives. They would thereby fulfil the goal of populating the open spaces of the country.

In March 1936 Cabinet approved more relaxed entry requirements for immigrants. Landing permits became available to various categories of people whose admission would not be detrimental to Australian workers. Dependent relatives of persons already settled in Australia could now enter if guarantees for their maintenance were provided. People with £50 landing money were allowed in if an individual or organisation in Australia would guarantee they would not become a charge on the state. Unguaranteed aliens with £200 landing money could also enter if they could show they would engage in trades and occupations which would not disadvantage Australian workers.[7]

The new regulations acknowledged the need to attract desirable 'white alien' immigrants to Australia. At the same time, government officials reiterated their aversion to any influx of Jews, a position first expressed by Cabinet in June 1933: 'Jews as a class are not desirable immigrants for the reason that they do not assimilate; speaking generally, they preserve their identity as Jews.'[8] With the relaxation in alien immigration regulations, pressure to resume assisted migration, the source of many British immigrants, now intensified. Despite little enthusiasm from the states, Cabinet announced in December 1936 the readiness of the Commonwealth government to support any state wishing to resume assisted migration. At the same time, contributions and assisted passages were resumed for children introduced by the Barnado Home in New South Wales, and extended to children for two new Fairbridge Farm Schools, in New South Wales and Victoria. Despite this financial backing, and evidence of a shortage of farm and domestic workers in some states, most states were reluctant to proceed at the pace desired. In a policy speech in September 1937 Prime Minister Lyons urged the states to support assisted migration, outlining the general picture: a declining birth rate ('We are losing more lives in one year than we lost in four years of the greatest war in all human history'); the loss of British immigrants ('For the four years from 1931 to 1934, 20 000 more people, mainly of our British kin, went out of the country than came into it'); the potential for an influx of alien immigrants and the implications of this for Australia ('It is important that we should renew a form of financial encouragement to British migrants so as to retain to the full the British character of our population. Our population is 99.1% of British nationality and we wish to keep it so.'[9]) Frustrated by the inability of the states to grapple with the problem, the Commonwealth took back full control of immigration in March 1938 and immediately resumed assisted migration. At the same time, Cabinet made decisions intended to restrict the flow of Jewish immigrants and to boost non-Jewish migration: the number of applicants the recently-formed Australian Jewish Welfare Society could guarantee was 'limited to 500 persons each year, with the added proviso that not more than twenty persons arrive on any one ship'. Furthermore, the landing money required by Scandinavians, Finns, Danes, Dutch and Germans of non-Jewish origin was reduced to £100. A further reduction to £50 was made for Dutch subjects whose application was approved by the Netherlands Migration Office; a rider that these concessions 'would not apply to persons of Jewish race' was attached.[10]

Not surprisingly, proposals to admit groups of refugee children or youth before assisted migration resumed in March 1938 were rejected. Although individual children could enter under the conditions outlined in March 1936, a ban on group migration effectively barred most children seeking refuge. The position was stated in 1936 and reaffirmed by Cabinet in its 1938 policy statement: 'No special facilities can be granted for the admission of groups of Jewish migrants, but each case will be considered on its merits ...'[11] Individual migration was generally not viable for children; nor, given the urgency of the situation from 1936, could it satisfy the growing demand for their resettlement overseas.

The formation of the Council for German Jewry in London in 1936 marked the beginning of successive attempts to move children to Australia. While other refugee organisations existed, the Council for German Jewry was particularly significant for Australia as it immediately forged links with Australian

Jewry, leading to the formation of the German Jewish Refugees Fund in Sydney, the forerunner of the Australian Jewish Welfare Society. The Australian government encouraged the development of a single organisation which could handle applications from Jewish refugees and the settlement of those who met the entry criteria. This saved the government from being bombarded with applications from numerous Jewish organisations. The German Jewish Refugees Fund, succeeded by the Australian Jewish Welfare Society, thus developed into a representative body, with committees in each state. It became part of a global network of organisations involved with Jewish refugees and a major channel through which pressure could be exerted on the Australian government on behalf of Jewish refugees.

Pressure also came directly from the Council for German Jewry, through deliberations with the Dominions Office or representatives of the Australian government in London. In this way Norman Bentwich, a presiding figure in the Council for German Jewry, began a campaign for the migration of German children and youth to Australia. Early in 1936 Bentwich approached the Dominions Office regarding the placement of German Jewish boys and girls in farm and domestic work in Australia. In March he submitted a proposal to set up a farm training school along the lines of Fairbridge, but for older boys who would go straight from German schools to Australia.[12] The Australian government refused the request on the grounds that assisted migration to Australia had not yet resumed and that the introduction of these children might prejudice the introduction of British children.[13]

While this position prevented the introduction of any scheme for young refugees before March 1938, Norman Bentwich continued to see Australia as the most likely of the dominions to contribute to Jewish emigration; he also saw the potential for child and youth migration under schemes similar to those implemented for British children and youth. Despite the rejection of his proposal, throughout 1937 he vigorously pursued the goal of youth migration to Australia and, through the Reichsvertretung in Germany, organised the selection and preparation of young Jews for future migration to Australia.[14]

Little information exists on the young people who came to Australia in 1938 as a result of these efforts. This may be no accident. In his 1936 proposal for the introduction of refugees, Bentwich emphasised his intention to keep any agreement quiet — no newspaper reports or any publicity that might lead to questions in parliament. Nevertheless, by the end of 1938, thirty-one boys and thirteen girls, mostly between the ages of fifteen and seventeen, did migrate to Australia,[15] the first seven boys arriving within weeks of the resumption of assisted migration. They expressed their gratitude to Norman Bentwich when he came to Australia later that year to attend the British Commonwealth Relations Conference: 'The seven Jewish boys from Germany now in Glen Innes thank you for all you have done for them'.[16] These seven had been placed on an experimental farm in Glen Innes; those who came later went immediately into farming and domestic positions, what the Reichsvertretung called the 'practical professions'.

One of the girls recalled how she was selected in Germany for this scheme:

> I read in the newspaper how Woburn House [the London headquarters for major relief organisations] was sending a delegation to select young people to go to Australia. They were to be tested in I.Q. and their ability to speak English and all kinds of things, and when they arrived in Australia they would be allowed to do anything they wanted, learn anything they wanted. I was very eager to study ... and so I was interviewed.

This was in 1937. Months later the delegation returned. This time 'they took us out to dinner to a simple place; they wanted to know whether we could eat decently'. More months passed, then a letter arrived giving her a week's notice to leave for England. Being at the time in hospital recovering from diphtheria, she escaped — climbed out the window at night, caught a train and arrived home without any luggage. From there to England, and thence Australia. Woburn House paid the passages and supplied the £50 landing money required by these young people. 'It was impressed on us that they were giving envelopes with £50 to the purser. "When you arrive you collect the envelope and give it to the Welfare Society. Don't open it." I never saw the cheque.'

The Children's Inter-Aid Committee, responsible for the placement of German and Austrian children in British homes and schools, was also casting around from 1937 'for opportunities of settlement for the children in overseas British countries'. The committee had been required to give an undertaking that the children would not stay in Britain when their education was finished. In 1937 a few of these children, of an undisclosed age, went on individual permits to Australia; in mid-1938 a further ten were placed in Australia as farm and domestic workers.

Each new crisis in Europe brought a flood of applications to the Australian government and to the refugee organisations, especially the Australian Jewish Welfare Society. The Australian government responded with policies that restricted rather than enabled Jewish migration. No overall quota existed before June 1938, but apart from the Jewish Welfare Society's 500 permits, the Department of the Interior was set to approve landing permits for approximately one thousand guaranteed Jewish applicants in 1938. Numerous other applications — about three hundred a week, each typically for several people — came from those in the unguaranteed category.[17] In June 1938 Cabinet approved a recommendation by the Minister for the Interior 'to limit the number of permits issued to Jewish applicants who have no guarantors in Australia to 300 persons per month'.[18] Thus, from June 1938, an unofficial quota for Jewish refugees was in place — 3600 unguaranteed persons a year and 1500 guaranteed. Recognising that a Jewish quota was out of keeping with the government's 'declared policy not to discriminate against nationality, race or religion', the Prime Minister advised that it was 'extremely desirable reference be not made to quota or to "Jews" in official communications or statements where restriction of entry is mentioned'.[19] The quota was not made public and went unannounced even at the Evian Conference in July 1938. Nevertheless, the spirit in which it was created was evident in the public pronouncement by Australia's representative at the conference, Colonel Thomas White: 'As we have no real racial problem we are not desirous of importing one by encouraging any scheme of large-scale foreign migration'.[20]

With a quota in place at least the government was prepared to make some concessions regarding the admission of young alien immigrants. In June, Cabinet revoked an earlier decision to refuse the admission of twenty Jewish boys from Poland.[21] At the same time, the German Emergency Fellowship Committee of the Society of Friends was given permission to admit twenty young 'non-Aryan' Christians for farm and domestic work. The Salvation Army was also permitted to introduce an unspecified number of Dutch migrants, including youths between fifteen and eighteen, on the proviso none were 'of Jewish race'.[22]

Cyril Bavin of the YMCA had raised the issue of 'non-Aryan' Christian refugees during a visit to Australia in January 1938. He indicated his organisation was prepared to train young 'German non-Aryans' who had become victims of Nazi persecution.[23] In Britain he

Some of the German and Austrian youths who came to Australia through the German Emergency Fellowship Committee (Society of Friends). Those identified are: Ernst Stein (second from end in back row, with cigarette), Raoul Krantz (next to Ernst), Keith Muenz (far left, front row, squatting) and Gerald Rieger (front row, playing recorder) Hans Eisler joined this group before they sailed. At fourteen he was the youngest; he was also the only Jewish boy. (Keith Muenz)

worked closely with the German Emergency Committee, while in Australia Camilla Wedgwood took up the cause.[24] Through her connections with the Society of Friends she became president of the Australian branch of the German Emergency Fellowship Committee, established in Sydney in 1937. In May 1938 she visited John McEwen, Minister for the Interior, and pleaded the case for the admission of young 'non-Aryan' Christians, an interview which led to the granting of the twenty permits.[25] Requests by both the London and Sydney committees for further concessions resulted in frustrating delays.[26] In late 1938 Cyril Bavin took fifty German and Austrian boys into his training scheme at Flint Hall Farm, Hambleden, anticipating approval for their migration to Australia. Delay followed delay. In April 1939 Camilla wrote that 'the Australian Government was proving very difficult to deal with'.[27] Cyril Bavin meanwhile arranged for sixteen boys to be interviewed at Australia House, and booked passages for 12 May. It was mid-May before permission finally came from the Department of the Interior 'to admit a limited number of refugee lads for work on the land — with £5 landing money'.[28] Without further delay, passages were re-booked on the *Orama* sailing on 17 June 1939.[29]

Hans Eisler, the Austrian lad who left Vienna on 'a rickety old plane' on 16 December 1938, was the only under-sixteen-year-old in the group. On his fourteenth birthday, after a fling in London, Hans was picked up by the police in Trafalgar Square and taken to the YMCA training farm at Hambleden. After a few weeks of basic farm training he was placed on a farm at Watlington. He remembers it as a wonderful experience, one he would gladly have continued had his emigration to Australia not been organised.

> I was working on the farm of Mr Butler, milking cows, sweeping ... I loved milking cows in the cold weather there — being close to them, cleaning up the stables ... The local teacher taught me English, even allowed me to hold hands with his daughter. The first thing the local parson did was put a cricket bat in my hand in the cold winter morning — made me learn to play cricket, which I loved. I entered the boxing tournament ... I got a new bike and went on tours with others on my days off. Mr Butler and the whole village were wonderful.

The hope of the German Emergency Committee to send many other boys to Australia, at the rate of twenty a month, never materialised. Earlier in 1939 they had sent thirteen youths on individual permits. Later

Hans Eisler at school in Austria in happier days. Hans is at the end of the second row from the back, in front of the teacher (Hans Eisler)

in 1939 they helped at least one fourteen-year-old, Alfred Hess, gain his release from Dachau and enter Australia.[30]

Britain's response to children from November 1938 was exemplary. Nevertheless, parents sent their children to Britain on the understanding that it was a temporary refuge. The Refugee Children's Movement believed it had a responsibility to provide a chance for the children 'to start a new life in a new land with the hope that, at some later and happier day, they themselves may be able to arrange for their parents to follow them'.[31] That Australia ranked high among those 'new lands' is certain. The report went on: 'It is hoped to find openings for these children in our own Colonies and Dominions'.

Britain softened its position on re-emigration when it became obvious that many of the children could be absorbed internally. The Home Office announced it was prepared 'to envisage the permanent unofficial adoption and residence of the younger children, and of girls who entered Domestic Service, or who married British citizens'.[32] Despite this change in position, in May 1939 it was estimated that it would still 'be necessary to emigrate 80% of the boys and 20% of the girls'.[33] The war interrupted these plans, but considerable pressure was put on Australia in the preceding months and during the early stages of the war, to relieve Britain of some of the children.

From late 1938 Australia was in a strong position to help, either by admitting some of the refugee children in Britain, or by taking children directly from the Continent. Migration was high on the Australian government's agenda and, as usual, children held a hallowed position among applicants — British children at least.

British child migration was then undergoing a boom period. Although Barnardo's and Fairbridge remained the two major organisations involved with children under twelve, after the resumption of assisted migration in March 1938 there was a proliferation of new schemes for children both under and over twelve. The Commonwealth government had facilitated this by agreeing to fund any organisation or religious body wishing 'to bring approved boys and girls from England to the Commonwealth, provided it is satisfied that [they] are able to provide satisfactorily for the children's after-care and place them in employment when they reach working age'.[34] In this period, for example, the Catholic institutions in Western Australia began their involvement in child migration, as did the Methodist Homes for Children in Western Australia, the Presbyterian Church in New South Wales and various other organisations. Others such as the Salvation Army, the YMCA and the Dreadnought Trust resumed and expanded their activities.

This increased demand for children, together with a falling birth rate and improved prospects for youth in Britain, meant it became increasingly difficult for organisations to fill their quotas. Consequently, many sailings of children to Australia were under quota. For example, the Presbyterian Church of New South Wales was unable to fill a quota for twenty-five children between five and ten years of age. In April 1939 Major Wheeler wrote from Australia House that seventeen children had sailed. 'Considerable difficulty was experienced in obtaining even this number of children, and it is not expected that any more will be sent.'[35] As early as July 1938 the Christian Brothers in Western Australia had highlighted this problem: 'We are finding it difficult to get 33 boys for the second batch ... I am very much concerned about the numbers available.'[36] A letter from Australia House in June 1939 shows the extent of the problem with respect to older children and youth:

> The voluntary organisations, such as Big Brother Movement, Salvation Army, Church of England Council and YMCA interested in lads up to 18 years, are scouring the countryside, and were it not for the fact that those organisations are advancing the whole or part of the passage money, in many cases the number shipped would be much less than they are to-day.[37]

This shortage of British child migrants reflected the continuing decline in British migration to Australia throughout the 1930s despite the resumption of assisted migration. For many at the forefront of migration affairs, the solution to the problem was obvious — open the doors to more non-British immigrants. 'We have got to get used to the idea that our new citizens will be chiefly non-British,' wrote W. D. Forsyth in the *Herald* on 17 October 1938. Forsyth was an outspoken critic of the migration of British children, claiming Britain should be keeping her children and improving their conditions. He saw refugee children as a timely and desirable alternative who 'ought to be regarded as a gift from the gods'.[38] Major Wheeler, a self-professed migrationist, and in charge of migration at Australia House in London, also believed Australia 'must be prepared to accept other migrants, provided they are the right type'.[39] In April 1939 he commented:

> There is little doubt as to Australia's capacity to absorb boys for farm work. At the present time, we have requisitions from interested organisations in Australia for 150 British lads per month; of these we are able to ship less than one third, and the prospects of increasing the flow to any appreciable degree are not encouraging.[40]

After interviewing the sixteen Austrian and German youths from the YMCA training farm, Wheeler made the wry comment, 'in my opinion the lads interviewed are superior physically and mentally to the type of British boy offering at the present time'.[41]

Despite the shortage of British children, most child and youth migration organisations gave little thought to the inclusion of refugee children in their schemes. The YMCA was an exception, as was the Fairbridge Farm School in Western Australia. Mami Bentwich visited the Fairbridge Farm schools when she and her husband, Norman, were in Australia from August to October 1938. Soon after their return to England they were at the forefront of the movement of children from Germany and Austria. She immediately established links with the Fairbridge Society in London. In December 1938 she approached the Society regarding the inclusion of Christian refugee children in Fairbridge parties sailing for Australia, but was informed that, under the terms of the Empire Settlement Act, only British children could be included. She nevertheless was asked to become a member of the Fairbridge Council, and so developed a formal link between British child migration and the movement of refugee children, a link which might facilitate future negotiations between the two. Meanwhile in Western Australia, members of the local branch of the Australian Jewish Welfare Society had approached Mr Joyner, chairman of the Fairbridge Farm School at Pinjarra, regarding the placement of German Jewish children. He advised them that 'the school was prepared to take twenty children on the understanding that these children would receive proper Jewish religious teaching'.[42] Negotiations were begun, but were aborted through procrastination by the Welfare Society, and any sense of urgency for the crisis facing European children.

Although the terms of the Empire Settlement Act would have precluded funding from the British government, this would not have prevented Commonwealth and state governments from supporting the inclusion of non-British children. A precedent was set in April 1938 when the Christian Brothers in Western Australia gained Cabinet approval to admit children from the Irish Free State. At the same time the government of Malta was negotiating with the Christian Brothers over the placement of boys between eight and twelve years in Catholic institutions in Western Australia. Financial arrangements included the government of Malta paying the customary twelve shillings per week for each child.[43]

No government in Australia was prepared to pay twelve shillings, or even less, for a refugee child. At the Evian Conference a resolution had been passed 'that the governments of the countries of refuge and settlement should not assume any obligations for the financing of involuntary emigration'.[44] Several governments, including those of France, Switzerland and Belgium, chose to ignore this. In 1941 Britain also began providing a per capita grant of up to eighteen shillings a week for refugee children.[45] The Australian government provided no financial support. It was left entirely to the voluntary organisations to finance the passages and maintenance of refugee children.

Camilla Wedgwood wrote scathingly of the government's attitude:

> With the Government's skilfully non-commital attitude and complete though suave refusal to take any responsibility whatever for the refugees coming out here, there is very little any voluntary association can do ... A supposedly generous government says with a grand gesture 'we will admit 15 000 in three years but all those 15 000 must have adequate means or be guaranteed by responsible citizens ...'[46]

Earlier in 1939 she expressed her sense of helplessness over how little her 'very amateur refugee committee' could do:

> It isn't the work that is exhausting, it is the sense of helplessness — how can one raise the necessary landing money and find openings for work! Each time a permit is granted and the money raised it seems like a separate miracle. But the nightmare is turning down the hopeless cases! In any case one feels like a mouse nibbling at a mountain. I have to keep reminding myself that every human being saved is one to the good.[47]

Despite its precarious financial position, the German Emergency Committee refused to appeal for public funds, fearing that publicity might bring a backlash from Australians. Other organisations which aligned themselves with the German Emergency Committee held appeals, but with little success. At the end of 1938 the Victorian International Refugee Emergency Council (VIREC), which had representatives from numerous churches and public organisations, launched a public appeal. Although sponsored by the Lord Mayor of Melbourne and the *Argus*, it raised only £2200. Compared with amounts the Australian Jewish Welfare Society raised from its small community, this was a pittance. For example, in April 1936 the New South Wales Jewish community launched an appeal to raise £20 000, its contribution to the £3 000 000 world appeal to help 100 000 young Germans emigrate. By August, £20 669 had been raised. Other appeals followed regularly, generally with similar success. Mindful of this discrepancy in fund-raising potential, the Australian Jewish Welfare Society opposed the formation of an interdenominational committee, the kind of committee most likely to have been effective in bringing to Australia large numbers of refugee children.

An interdenominational committee, modelled on the Refugee Children's Movement in Britain, would have reached mainstream Australia. Advertising, as used by the Jewish Welfare Society, and direct appeals to the public on behalf of children would almost certainly have resulted in many Australians offering to sponsor children and many others opening their homes to them. In Britain, the generosity of people was overwhelming when the Refugee Children's Movement appealed for homes and guarantors for children. Individuals in Britain rescued 6000 children by guaranteeing their maintenance. There is no reason to believe it would have been otherwise in Australia. As it was, the Australian public was never asked to help and, without a strong lobby group for children, the government was able to maintain a rather inflexible position on the entry of refugee children.

Unsolicited offers of help reached the Prime Minister. Most, like the letter sent by Mr and Mrs Jarvis on 6 January 1939 to Mr and Mrs Lyons, were offers by working-class Australians 'to do their bit' to help 'some of the little refugees that have been put in England through no fault of their own'. Mrs Jarvis offered to adopt two children, preferably twin girls, as long as their passages and any other necessary fees were paid.[48] Unrealistic as this particular request may have been, the government's response, and its delay for four months, were not conducive to child rescue. The Department of the Interior advised the Prime Minister 'that it is not considered advisable to furnish Mrs Jarvis with the names of the appropriate organisations for the purpose of assisting the reception and welfare of refugees'. The reason given was that none besides the Australian Jewish Welfare Society had sufficient funds to provide passages to Australia; furthermore, 'any refugee children brought to Australia by the Jewish Welfare Society would surely be placed in Jewish homes'.[49]

In England, numerous Jewish children were placed in gentile homes. The Refugee Children's Movement prescribed against proselytising and arranged either personal contact with a Jewish teacher or instruction by correspondence. Although the Jewish population in Australia was small — 23 553 in 1933 — it is probable many Jewish homes would have opened to refugee children had people been asked. Newly arrived refugees might also have helped had they been given the opportunity, but the Department of the Interior determined that 'nominations by refugees who had entered Australia be not accepted until the refugees had been in Australia for a period of three years'.[50] This decision was made at the recommendation of the Australian Jewish Welfare Society, and reflected its symbiotic relationship with the government. The Welfare Society wanted to maintain a tight control over Jewish immigration, not an unreasonable expectation given its responsibility for Jewish immigrants during their first five years in Australia.[51] Nevertheless, this stranglehold prevented other organisations helping Jewish child refugees. In February 1939, for example, the Child Refugees Welfare League in Melbourne proposed introducing 'a number of children who will be educated, placed in employment, or adopted by families'. The Department of the Interior urged the League to merge with the Jewish Welfare Society, claiming it wanted to deal with only one organisation in relation to Jewish refugees. The Welfare Society supported this stance and thereafter the government refused to consider any applications on behalf of Jewish refugees which were not endorsed by the Australian Jewish Welfare Society. Thus, by 1939 it was left entirely to the Australian Jewish Welfare Society to determine what action the Jewish community would take on behalf of Jewish refugee children.

Adolescents who could be self-supporting on arrival were always a good prospect. When a representation was made to the Australian Jewish Welfare Society in November 1938 to help twenty-seven boys and three girls from the Gross-Breesen training farm in Germany, 'it was decided that applications for landing permits be applied for on behalf of the entire number.'[52] Each committee member offered to guarantee three or four applicants, but the Department of the Interior insisted they be included in the Welfare Society's quota. The Jewish Welfare Society then moved that 'the Gross-Breesen applications go forward as part of our quota in preference to other applications.'[53] About the same time a number of Melbourne Jews fomented a plan for bringing German and Austrian youths to Australia for farm training. A separate organisation, the Welfare Guardian Society, which was endorsed and funded by the Australian Jewish Welfare Society, formed as a result. There is no evidence of government opposition to the proposal, which involved initially twenty boys. Fifteen of those selected came from the Dovercourt camp in England, having escaped Germany and Austria on kindertransports. One of the boys, Charlie Trainor, recalled how 'one day over the loudspeaker they asked if anyone wanted to go to Australia on the farm'. Tired of being in the camp, and barred from seeking employment in England, Charlie volunteered.

With five other boys selected in Germany, the Dovercourt group arrived in Melbourne on the *Jervis Bay* on 15 May 1939. Five of the boys were fifteen, the others mostly sixteen and seventeen.

From November 1938, the Executive Council of the Australian Jewish Welfare Society also received many expressions of interest in young children. These came from its own state branches and from individuals. On 8 December 1938, the Perth committee, following its negotiations with the Fairbridge Farm School, sent the following telegram to Sydney: 'This community prepared to be responsible for reception and care of fifty refugee Jewish children subject to Commonwealth approval'.[54] The executive of the Australian Jewish Welfare Society replied: 'Your idea sounds excellent and to assist us obtaining Commonwealth approval please send airmail full details your suggestions re financing fares, landing money, accommodation and maintenance'.

The Welfare Society was adamant that any arrangements would be made through established channels — committees at Woburn House or representative organisations in Germany and Austria. Its responses to Heinz Brent, who made a representation on behalf of twenty children in Germany, and to Hans Levi, who offered himself as an agent for the Reichsvertretung, express this intent: 'It [is] the policy of the Society to transact all its business direct with the organisations in Germany and Austria or through the medium of Woburn House'.[55]

A proposal from Frances Barkman, secretary of the Melbourne branch of the Australian Jewish Welfare Society, received more serious attention. Her interest in 'furthering the immigration of children' was discussed at a meeting on 13 December 1938, following which the Executive wrote to London 'requesting details of children desirous of emigrating'. Further consideration of this proposal was deferred, pending discussion at an interstate conference held on 1 January 1939.[56] Following this, Woburn House was asked to select desirable applicants and to make recommendations to the Australian Jewish Welfare Society. Only after this was the Australian government approached about a children's scheme.

The matter was explored during a January meeting with the Minister for the Interior. A report on that meeting states that 'the Department was prepared to receive proposals outlining a Children's Scheme covering all States'.[57] Not until 6 February 1939 was a formal request put to the government, 'for the admission of a limited number of children, outside the stated quota'. The Welfare Society couched the request in familiar child migration terms, pointing to the declining birth rate in Australia, the desirability of children as immigrants and the ease with which they would assimilate in Australia. It pointed out that the Perth, Melbourne and Sydney branches were interested in the scheme.[58] In a further meeting with the Department of the Interior, delegates of the Welfare Society asked that 750 children be admitted to Australia over a period of three years; also, that the children be admitted outside the quota and without the usual £50 landing money. They requested that if the children could not be excluded from the quota, 'could they be admitted without permits, provided that reputable persons could be found who would be willing to act as adopters'.[59]

On 15 March the Australian Jewish Welfare Society received approval to admit 250 Jewish refugee orphan children per annum for three years. According to the Department of the Interior, 'Consideration had been given to the question as to whether these should be included in the 15 000 refugees which the Commonwealth has indicated it will be prepared to admit over the three year period'.[60] Decisions were made that 'the children be included in the quota of 15 000'; they would require landing permits, but no landing money.

It was a small concession, scarcely a serious attempt to rescue children. Nevertheless, the Australian Jewish Welfare Society had a quota for 250 German and Austrian children for each of the next three years. The executive decided to allocate one hundred of the initial quota to New South Wales, one hundred to Victoria and fifty to Western Australia. Valuable time had been lost while these negotiations were proceeding, but swift action could still have saved several hundreds of children before the gates of Europe closed, ending most opportunities for overseas refuge. The action never came. Only nineteen of the permits were ever used.[61]

3

CHILDREN FROM GERMANY

17 April 1939: Berlin

My dears!

Just now I came from Rabbi Singermann. He is against that L goes to Australia ... he is still too young. But now the Reichsvertretung der Juden has approved the admission ... and the affair can hardly be cancelled now. S has to write a character reference for L and should bring it to us tomorrow. One doesn't know now what to do ... Kathe is very much for it. I'll miss him a lot, but whatever one does in life it's always wrong. L is so clever. Today he said: 'Daddy, it's a joke that the stork delivered me; I came out of Mummy's breast!!' Laughable, isn't it? Just now he said, 'Daddy, don't lift up the table or else you'll get a hernia one day and that will harm your stomach, then you'll throw up again'. He is so lovely, and him we must send so far away. Well, we'll see what fate has in store for us.

Greetings, Walter.[1]

Fate had nothing good in store for Walter Badrian and his wife Kathe. They were among the six million Jews murdered by the Nazis. Their beloved and only child would surely have joined them had they not decided in April 1939 to send him to Australia. By then time was running out for Walter and Kathe. Relatives had scattered across the globe to wherever a permit would take them — including three to Australia. But Walter and Kathe were trapped. They hoped for a permit to Australia, but without money or established family, their chances were slim. When they heard of a scheme to send children to Australia, they applied; but now the reality of separation was approaching ...

*   *   *

Laurie Badrian was one of the seventeen German Jewish children, aged between seven and twelve, who sailed on the *Orama* on 17 June 1939. It is not known how many other parents applied or would have sent their children had the opportunity offered. It is certain that tens of thousands of Jewish and other children at risk remained in Germany and its annexed territories before the outbreak of war. It has also been established that from November 1938 parents inundated the relief organisations with letters and personal representations pleading for the removal of their children.

How these seventeen were chosen is also unknown, as no written record of the process has been found. Nevertheless, patterns established for kindertransports to other countries, especially England, the collective memories of the children involved, and documents issued to them, provide considerable insight.

When the Movement for the Care of Children from Germany began, it had the task of selecting from the 60 000 children in Germany and Austria a limited number who could be admitted to England. 'It was decided that the only equitable method was to rely entirely on the judgment of the committees in Germany, except in the case of those children for whom guarantees were signed in England'.[2] Provincial offices of the Jewish social welfare department, the Judische Zentralwohlfahrtsstelle, were the first point of contact for parents of unguaranteed children. Parents submitted applications and photographs to the social worker, who

41

Laurie Badrian (seated, far left) and Alfred Stocks (standing, far left) with their Kindergarten class in Berlin, 1936. Both boys were among the seventeen children who came to Australia in 1939. (Laurie Badrian)

evaluated them for urgency, then forwarded them to the central office in Berlin, where further sorting occurred. Applications were so numerous that, according to one social worker, many were never read.[3] The final selection of children for England and the organisation of the transports were in the hands of the Kinderauswanderung Abteilung, a department of the Reichsvertretung der Juden devoted to child emigration.

The selection of children for Australia was made by the social welfare department, with official approval coming from the Reichsvertretung. When the Australian Jewish Welfare Society requested the Council for German Jewry in London to select some children the request would have proceeded along established communication channels. The Council always corresponded directly with the Reichsvertretung — in Austria, with the Kultusgemeinde — 'which in turn distributed the mail to their affiliated committees'.[4] In this way the social welfare department would have been asked to select some children for Australia.

Thirteen of the children came from Berlin, and four from provincial areas, indicating that the request was transmitted to at least some provincial welfare offices. Given the burdens on welfare staff and their limited resources, some offices may have received the information and not acted on it. Ellen Rothschild's mother, working at the welfare office in Kassel, was one who responded. She immediately applied to have Ellen included and 'travelled around trying to persuade other parents to send their children'. Ingrid and Marion Ehrlich's mother, living in Muhlhausen with her two daughters, was approached by a friend who worked for the Jewish welfare department. She was told of a children's transport going to Australia with an allowance for twenty children. In Berlin, having connections with the Reichsvertretung or the welfare department also gave people an edge in hearing about emigration schemes. Alfred

Stocks believes having a relative working for the Reichsvertretung was how his parents found out about the Australian scheme. His parents seized the opportunity, then proceeded to organise passages for themselves to Shanghai. In another case, a girl who had emigrated to Australia under an earlier youth scheme urged her mother to investigate opportunities for her young brother to join her. She provided her mother with names of Reichsvertretung contacts she had made through her own emigration and thus ensured that her brother's name was registered even before any definite scheme was announced. Others in her situation were not as fortunate. At the end of 1938 Reichsvertretung staff wrote that many of the forty-four young people who had emigrated to Australia that year had applied for brothers and sisters to join them. The Reichsvertretung was enthusiastic about the idea, but wondered 'whether this project [could] be carried out ... because of the events of November ... A large number of young people of this age group has been placed temporarily in England, so it may be feared that the English committees, through whose hands all applications for placement in Australia pass, will try in the first instance to have those young people who are already in England migrate on to Australia'.[5] The first group of children was chosen directly from Germany but, except for the case mentioned, applications of these earlier immigrants on behalf of younger siblings were overlooked.

The majority of Berlin children found out about the scheme through their Jewish schools, which distributed forms, sometimes to children identified as likely candidates. Margot Goldstein recalled being given a form and being told to go home and ask her parents if they were willing to send her to Australia. Ellen Lewinski (later Anderson), attending the same school, was elated by the offer: 'My teacher had said would I like to go to Australia, and I thought "What a gas that would be!" So I went home and asked my mother and she burst into tears, and I was surprised.' Three of the selected children attended this school, five others attended another school. At a third school, Betty Abrahamson (now Midalia) recalled the teacher saying: ' "Hands up those who'd like to migrate to Australia." That's what I remember though it might have been quite different. I thought, "This is goodo, this is good fun, to go somewhere." So I put my hand up and I got a note to take home.'

Parents might have found out about the proposed scheme any time after December 1938 when the Australian Jewish Welfare Society sent its initial request to the Council for German Jewry. Approval for a children's scheme was not given by the Australian government until 15 March 1939. Therefore, while parents may have applied earlier, the selection was not approved until after that date. Walter Badrian's 17 April letter, and other documents, show that this was done early in April. It is possible applications were not sought until after 15 March, in which case quick action by parents would have been a critical factor in the selection.

Few of the families had connections with Australia. 'I don't think they cared where they sent me; just to get out — England, Australia ... I don't think they cared where ... and I am sure they would have sent my sister and my brother,' commented Margot Goldstein. The age restriction of seven to twelve years excluded many siblings, but there was an expectation that these brothers and sisters would follow on later transports. This suggests that those involved in Germany hoped to negotiate more flexibility into the Australian offer, probably in line with the British scheme which included children from a few months to sixteen years. 'My brother was definitely supposed to follow,' said Betty Abrahamson. Letters from Margot Goldstein support this widely held belief. Two weeks after arriving in Australia she wrote to her family in Germany: 'Hopefully the next transport will leave soon and Ester with them. Then Ester and I would definitely bring you over.' A week later: 'What's happening with the next transport to Australia?' About the same time Hermann Levy's father wrote to Dr Falk in Melbourne about Hermann's sister being interviewed for Australia:

> Approximately three weeks ago our daughter Hanna was in Berlin to be introduced to a Gentleman from your country and we would be happy if she would be accepted there. Could you possibly support us in this? Hanna is fourteen years old, attends school in Hamburg and she's really a lovely girl <u>with all good characters</u>.

Like many children, Ellen Schaechter (now Osrtrower) believed that not only brothers and sisters, but the whole family would follow in a short time: 'The idea was that we would sail to Australia first and our families would follow in six months time. Now, it may not have been so, but that is what I believed.' If such promises were made, they were certainly not made by Australian authorities, either Jewish or government. Parents did not figure in their plans.

While it can be argued that by April 1939 all Jewish children were in need of rescue, applications were probably evaluated for degree of urgency, as occurred with applicants for England. Children in provincial towns were particularly at risk after November 1938. Those selected from these areas had all been terrorised by the Gestapo during Kristallnacht and had lost their fathers then or previously. Life after Kristallnacht was anxiety-ridden and lonely for many of these children, now barred from state schools and with no Jewish alternatives.

After the destruction of their flat, nine-year-old Hermann Levy and his mother picked up the broken pieces as best they could. 'We returned to our flat to attempt cleaning up the debris of glass, broken crockery etcetera. The kitchen cupboard now empty was leaning

Laurie Badrian on his first day of school, Germany 1938
(Laurie Badrian)

on to the opposite wall. The front door we nailed up with wood where the glass was formerly. Even a resemblance of order took several days.' The emotional trauma could not be patched up.

> Up to this point my father was for me the symbol of strength, maturity and responsibility ... now denigrated, arrested before my eyes and I am full of fear ... my mother was broken in the absence of my father. The men who took my father advised her no longer to send me to the local school ... I dared no longer play with or even speak to other children and never ventured on to the street unaccompanied. So mother and I lived alone for seven months until I emigrated.

Hermann does not know how he was selected for the Australian scheme, but in those seven months either his mother must have approached the local welfare office or someone from the office approached her, advising her to apply.

Urgent cases in Berlin included children whose families had always been poor and who had no reserves when forced into unemployment. Such families had no hope of emigrating. Betty Abrahamson's father, for example, had been a bootmaker, but became unemployed long before she left. The family survived on relief and on what her mother could earn through dressmaking. Families of Polish nationals who had been deported from Germany were also in a desperate situation by 1939. In February they received orders to leave Germany immediately. Children from these, as well as 'stateless' families, were selected for the Australian scheme.[6] Others were in households where fathers had disappeared — through hiding, incarceration or emigration — or were under threat of being picked up, but this phenomenon was so widespread by April 1939 that it alone would unlikely have constituted an urgent case. Given the 'potpourri' of children in the group of seventeen children — 'some were good students, some were not; some came from rich homes, some from poorer homes', Jo Lehmann (now Weinreb) remarked — it seems likely there was at least some effort to balance the group between urgent cases and those who could afford to pay. Intelligence and family background may also have played a part, as Ellen Schaechter discovered in a chance meeting at a New York cocktail party many years later: 'This man said that some of us were chosen because we were bright and of good families. This was so that we would make a good impression on Australian Jewry and that more children would be sponsored in the future.'

Money certainly played a role. George Dreyfus wrote: 'The arrangements were supposed to be for poor Jewish children who couldn't get out any other way, but my father donated some money and so was able to have us included. It was much easier for rich people to get out.'[7] In doing this, George's father facilitated the emigration of two other children whose families could not afford to pay. As a general principle, the Reichsvertretung required emigrants to contribute as much as possible toward their emigration, any subsidy being paid half from central funds and where possible half from funds of the local Jewish communities.[8] Considering the tremendous drain on funds at the time it is unlikely there would have been a departure from this policy for these children. Families who could pay, and a number could, must have been an attractive proposition.

That any of the seventeen was selected is remarkable — a fortunate misunderstanding perhaps. In its 15 March advice that it would admit 250 refugee children during each of the next three years, the Australian government stipulated that the children be orphans. The Australian Jewish Welfare Society itself had constantly used the term 'orphan' when discussing plans for refugee children. It used the term in its 6 February application to the government, referring to the children admitted to Great Britain as 'orphaned children from Central Europe'. It also mentioned the likelihood of many of the children being adopted. There seems little doubt that the Welfare Society had in mind children who were true orphans. This was never the intent of the London organisations. As the German Jewish Aid Committee in London later explained, 'what was intended was that 250 refugee children, who, through force of circumstances, had become parted from their parents — not 250 orphans — should be admitted'.[9] The premise was that the children's circumstances would be similar to those of children selected for England. It was with this understanding that the London organisation, and the welfare department in Germany, went about the first selection.

Having been selected, there began for the children and their families a period of waiting and preparation. Various documents had to be organised, both for leaving Germany and for

Laurie Badrian with his mother and father in Berlin, 10 June 1939, two days before he left for Australia. Both parents died during the Holocaust. (Laurie Badrian)

Marion and Ingrid Ehrlich with their mother on the rooftop garden of their house in Muhlhausen. Marion is on the left. Their parents escaped separately to Shanghai, their mother going overland by train through Russia after the outbreak of war. Both parents came to Australia after the war. (Marion Paul)

entering Australia. In some cases parents, hopeful of an offer from somewhere, not necessarily Australia, had already obtained passports for their children. Others now began this process. Betty Abrahamson recalled going to 'a very very big hall' where her emigration papers were processed. Boys as young as seven also had to prove they were exempt from the Hitler Youth before they could receive a passport. For Jewish children, gaining this exemption certificate was just another time-consuming formality.

To enter Australia, each child needed a landing permit. These were issued from Canberra on 21 April 1939. Parents also had to provide a character reference and proof of their child's sound physical and mental health.

All goods taken out of Germany underwent close scrutiny. Before leaving, a complete list of items had to be provided and authorised by the Reich. Every item included a cost price and its time of purchase. This did not prevent parents from outfitting their children with new clothes for the journey. Indeed, sewing machines worked overtime in many households, as mothers either sewed the clothes themselves or had dressmakers prepare new outfits. As Jo Lehmann recalled: 'We weren't allowed to take any gold with us — a certain amount of clothes only. I remember my mother being very conscientious about that — that I have new shoes, and my sister too. And clothes — we went to the dressmaker to get dresses made. We still had plenty of money'.

Even families with little money outfitted their children with special items. Betty Abrahamson's mother took her to a shop to buy a red woollen dress, her first piece of commercial clothing. 'I was thrilled, even though she could make far nicer clothes, being a dressmaker.' Apart from clothes, Edna Lehmann recalled her mother including some priceless treasures to help her feel at home in Australia: 'toys and teddy bears and books ... my very first books from kindergarten. She sent everything so that we should feel at home ...

She was a very good mother.' Walter and Kathe Badrian did likewise. As well as extensive clothing, Laurie took many toys including a petrol truck, two balls, a paintbox, coloured pencils and a colouring-in book and a harmonica.

Doctor Erna Falk, a specialist in child health in Berlin, was to escort the children to Australia. She interviewed parents before the completion of the arrangements and met most of them again at a farewell party for the children held in Berlin. That party was an opportunity for children and parents to meet. Jo Lehmann recalled the occasion — a long table, covered by a white cloth, and on it lots of biscuits and sweets which spelt out the word 'Melbourne'.

For the children, the preparations may have provided a welcome distraction in their otherwise unsettled lives. Despite the preparations, some of the younger children did not realise they were going on a long journey or leaving without their parents. Edna Lehmann was one of those: 'It didn't occur to me we wouldn't be back that night'. At the time of departure there was a sense of going on a journey, a holiday perhaps, and their parents joining them soon. 'Leaving wasn't that traumatic,' said Margot Goldstein. 'I mean even if you leave for a holiday you leave your parents ... I didn't know then that I wasn't going to see them again. It wasn't that kind of feeling at the time. I was sure that they were going to come later; they would say that you would be the first and then, in a few months, your sister, and then eventually everybody.' For Hermann Levy, alone with his ailing mother, the occasion was much sadder. He knew he was leaving, 'but it wasn't talked about at home too much because it would increase the sadness at home at the necessity of such a drastic step'. Hermann travelled alone to Bremerhaven, via Hamburg, where he farewelled his sister. 'I recall that the moment I was put on the train to Hamburg I felt that I'd never see my mother again. I waved until I could no longer identify her ... A passenger asked where I was going and the answer I recall was "half way around the world to Australia".'

For parents the moment of parting was invariably one of overwhelming sadness. 'I still see my parents on the day I left,' Ellen Lewinski recalled.

> It's made a deep impression — imprinted. Mother with her stony face to hide her emotion and my father in tears, and my saying 'What's the matter?', trying to comfort him where it hurt. And letting him hear the humming inside the new ball they'd just given

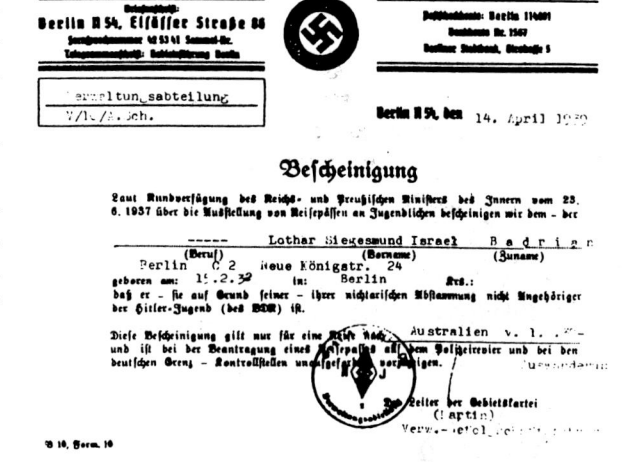

Certificate issued to Laurie (formerly Lothar) Badrian by the Berlin district of the Hitler Youth, 14 April 1939. Being Jewish, Laurie was excluded from the Hitler Youth and was thus eligible to apply for a passport. From 1936, membership of the Hitler Youth was compulsory for non-Jewish German youth but it was not enforced until April 1939. Emigration for non-Jewish youth thence became extremely difficult.

Translation: 'According to the laws of the Minister of Internal Affairs (law of 23 June 1937) re passports to youth ... Lothar Siegesmund Israel Badrian ... born on 15 February 1932 in Berlin ... is not a member of the Hitler Youth because he is not Aryan. This certificate is valid for one journey to Australia from 1 May 1939. This certificate must be presented when he applies for a passport and also when going through customs and crossing borders. He must present it without being asked.'

me, which I'd been bouncing; and being crushed in a hug much more firmly than I'd ever been hugged before, and his going on crying and mother trying to keep her face blank and looking stony. And my being puzzled by the reaction. I was going to Australia. I was going on the picnics, which is the way I'd brought home the invitation.

For Berlin children, farewells took place on the upstairs platform of the West Berlin railway station. 'I remember some of the children crying,' commented George Dreyfus. 'I was probably crying. I remember standing at the back of the train going to Bremerhaven thinking, "You're not going to come back here, are you".' The children met as a group in Bremen, where they stayed overnight at a hotel. Margot Goldstein recorded the occasion on a postcard to her family: 'Now we are in Bremen in a hotel. We stayed overnight in the hotel and on Tuesday the 13 June 1939 we go to Southampton.'

Few kindertransports left from German ports, but the Reich had given permission for about three hundred children to leave on the *Europa* from Bremen. According to Jo Lehmann, permission was given 'provided a lot of money was paid'.[10] It was an enormous ship — at 83 000 tons, Germany's largest. 'Never had I seen so many hundreds, perhaps thousands, of people who embarked on the *Europa*,' remarked Hermann Levy. As they were embarking, Ingrid and Marion Ehrlich's mother experienced an unexpected act of kindness. Because they were not from Berlin, their mother and grandmother had accompanied the girls to Bremen. Dressed alike in Shirley Temple dresses, the two little girls, aged nine and ten, attracted the attention and sympathy of an SS guard. Marion (now Marion Paul) recalled their departure:

> They wouldn't let my grandmother on the boat, but my mother went on, and then I think I started to cry because I knew she was leaving. My mother later told me that a nice SS man said, 'If you want to, stay on the boat'. Even though she didn't have a permit or fare or anything we think that he would have let her stay, but ... She should have.

It was the beginning of a long journey away from all that was familiar. For Ellen Lewinski, realisation of that now began:

> I didn't realise until I was at the port of Bremen that I'd made a mistake, that this party dress that I'd been allowed to get despite the fact that we couldn't afford it, and the cardigan that I'd so longed to have ... and the knee-length socks with pom poms, and patent leather shoes — an outfit I'd dreamed about having, and I'd nagged into getting. And I had more money in my pocket than I'd ever had before, because we were on relief by that time. I was on my way to the tuckshop and I suddenly realised that nobody gave a damn about the fact that I had all these things. The only people who really cared were the people I'd left behind. I'd made a mistake, and I didn't want to go. I felt desolate.

Betty Abrahamson, on the other hand, remained blissfully happy and unaware:

> I remember as clear as anything ... when we left Bremen Margot and I were in the same cabin. I remember we looked through the porthole and everyone was waving. And she was crying and crying. I was smiling and happy. I said, 'Why are you crying? We're going on a big adventure' ... perhaps she was just more aware than I. I didn't know. I don't know what I expected.

At Southampton the Australia-bound children, tagged and labelled, were separated from the others and taken by train to London. Memories linger of kindly volunteers offering sandwiches of fresh white bread — a luxury for German children, as were the freedom and absence of fear in the English people. In London the boys and girls were accommodated and entertained separately for several days. The girls recalled going to the zoo and visiting a maze.

Major Wheeler, in charge of migration at Australia House, was peeved that they were not presented for interviews and medical examinations at Australia House during their stay. He later complained to the Department of the Interior:

> It is really difficult to appreciate that British children, such as the Fairbridge children, must undergo a most rigorous test before being permitted to go to Australia, yet these German Jewish children are accepted evidently on the say-so of the German Jewish organisation.
>
> Might I suggest that if there is to be a continuance of the introduction of these children they should at least be passed by this Office and medically examined by the Commonwealth Medical Officer.[11]

One wonders what words might have been exchanged had Wheeler known the whole truth. During the journey from Bremen a girl with the British contingent came down with a sore throat and fever. Scarlet fever was suspected and most of the children were consequently quarantined at a Fever Hospital in London for several weeks. Fortunately for them, the Australia-bound children were whisked away on arrival in Southampton and were able to embark on the *Orama* as planned, several days later.

The day before leaving, an Austrian couple, also due to sail on the *Orama*, was called to Woburn House.

> They told us on the ship is a group of refugee children in the charge of a lady doctor [Erna Falk]. Her husband had committed suicide and she was in a very sorry state. They had some reservation whether this lady would be able to look after the children, and asked whether we could give her a hand. I had done a course of welfare work in Vienna. I suppose that is why they picked on us amongst all the many people ... somehow it developed that we were with the children all the time.[12]

In this way Hedi and Ferry Fixel began a long involvement with the seventeen children, one that extended into many of the children's adult lives.

★   ★   ★

The journey to Australia was generally a happy time, interspersed with bouts of homesickness — and seasickness. Hedi Fixel recalled: 'The captain and the crew, everybody was very kind to the children. Whenever there was a birthday in our group or in the Fairbridge group there was a party ... When we were in port there were outings and everything, like on a normal cruise ship.' The ship's interpreter later remarked: 'From the moment of departure the seventeen refugee children had been the life of the ship. Their healthy boisterousness made one wish that older folk were as carefree and as confident of the future.'[13]

This carefree abandonment was regulated by a daily routine: 8 o'clock breakfast, 12.30 dinner, 5 o'clock a 'last meal' and 7 o'clock bed. There were also organised games and activities and English lessons, during which the children learnt some of the popular English songs of the day, such as 'Daisy, Daisy'.

In this milieu, friendships quickly formed among the children and between the children and other passengers. Some of the older boys leaving without their families were drawn to the children; Jo Lehmann, a self-declared extrovert, recalled happy moments sitting on their laps and singing. But sibling relationships suffered their first blow, with siblings being separated in cabins and at the dining table. Ingrid Ehrlich recalled her sister, Marion, being moved to the other end of the dining table: 'Marion would look at what I was having for breakfast, then she'd order the same, so they moved her right down the other end of the table. It was cruel.' It was a pattern that was to continue when they arrived in Australia.

The time on board was relieved by brief jaunts ashore — at Toulon, Naples and

Ellen Rothschild (front, far right) with her family in 1937. Back row, left to right: Ellen's mother who survived underground in Berlin and came to Australia after the war; an uncle who died in the Warsaw ghetto; another uncle who escaped to England before the war, was interned there and was sent to Australia on the *Dunera* in 1940; an aunt who was murdered by the Nazis. Front row, left to right: a cousin, Ruth, who died in the gas chambers; Ellen's grandmother who committed suicide during Kristallnacht, November 1938, when Gestapo came to arrest her husband (she threw herself off a balcony); Ellen's grandfather, who was arrested during Kristallnacht and who died in Theresienstadt concentration camp. (Ellen Shafer)

Colombo. As often happens with children, the impressionable experiences were the simple and unplanned — going through a tunnel in a train, drinking coconut milk, gathering shells. A lasting memory for Margot Goldstein was going to the beach for the first time. 'I remember somebody bought me a bathing suit and I was afraid to go into the water. I sort of walked in a bit up to my knees. This overpowering feeling! This big beach! Some of the other children were a little scared [too].'

Each port was an opportunity to send and receive letters. Letters that have survived tell of an undercurrent of worry that pursued some of the children on their journey. Inquiries about the health of family members, about families having to move from their apartments, about the whereabouts of fathers ('Where is Papa actually?'), and about the prospects of permits and shipping ('What prospects are there for Papa to go to Shanghai?') quietly reveal the turmoil of the times and belie the age of the writers.[14] In Margot's letters, there was the constant reassurance of her own health and happiness: 'I am well. You don't have to worry about me because here I am fine.' The escorts would often add their own reassuring comments: 'Margot is very well. She isn't coughing any more at all. She is happy.'

* * *

The Australian Jewish Welfare Society proceeded with plans for the admission of other children, but with an extraordinary lack of urgency. The New South Wales branch of the Welfare Society moved on filling its quota in April 1939, when it sent a cable to London 'asking for applications for sixty children between the ages of seven and eleven to be submitted for selection in New South Wales after July this year'. It seems ludicrous that at such a time the Sydney Jewish community should choose to delay the removal of the children till they had built an expensive extension to the Montefiore Home at Hunters Hill, Sydney. But this was what happened. The foundation stone for the Isabella Lazarus Home was laid, and an appeal launched, in May 1939 at a ceremony filled with homilies about needy children and orphans.[15] The home was opened and consecrated in another official ceremony in late November, a home that would accommodate up to sixty children, half of them permanently.[16] By then, war with Germany had disrupted attempts to remove children from

Germany or its occupied or allied territories. The only refugee children housed at the Isabella Lazarus Home during the war had come to Australia with parents who, for various reasons, needed outside care for their children.[17]

The Western Australian Jewish community reneged on its December 1938 offer to take fifty refugee children. Having been notified by Sydney of the children's scheme for 250 children a year, and having been informed of the allocation of fifty children to Perth, the Perth committee advised Sydney: 'We are only prepared to take these children after selection at this end and at the rate of four a month'.[18] Even the Melbourne branch, which had expressed most interest in receiving children, moved slowly on its plans for more children. Originally its intention was to settle the first group of children, move them into private homes, then bring in another group. It was the end of August before the committee applied for further children, and then only ten — eight boys and two girls.[19] The composition of this group suggests the committee intended merging them with the original ten girls and seven boys; plans for fostering may already have been dwindling in the face of mounting difficulty to find children who met Australia's stringent requirements.

Despite the tardy response by the Australian Jewish Welfare Society, the orphan clause in the government's agreement crippled efforts to organise other groups of children. Realising that the first group of children were not orphans, the government insisted that any future children meet this criterion, that they have neither mother nor father living. Although undoubtedly there were Jewish orphans in Germany, it generally required the concern and commitment of a parent to organise a child's inclusion in a kindertransport. The majority of Jewish children in Germany in 1939 were not orphans. Most were in families where fathers were missing. Others had lost one parent through natural causes, suicide or divorce. Even children in the overcrowded orphanages were not necessarily orphans; often they were the offspring of destitute or despairing families.

In August the Welfare Society wrote to the Department of the Interior, appealing against the restriction:

> I should be most grateful if the Department would give further consideration to this matter as our London Committee is finding it extremely difficult to always forward us applications on behalf of children who are double orphans, that is to say, children who have neither father nor mother living.
>
> There are quite a number of children available who have lost one parent, and we would be most grateful if the Department would let us select children from this category, and in certain cases, even those who have both parents living.
>
> It is understood, of course, that we will inform our London organisation that in such cases the parent, or parents, shall be advised that if permits are granted for the child or children to migrate to Australia, it does not imply, or give them any encouragement to assume that they will also be admitted at a later date. The parent, or parents, will of course also be asked to sign a special undertaking placing the children under the control of this Society.[20]

Even with this undertaking, the Department of the Interior was not prepared to relax its terms:

> There is a great deal to be said in favour of the migration of young children who can be more readily assimilated than older people. Difficulties are, however, likely to arise if the Society's proposal is accepted, as, despite any undertaking which may be given by a parent, or parents, to the Society, we could not morally uphold the permanent separation of parents and children, and there is no doubt that a parent (say a widowed mother) who is

suffering hardships and indignities in Germany, and whose children have been admitted to Australia, would persistently seek to come out and be with them here. There is also the possibility of difficulties arising if parents are permitted to come out and then seek to regain control of the children, perhaps when the latter have reached the earning stage.[21]

Within two weeks of this correspondence Britain and Australia were at war with Germany. Although Germany allowed emigration until 23 October 1941,[22] Australian regulations forbidding the entry of residents from enemy or enemy-controlled territory prevented further admission of German refugees. Regardless of age or political or religious affiliation, the classification 'enemy alien' was now applied to 'German nationals including former Austrians, Czechs, Slovaks and Sudetan Germans who have become German nationals, also Stateless persons of German or Austrian origin'.[23] Female enemy aliens and children under eighteen, who were in the United Kingdom or neutral countries, could still gain permits for Australia. Therefore, the Australian Jewish Welfare Society now turned its attention to these children.

The Melbourne committee was most persistent. 'We have received numerous inquiries from our Victorian Committee regarding the migration of refugee children between seven and twelve years of age,' wrote the general secretary of the Welfare Society in November 1939. At the instigation of Frances Barkman, the Melbourne committee made a direct request to London in November for 'a further batch of twenty children up to the age of 12 years'.[24] With the completion of the Isabella Lazarus Home for Children, the Sydney committee was also anxious to receive children.[25] In December 1939, the Welfare Society approached the Department of the Interior for permission to bring in one hundred children who were not necessarily orphans — sixty for Sydney, twenty for Melbourne and ten each for Perth and Adelaide.

As all landing permits and quotas for aliens had been cancelled with the declaration of war,[26] this latest request was treated as a new application. It was given a lukewarm reception, passing from one official to the other in the Department of the Interior — from Peters to Garrett to Carrodus and finally to the Minister, Senator Foll. Carrodus voiced the general feeling when he recommended to the Minister: 'I would prefer to recommend that this application be not approved. As, however, the Society, in good faith, has incurred the expense of erecting a building to house and train these children, the recommendation that 50 be admitted during 1940 is submitted for approval.'[27]

In approving the recommendation, the Minister stipulated that the selected children should be complete orphans. However, a concession was made that 'failing complete orphans being available the balance selected should have only one living parent. The admission of any of these children to Australia cannot be used, at any time, to facilitate the entry of their relatives to the Commonwealth'.[28] The concession came with a price. The selected children were to be examined at Australia House, London, by authorities who reserved the right to issue or refuse permits. Other criteria for selection also tightened, although not necessarily at the behest of the government. The Sydney committee, which was to receive the fifty children, placed the selection in the hands of the Overseas Settlement Department at Bloomsbury House, London. It advised the London organisation:

> The children should be between 7 and 11 years of age — preferably between 7 and 9 years of age, AND THEY MUST BE FULLY JEWISH.
>
> I am sure you will realise how very essential it will be to select children who will create a good impression, not only with the officials

On board the *Orama* which left London for Australia on 17 June 1939. Standing, left to right: Marion Ehrlich (check shirt), Ilse Frank, Margot Goldstein (dress with tie belt), Ellen Schaechter, Ellen Rothschild (floral blouse and black skirt), Betty Abrahamson, Edna Lehmann (with hat), Jo Lehmann (hand on hip). Seated/kneeling, left to right: Herman Gold, Rolf Taylor, George Dreyfus (in front of Rolf), Richard Dreyfus, Laurie Badrian (in front of Richard), Ellen Lewinski, Alfred Stocks. Missing: Hermann Levy and Ingrid Ehrlich (Hedi Fixel)

of Australia House, but with the Commonwealth Authorities, on their arrival in Australia.

IT IS ALSO VITALLY NECESSARY THAT THESE CHILDREN BE OF SUCH A STANDARD THAT OUR OWN PEOPLE WILL BE DESIRABLY IMPRESSED — THEY BEING OUR MOST SEVERE CRITICS.

It then reminded those in the Overseas Settlement Department:

Upon your selection will depend whether the Commonwealth Government will give consideration to any further representation we might make for the admittance of further and larger numbers of children at later dates. The Melbourne Committee has advised their satisfaction with the children who arrived amongst the first batch last year. We hope to be equally satisfied.[29]

With such stringent requirements the Welfare Society was unable to fill even a quota of fifty. Young children who had arrived in England before the war were now settled in homes or hostels. Those needing homes were over eleven or not orphans.

Australia was given one final opportunity to help German children. In May 1940, after the fall of Holland and Belgium, the Australian Jewish Welfare Society received the following urgent cable from London: 'Refugee situation rendered serious by influx Dutch and Belgian refugees. Could you help by taking 500 German Jewish children 7 to 14 waiving orphan restrictions. Matter utmost urgency. Cable reply.'[30]

It is unclear whether the children referred to were German children who had taken refuge in Holland and Belgium or were children already in England whose places would be taken by Dutch and Belgian arrivals. In any case, the Melbourne committee made its position clear on the reception of further German children: 'On receipt of your telegram that Canberra will grant such permits will arrange to absorb 200 Dutch or Belgian, but not German, children'.[31]

This position might be explained by the government's announcement on 16 April 1940 that 'no more permits will be issued to German or former Austrian nationals during the war'. Nationals of other enemy-controlled territories would still be considered.[32] When making an application to the government for Dutch and Belgian children, the Welfare Society gave this as the reason for its amendment to the London request. The application was the beginning of a confused scenario between the Department of the Interior and the Jewish Welfare Society. The Department of the Interior acted on the request promptly, albeit ungenerously, granting permits for one hundred Dutch and Belgian children.[33] The age range of seven to fourteen, as requested, was accepted, as was waiving the orphan restriction, although the usual conditions on entry of parents and relatives applied. On receiving this offer from the Australian Jewish Welfare Society, the Overseas Settlement Department dropped a bombshell. It declared it could not be responsible for Dutch or Belgian children 'as our funds are collected only to provide for German and Austrian refugees'.[34] It was an ironic twist to a saga of aborted attempts to bring German Jewish children to Australia.

Faced with yet another unfilled quota, and at the request of London, the Australian Jewish Welfare Society approached the government again, asking that the age be raised to fourteen on its fifty permits for German children. The Minister refused to negotiate, declaring that the 'original decision must stand'.[35] By then, October 1940, civilian travel between Britain and Australia had all but ceased. Viable opportunities for Australia to help German Jewish children had ended. Efforts would be made periodically throughout the war to rescue German and other children from neutral countries and from countries threatened by German occupation. Australia would be involved in these efforts but, with the danger of sea travel, several years would pass before Australian refuge for child victims of the European war and of Nazi persecution was again tenable.

4

THE LOTTERY OF LIFE

School days at Rokitno, eastern Poland, 1935. Aleck Katz is at the end holding a stick. The many ethnic and religious groups of the border region are represented in the photograph: Jewish, Polish (Catholic), Ukranian and Russian (Orthodox) and German (Lutheran). Aleck's class teacher and headmaster stand at the rear. (Aleck Katz)

Racism and anti-semitism had a strong foothold in Poland long before the 1930s. Discrimination and violence over centuries had seen Jews relegated to the fringe of Polish society, separate from and subservient to Poles. Although many had fought alongside Poles for the independence of their country, the liberation of Poland after the First World War did not free them from the stigma of their caste.[1] Violence against Jews was rampant in 1918 and 1919, so much so that the allies made minority rights a condition of independence. The Minorities Treaty brought hope, followed by disillusionment and further violence. Poles, affronted by demands for pluralism, responded with hostility as ethnic minorities, especially Jews, strove for equality in the new Poland. The rise of fascism in Europe in the 1930s gave anti-semitism a mantle of respectability in Poland. As Celia Heller explained, 'In interwar Poland, anti-semitism was not simply the manifestation of the lunatic fringe; it was respectable and in the forefront of political affairs — a fact one must grasp in order to understand how pervasive Polish anti-semitism really was'.[2]

Thousands of Polish Jews emigrated to Germany after the First World War to escape persecution and poverty. Although life was often a struggle, economically and socially they were better off. 'People became somebody in Germany,' commented Max Nagel. 'That's what makes it tough for people who were satisfied living in Germany and did well, for Germany to do what it did. For the Poles to do what they did is understandable; they were much more anti-semitic than the Germans.'

As anti-semitism took hold in Germany some Polish nationals opted to return to Poland, but for many life in Germany remained preferable. Norman Schindler's family was one of those:

> My parents had left a small, primitive, poverty-stricken town in Poland in the early 1920s, looking for a better life, and it was a better life in Essen [Germany]. But soon anti-semitic policies began to be felt and they kept growing stronger and stronger ... In 1936 my mother, my sister and myself went back to Poland to stay with my grandfather in this little town; my father was going to come later. But my mother couldn't stand any more the primitiveness of the life there and after a few months we went back to Germany.

Oppressive poverty was the norm among Polish Jewry. Unable to own land, most lived in urban areas and worked as petty merchants or artisans.[3] Those in villages serviced the local peasants, their circumstances generally reflecting the poverty of their clientele. George Perl wrote of his childhood:

> My father was a cattle dealer and bought oxen and cows for resale from the neighbourhood peasants. In the past he had been well-off ... but then had lost his money in transporting wagonloads of oxen by rail to Warsaw. Now, occasionally he bought a single beast — an ox or a cow — and sold it to make a few zloty on the deal. From time to time father also brought some kerosene from town to the village, or a sack of salt, oil, matches, and pieces of cloth which were bartered for some corn, potatoes or swine bristles.

Jack Garbasz visited relatives in Rovno before leaving Poland for Australia in April 1939. All of these relatives, as well as Jack's parents and siblings, died in the Holocaust. Jack (wearing a cap) is in the back row with his uncles and aunts. In the front is Jack's grandmother, Sarah, his grandfather, Israel, and four of their grandchildren, Jack's cousins. (Jack Garbasz)

> The peasants would come to our home, take goods on account and pay for them once a year, at harvest time. Father kept an account, noting it all down in a book in Yiddish mixed with Hebrew words. The peasants listened to him make the reckoning and didn't understand how it was possible for them to have taken a total of so many litres of kerosene, so many packets of matches, so much salt.

People growing up in Poland in the 1920s and 30s recalled both town and village life as harsh and primitive. 'People were still wearing shoes from bark,' remarked Aleck Katz. 'They were still wrapping the feet with linen cloth ... and wearing flaxen shirts.' 'The extreme poverty in Poland for the Jews is difficult to imagine,' added Jack Garbasz, who lived in the town of Sarny, where his father taught carpentry.

> When the 1929 depression came it was such a shock to people who were just barely existing. The school was closed down. My father took some of the students on the side and they were making furniture, trying to keep themselves going. Mother and the children were packed off to my grandfather so he could

try and feed us. We were actually on the verge of starvation. I remember we had bread, oil and salt. On the bread you put a little oil, then salt. Listen, if you're hungry it's okay.

Yossel Birstein, who also grew up in these circumstances, recalled his father always telling him that the greatest good a man could do was to provide food for a day.

Apart from physical hardship, Jewish children were subjected to constant humiliation and harassment. Being attacked by adolescent gangs on the way to and from school was common. 'The fear for Jewish kids was terrible,' recalled Aleck Katz. 'Every day we used to be frightened that someone was going to bash us up.' Most attended Polish state schools, where they were exposed to what Celia Heller described as 'the crass anti-Semitism of their Polish classmates and the more obtuse anti-Semitism of their teachers'.[4] Jack Garbasz puzzled over the behaviour of his classmates:

Every week there was a religious lesson and the Catholics, my friends I used to play with during free periods, used to come up afterwards and beat us up because we Jews killed Christ. But the next free period we'd be playing again. It was such a contradiction. Why should they beat us up when they want to play with us later? Even worse was walking the street and a little kid would push you and you'd tell him 'get the hell out of here'. Then his big brother would run up and say, 'Ah! You've been hitting my little brother'. Bang! This provocation all along.

For Jack, fear turned to terror during an attempted pogrom in his town:

We had heard several days beforehand and were locked up in our house. Nobody was going out. I call it a miracle that we survived. Two Jewish blacksmiths, short, very hefty guys, saw the crowd assemble in the square and walk towards the Jewish quarter. They came up, each one with a heavy iron rod, and stood in the middle of the road and said, 'Anybody comes here gets killed'. The Poles knew them as they used to come and have their horses shod by those guys. They knew how heavy and how strong those guys were. They stopped, had a good look and went back. But for us, imagine you are a small kid and you are locked up and your parents are not able to do anything to help you. In fact, your parents are just as scared as you are. It was a very traumatic experience for me.

Jack's family had lived in that area for generations, but as a child he realised it held no future for him. 'As a small child I couldn't understand why they should hate me and want to harm me. That's when I started to feel that I didn't belong there.'

Along the borders of Poland, in what was formerly White Russia, Jewish families lived among other downtrodden minorities — mostly Ukrainians and Russians. The only Poles were industrialists, the military or government workers, brought in to look after the railway line, administration or the school. Relationships between Jews and other minorities were seldom close. 'My father and the whole household lived in fear of the gentiles,' wrote George Perl. 'Several Jewish families eked out an existence in a sea of peasantry; a whole village of peasants, more and more villages around.' 'There was no real friendship,' George explained. When he was a young child, his eldest brother was killed by a neighbour, a tragedy which overshadowed his relationships with the local gentiles. 'Everybody was watching me — not to play with non-Jewish boys. 'You don't know what's going to happen; they murder you, they kill you. Some people we knew and they respected us; we respected them ... but there was no closeness.'

Aleck Katz agreed. His family was 'a little bit higher' socially than the local peasants. Unlike most Jewish families, they lived on a thirty-hectare farm, leased to Aleck's grandfather after twenty-five years service in

Aleck Katz (standing, far right) with his mother, father and three brothers, Gedalie (far left), Aaron (centre back) and Ben-Zion (the youngest, standing next to his mother). After the German occupation of Poland, Aleck's father escaped death by fleeing into the forest and joining the Russian partisans; he died after the war in a displaced persons' camp in Germany. Aleck's mother and two younger brothers were gathered into a cattle truck with other Jews in the area and taken to a 'killing place', he thinks near Sarny. Aaron, the oldest brother, joined the Red Army; he survived the battle of Stalingrad but died later somewhere on the front line. (Aleck Katz)

This photograph was sent to Werner Teitel in Australia in 1942, but was not received until after the war, by which time all those in the photograph were dead. Pictured are Werner's mother and father, his sister, Waltraut, and the 'golden-haired' baby, Isilein, referred to in many of the letters that appear in this book. (Werner Teitel)

the Tzar's army. This enabled them to be reasonably self-sufficient.[5] 'We had our own potatoes and basic things. We had a sort of dairy business there; we had our own milk and cheese and enough to sell. Besides that, my father was working at a quarry as a foreman.' Despite his higher status there was always someone 'swinging' at Aleck. He recalled once hitting a Ukrainian boy and the boy's father coming at him with a knife.

> I hid under the bed, screaming away, shaking. The house was shaking. Luckily my mother was outside sweeping the dirt on the footpath, and she swang the broom at him. They respected my mother. Whenever they needed medicine or there was a sick person, they rushed to my mother. She used to help them.

Opportunities for Jewish youth to escape the shackles of poverty and anti-semitism were few. Formal education beyond primary school was only available at great personal and financial expense for Jewish children. Even with secondary or tertiary education, laws and discriminatory hiring practices introduced in the 1920s and '30s created barriers to employment in the civil service, industry, the professions, even in traditional artisan occupations. Attendance at university was also increasingly difficult as universities became the playing fields of radical nationalist groups bent on removing Jews from the professional and economic life of Poland. Informal quotas became common in the 1920s, as did violence against Jews who braved the atmosphere of hate. Although university administrators and government officials sometimes condemned the excesses, in time they yielded to the demands of the perpetrators. Stringent quotas became official in 1936, and in 1937 a seating ghetto was introduced — separate seating for Jewish students. Those who resisted became the victims of violent attacks, sometimes expulsion, even death. In 1937 any liberal influence within the Polish government ended and anti-semitic ideology became official.

Polish Jews were divided in their responses to anti-semitism. While orthodox Jews waited for the Messiah to deliver them to a better life, the non-orthodox, who included most young people, actively sought change through socialism or Zionism. Those who turned to socialism wanted to create a viable life for Jews in Poland, either through assimilation or separate nationhood, whereas Zionists saw emigration to their ancient homeland as the only solution. Emigration to Palestine was the expectation and hope of many Jewish children. 'We were educated for it and brought up as such,' explained Aleck Katz. 'I was brought up to speak and read Hebrew.' At the end of primary school, many children volunteered for hahsharah, a period of up to two years on a model kibbutz, where they prepared for life in Palestine. The 1931 British White Paper, restricting immigration to Palestine, had a devastating effect on Polish youth. Although many continued to prepare for Palestine, only a limited number could now hope to fulfil their dream. Further restrictions throughout the 1930s, together with the priority being given to German and Austrian youth, created a desperate situation for Jewish youth wanting to leave Poland.

Emigration overseas was also fraught with difficulties for Polish and other eastern European Jews. Although many had been able to emigrate before the Depression, including about 2000 to Australia,[6] as poor immigrants, of a perceptibly different culture, they were generally unwelcome throughout the world. Opportunities for emigration were further reduced as the refugee crisis of the 1930s unfolded and organisations focused on the plight of those formally classified as refugees.[7] Separate organisations for Polish Jews thus developed in the west in the 1930s, usually at the instigation of former eastern immigrants.

In Australia, a Polish Jewish Relief Fund formed in 1934.[8] Based in Melbourne, where the majority of Polish Jewish immigrants had settled, this voluntary organisation at first focused on sending money to Poland to alleviate the economic distress of some of its three million Jewish people. A brochure circulated by the Polish Jewish Relief Fund to raise money for this purpose described the situation of Jews in Poland as 'pitiful', with people living 'in misery and agony'; 'a whole community is starving'.[9] By 1937 it was realised that the money sent was insignificant compared with the need and offered no 'radical solution to the recipients of the charity'.[10] An alternative plan then evolved to bring Polish Jewish children to Australia.

Arthur Rose, the principal force behind this scheme, organised a meeting for 23 May 1937.[11] The plan that emerged was to bring from Poland up to twenty Jewish boys who had lost one or both parents. The boys were to be aged fourteen or under and to have completed primary school. On arrival in Australia they would receive six months intensive schooling to learn English, and would then be apprenticed to a trade or placed in agricultural work. While the Polish Jewish Relief Fund would care for the boys in Australia, individual guarantors would sponsor them and act as guardians.[12]

RELUCTANT REFUGE

Max Nagel and his family were among the Polish nationals deported from Germany to Zbonszyn Poland in October 1938. Max had been born in Germany but, by German law, held the nationality of his father. This photograph, taken in 1932 or '33, shows Max with his family in Altona (Hamburg). The entire family, except for Max, and including a younger child, Bernie, was murdered during the Holocaust. Left to right: Isidor Nagelberg (father), Willi (older boy), Max, Frieda Nagelberg (mother), Oscar (young child next to father), Adi. (Max Nagel)

Norman Schindler (seated in centre) with his mother, father, sister and her fiance. Taken in Zbonszyn, Poland, in March 1939 just before Norman left for Australia. Again, this is the only surviving photograph of Norman's family, all murdered during the Holocaust (Norman Schindler)

A rare photograph of Max Goldberg's parents and of his early life in Poland. For many former refugees, including Max, a single photograph is the only material link with the past. Some do not have even one photograph of their families. (Max Goldberg)

Amendments were made to this proposal before it was formally submitted to the Department of the Interior in September 1937. By then the age of the boys requested was fourteen to sixteen years. Numbers had also firmed; the plan was now that 'in the first instance, twenty children from the most needy and distressed Jewish families in Poland will be brought out here during the next twelve months, followed by a further twenty during the following twelve months'.[13] Despite the reference to needy and distressed families, the application stated that orphans would be given preference, although the term 'orphan' in this context seemed to include any child without a father.

Well-established prejudices toward Polish Jewish refugees and poor immigrants came to the fore as the Department of the Interior considered the proposal: 'Polish Jews who have come to Australia have not proved altogether satisfactory and, in the case of this scheme, the children will be selected from the most needy and distressed Jewish families in Poland. They are, therefore, less likely to prove desirable immigrants than those who have already come here.'[14]

Although Interior recommended the proposal not be approved, at the recommendation of Thomas White, Minister for Trade and Customs, it was passed to Cabinet for a decision.[15] This happened in November 1937,[16] but as with other proposals for the admission of groups of refugee children and youth, Cabinet took no action until after assisted immigration had resumed in March 1938. On 7 April Cabinet considered and rejected the proposal: 'It was decided that the Jewish Relief Fund be advised that Government does not approve of the introduction of a number of male Jewish children, preferably orphans, from Poland'. A clerical error created confusion over Cabinet's intent,[17] and the proposal went back to Cabinet for clarification. On 9 June 1938, following further discussion, Cabinet granted permission to the Polish Jewish Relief Fund 'to introduce up to twenty male Jewish children during the next twelve months, between the ages of fourteen and sixteen, on satisfactory guarantees for maintenance. No landing money stipulated.'[18]

By the end of the month the Polish Jewish Relief Fund had sent instructions on the selection of the children to the education organisation, ORT,[19] in Warsaw:

> Every boy that you select must be sound in mind, intelligent, physically fit, and with no bodily defects.
> Date of birth, standard of Jewish and Secular education, 2 photos, Health Certificate together with each boy's past record, if any, and any other information that you deem advisable, must be sent to us.
> When you select the boys care must be taken in regard to age. They must be between 14 and 16 years old, in accordance with the permit given by the Government.
> Care must be taken that no favouritism or influence is used in selecting any of the candidates.
> It would be advisable to make the selection from as wide an area as possible — not just from one or two cities.[20]

Lengthy delays occurred in Poland. The request was handed over to JEAS, the organisation responsible for Jewish emigration from Poland. JEAS wanted the Australian government to issue twenty blank landing permits, allowing the British consul in Warsaw to insert the names of the boys after they had been selected. This request caused further delay while it passed through the Australian network, only to be refused. As was common practice, the boys had to be selected before their permits would be issued.

Meanwhile, life for Polish-born Jews living in Germany had taken a dramatic turn. On 28 October 1938, over 16 000 were rounded up from across Germany, taken to the Polish border and dumped. In some towns, including Berlin, only the men were taken; in others, the arrests involved men, women and children, sometimes together as a family, sometimes separate. Werner Teitel's mother had recently had a baby. On the night the police came she had returned to hospital because of complications. Werner's eight-year-old sister was upstairs with the neighbours. She, her mother and baby brother thus escaped the deportation, at least temporarily. Not so fourteen-year-old Werner and his father, who were picked up separately. Werner, an apprentice butcher, was living on his work site when they came for him:

> They picked me up at five o'clock in the morning ... Policeman knocked on the door and said, 'Get up boy!' I sat up. 'What's up? What have I done?' He said, 'Nothing!' 'What has my father done?' He said, 'Nothing!' He said, 'Shut up and don't talk. Get up and get dressed because you've only got fifteen minutes. It concerns all Polish Jews in Germany.' He was an official policeman, not a Nazi or an SS man. He said, 'Take everything you've got. If you've got a case put it in.' I had nothing. I was fourteen years old. As we walked down the stairs — everybody wore jackboots in Germany, particularly in a job — he said, 'Any of these yours?' I said, 'Yes, that's my pair.' He said, 'Take them with you 'cause you won't be back.' He then said, 'This looks like a nice pair that'll fit you. Take them.' I said, 'It's not mine', and I was frightened. He says, 'Take it!' And I wouldn't take them, so he took them and gave them to me, 'cause he knew what was happening. He was a nice man. He said, 'The others'll get boots. You take them. You need them.' They came in handy 'cause I had a pair of boots for my father.

Werner was taken to a gymnasium in Essen, where many other Jews, including his friend Norman Schindler, had been herded. 'They marched us, with the few belongings that we had, to the railway station.' There people were searched for money. 'Nobody had more than ten marks. They took everything else. I got my week's wages, which was two marks fifty — two and sixpence. That's all I had. Then, in broken-down carriages — a goods train — we were shipped out to the border town of Benschen.'[21]

Norman Schindler continued:

> We were taken out of the sealed train, then with the German police and their dogs were marched across no man's land which was a few kilometres. People couldn't carry their belongings any more; they became heavier and heavier as they walked along. They had to drop them because the Germans were pushing them to walk as fast as they could. As far as the eye could see the place was strewn with cases, bed linen, and all sorts of boxes and personal belongings like you just can't imagine, all along the way. When we got to this town, Zbonszyn, nobody had any of their belongings; they were all strewn across the roads. The Poles took trucks later and gathered them all up and brought them into the town. We had to stand there and try to identify amongst thousands of articles.

The Polish government resisted the return of these Polish Jews.[22] Max Nagel recalled: 'There was a tug-of-war going on with Germany pushing us, I mean physically pushing us on that side, but the Poles wouldn't let us in. So the Germans started shooting ... a certain amount of panic started and the physical force itself made us go over the border.'

Trainload after trainload of people arrived, within hours of each other. They were taken into the small town of Zbonszyn, which was immediately surrounded by Polish soldiers. Werner Teitel had vivid memories of the first night: 'When we got there it was chaos. I finished up in a stable with another boy, another butcher. He had three sisters, a mother and a grandfather ... The first night I slept in the stable on the cobble stones. It was bitterly cold, and the grandfather of the friend died during the night.' Many other people also died of heart attack or exposure.

Days later, Werner found his father at the railway station. 'There was no more space in the township, so they sat on the floor in the railway station. He slept there, waiting for me. He knew if I was there I would find him ... I slept between his legs ... on the rippled stones. Seventeen people died in the several days I stayed there.' Later they were allocated space in a market building.

A normal-sized room slept twenty-five people. It was bug-infested, but at least you had a wooden floor. It wasn't quite as cold. By this time we had scrounged up two palliasses — two hessian bags which we stuffed with some straw, so we had something to sleep on. A sister slept against the wall, a brother slept next to her, I slept next to him, my father slept next to me, another man and his wife slept next to my father ...

Polish Jewry rallied to help these victims of Nazism. 'They arrived with trucks of bread and basic foodstuffs, and distributed this to the people,' recalled Werner. 'Over a period of time it became much more sophisticated ... they had a team of doctors who set up a clinic, and so on.' In time people developed the semblance of a life in Zbonszyn; those who could, occupied their days with food distribution, meetings and other community and cultural activities, anything to ward off the despair and depression to which it was so easy to succumb. Norman Schindler filled his days with such activities, helping to distribute food, volunteering to help around the town and at the clinic. 'It got me involved and gave me something to do, some reason to get up in the morning and to get going.' Werner Teitel found a job in the soup kitchen, Alwin Spiegel in the hospital. 'I didn't sit on my bottom and wait for something. I went and found something to do which kept me occupied. We didn't get paid, but I managed to make a bit of pocket money.'

In October 1938, the German government rounded up and deported over 16,000 Polish Jews who had been living in Germany. Most were dumped on the German border and forced across a no-man's land to the Polish town of Zbonszyn. (*Pix*, 4 February 1939)

A rare photograph from the refugee camp at Zbonszyn, Poland: Werner Teitel with his father, and a clever dog who knew where to find warmth and food. (Werner Teitel)

Such initiative probably helped these boys win what Norman Schindler called 'the lottery of life'. When ORT began selecting twenty boys for the Polish Jewish Relief Fund in Australia, it decided that half should come from Zbonszyn. Word of the scheme passed around town, as well as being advertised in a Jewish newsletter. Alwin Spiegel was tuned in to all rumours on emigration:

> You knew everything that was happening. There were rumours — a lot of people going here, going there. The idea when we were young kids was to have a rich uncle in America. There were no poor uncles. We didn't have one unfortunately, so we spent our time listening to rumours. Then one day someone in the hospital heard that they were going to pick out some boys between fourteen and sixteen to go to Australia. I came back to my parents and said, 'Can I go to Australia?' 'Where is it? What is Australia?' At that time Australia was like Africa. We'd never heard of it.

By then, families in Zbonszyn were powerless to support their children. Many consented to their sons' emigration as the only solution, and saw in it a glimmer of hope for the rest of the family. Norman Schindler said his mother wanted to keep the family together, but his father's argument prevailed: 'We have no way of getting out of here; at this point of time there doesn't seem to be any solution to this problem, so if we get him to go perhaps eventually he can organise something so that we can come too.'

Over five hundred boys were eligible, although no-one knows how many applied. Within several weeks at least some of those who had applied received letters inviting them to an interview. 'I was a strapping young lad,' said Werner Teitel, trying to explain his selection. 'I wasn't scared of anyone or anything. I was very outspoken, which didn't go against me. They asked, 'Do you know any English?' The little that I knew helped. Did I know my Bible? Yes, I knew my bible, which was one of the requisites at the time. I could read. I had basic schooling — eight years. I finished when I was thirteen years and nine months old.' Norman Schindler recalled also having to write an essay on his life; and having to have medical tests. 'At the end of another week or two I was told I was one of those selected to go.'

Those selected were aged fourteen or fifteen and had completed eight years of schooling. Most had also commenced a trade in Germany. Given the widespread unemployment among German youth, this made them somewhat exceptional, although, as Max Nagel's case shows, these apprenticeships were sometimes little more than slave labour: 'My main job consisted of being like a horse. We had a cart, a four-wheel cart with a harness in the front. They loaded it up with supplies, paint, ladders and such, and I got harnessed in. This is how I pulled the supplies from job to job.' Nevertheless, this foothold in a trade was important for their selection. It implied they could be self-supporting and would not become a charge on the state, a requirement for their entry into Australia.

Dates on documents suggest that the selection was made quickly. On 9 January 1939 the mayor of Zbonszyn issued the boys with certificates for emigration to Australia. By 27 January the Polish Jewish Relief Fund in Melbourne had received these and forwarded them, together with other required information, to the Department of the Interior. Eleven boys were selected from Zbonszyn although one, Herman Brecher, withdrew leaving ten permits to be distributed to Jewish boys in other parts of Poland.

By 8 February ORT had selected these ten boys from its technical schools in two towns on or near the Polish–Russian border — Sarny and Brest-Litovsk. In Sarny there was a notice on the wall, inviting those interested to apply in writing, with their parents' permission. George Perl read the notice and thought, '"I'm going." Most probably 60 to 70 per cent of boys in the school would have applied because everybody thought that a war was imminent.' Opportunities for emigration to Palestine were now almost nil for poor Polish youth. 'You could have gone to Palestine if you had something like a hundred pounds sterling, but who had a hundred pounds?' remarked George. 'It was a fortune.' Opportunities for employment were also negligible. 'I was in the third year of carpentry and I knew I was finishing, but what am I going to do next? Where am I going to go? Have I got a job? Have I got any opportunities? There was nothing.' George was officially fifteen, although in fact two years older; he was already two years old when his father registered his birth. 'That was maybe lucky for me; otherwise, I wouldn't have gone.' His parents gave their permission reluctantly. For them 'it was another tragedy for me to go on my own to God knows where'.

Aleck Katz remembered clearly the day he heard about the scheme. A young Jewish lawyer and youth leader, Menachem Begin, was in town to talk about the latest restrictions imposed by the British government on immigration to Palestine. Begin was travelling through Poland, denouncing the restrictions and encouraging illegal immigration to Palestine. Thinking the school would not allow him to attend, Aleck skipped classes so he could hear Begin. When the headmaster later called him to the office, Aleck assumed he was to be reprimanded for his absence. Instead, the headmaster drew his attention to the notice about Australia. 'He asked me, "Would you like to go to Australia?" He was amazed when I told him one of my friends was already there, because Australia was very very far away; we only knew it from geography lessons.'

Jack Schwartz and Jack Garbasz were also selected from Sarny. Jack Garbasz was still attending state school. His father was a teacher at the technical school, but had recently died. When Jack's mother heard of the opportunity for boys to emigrate to Australia, she put pressure on the school to include her son. Jack believes his inclusion was a gesture to compensate for the lack of any pension from the school. For his mother, as for others, the decision was a tremendous sacrifice. 'It was a self-sacrifice to give me a chance to survive.'

In Brest-Litovsk, Max Goldberg's mother also used some influence to have her son included. Her close friend was the wife of the ORT headmaster. Having heard about the scheme through this friend, Max's mother pushed to have her son selected. 'She was a very wise woman. My father was too deep in religion to know what was going on. He was hoping for the Messiah to come. But my mother must have had a notion that things were developing badly.'

Michael Porter recalled someone coming into his classroom and asking anyone who wanted to go to Australia to stand up. 'The whole class rose.'[23] His mother fainted when told her son 'had won the lottery and was going to Australia', explained Michael's wife, Betty. 'His parents argued long and loud over the pros and cons. Finally, his father and grandfather marched him off to Rabbi Isaac Ze'ev Ha-Levi Soloveitchik. Addressing himself to the two adults, the famous Talmudist asked, "God has pointed His finger at your son to go to Australia, and you are questioning?" That clinched it.'

Most families were too poor to contribute anything to their sons' emigration. Nor did the Polish Jewish Relief Fund in Melbourne intend the families to pay. However, a letter from JEAS to Aleck Katz's father shows that his family at least was asked for money:

> We have received the necessary documents and photographs, also the eighteen zloty. We have dispatched to the local government in Sarny the application for a passport for your son. In regards to that, we also have to establish that you were in Poland in 1921 and 1922, during the establishment of the Polish government.

To finalise the passport papers you must make one more application for your son's departure. The first application is held in Warsaw and is not released to the local government office.

Send us immediately the amount of 300 zlotys to cover the expenses for your son's departure. We have noticed that your son will have to leave no later than 10th or 11th of April. See that he is ready with everything so that there will be no hold-ups.[24]

There was no spare cash even in this household. To raise the money Aleck's mother sold her sewing machine for 170 zlotys; his uncle in Belgium sent the balance.

For boys like Aleck, who were living away from home, there was little time to spend with families before leaving. 'The trade school I was in was fifty kilometres from home. I wanted to go home and stay longer, but the headmaster was rather cautious, much to my disappointment. He didn't want us to stop school and cut off our education. They didn't give us longer than a couple of weeks.' The parting was wretched, but momentous. Aleck recalled visiting each Jewish household in his village, shaking hands and kissing every member of the families. 'At one a very religious elderly man put his hands on my head and blessed me and made me walk across the threshold with my right foot first to make it a safe journey. This was rather emotional. Some of my close friends followed me all the way to the station.' Aleck still has a little calendar a three-year-old child gave him as a farewell gift.

As they boarded trains for Warsaw, the boys knew they would not return, although hopes of families joining them were high. For Michael Porter the last memory as the train pulled out was of his mother's eyes: 'She wasn't crying; she was looking at me, looking at me and drinking in this last glimpse of her youngest son'.

In Zbonszyn, the same sadness prevailed, but people buoyed each other with optimistic talk of the future. Max Nagel's aunt in Germany wrote:

My poor loved ones, my letter is really for Maxi, the dear boy who is so brave and is going to Australia. Yes, you parents, it is hard to send a child so far away. May god help you and all of us, so that we will once more be together happily with our children. So Maxi is to prepare the way for you to a new world. Unfortunately I cannot give my dear sweet Godchild anything to take with him, no souvenir, nothing at all, but dear Maxi, so many good wishes will accompany you, and my wishes are added to them. Be good, and become the pride of your parents, sisters and brothers and all relatives, and be a real man, and don't any of you cry. It is a great blessing for Maxi, and God is above and He will and must see to it that parents and children are reunited. They belong together after all. Once more, everything, everything that is good and beautiful on earth for you my dear Maxi, and send a greeting from afar now and then to your old Aunt Eva. And you, dear parents, don't be sad. I have also sent my only child out into the world and I am quite alone. You are together and your little children will console you, so hold your heads high. So, until we meet again, wishing you a happy future. Many, many kisses, Eva. Don't be sad, it is sure to be a blessing for Maxi and for you.

Eva Weissman

Werner Teitel's mother wrote some parting words from Germany:

My dear good Werner.

I can imagine that you dear Werner would like to see us once more as much as I want to see you. But we have to put up with our fate which the dear God has imposed upon us. The dear God shall guard and protect you, that you beloved Werner grow in Australia into a respectable and honest human being ... Dear Werner stay healthy. It is a pity you can't see your little brother as the beloved child sits alone in the pram and plays with his feet. It is sheer delight to watch how our Isilein has developed. Now beloved Werner don't be disheartened, then everything will be all right. I wish you a pleasant journey. Keep a record of all your experiences so you can describe them to us. For the farewell I send you hearty regards and kisses from your mum who loves you.[25]

Werner's younger sister added a message, illustrated with many hearts:

Dear brother,

For the farewell I send you a lot of luck and health. On your far travels may the dear God guide and protect you. I'll always think of you. Your not to be forgotten sister Waltraut. I've got a good school report.

After a stopover in Warsaw, the boys from Zbonszyn and the Polish-born boys came together at the port of Gdynia. There, on 13 April 1939, they met their escort, Dr Lebenson,[26] and boarded the *Baltrover* for the journey to England. At Gdynia the Polish emigration authorities provided the ten Polish-born boys with a final indelible memory. 'We had to go through delousing, compulsory by the Polish government,' explained Aleck Katz. 'They put powder on us and went through our hair, then washing and showers.' The memory was bitter for Jack Garbasz: 'The Poles had a last chance at showing us their true colours. They shaved our heads before we were allowed to board the ship.'

Fear gave way to enormous relief as they passed through the Kiel canal, closely guarded by the Nazis. There was time then to relax and enjoy the sights of London before embarking on the *Oronsay* for Australia on 22 April 1939. The following five weeks were filled with interesting experiences. 'Everything was so new,' commented George Perl, 'especially coming from a village where everything was so primitive. Anything that I saw was totally different from what life was for me before then.' The excitement of the journey generally dispelled any homesickness: 'We were young kids,' reflected Jack Garbasz, 'and at that stage of your life you can usually shed your problems and be entertained and look on the adventurous side of it.'

Through letters and postcards, the boys shared their adventures with families insatiable for news of their welfare and details of their journey: 'It pleases us that you have described everything in such detail. Please always do it that way,' wrote Max Nagel's father; and later, 'Please write to us in full detail.' In Zbonszyn parents met regularly to share letters from their sons: 'We meet each time with the parents of the boys who left with you and everyone beams with pleasure when we get mail from you'.[27] Max's letters were often sent to him by airmail,[28] an expense impossible for some other families. 'In our little town even sending an ordinary letter was such an expense,' remarked Jack Garbasz. 'We never even heard of airmail.'

There was friction between the two groups of boys. Werner Teitel commented: 'We clashed early, until we came to Australia — and then we found we were all foreigners and it didn't matter where we came from. We were two different mentalities. We spoke different languages.'

Through a lifetime in Germany the German youths had become indoctrinated with German nationalism, despite their Jewish ancestry. Alwin Spiegel reflected on this: 'We believed we were superior of course. When you start as a German you are superior. The fact that Hitler comes and tells you you're a bloody Jew is bad, but before that we were superior. It was the same in Germany with the German Jews. We [eastern Jews] weren't good enough for them.' Alwin believes he bridged the gap to some extent; he belonged to the Betar, a Zionist group to which some of the Polish-born boys also belonged. He was also popular because he was the only one who could read the English menu.

The *Oronsay* reached Fremantle on 23 May

1939, exactly two years after the meeting called by Arthur Rose to discuss bringing Polish children to Australia. War interrupted plans to introduce another group of boys the following year. By then it was too late. That twenty boys found refuge in Australia is cause for both commiseration and celebration. Without the foresight and commitment of the Polish Jewish Relief Fund, they too would almost certainly have joined the one million Polish Jewish children murdered by the Nazis.

Children deported to Zbonszyn mostly shared this fate, although a small number found refuge in other countries. Before the camp was dissolved, 154 were taken to England by the Federation of Jewish Relief Organisations and were admitted on the understanding that permanent homes would be found for them elsewhere. With this in mind, Dr Machover, for many years the chairman of the Federation of Jewish Relief Organisations, travelled to Australia in August 1940 to investigate immigration possibilities. Once in Australia, he abandoned the idea, believing it was too dangerous for the children to travel, even if the Australian government gave permission for their entry.[29]

For children remaining in Zbonszyn, and for the families of the ten boys who had emigrated to Australia, there was a brief reprieve before the sinister events of the Holocaust overtook them. By May 1939 the Polish government had agreed they could move to inner Poland. The German government then began issuing permits allowing family representatives to return to Germany to liquidate assets and to gather such personal belongings as remained. On 20 June 1939, Max Nagel's father wrote to him about his return to Hamburg: 'Unfortunately I found very little of our things here ... the furniture and the bikes weren't there any more, but thank God clothing, linen, crockery, saucepans, your metal beds and the cot I still managed to rescue. If I had come a couple of days later that would all have been gone too.'

By 1 August the camp had been liquidated. Werner Teitel's mother delayed her departure from Germany as long as possible. On 30 July she left her home and travelled with her other two children to Zbonszyn. In a letter to Werner she described her journey and the appalling conditions in the camp: 'We left Herne on 30 July and at ten o'clock were at NeuBenschen. We were at the railway station all night and at ten o'clock in the morning arrived in Zbonszyn. It was a sad sight to see as old and young had taken up walking sticks. The children lay on the ground, on the stone floor. You had it even worse.'

The family, now reunited except for Werner, moved to Dabrowa in Poland. Their freedom was brief. Within weeks Dabrowa was under German occupation and the family forced into a ghetto existence, from which there was little hope of escape. Werner's mother continued:

> We live now in the Jewish quarters. Never before have I seen such poverty. Ten people live in one room. There's nothing like this in Germany. We have one bed, two men sleep on the floor. We spent two days looking for a flat. Flats are available but one can't pay the price. For two rooms with a kitchen, fifty zloty, paid one year in advance. Who can afford this? ... May dear God give us strength and health, then everything will be all right.

Other families moved from Zbonszyn to eastern Poland which, under the German-Soviet pact, was occupied by the Soviet army in September 1939. Jews in eastern Poland generally welcomed the arrival of the Soviets, and thousands of others fled east ahead of the German advance through western Poland.[30] Under Soviet occupation the families of the boys who had emigrated to Australia continued to eke out a living, and remained intact. That ended on 22 June 1941 when Germany invaded Russia and unleashed the floodgates of the Holocaust.

On board the *Oronsay* en route to Australia

Standing, left to right: Aleck Katz, Alwin Spiegel, Werner Teitel (with hand on Alwin's shoulder), Max Nagel, Michael Porter (dark coat and tie), Max Loftus (tall boy at back), Norman Schindler and Max Goldberg (two boys in centre with grey coats), Sigi Jaffe (behind Max), George Perl (dark cap and white shirt), Stanley Ball (at rear), Bill Baker (has a hand on his right shoulder), Sigmund Ettinger, Leon Getzler (facing left), Syd Miller. In front, left to right: Szymon Klitenik, Max Sheinfeld, Jack Garbasz, man in white coat (not one of the group), Max Juni, Jack Schwartz. (Jonas Pushett)

The Bulletin

Vol. 61.—No. 3152.   July 10, 1940.

ROOM, AND WELCOME!
"Australians are offering to take many more children from the danger zone than Britain can send."
"These are your cousins, the cubs, joeys, and there's a lot more coming. And the more the better!"

The enthusiasm in Australia at the prospect of receiving British evacuee children is evident in this front page of the *Bulletin*, 10 July 1940

5
Room, and Welcome

From 1 September 1939, British children experienced the upheaval if not the horror of war. As Hitler moved against Poland, Britain launched a long-planned evacuation of women and children from its cities to the country. This evacuation, the first of several in Britain, involved over one million children.[1] Many recently arrived refugee children were among them.

Movement of children overseas was also mooted in September. Among proposals which emerged was one from the British Orphans Adoption Society (BOAS) in Sydney for the transfer of British war orphans to Australia. BOAS promoted the legal adoption of British war orphans by Australian families as 'a new method of migration'. As the *Sydney Morning Herald* pointed out on 23 September, 'The arrival of large numbers of normal and healthy children would increase our population and would not cause any unemployment'. Taking British war orphans was also rationalised as 'a definite service on the part of Australia, and a contribution by those people who are not able to serve actively'.[2]

The September evacuation within Britain proved to be premature, attracting much criticism in ensuing months as people drifted home. By the end of the year about half the children who had been evacuated had returned home. While this quelled any immediate plans for overseas evacuation, the idea of receiving British children as a result of the war had been planted. It was an attractive proposition to many Australians unable to adopt an Australian child,[3] and to those wishing to see British migration continue throughout the war.[4] It required only the right circumstances to bring the idea to fruition.

Those circumstances were provided in May 1940. The ferocity and speed of the German advance along the western front brought to an abrupt halt any complacency about the war. Refugee organisations in Britain rallied to the support of a new wave of refugees from Belgium, Holland and France. In Britain and the dominions, arguments for the overseas evacuation of not only British, but also allied refugee children, gathered momentum.

The Commonwealth government now endorsed the proposal to transfer young British war orphans to Australia for adoption, and extended the proposal to include British children for the duration of the war. Department of the Interior officer, Joe Honeysett, was a major proponent of the scheme and provided a number of reasons for his position: it would increase the population in the best possible manner and would counteract the probable war wastage in the adult population; parents could be encouraged to join their children after the war by the offer of free passage; furthermore, it would 'obviate displacements of staff and other difficulties with which the Fairbridge Society and other organisations are having to meet as a result of the outbreak of war'.[5] The Department of the Interior consequently drew up a proposal for Cabinet for the transfer to Australia of 5000 children under the age of twelve. The children were to be of two classes — orphans for adoption, with any surplus going into institutions, and children who would be placed in private homes for the duration of the war.

In the proposal, any reference to British children was substituted by the phrase 'child population of Britain'.[6] It was a subtle but significant change as the child population of Britain then included numerous children from both allied and enemy countries.

With the deteriorating situation in Europe, the question was being asked publicly, 'Why only British? Dutch and Belgium children must also be taken into our homes.'[7] The question was also raised in parliament. On 28 May Archie Cameron, acting leader of the House of Representatives, committed the government to considering a scheme, proposed by the Country Party in Western Australia, 'to bring to Australia refugee children from Holland and Belgium'. This was the same week that Senator Foll, Minister for the Interior, had granted the Australian Jewish Welfare Society permission to introduce one hundred Dutch and Belgian children.

On the evening of 29 May, Cabinet discussed the Department of the Interior's proposal. The estimated expense to the Commonwealth was accepted without question — £75 000 for fares, £10 000 for 'maintenance in depots' and £5000 per annum for administrative expenses. Cabinet approved sending a cable to the High Commissioner for the United Kingdom 'asking him to ascertain if the offer to take 5000 children from Britain and place them in Australia would be acceptable to the British Government'. Prime Minister Robert Menzies took responsibility for sending the cable; his wording of it was to confine the scheme forever to British children:

> I would be glad if you would ascertain from British Government what its reaction would be if offer were made by Commonwealth to transport to Australia and take over the care of five thousand British children for the duration of the war and, if the United Kingdom Government is favourably disposed towards the proposal we would be glad of advice what transport facilities would be available, and the lowest rate for which the shipping companies would be prepared to carry the children.
>
> The children would be placed almost entirely in Australian homes and those not taken care of in this way would be placed in institutions such as Fairbridge and Doctor Barnado's Homes.
>
> Please inform the United Kingdom authorities that there is a strong public feeling in Australia that many homes here would be prepared to adopt orphan children.
>
> MENZIES[8]

Regardless of Menzies' wording of the cable, Senator Foll presented the idea to the Australian public in the broader context of 'British children and refugee children from Allied countries'. The response was so enthusiastic that, even in his first press statement on 31 May, Senator Foll was able to announce that he had received hundreds of letters. So buoyed was he by the response that he declared he 'would throw the whole of the machinery of the migration section of the Department of the Interior into the work of relieving Great Britain of portion of her terrible responsibility'.[9] Three days later he elaborated on some of the offers he had received for 'refugee children from Great Britain and allied countries':

> A resident of Newcastle offered to adopt one child and in addition to organise and bear all preliminary expenses in an effort to find homes for 100 children in Newcastle. This correspondent stated that the offer was absolutely without thought of remuneration.
>
> Mrs O. A. Hickins, State President of the Country Women's Association of Victoria promises to assist in every way possible to place refugee children in country homes throughout Victoria. The Association has a membership of 17 000.
>
> A telegram was received from the Secretary, Federal Council of Boy Scouts, in which the

Council offered to provide immediately scout homes for 1000 scout refugees.

While the government awaited a decision from Britain, offers continued to pour in — from individuals, organisations and community groups.

> From Cairns in the north to Hobart in the south, and from Perth in the west to Sydney in the east, places separated by thousands of miles in this vast continent, the people of Australia have indicated their desire to make available the loving kindness of their own households. This magnificent response is not confined to individuals, as organisations, representatives of all phases of the nation's life, have offered their active cooperation. As an example of this, at least two organisations have offered to provide 1000 homes for the children from overseas.[10]

Hobart Rotary Club even offered to assume the management of the entire scheme.

Many of the offers were without regard for nationality:

> I would willingly take into my family an orphaned boy or girl from one of the ravaged lands, and would endeavour to give that child a good education and a chance in life.

> Have available greater part large homestead in country on station property 90 miles from Melbourne. Am prepared accept ten children from England and or allied countries. Would want public-spirited woman volunteer to matron them.

> If your government decides to bring refugee orphans to Australia both my husband and myself would like very much to have one. We don't care what nationality it is or how old. I think the younger the better, and the sex does not matter either.

> In reference to the refugees, we would be willing to take one. I have three children ... I should like a girl about the same age as my own, 6 years. We have no room for more as we live in one of the South Australian Trust homes ... We are just a working family and trying to educate our family, and we live life very simply ... One does not miss a meal while cooking for 5, and if you would grant this favour we would be grateful to do such a wee mite for our wonderful country which we are very proud of.[11]

Even offers from refugee organisations were not necessarily exclusive to children of a particular creed or nationality. The Refugee Council of Tasmania, supported by the Tasmanian government, forwarded a proposal to the Prime Minister that 'in order to relieve the pressure placed upon Britain by the increasingly large numbers of refugees who are daily arriving from the war-stricken areas of Europe the Federal Government be urged to permit the entry into Australia of refugee children (orphans preferred) for legal adoption'.[12] The Migrants' Consultative Council, a sub-committee of the Australian Jewish Welfare Society, wrote that 'Jewish refugees in New South Wales are prepared to give a home to 100 to 150 children whom the Government of the Commonwealth may select to bring to Australia, either for the duration of the war or permanently, whatever the case may be, of any nationality, religion, or age, and to keep and educate them as their own children, to the best of our abilities'.[13]

The offers were so extensive and so inclusive of allied children that the Department of the Interior attempted to clarify and extend the original proposal. Thomas Garrett, assistant secretary of the department, composed a draft cable to the Australian High Commissioner in London, pointing out that the offer included 'refugee children such as Dutch, Belgian, Danish, Norwegian'.[14] It appears the cable was never transmitted, perhaps due to intervention by the Prime Minister. Menzies certainly remained lukewarm on the issue of allied children. In a letter to all state premiers on 10 June 1940 he pointed out that the plan being considered was restricted to British children, adding that further enquiries would be made with regard to others. Nevertheless, the issue remained confused by the Department of Interior's continued reference to allied refugee children.

* * *

The British response to this offer from Australia, and similar offers from other dominions, was to set up an inter-departmental committee under the chairmanship of Geoffrey Shakespeare, Parliamentary Under-Secretary of State to the Dominions Office. Its terms of reference were: 'To consider offers from overseas to house and care for children, whether accompanied or unaccompanied, from the European war zone, residing in Great Britain, including children orphaned by the war, and to make recommendations thereon'.[15]

Although initially opposed to any scheme which pandered to the weaker elements in the community or which implied defeatism, Shakespeare was converted to the position that to fortify itself Britain needed to remove its weaker members, the 'useless mouths'. He was also a self-confessed migrationist and recognised the opportunities of the scheme for Empire migration. He stated this position later in his autobiography, *Let Candles Be Brought In*: 'The clouds were surely big with mercy and were breaking with twin blessings on our heads — the gift of complete safety for our children and the resumption of migration'. The theme of Empire migration was to remain a strong motivating force for Shakespeare as he administered the scheme.

Within a week of its first meeting, the newly appointed committee was recommending that offers from the dominions and the United States should be accepted and a scheme, to be called the Children's Overseas Reception Board, developed for children who had turned five but not yet reached sixteen.[16] It was anticipated the United Kingdom government would pay the cost of sea transport and a per capita maintenance for the children, but parents would also be expected to contribute according to their means. It was recommended that 'the scheme should also apply in a similar manner, so far as overseas governments agree, to Allied refugee children who are not in employment (Belgian, Czecho-Slovakian, Dutch, French, Norwegian and Polish)'.[17]

On 17 June 1940 the report went before the British War Cabinet. Shakespeare later reflected in his autobiography:

> I shall not easily forget that historic occasion. I arrived soon after twelve-thirty p.m. and briefly explained the main features of the scheme. I had hardly finished when a messenger came in with a note for the Prime Minister. He read it, and announced to the Cabinet that France had capitulated. It can readily be imagined how all interest in the evacuation of children was eclipsed by the stark magnitude of this momentous event.

Of Churchill, Shakespeare commented: 'Winston Churchill did not appreciate what had happened. He was only present in the sense that his body was sunk in the Prime Minister's chair. His spirit was far away — soaring over the battlefields of France and witnessing her dying agony.'

Churchill later acknowledged as much himself and accepted responsibility for the question not being fully explored by the government:

> I must frankly admit that the full bearings of this question were not appreciated by His Majesty's Government at the time when it was first raised ... I take full responsibility for the steps which were originally taken, but I ask for the indulgence of the House on account of the many difficulties through which we have been passing.[18]

While discussion and interest in the evacuation of children may have been curtailed, the Cabinet secretary recorded in the minutes that the War Cabinet 'approved the recommendations ... and agreed that the scheme should be announced in Parliament the following Wednesday'.[19] Shakespeare had a mandate to proceed and so the Children's Overseas Reception Board, CORB, was born, with Shakespeare as its chairman. An Advisory Council, consisting of representatives of societies involved in child welfare and migration, was also appointed, its major responsibility being the selection of children and escorts.

The following day, 18 June 1940, Shakespeare talked to representatives of the governments concerned, outlining the scheme and seeking confirmation of their support before making an announcement in the House of Commons. Details of the scheme included:

- Children 5 to 16 years of age to be transferred.
- For the time being children would not be accompanied by parents but, if possible, special provision may be made later for war widows with children.
- Nominations by residents in Australia in favour of specific children will be included.
- Only sound and healthy children to be transferred.
- Medical examination to be conducted by school doctors in accordance with prescribed and approved standards.
- One matron or conductor will be provided for each 12 children. Applications from returning Australians are to be considered.
- Extra clothes necessary for local conditions to be provided by receiving body for which the United Kingdom Government would make available per capita grant possibly two or three pounds each.
- The United Kingdom Government will make a lump sum payment to the Australian Government at the rate of 5/- per week per child towards upkeep in Australia and will recover from contributions by parents here.
- The United Kingdom Government will arrange for and be responsible for the cost of passages to and from Australia.[20]

Having forwarded this information to Prime Minister Menzies, the Australian High Commissioner in London sent a second cable explaining that, after discussing the adoption of war orphans, it was decided that this phase of the scheme should be incorporated at a later date.[21] He also informed the Prime Minister that Canada was taking 10 000 children and New Zealand 2500, both subject to possible extension later. Menzies confirmed that the children would be welcome, though re-emphasised the large number of applications received for orphans. He acknowledged the British offer to make a lump sum payment to the Commonwealth but informed the High Commissioner that because 'unconditional offers to receive and care for children have been received from a large number of Australian parents who will not require payment, Australia would like the privilege of defraying the whole of the cost involved in caring for the children after arrival'.[22]

Senator Foll's announcement of the scheme on 20 June 1940 was another episode in a story which had been unfolding in the newspapers for several weeks. Since his statement on 31 May about Australia's offer to Britain, the newspapers carried almost daily coverage of plans and preparations to receive children. They fuelled public enthusiasm with headlines such as 'Care of War Orphans' and 'Bring Them Here', and with regular comment on the large number of offers received and the large number of children who would likely be available: 'Tentative plans for the reception of large numbers of refugee children from Great Britain and Allied countries are being prepared'[23]; 'More than 10 000 offers to care for British and Allied children have been received by Senator Foll from individuals and organisations.'[24] These articles often ran alongside reports from overseas correspondents, as happened on 22 June when the *Sydney Morning Herald* carried the following London report on CORB's first day of operation:

Thousands of parents besieged the offices of the newly-appointed Children's Overseas Reception Board yesterday, seeking to register children for evacuation to the Dominions.

A queue of 3000 was standing four-deep when the doors were opened at 9 a.m. after which the number grew throughout the morning.

The response by British parents was indeed feverish. As parents of children in private schools queued outside the CORB office in the Thomas Cook building in London, those with children in grant-aided or state schools inundated the offices of local education authorities.[25] In addition, about 7000 letters poured in daily to CORB. To cope with this formidable response, CORB staff expanded in a few weeks from thirty to over 500. In that time 211 448 applications were received, 94 per cent being for children in grant-aided schools.[26]

Churchill was not amused by the public hysteria which heralded CORB's launch, and expressed as much to the War Cabinet. To him, overseas evacuation reeked of defeatism. The War Cabinet immediately requested that a statement be broadcast to 'damp down' the scheme, pointing out that it 'was bound to be limited in scope owing mainly to the difficulties of providing transport ... and that the risks [to the children] might exceed the dangers to which they would be exposed by remaining in this country'.[27]

The public announcement fell to Shakespeare, whose enthusiasm for the scheme penetrated the sombre message intended by the War Cabinet. He pointed out that numbers would be limited by available shipping and by offers from the dominions, and that parents alone could make the decision on whether to avail themselves of the offer: 'You have to weigh the danger to which your child is exposed in this country, whether by invasion or by air raids, against the risks to which every ship that leaves these shores is subjected in war-time from enemy action, whether by air, by submarine or by mine'. At the same time he assured parents that the plan would be 'orderly, well planned' and that the children would be 'properly supervised, with all arrangements made for their welfare, their maintenance and their after-care at the end of their journey'. His concluding remarks can scarcely have had a 'damping down' effect:

> If you decide to take advantage of the benefits of this scheme, I know there will be much burning of heart at the thought of parting, but parents will not allow themselves to be influenced by selfish considerations where they believe the safety of their children is concerned. You will ask me for how long will the parting be? The answer is — our children will come back to us when we have secured final victory as inevitably we shall.[28]

In his speech Shakespeare had reminded listeners, perhaps inadvertently, of their gravest fear — the invasion. Even if Churchill had delivered the speech himself it is doubtful he could have allayed that fear. That the British public generally believed in the imminence of an attempted invasion seems irrefutable. In his Empire Day address to the nation, even the King had expressed his concern: 'The decisive struggle is now upon us ... the issue is now plain: it is life or death for us all'.[29]

His words came in the wake of the passing of the Emergency Powers Defence Bill, whereby Britons surrendered their personal and property rights for the sake of national security. This move was prompted by the belief, expressed in the War Cabinet on 21 May, that 'in view of past experience in Norway, Holland and France, it can be taken for granted that the Germans have the plan for the invasion of this country worked out to the last detail'. In this climate over 30 000 German and Austrian refugees in Britain, mostly men and youths between sixteen and seventy, were interned. Amongst them were one thousand youths who had fled to Britain as unaccompanied children with the Refugee Children's Movement. In July 1940, 201 of them were included among the 2542 internees sent to Australia on the *Dunera*.

After Dunkirk, the Prime Minister and the British War Cabinet seemed to believe the invasion was only a matter of time. In a secret document, the Joint Intelligence Sub-Committee reported that 'In accordance with the instruction of the Prime Minister we have had under urgent consideration the question of a German invasion of Great Britain'. They concluded that 'large-scale raids on the British Isles, involving all three arms, may take place at any moment. A full-scale invasion is unlikely to take place before the middle of July.'[30] While secret information was not available to the public, opinions on an invasion were expressed daily in the press and in parliamentary debates. On 4 June, for example, *The Times* printed a letter which summarised, with maps, an invasion plan outlined by Hitler's henchman, Professor Ewald Banse, in his book *Germany, Prepare for War!* The American ambassador, Joseph Kennedy, summed up the situation with this gloomy prognosis: 'To suppose the Allies have much to fight with except courage is fallacious'.[31] Surveys conducted by Mass Observation further reflect public opinion.[32] According to one report, only 50 per cent of the population expected Britain to fight alone after Dunkirk — 'everyone is going around looking as if they want to put their heads in a gas oven'. Opinions in Scotland were not much different. Mass Observation conducted a survey there in July amongst university students. To the question, 'What is likely to have happened to Britain by the end of this year?' most forecast that Germany would attempt an invasion. There was also considerable support for the notion that Ireland would be invaded. Little wonder that thousands of parents registered their children for overseas evacuation with the government scheme, or that those with the means arranged private evacuation.

Unable to stem the flow of applications by persuasion, Churchill and the War Cabinet decided on 1 July 1940 that the time had come to call a halt to the scheme and, without killing it, to ensure that it was kept to quite small proportions. Lists for the government scheme were thus to be closed, on the grounds that far more names had been received than could be dealt with. News received later that day played into Cabinet's hands. While crossing to Canada, the *Arandora Star*, a fast passenger liner, had been sunk, with many people, mostly internees, losing their lives. Although no CORB children were on the *Arandora Star*, it was a grim warning to Shakespeare, causing him to request that ships carrying CORB children be escorted. The War Cabinet consequently called a halt to any movement of CORB children on unescorted vessels. It was only a matter of days before this decision was taken a step further — to postponement. Having lost the services of the French fleet, and due to heavy engagement in anti-invasion duties, the British navy had few escorts available. Thus on 10 July the War Cabinet declared that the scheme 'must now be held in abeyance'.

On the same day, Stanley Bruce, the Australian High Commissioner in London, secretly informed Prime Minister Menzies of this probable outcome. By then organisation for the reception of the children in Australia was well under way. At a two-day conference between Commonwealth and state officials in late June, the groundwork for arrangements was laid. The children were to be introduced under the guardianship of the Commonwealth, with the Minister for the Interior being the legal guardian. The states, under his authority, would operate the scheme, being responsible for the reception, placement and after-care of the children through their child welfare departments. To facilitate this, the Attorney-General's Department began developing regulations under the National Security Act. Other decisions made at the conference related to the allocation of children to states on a population basis, allocation to families according to religion, the requirement that states keep an adequate record of each child, and a resolution that 'no placement of a child be permitted under circumstances less favourable than applying to an Australian child'.[33] Strong support emerged once more for the introduction of British war orphans and, in his report to the High Commissioner, Garrett requested urgent consideration of this phase. During the conference, aversion to the terms 'evacuee' and 'refugee' was also expressed, delegates opting for the term 'overseas children'. In Australia the scheme thus came to be called the Overseas Children's Scheme.

Offers of hospitality flowed in constantly. In the opening address at the conference, Department of the Interior personnel announced that they had received 1500 letters the previous day and that a further 1000 had already arrived that day. Included amongst the offers were many from professional groups wishing to help their associates in Britain; for example, the Chief Commissioner of Police in Victoria offered to provide homes for one hundred children of British police officials; the University Women's Association in Victoria offered homes to children of academics; the Australian Medical Association extended an offer to children of British doctors. Offers also came from various private schools, for example, a joint offer by five schools in Victoria to provide for one hundred British boys.

Throughout this phase, preparations continued to be made on the assumption that the scheme would include children from allied countries. This was despite Menzies' opposition to their inclusion. The Victorian representative at the conference indicated his state 'expected that a correct ratio between British and allied children should be observed'.[34] Numerous references in the newspapers and on the air alluded to British and allied children, application forms asked if people were 'prepared to take children not of British nationality', and thousands of people had indicated either a willingness to take, or a preference for, non-British children. Regardless of this, on 2 July the Australian Cabinet restricted the scheme to British children. Joseph Carrodus, Secretary of the Department of the Interior, tried to intercede, but to no avail. On 6 July Menzies sent the following cable to the Australian High Commissioner in London:

> In order that there may be no misunderstanding, wish to make it clear that approval of Commonwealth Government referred to British children, and did not include children from countries allied to Great Britain. Where reference is made to latter class in any cables from here, please delete. Glad if you would inform British Government.[35]

Deletions were subsequently made to Cabinet records. A line was drawn through the words 'and also refugee children such as French, Belgian and Dutch' in a cable that had been dispatched to London on 13 June.[36] No further reference was made to refugee children in relation to the government scheme.

It is unlikely the Children's Overseas Reception Board was disappointed with Australia's restriction. By July 1940 it too was trying to wriggle out of its commitment to allied children. On 17 June, at the request of Geoffrey Shakespeare, the British Foreign Office had sent letters to the consuls, or official representatives in Britain, of France, Belgium, Poland, the Netherlands, Norway and Czechoslovakia. They were given details of the scheme and informed that 'refugee parents of their nationality, or responsible persons in charge of children of their nationality not accompanied by parents' could avail themselves of the scheme by applying through their consuls. A commitment was made in the letter to the inclusion of these children without payment from parents, on the grounds that they were unlikely to be in a position to contribute.[37] Treasury was opposed to this and, by 2 July, the day the Australian Cabinet restricted its offer to British children, had still not approved the inclusion of non-British children. On that day, Thomas Dunlop, an official with CORB, informed the Foreign Office that 'the CORB scheme at present sanctioned by Treasury applies only to British children between 5 and 16 going to the British Dominions (and to British war widows wishing to accompany their children). CORB has not yet got Treasury authority to move any foreign children anywhere.'[38] Nor, according to this statement, had it obtained authority to send any children, British or foreign, to the United States.

Considering the commitments which had been made and which continued to be made, this was an astounding admission. To the Foreign Office it was a 'first class muddle',[39] and it urged CORB to rectify the matter by obtaining Treasury sanction immediately. The refusal of Australia to receive allied children probably came as a welcome relief to CORB. Nor would the Foreign Office have been too concerned with Australia's position. To the Foreign Office it was largely a matter of politics. Of particular importance was the strengthening of Anglo-French relations through the placement of French children in Canadian homes, and of Anglo-American relations through transferring to the United States both British and foreign children, as requested by their very influential child refugee committee, headed by Mrs Roosevelt. This position was articulated clearly in the British War Cabinet: 'the presence of our children in American households would be useful from a propaganda point of view'.[40]

Although the American committee sought to include German children, CORB's position on German and Austrian refugee children was quite clear. The Inter-Departmental Committee decided on 13 June that 'enemy aliens should not be included'. On 23 June Josiah Wedgwood, a champion for refugees, forced an admission from Shakespeare in the House of Commons that it was the British government, not the dominions, which had excluded German children:

> Colonel Wedgwood asked the Under-Secretary of State for Dominion Affairs whether the children of German Jews in this country are included in the benefits of the Dominions evacuation scheme?
> Mr Shakespeare: No, Sir. The scheme applies only to the children of Allied refugees.
> Colonel Wedgwood: Why does it not apply to those who are in greater need than we are?
> Mr Shakespeare: My immediate task is to administer this scheme in harmony with the wishes of the Dominion Governments.
> Colonel Wedgwood: Are we to understand from that reply that the Dominions make this distinction, and not the hon. Gentleman?
> Mr Shakespeare: No, Sir, that is not so; but in the discussions it was generally agreed that the first group should come from the children of Allied refugees.

Other members of parliament supported Wedgwood's position on the inclusion of German children. In a lengthy debate on 2 July, Mr Parker expressed his hope that the term 'allied refugee children' would not be interpreted too narrowly. 'I think anyone who is on our side in this war should be counted as an Ally. France has now gone out of the war, but we should treat the French children as Allies, and also treat the children of German and Austrian refugees as Allies for this purpose ... We should give every assistance to all of them to go to America or elsewhere if people are willing to receive them there.' Refugee organisations in Britain agreed and sent deputations to discuss the matter with Shakespeare and the Advisory Council. From these discussions it became clear to the Central Council of Jewish Refugees 'that refugee children would not be included in the

Government scheme',[41] although Shakespeare did suggest that a separate committee be set up to deal with questions concerning the evacuation of Jewish children. A committee of various refugee organisations was formed but, while it gathered considerable support, including that of the National Union of Teachers, it was never effective in altering CORB's position on alien children.

Another matter attracting considerable attention within the Jewish community was the evacuation of British Jewish children, but comments made in an Advisory Council meeting on 2 July suggest that CORB had little interest in the needs of Jewish children, be they allied, alien or British. On that occasion, the chairman reported on the deputations he had received, commenting that 'he had made it clear that children were being dealt with under the scheme as individuals and not as members of any particular groups'. To make his position clear, he added, 'care would be taken to prevent the inclusion of an undue proportion of Jews'.[42] CORB remained a very WASPish movement despite Shakespeare's insistence that the children were representative of a cross-section of British society. This fact was driven both by internal policy and by attitudes and policies in the various dominions. Apart from restrictions on Jewish children, Indian children were completely excluded, despite approaches on their behalf. Roman Catholics were also limited to 25 per cent of those going to any dominion.

Following the announcement of the scheme, the general secretary of the Australian Jewish Welfare Society had offered the services of his society to the government: 'I wish to extend to you the whole hearted co-operation of this Society in your efforts and can assure you that the allocation, if possible, of Jewish children will be cared for by my Society in all States.'[43] He requested that the 150 children for whom the Welfare Society held permits be included in CORB sailings. The Jewish Welfare Guardian Society, which had brought twenty adolescent German and Austrian boys to Melbourne in 1939, also expressed an interest in CORB: 'The Society is wishing to identify itself as far as possible with the Government scheme and to do its utmost to give the fullest co-operation to the evacuation of Jewish children to Victoria'.[44] By then the Australian government had not only restricted the scheme to British children, but had imposed a limit of 10 per cent on the number of unnominated Jewish children who could be included.[45]

As Prime Minister Menzies was cabling the Australian High Commissioner in London on 6 July regarding the restriction of the scheme to British children, the High Commissioner was sending him the long-awaited news: 'Four hundred children so far approved ... First party should sail approximately 18th July.'[46] For security reasons the news was not relayed to the public. Having received the information, Cabinet met on 10 July and, by agreeing that 'nominated children should not be included in the 5000', approved the admission of virtually an unlimited number of British children. A cable was immediately sent to the High Commissioner in London informing him of this amendment and of the fact that over thirty thousand offers had been received from Australian citizens. The front page of *The Bulletin* that day expressed Australia's jubilation over the prospect of receiving many thousands of British children: 'Room, and Welcome', the caption read. The decision made almost simultaneously in Britain to postpone the scheme shattered the euphoria — although it was 15 July before any official announcement of this decision was made in either Britain or Australia.

Churchill mused over Cabinet's 10 July decision that the scheme 'be held in abeyance', clearly piqued at the compromising position in which CORB had placed him:

> I have always been against this scheme for the evacuation of children ... from the word 'Go',

but I cannot think that the proposed abandonment of it at this stage is right. The facts are that a large number of children belonging to the wealthier classes have already gone and their going has been much publicised. Only the other day I saw a snippet in one of the papers saying that Lady So-and-So had received the offer of a hundred places and that she had filled them all from amongst her friends. If now we shut down altogether on the sending of children under a Government scheme which would enable the poor to participate, the whole business has a most unpleasant smell.

It will probably look as if those who should be the natural leaders of the people have run away like rats from a sinking ship; that there is still a loop-hole for those who have money to go, but there is now no chance for the poorer classes.

Surely we ought to say that there is an inevitable risk in sending children, vide the 'Arandora Star'; that there can only be a limited number of places for financial and other obvious reasons and that those who will be sent will be chosen by lot from applicants who are prepared to run the risk. The Government would pay for those who cannot afford to pay for themselves.

The whole scheme is misconceived, but I cannot see any other way out of it now.[47]

Confusion reigned the following week. Was the scheme on or was it off? The War Cabinet had directed the Lord President of the Council to prepare an answer to be given in parliament on 16 July. In view of the rumours circulating in the press, the Minister of Information was authorised to disclose the contents of that answer to the press before its delivery in parliament. The message conveyed to the public and the parliament was that the scheme was postponed, not because of any shortage of shipping, but because naval protection was not available to ensure the safety of the children. Children could still be conveyed under private arrangements on regular passenger vessels, but the government would not assume any responsibility for these children. Three days of exhaustive debate followed the delivery of this answer in the House of Commons. Emerging from the discussion was a clear indication that, although the scheme as planned, for 10 000 children a month, was temporarily postponed, a limited scheme, according to the availability of convoys, was to proceed.[48] Furthermore, Churchill made it clear that any government evacuation would be for the purpose of equity and not to remove 'useless mouths' or to facilitate turning Britain into a fortress:

> It is most undesirable that anything in the nature of a large-scale exodus from this country should take place, and I do not believe that the military situation requires or justifies such a proceeding, having regard to the relative dangers of going and staying. Nor is it physically possible. His Majesty's Government have been deeply touched by the kindly offers of hospitality received from the Dominions and the United States. They will take pains to make sure that in the use that is made of these offers there shall be no question of rich people having an advantage, if advantage there be, over poor. The scheme has been postponed, not abandoned, but any further emigration that may be possible, as opportunity serves, will be regulated, with a view to restoring the balance between classes, and not in pursuance of any policy of reducing the number of persons in this well-defended island.

Churchill had saved face by changing the purpose of the government overseas evacuation scheme. It was a political move, but one based on fact. Private evacuation had been proceeding at a staggering rate — 3 000 children a month according to Geoffrey Shakespeare's estimates. Shakespeare accepted the new conditions of CORB as a challenge — how best to give effect to the Prime Minister's assurance that any future emigration of children would serve to restore the balance between the classes. He had been investigating the convoy situation since early July and, at a meeting on 1 August 1940, indicated that about 2000 children a month could be sent in ships in slow convoy. The situation was aggravated by the priority being given to internees being deported to Australia and Canada. While Shakespeare recommended limiting the number of children travelling privately on fast liners, he also urged the meeting to approach the Minister of Shipping to see if Dutch ships could be made available for the transport of children under the government scheme.[49] Both Dutch and Polish ships were subsequently made available for CORB children.

Although the original scheme was postponed, CORB quietly went ahead with this alternative plan. The first group of eighty-six children sailed for Canada on 20 July 1940, creating further public confusion about the state of the scheme. Despite the risks, parents generally wanted the scheme to continue. There were inevitably some cancellations between selection and sailing, but there was never any difficulty filling the vacancies. It seems parents continued to see the risks of sea travel as less than those of staying at home — at least till ships with children aboard became the targets of torpedoes.

*   *   *

In Australia rumours of the postponement were confirmed in the newspapers on 15 July. The following day the Department of the Interior was notified that the sailing of the first party, scheduled for 18 July, was postponed. State premiers were requested to convey this information to people who had offered homes to children. While some states probably proceeded with arrangements, officially 'the organisation for the reception, placement and after-care of the children was suspended'.[50] The first wind of any change came about two weeks later when the High Commissioner for the United Kingdom in Australia notified the Prime Minister that Mr W. J. Garnett had been appointed CORB's representative in Australia

and would 'sail early in August with the first party of children'. A cable on 31 July confirmed the sailing: 'First party approximately 520 children expect to sail 5th August.'

For security reasons the Australian government received a minimum of information until after the children's departure, the Australian public received even less. Confirmation that the first party was on its way arrived on 11 August: '477 sailed *Batory* 5th August, Orient Company Australian agents. Imperative no public announcement be made until arrival of children. Next party of 71 expected to sail 19th August.'

Containing the rumours was impossible. Many Australians began receiving cables from relatives in Britain regarding the evacuation of their children, and reports from London correspondents began appearing in the press. The Department of the Interior consequently released a press statement, giving some statistics on the first party. The Prime Minister was kept informed of all sailings. Several days after the second party left England, he received the following cable: 'Eighty-two sailed *Nestor* 23 August; next parties of eighteen and one hundred and fifty-five respectively expected sail about 11th September'.

Late in September authorities in London cabled that 'the Blue Funnel boat *Diomed*, carrying eighteen boys, sailed on 12th September'.[51] No public announcements were made about these later groups of children until the ships had reached their first Australian port.

Details of the children on the ships, and of families nominated to receive them, arrived some time after the children's departure. Although 3000 children had been nominated by friends or relatives in Australia, very few of these children were included on account of CORB's giving priority to children in vulnerable areas. Most of the children were unofficially nominated — they were going to relatives and friends in Australia whose names had been supplied by parents but who had not lodged an application for them. As was explained to state premiers, 'when the movement was commenced the general impression was that if a child could furnish the name of a friend or relative in Australia he would receive preference in booking. On that account it is believed that many of the addresses furnished may relate to persons who have not been consulted and may not be in a position to provide for extra children'.[52] Of the 477 children on the *Batory*, 331 were nominated, but only fifteen officially; on the *Nestor* seventy-six children were nominated but only two of them officially; on the *Diomed* thirteen children were nominated; it is not known if any were official nominations.[53]

Advising people that they had been nominated became a priority for state committees. Many families had already received cables from Britain before the children's departure and confirmed their willingness to accept the children. Audrey Dickenson's (now Watson) aunt recalled receiving a cable from Audrey's mother and having to make a snap decision. 'The boy stood at the door because the reply was pre-paid. She had to let them know straight away.' For others their nomination was a complete surprise. In some cases the Australian relatives could not be traced; of those who could, many welcomed the opportunity afforded them, others were unwilling or unable to take the children. A Victorian nominee wrote to the Child Welfare Department:

Dear Sir,

I wish to state that I am an assisted mother and I have to go out to work myself. My husband is on an invalid pension which has been reduced because of my earnings. I have only got two bedrooms for the children and the other for self and husband. I regret I am not in a position to take my brother's three children.[54]

'In quite a number of cases,' as was pointed out to the High Commissioner in London, 'nominated guardians indicated that they are prepared to receive the children but will require financial assistance towards their maintenance.'[55] 'I can house quite comfortably five or six kiddies and can give them separate rooms,' wrote one Victorian who agreed to take all her sister's children. 'But I cannot keep them altogether. I should need an allowance to cover their feeding.'[56] The High Commissioner acknowledged that CORB was receiving payments from parents averaging five shillings a week per child, but that this money was considered 'a contribution towards the cost of the scheme as a whole and not only towards maintenance'. He indicated that CORB was still prepared to contribute up to five shillings a week for each child, but advised the Department of the Interior to ignore parents' wishes if money was an issue: 'There is no need for the Australian authorities to send children to nominated homes if they are unable to provide for children; would prefer children be placed in other homes, prepared to take them without payment'.[57]

Walter Hare was probably not the only British parent shocked at announcements on the wireless and in the press that his children might not be sent to the relative he had nominated. 'It has made me feel very uneasy,' he wrote to his brother in Australia, 'and I shall be eagerly waiting to hear from you. Will you let me down?'[58] Walter's brother was in no position to care for four extra children; as for many other children, alternative arrangements had to be made.

Changes to their arrangements may have been immaterial to many children. In most cases they were proceeding to relatives unknown to them except by name or photograph. Patricia Greening (now Duffy), from whose family five children were evacuated, commented on a change made to their arrangements: 'They came aboard in Cape

Town and said that my grandmother had died and they didn't know what was going to happen to us. I thought, "I am sorry that I'm not going to meet my grandmother, but then I never knew about her anyway". I told the others, but they didn't care because they didn't know her.'

There were many children who had no family connections in Australia and who were proceeding to some of the thousands of households which had applied for children. Freda Morgan described what prompted her parents to send their three youngest children to strangers in Australia: 'We lived in Liverpool right by the docks. Children in the schools there were evacuated to Wales, but my father said that is too close. If we were to go away it would be far. He forced the decision. It was not against my mother's wishes, but she was upset of course at losing all her little ones.'

One parent frequently commandeered the decision, often against the wishes of the other. Alan Timmins said his father begged his mother not to send him away. Alan is one of a small number of evacuees who believes, with some justification, that his mother sent him away to be rid of him. His first knowledge of his pending departure was being told shortly beforehand, 'You're going to Australia. What do you think?'

Few children were consulted about the evacuation. Derek Simpson was, but said 'it was like asking a child if he wanted an ice-cream'. Ken Gregory thought 'it seemed like a bit of a lark', so of course agreed he would like to go. Eric Ward had only a couple of days notice of his evacuation, but recalled 'lying in bed romanticising about Australia and their sheep, as little boys will do, hanging under the bellies of the sheep and going from one property to another and doing all sorts of stupid things'. Not all children took the news so positively. 'At first I was very angry,' commented Patricia Greening. 'I thought, "my father hates me; he wants to get rid of me".' Rightly or wrongly, a number of children interpreted the decision as a rejection by one or both parents. Nevertheless, few questioned their parents' decision.

Freda Morgan with her family in Liverpool, 1940, just before she and her two brothers, Percy and Maurice, were evacuated to Australia. At back, with glasses, is brother Cyril. Middle row: sister Olga, mother, Percy. In front: Freda with dog, Peggy, and Maurice. In 1941, their Liverpool home was flattened. The remaining family, although not seriously injured, was forced to move in with relatives. Peggy met the fate of numerous pets in Britain. Freda's father wrote in May 1941, 'we had to get Peggy destroyed — suffering from shock'. Percy left Australia in 1944 to join the Indian Army. (Freda Morgan Welsh)

The war had by then greatly disrupted child and family life in Britain. Many children were 'used to the idea of not living at home', having been evacuated one or several times previously. School life had also been seriously interrupted. In many areas of evacuation the pressure on schools was so great that local children attended in the morning and evacuees in the afternoon. Those who remained in danger zones experienced other changes. Freda Morgan remembered attending school in houses in

Mrs Kitty Schultz with her four young children in London, 1940. The oldest two children, Phillip, seven, and Rosalie, five, were evacuated to Australia later that year. They were two of a very small number of British Jewish children evacuated through the Children's Overseas Reception Board. Left to right: Phillip, Freda, Rosalie, Mrs Schultz, Sandra (in pram). (Sandra Jacobsohn)

Evacuation overseas began with children leaving home and assembling at selected schools in Britain. From there they travelled by train to Liverpool. Parents frequently accompanied children to assembly points, but not beyond. The photo shows children assembled at Twickenham County Secondary School. It includes Anne Vincent (second row from front, second from end), Marjory Ursell (with striped tie on Anne's right), Reg Farquharson (on Anne's left), Eileen Edwards (behind Anne, to her left), Daphne le Gros (girl at back), and Paul Farquharson (end of third row from front, with curly hair). This group of children travelled to Australia on the *Batory* which left Liverpool on 5 August 1940. (Anne Lowden)

Liverpool: 'Rather than having a lot of children in a school the teachers used to go round the houses; my mother had six or eight of us at a time'. The war had intruded into children's lives in numerous other ways — through family members joining the services, and the frequent preoccupation of parents with voluntary service; and through restrictions imposed for the sake of national and personal safety. While large-scale raids on British cities did not occur until after most children had left, air raids were common in some areas, to the extent children often became quite blasé about them: 'It was nothing to have the sirens go while you were in school,' commented Peggy McLeish (now Cox). 'I used to ride my bike back and forth to school. I had instructions to get in the gutter if the sirens went.'

For all, the leaving was sudden, two or three days notice being typical. In a letter to his brother in Australia, Walter Hare described the process: 'I found out by post the children were selected. Particulars were kept secret even from me. All that I received was a list of clothing that I was to get for each child ... and later I received two days notice to have the children at Romford station at 8.30 a.m.'

Walter described the parting as 'terrible', a feeling no doubt shared by most parents. Many contained their emotions until the children had left. Audrey Dickenson later heard her mother collapsed after seeing her wave goodbye from the bus. Many children thought the separation would be brief. Others had not been told they were going overseas. Joan Hodgson (now Sullivan) thought she was going on a short train journey and recalled calling her older sister a 'baby' because she was crying. In tears or in good cheer they travelled by foot, bus or train to specified schools to assemble. 'We all walked off around the corner singing "There'll always be an England", got on the bus and went to this school at Twickenham,' Anne Vincent (now Lowden) recalled. From these assembly points the children travelled by train to Liverpool.

Waiting in Liverpool was often a daunting experience. For the 477 children sailing in the first party to Australia, the days stretched into four as air raids postponed their departure. They were scattered across four schools, ill-equipped for their needs. 'Such a scene I am sure the school had never witnessed before,' recorded escort, Isabella Brown (now Lupton), in her diary. 'Palliasses rows upon rows in the main hall.' Anne Vincent, an evacuee in another school, added: 'We slept on the floor. We had straw palliasses which we spread around the room, and we rested our heads on the radiator. We didn't bother to get undressed because every night the air raid sirens went and we all had to get up and go to the air raid shelters.'

The *Nestor* and *Diomed* contingents stayed at Fazackerley Cottage Homes, an orphanage from which the resident children had been evacuated. It was a grim place, its starkness a lingering memory for many evacuees, Beryl Minter (now Smith) included: 'I don't think there was a tree in sight, and there was asphalt everywhere. We slept in dormitories on straw mattresses. We drank out of enamel mugs and we ate off enamel plates and the cutlery was the cheapest — shiny metal, but pitted.'

While in Liverpool, children with doubtful medical certificates underwent further examinations by Dr Park on behalf of the Australian government. As a result, thirteen from the *Batory* contingent and two from the *Nestor* were sent home rather than to Australia.

The ships' names remained secret until the time of embarkation. Despite this concession to safety, a rousing farewell was given the 477 children who left for Australia on 5 August 1940. In a speech, much publicised after their departure, Geoffrey Shakespeare referred to them as 'England's Crown Jewels'. In more auspicious times, the crown jewels might have been conveyed more regally. As it happened, plans to embark them on P&O liner *Orion* were changed at the last moment due to engine

The *Batory*, on which 477 British children travelled to Australia (Joyce Beeston Turnbull)

trouble. The Ministry of Shipping decided to substitute the *Batory*, a Polish ship of the Gdynia-America Shipping Line which, being at sea at the outbreak of war, had joined forces with the British fleet. Although built with accommodation for about 800 passengers, the *Batory* had been converted to a troop ship, whose priority for this trip was 'the carriage of troops [who] must be at a certain place by a certain date'.[59] It was in the mixed company of 800 troops, one hundred first class passengers and a compliment of officers and crew that the children and their escorts left Liverpool on 5 August.

The second group of evacuees for Australia left on the *Nestor* on 23 August. Heavy bombing of Liverpool harbour may have caused officials to stagger the children's embarkation. Freda Morgan recalled going by coach to the docks early the previous morning and having to wait quietly all day in a shed. They boarded in time for tea, although the ship remained anchored in mid-stream until the morning tide. Other children embarked during that time. Climbing aboard was a fearful experience for some of them. 'I can remember cold, damp, rain,' wrote Sheila Hammond (now Slight). 'We went out on a small boat to the *Nestor*. I was terrified climbing up the "stairway" lugging my heavy case. I still have an injured neck due to this.' Joan Hodgson also found it an unforgettable experience:

> We climbed a rope ladder ... small wooden steps fastened together by rope, and rope to hang on to for grim death ... I remember being told to look up, NOT DOWN, but I did look down at one stage. It was a long way. The launch was against the ship, then the swell took it away a few feet, then carried it back again.

On the ship children were divided into sections, each with an escort, many of whom were Australians returning from overseas. The photo shows Australian escort Isabella Brown with five of her charges on the *Batory*. From left to right: Margaret Bell, Enid Burrow, Sheila Jones, Nora Lupton and Rita Patterson. (Isabella Lupton)

Boys on the *Nestor*. (Ian Paterson)

Dawn was breaking as the *Nestor* pulled out of Liverpool harbour. Across Britain people were waking to the news that overnight bombs had fallen on central London for the first time.

As the bombing increased in the following weeks, some parents took comfort in the fact they had sent their children to safety. One parent wrote to Isabella Brown:

> I have been very worried about Nora as it is the first time we have been parted. You see I love Nora so much that I really wonder sometimes whether I did the right thing in letting her go so far from home. Then, when the air raid sirens go, I am thankful that I did, as I think that after this war is over a lot of children will be just a bundle of nerves if not crippled ... I would never have forgiven myself if I hadn't given her the chance to be safe.

Even the torpedoing of the Dutch liner *Volendam* on its way to New York on 30 August did not dampen enthusiasm for overseas evacuation. Incredibly, there was no loss of passenger life, the 321 children being picked up in lifeboats and transferred safely to other ships. Rather than diminish confidence in CORB, the incident was heralded as another British triumph in the face of overwhelming odds. Parents who wished to send their children away were not discouraged. As the Battle of Britain moved into its most critical phase — the week of 7–15 September — parents continued to pack their children off to Liverpool for evacuation overseas. On Thursday 12 September eighteen Lancashire boys boarded the *Diomed*, a small ship of the Blue Funnel Line, which was sailing for Australia. Nearby, ninety Canada-bound CORB children boarded the *City of Benares*. Both ships were to leave in convoy OB213 the following morning. Donald Mitchell, an evacuee on the *Diomed*, believes the *Diomed* was to have been the commodore or leading ship.[60] A burst boiler changed this plan. The boys on the *Diomed* woke the following morning to find themselves in dock. The convoy had left without them, with the *City of Benares* as the commodore ship. After repairs, the *Diomed* sailed on 17 September. That night disaster struck the earlier convoy, now four days ahead. The *City of Benares* was torpedoed. Seventy-seven children and six escorts died, the majority of deaths occurring while abandoning ship or from exposure during long hours in cold, rough water.[61]

Although shocked by the tragedy, Shakespeare resisted total suspension of the scheme. He recommended that evacuation on the north Atlantic route be suspended during the winter, except in the case of fast escorted liners; he also recommended that CORB 'continue sending children to the other three Dominions, provided convoys are available'.[62] Arguments for and against suspension ensued, with the War Cabinet taking the middle ground on 30 September: 'The scheme should be suspended for the time being without prejudice to the possibility of its being resumed next year.'[63] A public announcement to this effect was made on 2 October.

While this debate continued, various groups of children were disembarked from ships in Liverpool and sent home. Among them were 155 children due to sail on the *Largs Bay* for Australia on 25 September. A group of children for New Zealand was also removed from the *Rangitane,* which sailed in the same convoy. The Australian government's hopes of receiving large numbers of children seemed dashed. Yet hope prevailed that the suspension would be temporary. In the meantime, private evacuation was still possible, although dangerous, and the Department of the Interior encouraged organisations to bring British children to Australia by this means.

There is little doubt that if CORB had resumed it would have accommodated permanent child migrants. During 1940, the Fairbridge Society pushed for the continued transfer of children to its farm schools. In March 1940 the Department of the Interior approved the entry of fifty-six children, selected by Fairbridge before the war. Twenty-eight of those children arrived in Sydney on the *Aorangi* on 31 August 1940, having travelled to Australia via Canada. By September, Fairbridge had convinced the Dominions Office that Fairbridge children should be included in future CORB sailings: 'The work that the Fairbridge Farm Society render is more valuable to the Empire than that of CORB ... the children sent out by CORB are only birds of passage, though it may be hoped that some will remain permanently in the Dominion'.[64]

When the matter was brought to Shakespeare's attention, he agreed that space should be allocated to Fairbridge children in future, the number of CORB children being reduced accordingly. Despite this support for traditional child migration schemes, Shakespeare continued to promote CORB as another form of migration:

> This is the first chapter in a new volume of Overseas Settlement conceived on wise lines ... Not for the first time has war unexpectedly led to developments that no-one could foresee and the benefits of which have enriched the nations. Suspended the scheme may be, but we have lit a candle that will not easily be put out. From this war the Empire will emerge closer knit, its people tempered in the fires of sacrifice ... The children evacuated overseas ... will have played no small part.[65]

Australia's interest in orphans also continued after the suspension of CORB. The Department of the Interior was merely awaiting the arrival of the first group of children before launching a further request for this phase of the scheme. On hearing of the suspension of CORB, Menzies wrote: 'The people of Australia will still be pleased to welcome war orphans if in the future it should

Escort Doris Beeston on board the *Batory* with some of her boys. One of Doris' boys wrote the following address at the top of a letter: Some Wear at Sea. In a letter home Doris made the wry comment 'which is more than true'. Doris Beeston died when the ship on which she was returning to England was sunk by a German raider, November 1940. (Joyce Beeston Turnbull)

be found possible to send them'.[66] It was a position pursued rather aggressively in the following months. Meanwhile, preparations went ahead to receive the 577 'birds of passage' then at sea.[67]

★ ★ ★

The *Batory* was at sea for ten weeks, the *Nestor* and the *Diomed* seven. After travelling around the north coast of Ireland the ships left the main convoys and headed south. The *Batory* was one of twenty-seven ships, the largest convoy to leave Liverpool, and retained a Royal Navy escort until Cape Town. Not so the other ships which were soon without protection. Five days out of Liverpool, Sheila Hammond, on board the *Nestor*, noted in her diary, 'Convoy gone'. In wartime conditions danger was a constant companion, but one which irked more than worried the children. 'There was a time when we slept in coats and life jackets,' recalled Beryl Minter. 'We must have stunk because I'm sure we didn't have any baths.' Even when life jackets were no longer required sleepwear, they were the bane of the children's lives, the children being obliged to take them everywhere. Lifeboat drill was another tedious necessity. On the *Batory* 'we had lifeboat drill every day,' commented Phyllis Ward (now Thatcher). 'The escort was responsible for getting her children to the allocated boat station.' 'And then you'd stand there for hours,' added her brother, Eric. For Joan Hodgson, sailing on the *Nestor*, the memory of being put in the lifeboat for practice still haunts her.

The journeys were clouded in secrecy. While children were encouraged to write home, letters were censored to ensure no details of the ships or their whereabouts were disclosed. They were always 'somewhere at sea'. Comments written in the foreword of the *Albatross*, a magazine published by children on the *Batory*, reflect the good humour and spirit with which some children and escorts tackled these inconveniences:

> We trust that these pages are now sufficiently vague and innocuous; we believe that we have given away nothing except the obvious fact that we left the old world some time in August 1940 and, proceeding by devious routes, hope to arrive in the new world one sunny day.
>
> It is never forbidden to hope.
>
> This leaving the old world is not easy, but like the Albatross we know that our sanctuary lies in southern waters.
>
> Before us is a great adventure, and we hope that this magazine may be one of the reminders of friendships made on a voyage which has proved unique for reasons we all know but can't disclose.

Escorts organised the children into regular routines, although the *Batory*, with its large contingent of children and its overcrowded quarters, inevitably presented a greater need for routine and organised activity. Music featured significantly in these activities. Sing-alongs and concerts were held most evenings, with crew and other passengers often participating. At the end of the journey, Meta Maclean, the pianist on these occasions, immortalised the journey of the *Batory* in her book, *The Singing Ship*. While her book captured many precious moments, it tells little of the seamy side of living for ten weeks with 477 children and their 'keepers', 800 troops and 100 private passengers in an enclosed space. Diaries, memories and more recent writings perhaps balance the picture. Nurse Frazer-Allen recorded these entries in her diary:

7 July
The male escorts do not seem to know that a child's body needs a good scrub before bed.

Later
The Dominions Doctors who passed some of these kiddies ought to be shot!!!!

1 September
One of the escorts in the past week rather lost her head and beat one of the children unmercifully, result being a battered infant carried to surgery and a couple of very indignant soldiers who witnessed the whole affair, also great indignation by private passengers who also saw it happen.

The conditions of the children's cabins and their clothes are worse than sordid.

The boat rocked much in the night, several children fell out of bed. One more very badly concussed. Five escorts off sick … Depression

Each evacuee had a number which was inscribed on a badge, to be worn at all times. This badge belonged to Maurice Morgan, number 2550. (Freda Morgan)

The eighteen *Diomed* boys with the ship's Captain and the Chief Engineer. Tony Houghton is behind and between the two officers; Donald Mitchell is on Tony's right and Cliff Humphreys on his left. In the front row, left end, is Arthur Beech and on the right end John Cardy. Frederick Boyce is the younger of the two escorts; the other is Horace Chesney. (Cliff Humphreys)

always sets in on night duty but the round of the Children's Cabins and the smell of unwashed humanity!!!! just finishes everything. (On the following page she quotes Chief Escort Kilby: 'You can find your way around the ship from the smells'.)

Later
More than half the children are now out-patients — measles and chicken pox increasing in leaps and bounds. Many with impetigo and heat rash; athletes foot and ringworm also rife.[68]

Frazer-Allen conceded that escorts were working under extreme conditions: 'No provision was made for extra escorts for the purpose of relief ... If they go off sick the children are divided among other escorts which means it is almost impossible for them to manage even if they are folk with initiative and good capabilities.' Escorts who did manage well brought to the job a blend of kindness, good humour and efficiency. Ken Gregory recalled that his escort, Doris Beeston, 'checked on us pretty constantly and made sure we kept ourselves clean. She made sure we had a bath and she used to check the cabins. She kept us pretty well under control.' In a letter home Doris Beeston wrote, 'a family of 16 keeps you busy with washing and mending!! However, some of the older girls and sisters are giving us a hand now, which eases the situation quite a bit.' The children were in multiple-age groups, with fourteen to sixteen boys or girls allocated to each escort. The older girls carried a lot of responsibility for the care of the younger ones. Peggy McLeish felt their needs were often neglected during the journey: 'Because I was the eldest I was expected not to want any attention or care. This was hard.'

Seasickness plagued many of the children. 'I was violently seasick all the time, day in day out, for ten weeks,' commented Phyllis Ward. 'Washing was only in salt water so the poor clothes were washed silly and vomited on silly ... I chucked most of my clothes overboard on the trip.' CORB had not been very far-sighted, according to Ian Paterson, when issuing the lists of clothing for children to take: 'Before we even got below the Azores some of the shoes were worn out; and the kids had no hats worth speaking of'. When the *Nestor* pulled into Takoradi, on the west coast of Africa, none of the escorts was keen to go ashore on account of an outbreak of yellow fever, so they drew lots. Ian drew one of the short straws. 'We went up to Freetown and bought all the hats and shoes we could find ... The girls took one look at those hats and they didn't like them at all. But they were told to wear them, so they wore them all right. They just walked out on deck and let the wind blow them off. So that fixed that.' In Bombay, Bill Oats had a similar shopping expedition for *Batory* children, combing the bazaars for eighty-seven pairs of sandals and an array of other items.

The ports of call relieved the monotony of shipboard life and exposed the children to people, places and experiences most could never have imagined. After brief stops at Takoradi or Freetown, all three ships crossed the Equator and headed for Cape Town. The *Batory* was delayed in Cape Town for six days while its de-gaussing equipment was repaired. Neither the children nor the escorts minded. The South Africans feted the children during their stay, and gave the escorts some much-needed respite. Bill Oats recorded the incredible amount the *Batory* children consumed at a civic reception there: '8000 oranges (not all eaten on the spot, but brought back to the ship), 2000 bananas, 1000 apples, 3000 buns, 2000 cakes, 2000 ice creams, 300 pounds of sweets, 160 dozen mineral waters, and all this was in addition to personal lunch-boxes'. The same overwhelming hospitality was extended to all the children in Cape Town. After that, their routes varied, the *Nestor* and the *Diomed* heading for Fremantle, via Durban, while the *Batory* turned north.

One hundred airmen left the *Batory* at Cape Town, but there remained on board at least 700 officers and soldiers, mainly from the Manchester Regiment and the Gordon Highlanders. Over the weeks, and despite military orders to the contrary, relationships developed between the soldiers and the children. 'You would see them cuddling and playing with the little ones,' commented Peggy McLeish. 'They would go to the canteen and buy chocolate and sweets, and would go ashore and buy things.' 'They were fantastic,' added Patricia Greening. 'If any of the kids were homesick or things like that they would talk to them. In a way they looked after the kids.' Many of the soldiers were barely beyond childhood themselves, and also homesick. Patricia Greening has a vivid memory of one eighteen-year-old soldier: 'He was crying. We were not supposed to talk to them, but I couldn't stand it and went up and asked him what's the matter. He said to me, "I was at Dunkirk and I'm now going out somewhere else and I haven't even seen my parents. My parents don't know where I am".'

Most interviewees spoke also of the kindness of the crew and of the many illicit treats they scored, especially from the stewards. John Hare recalled forbidden visits to the troops mess on the *Batory*: 'Some of the stewards would take us down. They used to give us tinned bully beef and condensed milk in tins. I remember they'd put a couple of holes in it ... and I used to drink it out of the tin and eat corned beef slices ... that was a luxury.' This kindness ensured that the journeys were generally happy events, despite the homesickness which nagged many of the children.

The *Batory* hugged the coast on its way north, alerted to the probability of raiders in the Indian ocean. After a stopover in Bombay, it sailed to Singapore, where the soldiers left the ship, which then commenced the final leg of its long journey to Australia. Its passengers had not been alone in this ordeal, as several other ships, including the *Stratheden*, the commodore ship, remained in the convoy all the way from Liverpool. The *Stratheden* also had children on board — not CORB children, but private evacuees. Anne Dawkins, travelling with her mother, was one of those children:

> Our vessel sailed next to the *Batory*, which was filled with children. Their carers often got them together to sing — and we could hear their singing across the water. On the *Stratheden* there were many children, who had been at boarding schools in England, being sent home to Burma for safety. My mother often wondered what became of them when the Japanese occupied Burma.

Ian Paterson, centre back, with some of the girls on the *Nestor*. 82 British children travelled to Australia on the *Nestor*. (Ian Paterson)

6
RESCUE ATTEMPTS

The outbreak of war ended the emigration hopes of most people wanting to leave Germany or Nazi-occupied Europe. Families who had sent their children overseas now faced the realisation that early reunion was unlikely. 'At the outbreak of the war ... a vast sadness took hold of the Jews, as from this moment on any chance to emigrate was taken from us'.[1] Chances were limited as much by other countries as by Germany. The Reich allowed emigration until October 1941, but few people had the money or visas necessary to take advantage of the few available escape routes. By December 1940 only two official emigration routes remained open — via Lisbon and via Japan. In both cases, the cost was prohibitive. By January 1941 the Japanese route had closed, having become too expensive and too troublesome. In 1939 and 1940 Lloyd Triestino also continued to operate a ferry service between Italy and Shanghai, dumping thousands of mostly Jewish refugees on the Shanghai waterfront. For Poles, opportunities for escape were even more limited. With the outbreak of war, Polish passports were no longer recognised in surrounding countries, so emigration from Poland became impossible, except from the Russian-occupied sector and for residents with foreign passports. Even then, gaining an exit visa from Russia was almost as difficult as gaining an entry visa for another country.[2] Between September 1939 and June 1941 more Poles left through deportation than through emigration. It is estimated that over one million persons, including many children, were forcibly resettled in the Soviet Union in that period; about one-third of them were Jewish.[3] Others fled in June 1941 with the retreating Russian army, ahead of the German advance.

The German army slaughtered tens of thousands of Jews during its advance through Russian-occupied territory.[4] Surviving Jews were interned in ghettos and forced into slave labour. Educated Poles were also marked for extermination. Others were forced into slave labour and often deported to make way for German settlers.[5] In late 1941, now with a massive Jewish population under its jurisdiction, Germany's position on emigration changed. On 23 October 1941 Himmler decreed that the emigration of Jews should be stopped immediately,[6] thereby ending all opportunity for escape from Germany and Nazi-occupied Europe. The decision to remove all Jews by extermination rather than emigration had been made.[7]

* * *

As the territory under Nazi occupation increased, the attention of the British government turned to British and allied nationals in countries threatened by the enemy — Yugoslavia, Romania, Turkey, and even, by January 1941, Japan and Portugal. The Foreign Office, believing it would incur criticism if it provided only for its own nationals, and claiming Britain could not absorb any more refugees, requested the British dominions and colonies to provide refuge to these allied nationals for the duration of the war. Most urgent was the case of hundreds of Poles in Romania and Yugoslavia, including a group of 150 Polish Boy Scouts in Romania. In December 1940 a request on their behalf was sent to Stanley Bruce, the Australian High Commissioner in London. On 23 December, ten days after receiving the request, Bruce sent the following cable to Prime Minister Menzies:

> Most of these boys are Scouts and Roman Catholics, less than ten per cent being Jews. Aged fourteen to eighteen. Nearly all belong to the Polish intellectual class which is singled out for persecution by Germans. British Minister at Bucharest reports that the boys are of good stamp and will be in serious danger if left where they are ... Proposal is that boys be given agricultural training in Australia for the period of the war and after the war be given the option of remaining in Australia if they have made good, or of returning to Poland. All expenses to be borne by Polish Government.[8]

Cabinet approved the request, but refused entry to any other Polish or Czech nationals for whom the British Foreign Office was seeking refuge. The admission of the boys was conditional on their being of sound health, all expenses being borne by the Polish government, and undertakings being made by welfare organisations for their care and maintenance in Australia.

Every day was critical in these emergencies, a fact which seems not to have been appreciated by the Australian government. It took another urgent cable before the welfare organisations were contacted: 'Matter is now one of great urgency having regard to recent developments in Rumania. Please telegraph on January 27 if possible whether or not welfare organizations will be able to undertake care.'[9] Within a week offers came from the Australian Jewish Welfare Society in Sydney for the twenty Jewish boys in the group, from the Continental Catholic Migrants Welfare Committee for the Catholic boys, and from the New Settlers' League in Queensland for any others. By the time this information reached London it was too late. The British consul had left Romania for Istanbul, having issued permits to only twenty boys. Efforts to rescue at least these twenty via Istanbul proved futile.

Although correspondence on the boys continued for several months, nothing more was heard of them. A statement on 18 June 1941 summarised the situation:

> The sequel to the offer to take the group of 150 boys was that visas were issued for a small number before we broke off diplomatic relations with Rumania. None, however, succeeded in leaving the Balkans and in May the Polish Embassy in Turkey said that none of them had yet succeeded in reaching there. It is improbable that any will manage to get through now and the whole scheme is, therefore, in abeyance.[10]

British Foreign Office personnel criticised the Australian government for its slack response, expressing the view that Australia should not be thanked for its offer: 'As it now seems doubtful whether the boys will have been got out before our Legation left — and they might have been if the Commonwealth had replied promptly to the request we made in December — it seems unnecessary to repeat these thanks'.[11]

Polish officials persistently requested Australia to open its doors to other Polish refugees, especially to those in Japan. In May 1941 the Department of the Interior authorised permits for sixty-six refugees in Japan. In July a further one hundred permits were issued on a guarantee from the Australian Jewish Welfare Society that it would take full responsibility for the refugees. None of these arrivals were unaccompanied children. Only later would unaccompanied Polish children again feature in requests for refuge.

* * *

On 17 December 1942, rumours that the Nazis were systematically exterminating the Jews of

Europe were confirmed in Britain's House of Commons and communicated to the world. Public sympathy was high, but the official response was ambiguous. The British government invited the United States to a private conference to discuss possible solutions to the refugee problem, but warned of 'the possibility that Germans or their satellites may change over from the policy of extermination to one of extrusion and aim, as they did before the war, at embarrassing other countries by flooding them with alien immigrants'.[12] Overshadowed by such thinking, the resulting Bermuda conference, held in April 1943, offered no help for those trapped in Nazi-occupied Europe. At most, it drew attention to pockets of refugees, Jewish and other, who had escaped to neutral countries, and on ways to relieve neutral countries of their burden. Australia was to be involved in the rescue of some of those refugees, among them children who had managed to leave Vichy France before the German occupation of that sector in November 1942, and children who might still be smuggled over the borders of occupied Europe.

When the Germans arrived in June 1940, France was crammed with refugees. During the early days of occupation, and the division of the country into occupied and free zones, there was a mass exodus to the south. Internment camps built for Spanish refugees quickly filled with these latest arrivals. Camps such as Gurs were described as 'worse than a Nazi concentration camp ... with people compelled to sleep on the cold, frozen ground ... and where hunger and disease were rampant'.[13] While refugee organisations succeeded in removing many children to orphanages and homes, there remained so many homeless and destitute children in Vichy France that the greatest problem for the relief organisations was deciding 'who to save ... how much to spend on one case when you knew it meant sacrificing another'.[14] When deportations to the east began in July 1942, efforts to acquire visas for children intensified.[15] While a small number of children left for the United States,[16] negotiations to admit up to 5000 to the United States and 500 to Britain, broke down when Vichy authorities refused to grant exit visas to the children. After the German occupation of the free zone in November 1942, attention turned to children who had already reached neutral countries and to clandestine ways of increasing their numbers.

In November 1942, Otto Schiff, chairman of the Council for German Jewry in London, requested the Australian Jewish Welfare Society to approach the Commonwealth government 'with the view of securing permits so that any children who might be rescued through Spain or Portugal could be given a haven'.[17] In March 1943 the government granted the Australian Jewish Welfare Society permits for 150 children from seven to fourteen years of age. The scenario that followed was reminiscent of earlier responses. Excessive delays occurred while committees were formed and appeals launched.[18] This time the delays may have been immaterial. Transport for the children was not available, although the Department of the Interior requested the Prime Minister, now John Curtin, to intervene on behalf of the Welfare Society.

Smuggling children across the borders of occupied Europe became a priority for many refugee organisations. At $400 a head, it was an expensive operation, and the children's arrival in neutral countries an increasing burden. Following a recommendation of the Bermuda conference, the Swiss government responded to the dilemma by agreeing to admit any children whose future resettlement in another country was guaranteed by a permit. With this information, the Australian Jewish Welfare Society applied for, and was granted in February 1944, a further 150 permits for children. Within a short time all 300 permits then held by the Welfare Society were offered to children entering Switzerland. In a July meeting of the Welfare Society it was reported that '374 children had entered Geneva on the 300 permits'. This valuable contribution to the rescue of European children might have been much greater had the government accompanied its offer with financial support. The Jewish Welfare Society had indicated it would receive thousands of children if given a subsidy.[19] There was no subsidy; rather, the government insisted on 'a guarantee of money for the 300 children for whom permits had been obtained'.[20]

Nevertheless, government attitudes to the admission of foreign children were changing, in line with public opinion[21] and the need to address the issue of postwar migration. Throughout 1944, possibly prompted by the presence of so many homeless children in Europe, the government began formulating plans for postwar child migration. The plan announced at the end of the year reiterated the desirability of children as migrants and proposed seizing the opportunity offered by the war and exploiting it in the next two or three years.[22] In this frame of mind, the government supported the Jewish Welfare Guardian Society's proposal to admit 1000 boys between fourteen and seventeen years of age after the war, giving approval in April 1944 for the first one hundred. This changing attitude did little to save lives; at most it indicated a readiness to offer permits to a limited number of foreign children who could be screened and selected using normal migration criteria. The government remained opposed to introducing children on any other terms, a position clearly articulated when responding in 1944 to a request to admit 700 Polish children from camps in Iran.

*　　*　　*

In August 1941, soon after the German invasion of Russia, Stalin granted an amnesty to Poles who had been deported to Russia.

Krstyna Skwarko, a deportee, described what followed:

> As soon as the political amnesty was announced there began an amazing exodus. From all the corners of Russia, from Northern Europe, Arkhangelsk and Vorkuta, down from the Ural Mountains, from Northern Asia, from Kolyma, from Siberia, Novosybirsk, Irkutsk, from Central Asia, from Kazakhstan, from all the forced labour camps, mines, prisons, from forests and other places of their exile, almost a million-strong mass of Polish people travelled in goods trains, sick, hungry and in rags to reach the south and the Caspian Sea.
>
> They had heard that a Polish army was being formed there. They hoped to join it. They hoped to be able to cross the border to Persia.[23]

As it eventuated, Stalin allowed only about 100 000 deportees to leave, among them fifteen to twenty thousand children who were resettled in camps in Iran.[24] These were children who had survived the misery of Russian labour camps or whose parents had delivered them to Polish orphanages established in Russia for deportees. 'To the question about parents the most frequent answer we heard was: "Mum is dead, Dad joined the army", or "Both Mum and Dad are dead".'[25] In Iran they were placed in camps and boarding schools, under the care of the British army. Children continued to arrive throughout 1943: 'The small children arrived half-starved, their bodies just skin and bone ... Many told how, unable to be fed by their mothers in Russia, they were pushed onto passing trains that were carrying orphans south in order to save them from certain death.'[26]

Other children began leaving, to countries which extended invitations to them in numbers up to 700 — Rhodesia, Tanganyika, Kenya, South Africa, Mexico, India and New Zealand. By December 1944, when the British and Polish armies were preparing to move out of Iran, only 700 children remained in the

Jewish women working for the Germans in the Sarny ghetto, Poland, about 1942. All surviving Jewish families were forced into ghetto life after the German occupation of Poland from June 1941. Jack Garbasz, who provided the photo, was unable to identify his two sisters although they are present. The ghetto was liquidated on 28 August 1942. (Jack Garbasz)

camps. The Polish consul approached the Australian government about admitting the remaining 700 children 'for the duration of the war'.[27] The matter was given serious consideration, to the extent that suitable camps for accommodating the group were investigated.[28] However, a decision was deferred on the grounds that the new Polish provisional government might refuse to honour financial undertakings given by the Polish government in London.

> This might not be regarded as serious if all the party brought out from Iran were in sound health and of good type ... as the children could be regarded as a contribution to the child migration scheme. As, however, it will not be practicable to have them properly examined by competent Australian authorities ... it is possible that a number of the party will not be suitable for permanent residence.[29]

While the Australian government procrastinated, the 700 children were transferred from Iran to Syria.

Had large numbers of Jewish children been released from Nazi-occupied Europe, Australia would almost certainly have been asked to play a bigger role in child rescue during the war. Britain carried on negotiations with this understanding. For example, early in 1944 the British government called on the German government to negotiate the emigration to Palestine of 5000 children from Poland, Lithuania and Latvia.[30] The Germans' refusal to consider any proposal involving Palestine led the British government to agree they would admit the children into the British Empire, 'with the exception of Palestine and the Near East'.[31] No agreement was reached and the proposal merged with an even bigger one, for the release of surviving Hungarian Jews, the so-called Horthy plan. With an Anglo-American agreement having been made in

August 1944 for their resettlement, Horthy recommended the release of Hungarian Jews, initially Jewish children under ten who had visas for foreign countries, and adults and children eligible for admission into Palestine. Informed of this, Australian Jewry urged the government to make visas available for 3000 adults and 5000 children.[32] The Reich opposed Horthy's plan, releasing only a small number of Hungarian Jews. With advice from London that there was 'provision for many more than those who had escaped',[33] the Australian government was not called on to help. Had large numbers of children been released, transport to Australia would have been a problem, but not the insurmountable one it was always claimed to be. New Zealand's feat in transporting 733 Polish children and 140 Polish adults from Iran in October 1944 undermined that argument.[34] Under pressure, British and United States authorities could have arranged shipping and safe conduct by 1944. It was a matter of priorities.

*   *   *

Following the Anglo-American agreement on Hungarian Jews, the British War Cabinet prepared a report for the United States government outlining Britain's contribution to refugees, and the contribution of its dominions and colonies. In responding to a draft of this report, the Australian government highlighted its contribution in the Pacific region where it had assumed a major portion of the refugee burden.[35]

Australia began receiving refugees from this region from July 1940, when British evacuees arrived from Hong Kong. They included 800 children by February 1941, although officially these children were accompanied by a parent or guardian.[36] Throughout 1941 a steady flow of women and children, including many Australian citizens, arrived from New Guinea and elsewhere in the region. Following the declaration of war with Japan in December 1941, this flow increased. Australia now became the major destination of women and children from Malaya, the East Indies and the Pacific islands. Although entry for non-British evacuees was controlled,[37] the Australia government displayed a flexibility with its neighbours that was missing with more distant European refugees. The Minister for the Interior commented:

> At a critical time such as this, the Commonwealth should not adopt what might be considered a rigid and ungenerous attitude in regard to admitting women and children from a threatened area such as Malaya. Too much insistence upon written undertakings might react detrimentally so far as Australia's relations with some of her allies are concerned.[38]

In January 1942 Cabinet also relaxed the immigration laws to allow 'a limited number of Chinese men and European Chinese, Chinese, and Eurasian women and child refugees to be given temporary homes in Australia'.[39] With the advance of the Japanese through countries in the Pacific region, even these restrictions were often overlooked — indeed they became impossible to enforce. As emergency evacuations occurred, people scrambled onto whatever transport was available to escape the advancing Japanese army.

With the emphasis on the evacuation of women and children, there was no organised evacuation of unaccompanied children in this region. Nevertheless, passenger lists show a number of children travelling to Australia by themselves between 1940 and 1942. One headmaster took the initiative to evacuate nineteen children from his school in Sumatra without waiting for approval from either Australian authorities or parents.[40] His action probably saved lives, as the Japanese arrived within weeks of the children's departure.

Among the evacuees were children who had returned to the colonies from boarding schools in England. While the much publicised CORB scheme was being planned, another unreported evacuation was under way in Britain; the British government was urging parents who lived in the colonies to evacuate their children. Pat McEvoy was one child who joined this wave of evacuees from England. Her father, Arthur McEvoy, had lived in Penang since 1924; his wife joined him after their marriage in 1929. When their children reached school age, the McEvoys followed the colonial practice of sending them to boarding school. In June 1940 the municipality of Penang offered to pay the passages of children returning to Penang. In a letter to his in-laws in England, Arthur McEvoy weighed the pros and cons of evacuation as opposed to leaving the children in England. 'A decision must be made,' he concluded. 'We have to choose between the comparatively short gamble of a dangerous sea voyage and the continuous and increasing risk of bombs.'[41] He eventually decided on evacuation and Pat and her brother travelled to Penang on the *Sarpedon* in July 1940. Pat recalled the journey: 'It was a long journey ... around the Cape. Though the convoy was attacked by subs we all thought it great fun! I was ten and my brother eight. We were "chaperoned" by a lady taking her two children to Malaya. She also had two other boys with her.'

Penang became a precarious refuge after the Japanese attack on Pearl Harbor. Days later, on 13 December 1941, European women and children were evacuated from Penang, among them the McEvoy children and their mother. After arriving in Singapore, they sailed immediately to Batavia and thence to Australia. Not all parents left promptly. Many delayed their departure until the eleventh hour, often with disastrous results. Children died, were separated, interned and orphaned as a result of these delays.

At Tulagi, in the Solomon Islands, Andrea Wilson's (now Bannantyne) mother refused to leave, or to send her daughter away until the last minute. Unlike most children from colonial families, Andrea had lived at home throughout her childhood. 'It was always thought necessary to send your children away ... but when I was born I was fat, happy and healthy. It was seen that I didn't need to be sent away.' Andrea thrived in the tropical environment: 'I grew happier and fatter and the mosquitos didn't give me malaria, and when there was an earthquake I thrived on it — I used to scream with laughter and think it was lovely, whereas this was my brother's main terror.'

Talk of a Japanese invasion was regular fare for Andrea as a child.

> We'd always had Japanese trawlers in the harbour and my father, the resident commissioner in the British Colonial Service, would say, 'they're not diving for trochus, they're mapping the floor of the ocean and the harbour so that they can invade.' Everyone would see him battering away at his old typewriter out on the verandah, sending away letters marked 'Top Secret'. Mother would go and peep over his shoulder and say, 'Oh yes, he's writing another letter saying the Japs are invading.' He would get quite hysterical about these Japanese because he would order them into the harbour to look at their boats. He would go into the galley and find these mapping tables just folded down quickly, still with the black linen on them, with the charting.

The warnings of her father, Alexander (Spareline) Wilson, went unheeded. Even at the end people could not believe the Japanese were coming. 'Everyone was packing their lovely possessions ... The wharf was absolutely littered with cases of silver and valuables — all these lovely collections of anthropological stuff, and personal possessions.' When the ship failed to come, the women and children left in a missionary vessel without their possessions, and without Andrea and her mother: 'My mother refused to go on it and wouldn't send me ...

Though they didn't know what the deadline was, my father kept saying that they were coming … He evacuated all the Chinese population — sent them all to Sydney in a government schooner and another boat.'

Andrea's turn came when another missionary family came across in their boat, saying that this was positively the last boat. It was the beginning of an extraordinary journey to Australia.

> It was a very small boat. We had to black the windows out — paint them, then cover them with black tissue paper. We had to take turns to watch for submarines, day and night, two adults and two children. We didn't know that the place was absolutely stuffed with submarines. I didn't know what had happened to my mother and father, but I was quite happy. My mother had said, 'Don't worry, we'll be all right', so I was thoroughly enjoying it. I resented very much being woken up and having to sit on deck, but even that was fun … I remember once facing the other way to everybody else and up came this black bit of submarine not too far away. I looked at it and I thought, 'Well now, that must be a submarine. What will I do?' I didn't say anything. I just sat and looked at it. I thought, 'It doesn't look very big … and it doesn't look like it will send depth charges at us. If I tell them I've seen it, by the time they turn around it won't be there and they won't believe me.' So I just watched it and it went away and I never told a soul. It had little impact on me until I was grown up. I thought it was a nice little submarine. Children can be quite incredible.

In the final panic, Andrea's mother had been thrust onto another boat. Unable to cross the Coral Sea, it headed north to China. In Tulagi, her father, abandoned by his staff, rushed around detonating the records and anything likely to be of value to the Japanese. Then, having sent away the locals, he waited on the wharf for the ship to collect him. 'Suddenly, out of the blue, came the Japanese planes … They came down, strafing the wharf and everything on it.' He escaped by jumping into the water and staying there for two days, after which the locals returned and took him into the jungle. 'He lived in the jungle with them, in hand to hand combat with the Japanese.' Andrea only discovered the whereabouts of her parents much later. In the meantime she became another child cast adrift from her family.

* * *

For all these children who came alone to Australia, the journey was like a rite of passage. Although their backgrounds differed, as did the traumas they had suffered before departure, a common thread bound them. All had been uprooted from their familiar worlds, separated from parents and thrust into situations where they would have to cope without the support of their families. Australia had offered them a haven. How they would fare there remained to be seen.

7

LARINO

23 July 1939. SS Orama

Tomorrow 24 July we will leave the ship. We already arrived in Melbourne today, but only at 10 o'clock in the evening. You can't imagine how much I look forward to Melbourne. They say it's a big house in a healthy neighbourhood and the tram stops just before the door. Hopefully you too will come soon.

Many regards and 1 000 000 kisses.[1]

En route to Melbourne the *Orama* berthed in Fremantle and Adelaide. On both occasions the Jewish communities gave warm welcomes to the young German children. The Perth reception was particularly memorable, and well recorded. A committee member later wrote:

> A few of us went down to the boat to bring them up to Perth. Beautiful children, all of them ... with happy, smiling faces, and eyes almost popping out of their heads in excitement of their new adventure ... I had four girls and one boy [George] in my car. George was thrilled with everything, especially the football grounds at Claremont and Subiaco. Passing a music shop he noticed some saxophones in the window. 'My father has one of those,' he told me, 'but,' he added, confidentially, 'he can't play it.' He kept making signals to me and pointing to the cars in front. I couldn't follow him, so, like a flash, out came his German—English pocket dictionary. His finger ran down the pages. 'Overtake,' he announced triumphantly. I 'overtook', much to his delight.[2]

The children were taken to the synagogue where, Betty Abrahamson recalled, Rabbi Freedman giving them a welcoming speech.

'He couldn't speak German, so he talked Yiddish — and I remember we were all trying not to giggle, 'cause we thought it funny, this little man giving us a speech in Yiddish ... but we got the meaning.' Then to a sumptuous lunch at the Brecklers, a wealthy Perth family, who offered them treats to delight any child. 'At such a table I have never eaten,' wrote Margot Goldstein to her family. 'Next to one was a plate with bread, before another was candy cake, and fruit was on the table. You could eat what you wanted.' After eating, there was time to play — 'the boys played football, but laughed scornfully at the shape of the ball' — and perform; they delighted their Australian audience with 'German folk songs, followed by traditional Hebrew melodies ... then proceeded to "put one over us" by gleefully singing "Daisy", which they had learnt on the boat coming over.'[3] Betty Abrahamson also recalled the Breckler's daughter, Shirley, teaching them the Lambeth Walk. The day over, they returned to the ship, which proceeded to Adelaide, then Melbourne.

In Melbourne another reception awaited them. The Ladies' Auxiliary of the Australian Jewish Welfare Society met many ships, but few aroused such interest as the *Orama* and these seventeen child passengers. Their arrival was the culmination of months of planning and preparation, and the women were there in large numbers to greet their charges.[4] Amongst them was the secretary of the Welfare Society, Frances Barkman, who had been largely responsible for initiating the scheme to bring refugee children to Australia.

Frances Barkman habitually imposed name

changes on newly arrived refugees, a ritual which the children now underwent. The majority received anglicised versions or abbreviated forms of their family names. For example, Ehrlich became Earl, Lewinski became Lewin, Abrahamson, Abraham. Ellen Schaechter vividly recalls Miss Barkman sitting at a table, a porthole over her left shoulder, saying, 'Ellen Schaechter, now you are Ellen Chester', and the feeling of her past seeming to disappear. Other children had little reaction to the procedure, perhaps not comprehending what was going on.

From the docks the children were taken to their new home at Balwyn, a few miles outside the city of Melbourne. This large Federation-style house, named Larino, had recently been saved from demolition, renovated and rented to the Jewish Welfare Society by Samuel Meyers, husband of one of the women on the Ladies' Auxiliary. Hedi and Ferry Fixel, whose plans to proceed immediately to Tasmania had fallen through, accompanied the children.

> We were a little bit in limbo about what to do. At the same time, we were welcomed by the Welfare Society in Melbourne. They told us, 'It is hard for the children; they are used to you. Come with us into the children's home for the time being and see what happens.' So we came into the children's home and that was like a dream — a beautiful old home, done up, with a big garden; and there were big rooms for the children, very nicely furnished. There was quite a big domestic staff there — a cook, housekeeper, handyman and pantry maid.

The children, accustomed to European apartment living, were equally impressed with the home, many describing it as a 'palace'. 'I remember when we first arrived,' commented Edna Lehmann. 'There was this magnificent house. It was like a palace. We thought everyone in Australia must live like that.' There were numerous rooms, twenty-eight according to Hermann Levy. In a letter home, Margot Goldstein described the use of some of those rooms: 'The girls have two bedrooms. Six children sleep in one. I am in the other room where four sleep. We bathe or shower every day. Then we have a dining room and also a writing room. And then a completely empty space with only two benches in it. And then a boys' bedroom and a big garden.'

Inscribed in the stained glass of the front door were the words, 'How like a winter hath thine absence been'. A reporter commented on their aptness: 'Surely it has been winter in the hearts of those parents who sent their sons and daughters to find a new and better life in Australia'.[5] For the children, their arrival at Larino was certainly the beginning of a new life; for most it would be the only home they would know for many years.

* * *

After a day to explore and settle into their new environment, the seventeen children were enrolled at Balwyn State School, an event which received front page coverage in the *Sun News-Pictorial*. Arrangements had been made for them to spend a short time together before entering regular classes. It was the first school experience for some children since being barred from state schools in Germany, and it provided a happy contrast to their treatment in their homeland. 'I remember the beautiful way we were accepted by all when we first went to school', commented Hermann Levy. For Betty Abrahamson, a neighbour dropping off a bag of oranges for the children was a highlight: 'On our first day at school there were these beautiful big oranges sitting on our desks ... I'd never seen beautiful oranges like that. They really impressed me ... my eyes popped. It was said these lovely people next door had an orange tree and had given them to us ... I thought that was such a wonderful thing.'

Larino, a beautiful old house situated at 23 Maleela Avenue, Balwyn, which was converted into a home for the children. In 1946 the name was changed to the Frances Barkman Home. In 1965 the Frances Barkman Home was relocated and began operating elsewhere as a family group scheme. The original house was almost completely destroyed by fire and now displays none of its previous grandeur. In recent years it has been a home for elderly and disabled people. (*Australian Jewish News*, 5 October 1990)

Bob Payne, whose parents were responsible for this gesture, was then seven years old and also attending the school.

Mum explained to me that we must be kind to these children because they had suffered a lot. She was a Quaker, and many displaced Europeans passed through our open front and back doors in those days, some for a meal, some for help, some just bringing a friend. They were not only welcomed but made to feel at home. Our home was next door to the school and Mum encouraged the children to drop in for something to eat on the way home after school.

Mrs Payne also supported the Fixels by familiarising them with life in Australia and by helping Hedi hone her cooking skills.

Their warm reception at Balwyn State School was due largely to the excellent leadership provided by the principal, Mr Carter. He retains a special place in the children's memories. 'We all adored him,' commented Ellen Schaechter. 'Mr Carter was a darling,' confirmed Betty Abrahamson, 'He was an absolutely wonderful person.' Nevertheless, he caused a great deal of hysteria among some of the children when they saw an ash tray with a swastika on his desk. Although they spoke no English at the time, he managed to explain that it was an ancient symbol and for him had no connection with the Nazis. The fact that his daughter was on a music scholarship in Germany undoubtedly strengthened Mr Carter's interest in the children. Under his guidance much kindness was extended to

Above: A day after arriving in Melbourne, the children began school at Balwyn State School. Here Richard Dreyfus bows to the school principal, Mr Carter. Other children, from left to right, are: Alfred Stocks, Hermann Levy, Herman Gold, Ellen Lewinski and Ingrid Ehrlich.

Left: Richard Dreyfus attracts amazed looks as he makes contact with an Australian football, a very odd-looking ball indeed to a German child. (*Sun News-Pictorial*, 27 July 1939)

them. 'The kids and teachers could not have been nicer or kinder,' commented Ellen Schaechter. 'We told them incredible fibs about Germany and the wildest stories when it was our turn for "morning observations". They pretended to believe us and tried to befriend us. Not many succeeded because of language problems, and because we went home for lunch.' Ingrid Ehrlich also commented on efforts by the other children to befriend them: 'The children were marvellous. They used to take us into the shelter sheds and make us read English and read with us. They were very kind to us, they really were.' Bob Payne commented, 'I think we children at Balwyn State School accepted the Larino children as we did other Aussies — that is, we all got no more nor less than we deserved'. Memories and media reports support the conclusion that the Australian public welcomed the children and would happily have received many others like them. A taxi-driver who called at Larino during their first week was overheard saying: 'Australia is really lucky getting settlers like them. When you see them, you sort of realise what a swine Hitler must be. Yet he must be a —— fool into the bargain. If those are the sort of people he drives out, the crowd that's left must be a pretty —— mob'.[6]

Despite the good-will, the children's introduction to Australian society was not without its difficulties. Movement into mainstream classes brought confusion and misunderstanding, as Edna Lehmann illustrated: 'It was a hard time because we didn't understand English. For example, once the teacher said, "Now we'll do mental arithmetic." To me "mental" sounded like 'mantle', a coat. It was winter by then and we had our coats slung over the backs of the seats. So I put my coat on.' Edna also felt embarrassment at having to speak in front of others, and at some of their German customs. 'All the boys had been taught the German custom to bow; the girls did a little curtsy. It was polite. Of course, the Australian kids ragged us like mad because they thought this was very funny.'

To help with their English, Mr Carter gave them special sessions in his room. 'He tried very hard to make us speak like Australians. He had groups of us and we had to repeat words and so forth' recalled Frances Kochen (now Rothschild). The children were also given English classes at Larino three times a week. Ellen Schaechter remembered Elsa Haas teaching them phonetic verses to practise certain vowels and consonants. Ellen said it was not uncommon to go to sleep reciting verses such as:

> Lippy and Loppy are two little rabbits
> Lippety loppety down to the bottom
> Lippety loppety back to the top
> Lippety loppety loppety lippety loppety loo

Despite Mr Carter's efforts, attitudes of the wider Australian community towards Germans inevitably penetrated the school playground. The fact that as Jews they had been driven out of Germany was not generally appreciated. 'I don't think they knew what we were about. They knew there was a war going on and that the Germans were the baddies.' 'Hate for the Germans was so strong,' said Margot Goldstein. 'I remember one girl coming up to me and saying, "You Germans, you were preparing for this war for years. You got your arms and everything." I remember the "you Germans"; it sticks in my mind. Like, all of a sudden I realised she thought of us as German and I myself never thought I was German.'

'Don't be foreign' was instilled in them by the Welfare Society. 'We weren't allowed to speak German after a few months in the home,' commented Marion Ehrlich. Lapses inevitably occurred, and for these the children were reprimanded. Much of their German clothing — the dirndl dresses and the lederhosen — were likewise taboo outside Larino. 'We weren't allowed to wear them here — it would have looked too Germanic.'[7] 'After all, there

The seventeen new arrivals joined other children for a picnic in the Australian bush near Melbourne. (Hedi Fixel)

Ferry Fixel, although not employed at the home, lived in, and is remembered for his kindness and gentleness. He is pictured here with Laurie Badrian, Wally Pratt (a short term resident) and Hermann Levy. (Hedi Fixel)

Hedi Fixel, who was matron at Larino from July 1939 until mid-1941. (Frances Rothschild) was a war on,' conceded Margot Goldstein. In wartime Australia, speaking German was not only unfashionable, it was against regulations in some circumstances, as Hedi Fixel pointed out: 'During the war if you spoke German on the phone they would cut in on you and tell you to speak English'. The Welfare Society, ever conscious of enforcing government regulations, displayed notices in its office 'warning refugees against speaking anything but English on the telephone and advising them that a breach of the regulations would result in the telephone in question being disconnected'. While embracing a new language and culture may have been easier for the children than for many adult refugees, becoming 100 per cent Australian and 100 per cent Jewish, as their rabbi admonished them to do, was a tall order and caused additional stress during an already highly emotional time.

* * *

Originally it was intended that Larino be a transit home. The children would stay there for about three months to become acclimatised and learn English, then be fostered into private homes. According to one source, this was why the children had their tonsils out soon after arrival. Two boys escaped this ordeal; the other children spent part of their first school holiday in hospital. Betty Abrahamson recalled the terror of that ordeal:

> We weren't told we were having our tonsils out. They put us in groups ... The first group disappeared. 'Where are they?' 'Oh, you know, mmm.' Nothing was said. Then they took our group ... we went to the hospital ... we didn't know what was going on ... and suddenly we saw the other group ... they came and they waved, but they couldn't talk ... Nothing was explained. Nothing was said. We were taken to this place from Germany, where we knew people disappeared, and these kids came out and they haven't got any voices. I was terrified. In those days they had masks which they poured anaesthetic on. Well, you've never heard anyone scream the way I screamed, and kicked, when they put that thing on me. I think because I screamed and kicked so much I bled very badly afterwards ... I thought I was being murdered ... Afterwards wasn't as bad because they came around with ice-cream. You don't come around with ice-cream if you're trying to kill someone.

The children underwent various other medical examinations and treatments soon after their arrival. Margot Goldstein wrote that they all had their feet examined. Betty Abrahamson recalled a visit to the dentist, again with no explanation.

> This dentist tried everything to make me smile — he made funny faces, he put my hat on his head (I wasn't impressed) and I started screaming and yelling ... Again, just scared ... In the end, his sister, who was the nurse, took my hand and she took me out and bought me an ice-cream. She explained what he was going to do and I was quite all right after that.

As the likelihood of receiving other refugee children dimmed, plans to foster the original group were abandoned. Shortly after their arrival these seventeen were joined by Paula and Frances Kochen whose mother was unable to maintain them in her live-in position at Samuel Wynn's. Later in the year, Richard and George Dreyfus left to join their parents who had arrived in Australia, having left Germany the day after war was declared. The others settled down for the duration — and beyond.

The outbreak of war soon after the children's arrival not only shattered all hope of imminent family reunion, for most it also severed links with families in Germany. Children with families in Shanghai could still correspond; a few others received family mail or news via relatives in the United States. In December 1941, when the United States entered the war, that avenue also closed. Thereafter Red Cross messages of twenty-five words became the only means of communication between children and parents in Germany.

Surviving letters tell a story of dwindling hope, and of the pain and worry caused by separation. Laurie Badrian's letters from his parents illustrate this:

15 August 1939

My beloved child!

You always crossed your fingers for me and wished Masseltow. Tomorrow I'll be at the aid association, so you can cross your fingers again (in thought). Maybe we'll be able to come soon. Write your dear parents what you're doing all the time. Stay healthy. Greetings to Fredi and Ilse and all the ladies and gentlemen.

100 000 kisses from your good daddy.

16 August 1939.

My beloved golden boy!

Since you wanted to know how much money daddy brings home I can tell you that mummy now works in a Jewish office and brings home money every month. Daddy, in the meantime, does the cooking at home and makes the beds. Please always write the date on your mail because I always like to know when you wrote. Did you receive mail from grandma Minna and grandma Emma?

Hearty kisses to you dear Lothar from your sweet mummy.

26 August 1939.

Only beloved child.

From far we send you hearty greetings and kisses. Always think of your dear parents who have troublesome days ahead. Pray to our dear Lord that he keeps your parents healthy, so that we can see you again healthy in life, also the dear people close to you. Enjoy it that you can live in peace and gladness there. Always look after yourself well and stay happy and content. Write to us soon. We'll write to you again as soon as it's possible for us. The grandmas send their regards, also Simons and all the people who know you. Also send us photos of you. A thousand greetings and kisses my beloved Pumpele and Patschele from your good parents,

Walter and Kathe

Margot Goldstein's letters to her family express the optimism of childhood that must have buoyed many children through this period. They reveal also a maturity beyond her years. Here is a child supporting her parents through constant reassurances of her well-being, even reversing the roles and intervening to help a parent:

Dear parents, sister and brother

I received your letter 31 December 1940 the day before yesterday and was very happy. I heard that Papa would go to Shanghai and that there's not quite enough money. I told Mrs Fixel all about it and she said she would talk to the Committee.

Unfortunately, as Mrs Fixel explained in an attached note, there was nothing she could do:

Dear Madam

Margot is very well and is developing splendidly. You have nothing to worry about in this respect. Otherwise there is unfortunately nothing we can undertake here. I hope very much that everything with you is all right.

While children who knew their parents had escaped to Palestine or Shanghai may have had less cause to worry, it is doubtful if this made much difference for those who were very young. The physical absence of parents was the most salient factor and disturbed the children regardless of their parents' whereabouts. Marion Ehrlich, for example, knew her parents were in Shanghai, yet occasionally on the way to school 'would see a lady on the other side of the street. It looked like my mother, a tall, thin lady. I knew it wasn't my mother, but I thought it could be. I would look and run up and, no, it wasn't her.'

Some former child refugees do not recall the early period as being particularly stressful, nor of being particularly homesick. They often missed their familiar worlds and others within it as much as they missed their parents. 'I missed our dog, a fox terrier called Pitt, almost as much as I missed our mother and kept asking after the dog in our Red Cross messages,' recalled Jo Lehmann. Their emotional behaviour may be the best indicator of their reactions to their situation, both then and later. Most can refer to emotional disorders in themselves or others, such as bed-wetting, stammering, blushing and nightmares. Hedi Fixel commented on emotional scenes, especially when war was declared and the children realised they would not have contact with their families. Ellen Lewinski, recounting incidents of cruelty and bullying in the first year, believed they must have been 'terribly disturbed' to behave so aggressively. Commenting on this, Betty Abrahamson said a ringleader 'organised for people to get teased ... that person would get a hell of a time ... Mine didn't last for long, but I remember teasing Ingrid because I was told to. I remember her crying in the night. Somebody said, 'Oh, go and slap her face. Go on Betty.' I went over and I didn't want to slap her face. She was crying. I remember clapping my hands together and going back to bed.' Ellen Lewinski spoke of how Ferry Fixel supported them through this stage. On one occasion 'we were all told to lie on the floor and swim in the tears of the two who were being victimised. And he sat on the couch in the downstairs playroom with one arm around each of the victims, and he looked sad, while the rest of us were swimming on the floor, pretending to swim in the tears.'

Hedi Fixel became matron soon after the move to Larino. Her husband, Ferry, lived there in an unofficial capacity. The children remember them as kind people, committed to their care. While Hedi, as matron, had numerous demands on her time, Ferry devoted

Hedi Fixel captioned this photograph 'Girls with dolls from Santa Claus, January 1940'. From left to right: Ellen Schaechter, Ingrid Ehrlich, Marion Ehrlich, Paula Kochen. (Hedi Fixel)

Ferry Fixel organised many valuable experiences for the children, including bringing in chickens for the boys to care for. Hermann Levy, whose letters from home show he had a vast knowledge of poultry when he arrived, is pictured with one of his charges. (Hedi Fixel)

himself to the children, responding sensitively to their needs. A former refugee commented on how the Fixels supported her brother:

> My brother was very very difficult. He didn't steal or hit anybody, just rebelled against everything. His attitude was 'If they want to speak to me they'll just have to learn German, won't they!' The Fixels were really wonderful. I often spoke to her because my brother was so difficult. But they tried. He was interested in anything agricultural so they especially got chickens that he could feed.

With Marion Ehrlich it was gardening. 'He was a gardener and he used to encourage us to garden. I had a plot with Ellen with pansies. It was really exciting for us to see them bloom; we used to love that. He was very kind.'

The Fixels had their own life to make in their new country. In time Ferry left for work in Tasmania. Hedi stayed on a while, but it was a difficult job for a woman alone and she left by mid-1941. In the preceding months, the children's behaviour was a major topic of discussion at meetings of the Australian Jewish Welfare Society. The House Committee criticised Hedi for her 'lack of disciplinary control' and for indulging the children, to whom, they complained, 'she gave far too much consideration'. The complaints say much about the committee's attitudes: 'On one occasion a child sucked an egg at the table and on others children had resorted to the use of their fingers and neglected to use the cutlery provided'. 'Apart from that they were known to lapse into German.' Hedi Fixel was also taxed 'with neglecting to enforce certain rules such as arranging for children to wash some of their own socks as suggested by the House Committee'.

Hedi Fixel acknowledged that some of the children were being difficult, but pointed to a situation which the committee had overlooked; the children had been confined to Larino for three months due to an epidemic of scarlet fever. After a visit to Larino, Frances Barkman agreed the troublesome behaviour could well

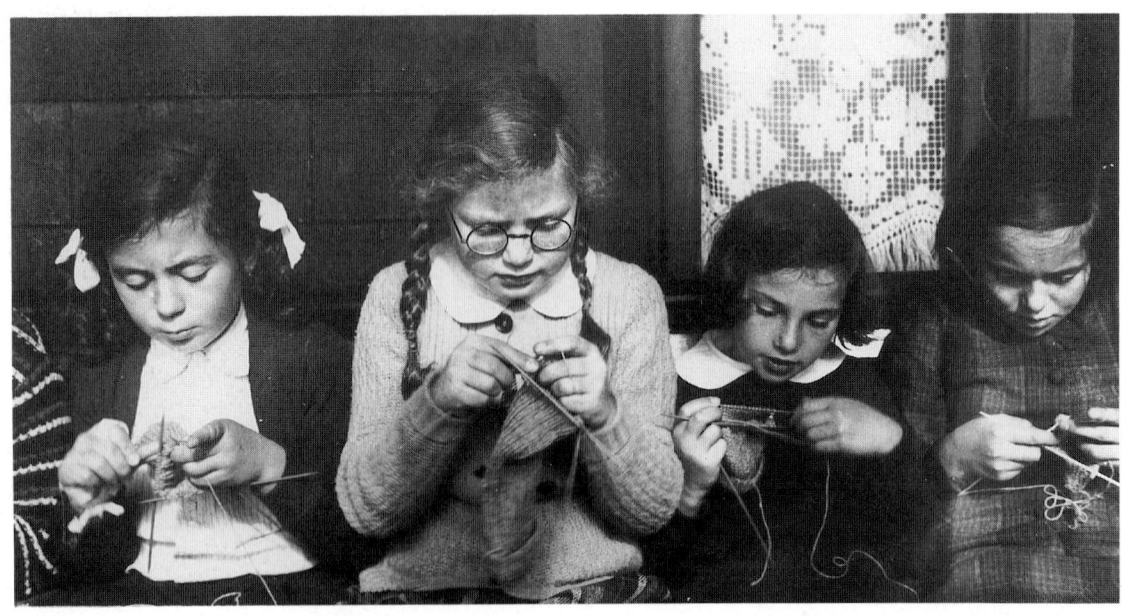

Both boys and girls at Larino knitted for the war effort. Above, left to right: Margot Goldstein, Jo Lehmann, Ellen Rothschild and Ellen Lewinski. (Marion Paul)

be related to their confinement, the children being bored through lack of variety, not seeing anyone from outside, and being free of all school discipline. She also pointed to the recent arrival of three children from Tatura internment camp and their effect on the group.[8] Attention was drawn particularly to the boys' behaviour, although certain girls were said to be teasing the boys and provoking their misbehaviour. Frances Barkman suggested the time might be ripe to consider separating the boys and the girls, and perhaps of combining girls and boys of the Jewish Welfare Society and the Jewish Orphan Society.

Hedi Fixel resigned about this time. The Welfare Society's response was to cast around for a matron 'with experience in institutional management'. An advertisement was placed in several papers, 'inviting applications from one individual or a couple qualified to take over the supervision and control of the children and the management of the staff'. Mrs Samuels was offered the position with the understanding that her husband would live on the premises 'to help with the discipline of the boys'.

So began a dark period for the children. Dr Samuels took seriously the Welfare Society's request that he discipline the boys. According to Alfred Stocks, Dr Samuels ran the place like the army, administering corporal punishment liberally. Alfred recalled an incident of excessive humiliation for him during this regime. Although the children received threepence a week pocket money, a penny went towards war bonds and another penny to Jewish welfare. 'We ended up with a penny. I remember the other kids went into the shops and bought chips and things after school. Once I took some money out of the telephone box. First I didn't own up, but when I got found out they did a very drastic thing to me; they got the rabbi to speak to me. I'll never forget that.' The matter was reported to the directors of the Welfare Society, who took it a step further. They advised the matron 'to speak informally to the policeman of the district and arrange with him that the child should be given a thorough fright at the Police Station. This would impress him

Beating the Australian heat (Hedi Fixel)

sufficiently and exclude the possibility of a recurrence of such offences in the future.'

As might be expected from earlier complaints, behaviour in the dining room came under particular surveillance. At this stage the children were still getting used to institutional cooking — often mushy and overcooked — as well as in many cases getting used to kosher food — endless boring, dry sandwiches, according to Marion Ehrlich. Regardless, they were now forced to eat everything on their plates. Jo Lehmann recalled her sister being slapped for not eating her porridge, as well as other unpleasant food-related incidents: 'I remember one particularly unpleasant incident when Dr Samuels insisted we eat the cauliflower which, perhaps unknown to him, was full of caterpillars!' Betty Abrahamson laughed in retrospect at a similar incident: 'We got this terrible soup and it was full of ants. We used to get Argentine ants in those days ... you had to put things — the table and so on — in water ... but the ants got through that time.

There are other unpleasant memories of this period:

> He used to make us get up in the cold of winter and strip into our underclothes and do PT at six o'clock in the morning. I don't know if he wanted to see us jumping about in our undies, or if it was concern for physical exercise, but we all resented this terribly. The days were quite long enough.

Some of the girls recalled how Dr Samuels would walk in on them when they were bathing. He embarrassed and disgusted them, although in retrospect they judge the behaviour as misguided, not necessarily perverse. He was a medical doctor and a few of them were on the verge of puberty. One of the girls reported that after this infringement of her privacy he took her aside and told her the 'facts of life'. Fortunately Dr Samuels left Larino after about three months, although his wife stayed a while longer.

When the Welfare Society sought a replacement for this couple, they chose a young woman, Ursula Kaye, who came from the same background and circumstances as the children. Ursula considers she had had a 'good and easy' life since her arrival in Australia, working in the household of Sir John and Lady Latham. In 1941 she left their employ to return to office work. While she was between jobs she was enticed into inquiring about the position of matron at Larino. Her acceptance came reluctantly. 'I didn't want to go to the home ... When the committee asked I said, "Look, I don't know whether I can do the job. I come from a liberal household." ' The previous matron was also unsure, Ursula being a smoker, with red-painted fingernails and a boyfriend. 'She said to me, "You won't last here, not with those fingernails and a boyfriend".' Ursula did last — till 1946.

* * *

Group living inevitably meant having routines and practices unnecessary in a family home. The Fixels tried to keep these as individual as possible; for example, Hedi explained, 'In the bathroom the towels and everything were numbered so that the same child got the same towel'. They tried to implement other routines in a spirit of fun and competition. 'The children had to make their own beds and straighten things out, then they got a prize when it was well done. Ferry organised all that.' Later staff did not necessarily follow this child-centred approach to chores. Alfred Stocks remembered later room inspections: 'There were weekly inspections — our room against the girls' rooms. There was not allowed to be a dip in the middle of the bed and the cover had to be nice and straight. And the cupboards were looked at. Things couldn't be just thrown in; they had to be tidy.'

The toilet routine was perhaps more extraordinary. The children had to mark crosses under their names in the toilet so that a check could be made on their bowel movements. The castor oil bottle came out if there was no action for three or four days, although Jo Lehmann recalled a kinder treatment for constipation — receiving an apple.

A diary kept by Ellen Lewinski in February and March 1940 provides an irrefutable record of the monotonous routine into which the children's lives quickly fell. The institutional bells echo through the pages:

Thursday, 7 March 1940

After breakfast we went to school. Then the bell rang to queue up and we went into the classroom. Then it rang for the break and then it rang to march — can't remember who came first. Then we went back into class. Then the bell rang again and we went home and had lunch. Then we went back to school. Then it rang for the break. Then it rang again for the lesson and then to go home. Then we did our homework and after we went into the garden and played. Then it rang for supper and after we played. Then it rang again for milk and we went upstairs to bathe and went to bed.

Within a short time the children became conspicuous as much from their institutional bearing as from their foreignness; they became the children from the home. The girls sorely remember the hand-me-down clothes that soon replaced what they had brought from Germany. Even in primary school the lack of proper school uniforms set them apart from the other children. Ann Creber, a fellow student at Balwyn State School, later commented to Ellen Lewinski that the Larino girls looked like a lot of black crows on a fence. 'We wore black stockings and navy tunics and none of us had ribbons or the proper school tie. We just had black ties. So we looked somewhat dark in our apparel.' In addition, they never had summer uniforms. 'We had to wear the heavy dark winter tunics with white shirts summer and winter.'

Nevertheless, Betty Abrahamson believes they fared well compared with another group of children at Balwyn school. These were boys from an institution. 'They all came without shoes. We used to think "those poor children", but were later told it was normal for Australian children to go without shoes.'

Socially and physically the German children became very insular. 'We were an island,' explained Frances Kochen. 'We went to school and we went home. We were taken places occasionally, but always as a group.' While some of the children made friends at school, outside school there was little socialising. In the six weeks she kept her diary, Ellen Lewinski recorded one incident of local children visiting to play, although she does record it as an unremarkable event:

Saturday, 17 February 1940

After breakfast we went to the temple and after we came home we ate lunch and then I tidied up my wardrobe. Then I went down into the garden and, as I came out of the house, there were two girls from our school. Then we played.

Jo Lehmann speculated on the reasons she and Ellen Lewinski may have made friends more easily than some of the children. They were both blonde, both extroverts, they learnt English fairly quickly and neither had an orthodox background, so had no compunction about mixing with gentiles. Religion may have hampered more orthodox children from forming friendships with Australians, and all children from socialising outside of school hours. A relative of one of the children commented: 'They had no opportunity to mix. They had to come straight home after school. Even if they were invited they were not allowed to go. I don't know why, but probably in case somebody gave them non-kosher food.'

Ingrid Ehrlich commented, 'We wanted to integrate but at the same time we wanted to stay Jewish. We had a very Jewish upbringing in the home.' Betty Abrahamson believes the Australian children were justified in considering them 'clicky'. 'We all walked to school together, we all came home together, we all played together, we all ate together ... Really, we were like brothers and sisters.' Betty's enjoyment of sport and of being outdoors probably helped her break down some of the barriers. She always had friends at school. 'I liked sports better than I liked school and being inside.' Alfred Stocks also breached the gap through sport:

> I always liked my sport and, because Australians liked their sports, I had no problem. I played in the cricket team at the state school. Later I played in the football team at Box Hill technical school. So I got on with everybody ... As a matter of fact, I was class captain in the technical school. Stocksy was my name — very Australian.

Even so, Alfred's sporting activities were confined to school hours, or to the spacious grounds of Larino.

Swimming was one sporting activity in which all the children engaged. In summer it was a weekly event at Balwyn State School. Ellen Lewinski wrote in her diary:

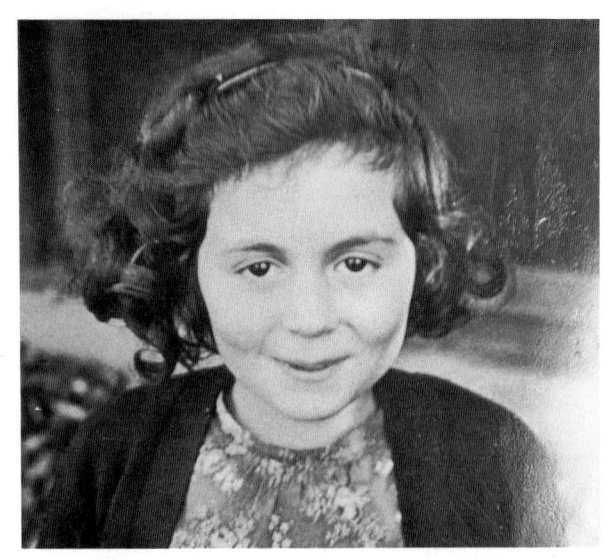

Hedi Fixel playing ball with the girls in the expansive grounds of Larino. (Hedi Fixel)

Hedi Fixel with, from left, Ilse Frank, Ellen Rothschild and Ellen Schaechter (Hedi Fixel)

Margot Goldstein, whose letters to her family appear throughout the book (Margot Herschenbaum)

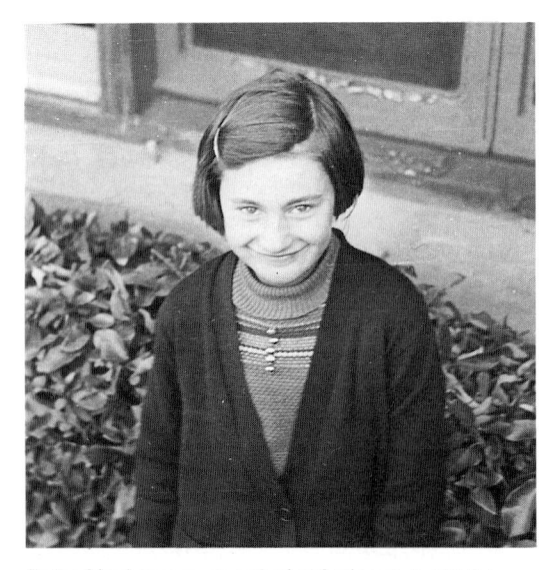

Betty Abrahamson on arrival at Larino (Betty Midalia)

Monday, 26 February 1940

After breakfast we went to school and handed over our money for swimming. Then the bell rang for us to queue up and we went into the classroom. In class we said a poem and then Miss White gave us our tickets for swimming and then we went. The only thing I didn't dare do was to float on water.

Monday, 4 March 1940

After breakfast we got ready the things we needed for school and swimming. Then we went to school and paid for the swimming and soon we went off to swim.

At home they drew upon each other for companionship. In her diary, Ellen Lewinski captured some of their shared fun and mischief which many others have long since forgotten:

Saturday, 24 February 1940

After breakfast we played baseball and something else and then the bell rang for lunch. After lunch we went back into the garden and jumped with the skipping rope, and the boys threw acorns. Then of course we threw too, and soon it was a real fight.

Sunday, 24 March 1940

We were still sleeping when, in the morning, the children from the other room came in with a bucketful of water and woke us up by bespattering us with water. Then the bell rang to get up and they bespattered us some more.

In later years, Ellen recalled the games they played together: 'We played tremendous games. We could play cricket if we could get the cook and the handyman to join in. We played football, we played wonderful hide-and-seek games, and the matron joined in.' A home movie made on an excursion to the Dandenongs in 1939 provides some delightful scenes of the children playing cricket in a bush environment.[9] As time passed, the girls generally showed little enthusiasm for sport. Betty Abrahamson was an exception. 'I was the girl the boys would pick first for cricket and football. They wouldn't admit that a girl could be better than any other ... I remember being in my room and I used to wait ... the boys used to call out "Betty, do you want to play football with us?" I really loved it.'

Music and creative activities filled many hours. They were given piano lessons and had considerable opportunity for drama activities. 'We created our own plays,' Paula Kochen (now Boltman) recalled, 'For every sort of occasion we made up plays which we performed in front of people, at first in German and, when that was forbidden, we did them in English. That's how I became very interested in the theatre'. Not all children were so enamoured of these performances; in fact, some dreaded performing in front of others. Edna Lehmann, who developed a stammer after her arrival in Australia, said even if she knew her lines perfectly they would not come out. 'The only acting parts I got were to do some mime or where I got killed off in the first scene.'

Always there were homework and chores. A short time after their arrival the staff was reduced to a cook and a handyman, the result being that more housework fell to the children. 'We had our turn at washing dishes and drying up,' recalled Ellen Rothschild. 'We washed and scrubbed the floors. They were timber floors and quite a job to wash.' Like many Australian children, both boys and girls at Larino also spent many hours knitting for the war effort. 'We listened to the radio and knitted,' said Ingrid Ehrlich. Margot Goldstein remembered receiving a doll for being the best sock-knitter. She also recalled the children going to a Red Cross centre at one time to untie string from parcels.

Friday nights were always special. The children would change into their good clothes for service, followed by dinner. Marion Ehrlich recalled that 'Friday nights we always used to have fried fish and mashed potato and peas, and I loved that.' This was followed by dessert, which Ellen Lewinski remembered as being 'ice cream and fruit salad in the summer, and in the winter lemon snow with custard'. While he was there, Ferry Fixel held the service. Afterwards the children would put on performances for which he would give prizes. Later, in the absence of a man at Larino, Mr Glass, from the Australian Jewish Welfare Society, would visit every Friday fortnight. Ursula Kaye recalled these visits: 'He always brought a big bag of lollies. We put the lollies in glass dishes and after the service and dinner we sat around and talked and passed around the lollies.'

From an Australian Jewish point of view, Larino was, in the words of the *Australian Jewish Herald*, 'run on strictly Jewish lines'. The Welfare Society hired a young teacher, Miss Judd, herself a refugee, to assist in this. Hedi Fixel explained:

> She had come from Hamburg from a very orthodox family. She was a marvellous teacher in every way. She was very careful with her food because she would only be strictly kosher. The home was kosher, but not so strictly. It was what was said at the time Anglo-Jewish Australian ... She gave the children and me a very good basis, because I knew very little, and also she was very strict. For instance, according to strict Jewish law you can't do certain things on the sabbath, amongst them tearing paper. So the children prepared their toilet paper before; it was the greatest nuisance.

At one time, objections were made by the House Committee 'to the ultra orthodoxy of the Hebrew teacher and the foreign influence wielded by her' and it was suggested she should be replaced. Both Rabbi Danglow and Frances Barkman defended her, pointing to the high standard achieved by the Larino children in their examinations, 'up to and even above that for pupils at the Hebrew school'.[10] The matter was dropped and Miss Judd stayed with the children for many years. To some children, especially Hermann Levy, she became a guiding influence and a staunch friend. 'I noticed her the first week and she has never left me since.'

Living in Balwyn, then an outer suburb of Melbourne, they were isolated from the Jewish community. With the nearest synagogue at St Kilda, the children attended only every second Saturday. It was a major trek, consuming most of the day — two hours by tram. 'You had to wear your hat and behave properly, or somebody was sure to complain,' commented Ellen Rothschild. Heavy rain provided one of the few excuses for absence. So 'every two weeks I was praying it would pour'. Ellen's friend, Marion Ehrlich, likewise dreaded these occasions: 'I used to hate it. I used to get motion sickness. I would vomit and they had to get me some soda water.' For Herman Gold, the need to travel presented a problem of a different ilk. As Hedi Fixel explained, 'According to strict Jewish rules you should not travel on the sabbath; you should only walk. Rabbi Danglow was very considerate. But there was one boy who objected.' Occasionally provision was made for him to stay near the synagogue on Friday nights, but no permanent arrangement of this nature was made until much later. For him the only option was not to attend the synagogue, a situation which caused considerable trauma. When the matter of allowing him to stay on Friday nights with an Australian Jewish family was discussed by the Welfare Society, the directors refused on the grounds that it could be seen as a privilege to a boy whose behaviour had been quite unsatisfactory over a period of time. They agreed he could spend the evening at the Jewish orphanage if suitable arrangements could be made.

Far from being a homogeneous group, the children came from families whose observance of Jewish religion varied greatly — from strict orthodoxy to the extreme liberalism adopted by many modern German Jewish families. Few found at Larino a continuation of their family practices and had to adjust to the new situation. Peer pressure seems to have aided the process, with some of the boys playing an overseeing role. Ellen Lewinski recorded one incident in her diary. It was a Saturday on which, for some reason, the girls had not gone to the synagogue:

> The boys went to the synagogue but H didn't go because he doesn't drive on Saturday. We girls wanted to practice the performance for Purim, but H overheard us and so we had a quarrel. Then the boys came back from the synagogue and the dispute became even bigger.

Jo Lehmann also recalled sometimes being 'told off' by the boys: 'Once, on a Saturday, I picked up the scissors or something from the floor and we were not allowed to do that. It was difficult for me to be so strictly religious. I was forced to become religious when I wasn't.'

Ursula Kaye said she 'asked someone once why the children were brought up so religious when most of them came from homes that were more liberal. He replied that it was much better because later on they would have something to drop.' In hindsight, many agree that was a wise decision. Yet Hermann Levy is critical of the home for not being more religious. He commented that he never went to a wedding or a circumcision and thus never learnt how to behave on such occasions. As a consequence, he was later made a 'laughing stock' at his own wedding through not knowing what to do. Hermann's criticism reveals a deprivation broader than the learning of religious ritual. Living in a group home, the children were deprived of much social and cultural learning that occurs in a family in the course of daily life.

Cloistered in the home, the children had

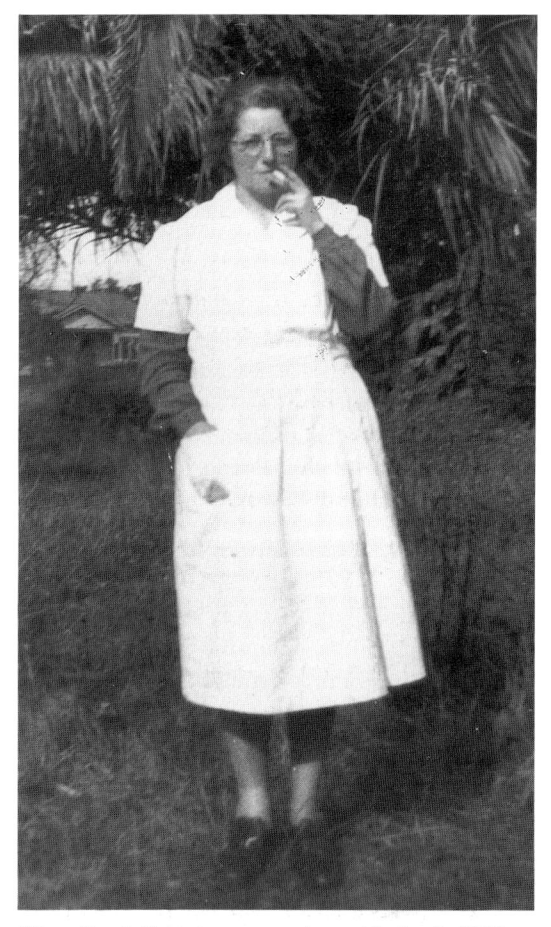

When Ursula Kaye became matron at Larino in 1941, the former matron looked at her red-painted fingernails and declared, 'You won't last here, not with those finger nails and a boyfriend'. Unperturbed, Ursula accepted the challenge and remained matron until 1946. (Ellen Shafer)

little opportunity to experience family life. Even when they went to synagogue there was little socialising. Occasionally they would be taken on outings, perhaps to the beach, but, according to Jo Lehmann, 'that was as rare a treat as a meal in a restaurant or eating chocolate'. In later years they were sometimes invited individually or in small groups to someone's home for a meal. 'By then,' remarked Edna Lehmann, 'I didn't appreciate it. I wanted to be with our own gang, and not have to say "thank you" and be grateful.' Marion Ehrlich enjoyed these rare occasions, but the memories are bitter-sweet:

> Occasionally we would be invited to a Jewish family for lunch and I enjoyed that. Sometimes we would go to the pictures afterwards with the other children, as they would have children of their own. They would take us to the pictures and that was exciting ... They were kind to us, but we felt a bit out of it. They were usually fairly young families — doctors and dentists — Australian Jewish families, and we would notice that they had new clothes. They were brought up differently from us. We had hand-me-downs. People used to send suitcases of their old clothes for us.

Attitudes of established, Anglicised Jewry to the refugees have often been described as hostile and patronising. Paul Cullen, commenting on his father Sir Samuel Cohen, founding president of the Australian Jewish Welfare Society, summarised these attitudes, and the treatment refugees received:

> There was a stuffiness of behaviour whether they were Jews or non-Jews. My father wanted to help the refugees but not mix with them. He would do anything on an official basis but little on a personal basis. This was a snobbish attitude but it was shared by the majority of the established Jewish families. The greater the degree of establishment, the greater the elitism.[11]

For German and Austrian refugees in Melbourne the situation was exacerbated by the presence of many eastern Jews in the established community. They also kept their distance socially from the new arrivals from Germany. Ursula Kaye rationalised their behaviour as a form of retribution: 'We weren't so nice to them when they came to Germany.'

Despite kindness by individuals, the children regularly experienced this 'snobbish attitude' and the aloof philanthropy. Edna Lehmann said as a child she sensed 'that those who had assimilated well didn't want to be associated with us particularly. I suppose they must have contributed funds ... but I don't think any of them felt any compassion for these parentless children'.

The kindness was often dulled by an overwhelming sense of their lowly status as refugees. This perception was enhanced by verbal reminders of their status and by the expectation of perpetual gratitude. Even at the boys' bar mitzvahs, Ursula Kaye recalled, 'Every boy was told how lucky he was to be out here and how grateful he should be to the Welfare Society and Australia ... It was not said by the rabbi "how heartbreaking it is that your parents aren't here!" He didn't say that.'

Camilla Wedgwood recognised the dilemma for those helping refugees; in 1939 she wrote of how easy it was 'to feel like God and want to arrange people's lives for them. So far I have avoided the damnable sin of wanting people to be grateful, but when one really has been instrumental in saving a person's life or sanity it is pitifully easy to feel as though one had some sort of ownership of them, as though they were one's own creation.'[12]

As wards of the Australian Jewish Welfare Society, the children were seen as the property of the Society, whose mission was to turn them into good Jewish Australians. This position was particularly obvious when the committee women gathered for monthly meetings at Larino. At each meeting the matron reported on her many areas of responsibility — the children, the staff and the budget. Ursula Kaye found it a gruelling experience: 'I was frightened of the committee. There were twelve people sitting around the table, and you were the one who was responsible, sitting there on the short side, all on your own. You had the feeling they were putting the hooks into you.'

The meeting over, it was the children's turn. Margot Goldstein remembers: 'We showed them what good Australians we were and sang "There'll Always be an England" and other songs like that'. The children hated this, although as Ingrid Ehrlich pointed out: 'We were in awe when they did come once a month ... but we were in awe in Germany too. That was the generation.' Edna Lehmann particularly dreaded the occasions. As the smallest she always received a kiss from Frances Barkman at the end of the performance. 'I hated being kissed by her. I used to take out my handkerchief and wait till she was out of the way, then wipe it away. I hated being treated like a puppy dog. The smallest always got patted on the head or kissed or something.'

Edna recalled with amusement that 'some of the old ladies had stubbly chins and a bit of a beard'. She also remembered how the children used to imitate Frances Barkman's walk: 'posterior protruding and sort of sliding along ... It wasn't malicious, just childish.' In fact, Edna remembers Frances Barkman a little more kindly than most of the children: 'She was a real go-getter. She used to battle to get funds for us to have music lessons and other privileges. She was a very kind-hearted woman, but she was very severe.'

Some children never saw beyond the severity with which Fanny Barkman, as she was called, was obviously well-endowed. All acknowledged that the committee women were probably well-intentioned, but believe those who wielded the power lacked an understanding of the needs of young children and adolescents. Nevertheless, some of the women, Frances Barkman included, gave a lot of their time to the children, a fact emphasised by Ellen Lewinski: 'I wouldn't want anyone to minimise what they did. It was an enormous effort and it was an ongoing effort.' As a young woman with an accountancy degree, Molly Elvish was asked to be the secretary–treasurer of the House Committee. She confirmed how demanding the work was for her as a mother of two very young children. Unlike many of the women, she was not wealthy. She and her husband and their two children lived at the time on his student allowance.

The emotional void experienced by the children could probably have been filled by refugee families, but attitudes of Australian Jewry to the refugees prevented the children from socialising with other refugees. Mixing with refugees was seen as detrimental to their assimilation into Australian society. One case was recorded of a child being prevented from leaving Larino to live with a refugee family. When the matter was discussed in December 1943, directors of the Welfare Society questioned 'whether it would be the right environment for a boy for whom the Society had been doing everything to acclimatise to an Australian environment'. Hermann Levy also recorded that he was not allowed to visit their Hebrew teacher 'because she was a foreigner like us and not a dinkum Aussie'. In later years this policy obviously was relaxed as some children did stay with relatives for weekends. Relatives and friends visited Larino, but such visits were limited by the austerity of war and by personal circumstances. Gisella Schneider talked of the commitment involved in visiting her brother Rolf:

> All the time I had off work was half a day on Sunday afternoon, and I never went anywhere else. I was earning about twenty shillings a week and for me it was a fortune to spend the fare out there ... Although I didn't have any money I always took out at least one or two others. We would just go walking and I would buy ice-cream. Occasionally I took them to the circus or the movies.

Frances and Paula Kochen's mother also visited fortnightly while they were at Larino. According to Hedi Fixel she was very tactful, and sensitive to the other children. Nevertheless, visits by parents and siblings, no matter how discreet, must have been a sad reminder to the other children of their missing families.

Although the absence of their families was not something on which the children

George (left) and Richard Dreyfus. Their parents left Germany the day after war was declared. The two boys were reunited with their parents in Melbourne at the end of 1939. (Hedi Fixel)

consciously dwelt, it was a reality which rippled through their lives. Edna Lehmann believes they became used to being on their own, yet recalled behaviour which indicated to her how starved they must have been for love:

> We always wanted to sit next to matron. When we went to the pictures, which was very rare — about three times a year — we used to plan it: 'I'm going to sit next to matron, then I'm going to sit next to you, and then I'm going to sit next to you ... ' The furthest you got away from matron that was the worst. A pecking order.

Outwardly they may have appeared cheerful and happy; indeed some were. But even for extroverts like Jo Lehmann, the smile of childhood often disguised an inner sadness which was expressed in the quiet of night. 'I used to cry sometimes at night. We wanted someone to hug us and kiss us.' The boys may not have allowed themselves even this privilege. Some of the girls, including Margot Goldstein, were also embarrassed to be seen or heard crying. 'I didn't want anyone to see me cry, but I don't know why. I remember getting under the blanket and crying in a way that nobody could hear me. I had a system: you sort of swallowed the tears and nobody heard you'. Ellen Lewinski commented on the inability of group care to provide the love and the cuddles which they craved: 'There was a desolation because there was no love. There couldn't be ... You need to be able to say to a child, "You're my special one"'. When the letters stopped there was no-one to tell them this.'

Red Cross letters stopped by early 1943. By then Hermann Levy knew that he was an orphan. This was his father's last letter, written on 19 October 1941:

Dear Hermann

We think of you often and hope that you continue to be well and learn well at school. I'd like to tell you a number of facts about the hens ... This year the hens have not laid so vigorously. Nevertheless the eggs reached 1400. Just now only one is laying, the others are moulting and look a terrible sight. How are the hens you are looking after? Do you enjoy looking after them? Do you distinguish which hen lays which eggs? Hannah still does not understand how to care for the hens as well as you did. Pity you can't see the hens now. They are white leghorns. We often view the single photo you posted to us. Enough for this time. Hopefully you will soon let us hear from you. Be healthy. Best regards. Your loving father.

Two weeks later Martin Levy, widowed, persecuted and ostracised by those around him, jumped from a window of his apartment block. Hermann heard of his father's death on 16

April 1942, but only in 1988 did he discover how his parents had died.

Ellen Lewinski heard in 1943 that her mother had died from peritonitis early in the war. News of other parents, including those transported east to concentration camps, generally did not arrive until after the war. Although often fearing the worst, children continued to send the precious twenty-five word messages. Margot Goldstein wrote in August 1944:

> Darlings,
>
> No word this year. Trust all well with you as with me. Top of Form. Happy returns father. Best wishes New Year. All love.

It was a period of intense worry and depression for some children and was aggravated by the fact it frequently coincided with the onset of adolescence, a time when many were missing their parents greatly. Ellen Lewinski recalled: 'It was a desolate time. Matron gave us as much guidance as she could, but I was often miserable ... I often missed my parents and my family to such a degree that there was a hole there that nobody could fill.'

Some children found comfort in solitude, a rare commodity in a group home: 'One time I went into the linen closet. I closed the door and had a big cry.' Many escaped into books. Edna Lehmann commented, 'I would take a book, climb a tree and sit there for hours, till it was time for meals or chores'. A few found supportive adults to befriend them. Betty Abrahamson, for example, cultivated the friendship of the cook. 'I was cook's special. She took me to the races a few times and took me out a few times. We had a good relationship ... There was cigarette rationing and she used to send me on the queue ... she'd be behind me and we'd pretend we didn't know each other.' The friendship by no means replaced Betty's absent parents. She too recalled a long period of going under the blankets at night, of crying and thinking, 'I wish my mum was here'.

Study and school life provided new interests and friends in this time of need. From Balwyn State School the girls moved to East Camberwell Girls' High, the boys to Box Hill High School or Technical School. Although many formed close friendships at school, there was still little overlap between life at school and that at home. Jo Lehmann commented on her routine:

> I only saw the Australian schoolchildren at school and never after school hours ... I had an hour's tram ride home from school and, once I arrived at five p.m., I quickly found myself a chair and space at the long table in the study and started on my homework. Barring a supper break, and provided I didn't have kitchen duty, I kept at my books till 11p.m. Not much time left to socialise.

As the years passed, Jo capitalised on her strengths. Unlike most other children, she retained a strong European identity and a pride in her German origins. For her 'it wasn't a stigma. It was something that made me interesting to the Australians who wanted either German lessons or to hear about things in Germany. Since I couldn't show off my clothes ... all I had was knowledge of Europe and another language.' She would barter German lessons for lessons in Latin or whatever else she wanted to learn.

Life was more difficult for the boys. 'They got the raw end of the deal,' Ellen Rothschild thought. Since early 1941 there had been many discussions on moving the boys to a separate home — even thoughts of combining with the Jewish orphanage for this purpose. There was talk of building a joint home in the grounds of the Jewish nursing home, Montefiore, as had happened in Sydney. The time was considered inopportune and, instead, a proposal went forward 'to find a large home, or two adjacent houses, reasonably near to a synagogue, which would be leased and converted to a suitable home for all the children'.[13] Nothing came of this. There was perhaps opposition to the idea of combining the children, as the following incident, reported by Ursula Kaye, suggests:

> Once I spoke to one of the men at the synagogue and asked him why he didn't throw the orphanage and the Larino children together. I thought they were so isolated and another ten children wouldn't make much difference. He said, 'Oh no, my dear'. 'Why?' I asked. He replied, 'Your children are brought up in too high a fashion'. 'Oh my word', I thought.

Although the idea of combining the two groups was dropped, that of moving the Larino boys remained under consideration.[14] The Welfare Society also tried to make the boys self-supporting as soon as possible and seized opportunities for their employment, usually at the expense of their education. At the beginning of 1943 several boys were ready to transfer to either Box Hill High School or Box Hill Technical School. Herman Gold never made it; he was forced to accept a position in a carpentry firm, with the understanding he would be apprenticed when he turned fifteen. During 1943 approaches were also made to the Welfare Guardian Society about some of the boys becoming its wards.[15] After visiting Larino the executive of the Guardian Society concluded that Larino offered 'an opportunity for selecting potential farmers and arranging direction of their initial education' in this regard.[16] But the guardians were not prepared to accept boys who were unwilling to go farming. On those grounds, they refused to accept Herman Gold. Rolf Taylor was given serious consideration and, at the beginning of 1944, 'a guardian was appointed to take a friendly interest in the boy until such time as the Society accepts him as a ward'.[17] His sister claimed that at thirteen her brother 'wanted nothing else but to be on a farm' and, despite the advice of his guardian, a Melbourne doctor, Rolf insisted on leaving school. A compromise was reached. At the beginning of 1945 he became a ward of the Welfare Guardian Society and enrolled at Wangaratta Technical School where many of the Welfare Guardian boys who arrived in 1939 had attended. With that his links with Larino were severed and his life alone, and on the land, began.

None of the other boys followed this path although, according to Alfred Stocks, Frances Barkman wanted them all to become farmers. Instead they left school after the Intermediate to work with tradesmen who often treated them as little more than cheap labour — sorting screws and nails, doing the shopping, cleaning the house. Even Hermann Levy, who was identified at the end of primary school as being 'of more than average intelligence', was forced to leave school after the Intermediate. As the only Jewish boy at Box Hill High School, his high school days were not particularly happy. Hermann believes this may have affected his performance. 'The lady in charge at Larino took me out of school on the strength of mid-term marks even though I passed all subjects at the end of the year. I was put to work with a watch repairer where I sat with one person day in day out for five of perhaps the most formative years of my life.' The experience was, he believes, socially crippling, and has continued to complicate his already traumatised life.

Hermann envied the girls for their greater opportunities. Several girls went beyond the Intermediate certificate, moving to MacRobertson High School for their Leaving. Jo Lehmann commended Frances Barkman, who was the senior French teacher at MacRobertson High, for supporting her in this endeavour: 'She recognised and encouraged my academic potential and allowed me to continue to Matric, though she made me do ten hours weekly of pure and applied maths, chemistry and physics when I would really rather have studied arts, especially literature.'

Although Jo was undoubtedly an excellent student, she acknowledged that her father in

Ursula Kaye always made birthdays a special time at Larino. 'There used to be a mug of cocoa plus an Adams birthday cake ... and we'd sit around the table and Ursula would tell us the story of a film she'd seen. They were so detailed ... if you saw the film later you knew if things had been cut out.' Here the tables are turned as the children help Ursula celebrate her birthday, October 1946

Palestine was sending money to Larino and wondered to what extent that influenced the committee's readiness to support her continued studies. Despite some advantages, most of the girls were forced to leave school earlier than they would have liked. Betty Abrahamson thinks she was probably 'the only girl who didn't cry because school was finished ... I was delighted.' Most went into clerical work or apprenticeships not necessarily of their choosing. Ellen Lewinski, 'the blonde butterfly' as she was called, was apprenticed as a dressmaker for a year, 'until I got fired for being inept. Then they put me back into commercial college, so I became a secretary.' Several of the girls completed the Leaving Certificate at night school and went on later, as did some of the boys, to tertiary study.

There are regrets over aborted education and career opportunities, but these, like many of the children's experiences at Larino, have to be judged within the context of wartime Australia and against the many financial demands on the Welfare Society at the time. As children who were neither British subjects nor the children of British subjects, they were ineligible for government scholarships. An enquiry was made in late 1942 'as to whether these children, who were wards of the Australian Jewish Welfare Society, could not be regarded in any special category with a view to naturalisation'.[18] The government made no concessions. This meant they could not become Australian citizens until they were twenty-one, and only then would they be eligible for scholarships. Jo Lehmann went

Of the seven boys who arrived from Germany in 1939, four remained at Larino until 1946. They are pictured here with Harry Bader (centre front), whose parents were interned at Tatura and who came to Larino in 1941. Children of internees were allowed to leave the camp and, as a result, a number had brief stays at Larino. Only Harry stayed for the duration. Taken in October 1945 and showing from left to right around Harry: Laurie Badrian, Herman Gold, Hermann Levy and Alfred Stocks. (Ellen Shafer)

through school knowing that, even if she received excellent results, she would not be allowed to accept any prizes or scholarships. 'The Australian government did not permit us refugee children to accept prizes. They were not for us. In that respect we were not the same as the other Australians.'

The Jewish Welfare Society's hopes of receiving other child refugees were rekindled at various times throughout the war, another factor which impacted on the children at Larino and on pressure to make them self-supporting as soon as possible. While these attempts were aborted, from early 1944 the Welfare Society was involved in plans for postwar child migration and in related fund-raising. It was just a matter of time till more children arrived — children who had escaped earlier to Switzerland or who had survived the concentration camps and untold horrors.

In assessing the care they received in Australia, the 'Larinoites', as they now call themselves, acknowledged how lucky they were to have been snatched from those horrors. Their criticism is tempered with the knowledge that the Welfare Society saved their lives. In that sense, Larino was certainly the safe haven George Dreyfus named it in his composition, *Larino, Safe Haven*.[19] 'All of us, not all the time, but a lot of the time, were unhappy. But we were lucky to be alive at all,' commented Jo Lehmann. Given the circumstances, most concluded that those in charge of them 'did their best'. 'That we were away from our parents was nobody's fault except Hitler's,' commented Marion Ehrlich. 'We were lucky to be here. We probably would have been gassed otherwise.' There is no question that the children's physical needs were well met, but the scars of unmet social, emotional and psychological needs still plague some of the former Larino children. The extent to which these reflect traumas inflicted by persecution, separation from families or by the Holocaust generally, as opposed to their upbringing at Larino, is difficult to assess. It is obvious though that the institutional life of Larino did not provide the nurturing environment needed to heal past wounds or to support the children through the tragic loss of their families.

Ursula Kaye, their matron for many years, reflected on her role and on the burden of her responsibility:

> It was quite wrong that I was the only one there. When I went to the home I was twenty-six and not married and had no children, and I related to the girls more than I could relate to the boys. I was much too young to be there.

Ellen Lewinski, who said she was often referred to as the 'blonde butterfly'.
(Frances Rothschild)

It should have been a couple around forty who had children themselves.

Shortcomings there were, but Ursula had a powerful influence on many of the children, as Ellen Lewinski commented:

> She set rules that made sense and she enforced them fairly. She gave us a sense of 'esprit de corps'. There were people who sought her out and, if she encouraged them, one would say she had favourites, but I was never aware that she encouraged them. I was not one of her favourites, but she would let me lay out her clothes. I was particularly fussy about clothes, and if she was coming to school to represent us I wanted to make quite sure she was dressed properly ... She entertained us — took us for evening walks to get rid of the energy, and told us stories. For every birthday there used to be a mug of cocoa and an Adams birthday cake. We'd sit around the table and Ursula would tell us the story of a film she'd seen. They were so detailed that, if we saw the film later, we'd recognise if things had been cut out.

When Ursula left Larino in 1946 the children presented her with a leather-bound book which they compiled in her honour — *Ye Olde Booke of Humour*, compiled during the reign of Her Gracious Majesty our matron, Ursula Kaye 1941–1946. It is full of reminders of their life together and of their shared experiences.

Dreams of a better life occupied all the children. Families were central to those dreams. For children who knew they had even one surviving parent, such dreams had some foundation and maybe, Jo Lehmann thinks, liberated them to enjoy what Australia had to offer and to make more friends. 'If the others clung to their uniqueness and didn't mix with the Australians it may be because they were actually clinging to memories of home and of their parents. I was more outgoing because I could afford to be.'[20]

In the absence of their own families, all craved a family environment and suffered for the lack of it. Whether living with families rather than at Larino would have made them happier remains unknown, but can be considered in light of the experiences of the British evacuees in Australia. That there were families willing to absorb young refugee children is proven from the many letters received by the Welfare Society and by the Australian government before and during the war. Most of those offers came from the general public or from refugee families, but some also came from established Jewish families. While some children would surely have fared well in these families, and have had their horizons and opportunities greatly expanded, the consensus seems to be that they were better off at Larino. At least there, said Edna Lehmann, 'we had one another for comfort and support.' This did not stop them dreaming of how life might be:

'I remember going for walks when I was a bit older,' Marion Ehrlich recalled, 'I'd go along the streets and I'd look into a house and see the lights on and I'd wish I could live in a little house like that and have a normal family life. I did miss it.'

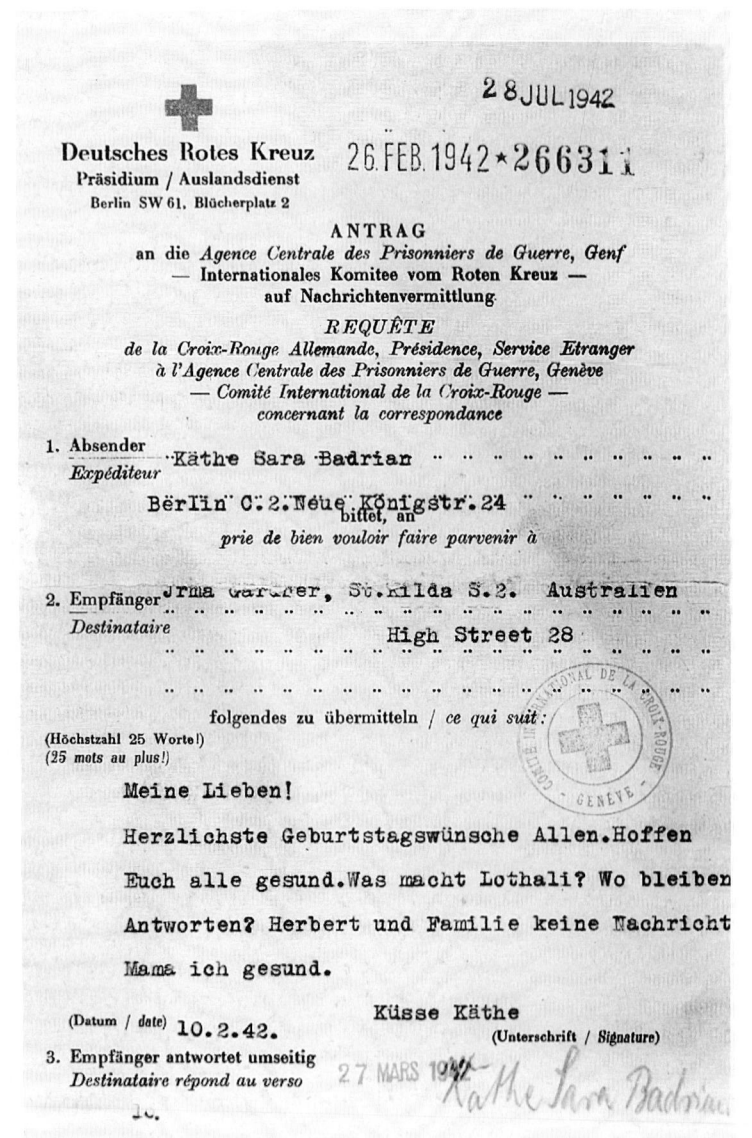

A Red Cross message sent to Laurie Badrian by his mother Kathe in February 1942. These 25-word messages were the only direct link between children and their families after the outbreak of war.

8
Borrowed Families

As the *Batory* arrived in Melbourne, on 14 October 1940, the children sang some of the songs they had learnt during the voyage. The girl with plaits, near the end of the second row and in front of the teddy bear, is Jean Schultz. (Jean Saltzman)

Joe Honeysett had a long wait for the British evacuees. As the Commonwealth liaison officer for the Overseas Children's Scheme, he arrived in Perth on 18 September 1940 to meet the *Batory* and to supervise the disembarkation of the children at the various ports. Wartime precautions complicated the arrangements. The movement of ships being top secret, dates of arrival were speculative. The navy requested that the arrival of ships with children should not be mentioned in the press, over the air or in newsreels until the ships had arrived at their final port of call and all the children had disembarked. The Department of Information thus imposed 'delayed release' conditions on all related publicity. When permission for release was given on 16 October, the *Batory* had already unloaded children in Fremantle and Melbourne, the South Australian contingent had arrived by train from Melbourne, and the ship had arrived safely in Sydney.

The delay in publicity was criticised, but did not diminish extensive reporting of the children's arrival:

CHILD EVACUEES ARRIVE IN SINGING SHIP

A cargo more precious than any treasure trove was safely landed in Sydney yesterday, when the first shipload of British evacuated children to reach Australia swung into the harbour in a big grey-painted liner, which all along its route has been called 'the singing ship'.[1]

Newspapers and magazines around Australia carried pages of stories, accompanied by captivating captions and photographs of the children embracing their new country and their new families: '477 Little Britons Arrive', 'Britons Young and Free', 'Well... Here We Are'. A perception of the scheme as 'one of the greatest Empire-binding moves that has ever been made'[2] underscored many of the stories, to the extent that the children's reason for leaving home was often lost:

Australia is proud to welcome the British children sent to this country for safety during the war. Already the youngsters have impressed us with their brave bearing, their pluck and cheerfulness. To so many of them this is a dream country, and we can make their dreams come true. One little girl said on sighting an Australian city from the porthole of a ship, 'This must be the Promised Land'. So we must see that every promise made in our hearts for their happiness is fulfilled. We must make them feel at home. For a start we can forget that dreadful word 'evacuees'... It is a defeatist word. These dimpled girls, these sturdy, suntanned boys are merely changing homes within the Empire. Let's think of them as pioneers of a better day and a better Empire understanding. Like young Joshuas they will return to England after the war with news of a great land they had visited — a land of kindly people — a country of prosperity to which they will all want to return.[3]

The children were treated like celebrities, although the thirty-five headed for Queensland received the most overwhelming welcome. Travelling by train from Sydney, they were greeted at railway stations along the line by Voluntary Aid Detachment (VAD) workers with refreshments and gifts. Local schools gathered at the stations to cheer and wave. In Brisbane the children were paraded through the streets:

'Good luck to you', 'Welcome to Australia', 'We're glad you're here', cried hundreds of men, women and children who lined the street. Business girls and men leaned over balconies to give coo-ees of welcome. Women rushed up to the cars and shook hands with the children. Into the cars eager hands thrust sweets, flags and streamers, and one group of business girls handed envelopes of 'pocket money' to each carload as it passed. At Kangaroo Point the cars, on their way to a hostel prepared for the children, drove through lines of flag-waving, cheering children from the Kangaroo Point State School.[4]

It was 'a magnificent reception', Honeysett reported, adding 'it was not possible for the other capital cities to afford a similarly enthusiastic welcome owing to the censorship restrictions in force'.[5]

The same censorship restrictions were in place for the arrival of the *Nestor* and the *Diomed*. The *Nestor* reached Sydney on 24 October. Danger of mines in Bass Strait forced the boys on the *Diomed* to disembark in Adelaide on 8 November; from there twelve travelled east by train. Reporters had had their field day by then and the arrivals attracted little publicity.

Censorship meant that custodians had little warning of the children's arrival. The Victorian situation provides an insight into this. On 24

August 1940 the Victorian committee of the Overseas Children's Scheme informed families nominated for the *Batory* children that the children were on their way. On 7 October the committee sent a second letter stating that the ship would probably arrive in Melbourne on 14 October. Families were asked to be ready to attend at short notice to take custody of the children on or about that date. Little wonder if some custodians were ill-prepared for their guests. Plans to build a sleep-out or otherwise to modify homes to accommodate the children rarely had time to materialise.

Arrangements on arrival varied across states. In South Australia the children were taken to the Cheer-up Hut near the Adelaide railway station, where they were given an official welcome, a meal and a mandatory medical check. From there, both nominated and unnominated children were picked up on the same day by foster families. Children disembarking in Victoria were given a party at the United Services cafe, on the corner of Swanson and Collins streets. Many people came there to pick up children or just to look. John Hare recalled having the first inkling of worry as he climbed the stairs leading out of the cafe: 'I can vividly remember coming back up the stairs — lined with people looking at this shipload of Pommy kids ... and people saying, "I'd like that one".'

John was one of a large family of evacuees — three older sisters and himself, a seven-year-old. Their father sent them to Australia on the understanding they would not be separated. He wrote to his stepbrother in Australia: 'I was assured the children would not be separated. If I had had any doubts I should have taken them home again as the parting was terrible.' Neither their Uncle Claude nor any other Victorian family was able to accommodate four children. Of the thousands of applications received in Victoria, only one was for more than two children. When they left the United Services cafe, the four Hare children went with other children requiring placements to hostels in Melbourne, boys to the Travellers' Aid Society hostel and girls to the Child Welfare Department depot at Royal Park.

In New South Wales, the North Head Quarantine Station was used for temporary accommodation, the children being cared for by a staff of VADs and some officers of the Child Welfare Department. Phyllis and Eric Ward were at the Quarantine Station a week before their foster parents arrived from the country to pick them up: 'It was a bit sad because you would be playing down on the beach or wherever, and at evening meal you'd find that another four or five had gone, but no-one had come and told you, so you never had a chance to say goodbye to anyone. Then of course that happened to us after we'd been there for about a week.'

Despite minor delays, within a short time of arrival the 577 British evacuees had dispersed to families all across Australia, except the Northern Territory, which was exluded on the grounds of transportation expenses and the demands of the climate. In doing so, they entered physical and social environments of immense diversity. The physical environment both delighted and challenged. Beryl Minter recalled driving to her home, set in the vineyards of South Australia: 'We drove in an old Ford with a dicky seat, and I sat in the back. We went down to McLaren Vale, which at that time was very rural, and I remember coming over the hill and seeing this marvellous almond blossom on the foothills, and the Mount Lofty Ranges. That was fantastic.'

By contrast, Peggy McLeish went to an uncle in Paxton, a small coalmining community in the Hunter Valley of New South Wales. Travelling to school in nearby Cessnock remains a vivid memory: 'We travelled on this rickety old bus — rattling along on a dirt track. It was so dirty and dusty. Your school tunic would be covered in brown dust. I wondered what had hit me ... It was a real hellhole for

RELUCTANT REFUGE

Peggy McLeish outside her uncle and aunt's one bedroom miner's cottage at Paxton where she and her cousin Margaret Bell were given a home. There was no running water or sewerage. The photo shows a rain water tank and, next to it, a copper for washing clothes. (Peggy Cox)

me.' Conditions in Peggy's foster home exacerbated the situation:

> We had only one bedroom. They had a little verandah; it had a bit of lattice around it and canvas around the outside for a bit of privacy — and for two of us. I'd always had a room to myself. Now I had my little cousin with me, in the same bed. No sewer. We had to walk up the paddock to an outside toilet. There'd be cows around and I was scared because I wasn't a country girl ... There was only a tank for water — a copper outside for washing clothes and an aluminium dish in the kitchen for washing up. A tin bath was put in the kitchen on Friday night and the cleanest went first.

The heat was a particular challenge. 'That first summer was very hot and dry,' recalled Eric Ward. 'I remember walking on asphalt in bare feet and not being able to tolerate it.' 'We hated the heat,' Freda Morgan remarked. 'Two o'clock every day at school my brother and I would be at the troughs with a nose bleed. We'd meet out there. But that soon went.' Freda, who came from Liverpool to Murray Bridge, soon began to appreciate the fringe benefits of living in a warm climate. 'It was a wonderful life. Milking cows and riding horses. We used to run down at six o'clock in the morning and swim the river and back before we did our chores. It was just absolutely marvellous.' Children in the cities also generally appreciated the warmth, the space and the informal lifestyle.

Their social environments often demanded greater adjustment. Following the first flurry of publicity, officials appealed to the media to leave the children alone. 'The interest of the children is our first concern and that is best accomplished by allowing them to be quietly absorbed into our population and not treated as a special class.'[6] It was an unrealistic expectation. The children were novelties and, in country towns particularly, their arrival was a matter of communal interest. When the three Morgan children arrived in Murray Bridge the town was at the railway station to greet them. Freda Morgan recounted what happened next: 'This man, whom I didn't know, picked me up and hugged me. I was horrified. Then we all walked up the hill to the bank where dad was the manager.' Phyllis Ward recalled her arrival: 'Even before we got to Yass everybody knew about these two English children coming, so they all knew us but we didn't know who the heck they were. I felt constantly on show. We were a real novelty and of course we had strong Liverpudlian accents.'

The children's accents immediately set them

The Morgan children with their Australian foster siblings. Back row: Stow Kentish, Dorothy Kentish, Freda Morgan, David Kentish. Front: Maurice Morgan and Margaret Kentish. Percy Morgan, the eldest of the three Morgan children to be evacuated, lived with another family, a short distance from Murray Bridge. He formed strong bonds with his foster family, to the extent that the family offered him a share in their property if he stayed in Australia. The lure of the army was greater, and Percy left in 1944 for India.

apart. Alan Timmins had a broad Geordie accent. 'For about a year no-one seemed to understand what I was saying. Some people kept me talking just to hear me.' The attention was not without its rewards: 'The first Christmas I was at the school in Hamley Bridge I can remember singing "The Quartermaster's Store" on the stage. They all thought that was marvellous. They'd never heard anything like it and wouldn't let me off the stage. They kept plying me with ice-cream afterwards.'

For Alan, as for other children, the novelty phase passed. He became part of the community, singing in the church choir, playing the drums in the school band and joining forces with his Australian cousin to earn money for the war effort.

> We were always busy, going around the houses selling badges. He would do one half of the town and I would do the other. We collected paper, bones and batteries for the Schools' Patriotic Fund. I remember climbing out the window in the early hours of the morning to collect beer bottles after dances at the Institute. We'd get a farthing for the empty ones and the full ones we sold back to the pub. We were always getting into trouble for that.

Being English enhanced the status of some children. As the only British evacuee at Lee Street school in North Carlton, Melbourne, Jean Schultz was the centre of attention: 'I was made a fuss of because I was from England and I'd come all that way on my own. I was the headmaster's pet and had the job of putting on the marching music for the flag ceremony.' Beryl Minter also commented on how her social standing 'went up two notches' amongst the vignerons of McLaren Vale, just because she was English. She joined the long-sock brigade at the local school: 'Long socks were the social mark, a definite indication that you were middle class. If you wore long socks instead of short socks, or no socks, you were actually a social grade higher.'

Other children found their accents and their origins a cause of misery and embarrassment. Anne Vincent's working-class relatives were uneasy with her well-spoken English. Anne, like many children, also recalled being laughed at at school. The teasing particularly affected children whose self-confidence was already undergoing a battering — those deeply affected by the separation from their families or now in homes where they felt unwanted. 'At school they treated me like a freak for a long time,' commented Peggy McLeish. 'They'd all crowd around to make me talk. Of course, I'd clamp up even more then.' Maureen Greening (now Norling) was driven into isolation by the taunts: 'I wanted to be nice to them but they would go away and laugh. So I would sit in a corner and have nothing to do with them. I thought, well they poke fun at me so if I sit here and don't say anything ... '

Boys were more likely to be bullied and provoked into fighting. This was the case for Peter Barnard: 'Eventually I got fed up with someone who was always taunting me when I went to the local school. I suppose it was the usual thing — Pommy bastards or something. I eventually thumped him. The teacher was upset about this and decided that I was a bully. So it got back to my uncle.' Fortunately Peter had the support of his uncle in weathering this storm; as a postwar British migrant he had already run the gauntlet as a 'Pommy bastard', so could empathise with his nephew. John Hare's foster father at the time, an ex diamond miner, also supported him through a bullying phase. 'I was always coming home with a black eye. One day he said, "If we're going to keep you we might as well teach you to survive". So he taught me to box.'

Supportive, caring foster families were able to help children make the necessary adjustments. Some children found such families in their first placements, among both relatives and strangers. Some never did. Experiences within these families were as diverse as the children and families who embarked on the relationships.

For the majority of children, placements were predetermined when parents nominated Australian relatives. While some relatives declined the request, others took the children under duress, perhaps as an obligation to family or empire in time of war. Many welcomed the opportunity to receive the children, although at times this involved considerable personal sacrifice. Peggy McLeish's uncle, who came to Australia after being gassed in the First World War, had never been able to work. 'He shouldn't have been working, but before we were allowed to go there he had to get work. He had to go down the mine again.' Alf Downes, a tram driver, had to battle with the Child Welfare Department over his niece, Anne Vincent: 'They said I couldn't keep her, but I insisted on taking her'. As happened with many men, Alf left for the Middle East almost immediately after his niece arrived, leaving his wife the responsibility of caring for another child on a very meagre allowance. Children in these circumstances have mixed feelings over their placements. While acknowledging the sacrifices of their relatives, they admit they lived in conditions well below those to which they had been accustomed. When nominating relatives, parents were often unaware of their circumstances. Glowing letters from Australia over the years probably misled many into believing their relatives had found health and prosperity in Australia. While some had, others were struggling to make ends meet.

Unnominated children often fared better economically. With so many homes offered, state committees could afford to be selective when choosing homes for these children. Before the children's arrival, welfare officials visited applicants, choosing those who seemed to have the commitment and the means to maintain the children 'gratuitously for the duration of the war'. Cyril Bavin, who succeeded Wilf Garnett as CORB's representative in Australia, wrote: 'In many cases nominated homes are not on a par with the homes offered by generously-minded citizens to the unspecified children'.[7] This did not mean that a higher socioeconomic status guaranteed the success of a placement. Bavin acknowledged that relationships counted for much. Relationships aside, evidence suggests that children fared best in homes of at least equivalent or somewhat higher socioeconomic status than that of their families. Placements in homes vastly different were often unsuccessful.[8]

Nominations were generally made by parents in the belief that their contributions to CORB would be transmitted to custodians in Australia. Despite a press release and a circular to all parents explaining the situation, many continued to think custodians were receiving their six shillings a week.[9] In fact, custodians at first received no monetary assistance unless parents sent money over and above their contribution to CORB. The decision by Cabinet in July 1941 to offer them child endowment was the first acknowledgment that many foster parents needed financial support in maintaining their guests. At the end of 1941 the British government asked the Australian government to reconsider the voluntary basis of the scheme. The High Commissioner for the United Kingdom pointed out:

> Parents are increasingly critical of arrangements under which compulsory contributions are collected but not applied to the maintenance of their children. This feeling is enhanced by the knowledge that custodians of child evacuees within the United Kingdom receive a weekly official maintenance allowance. It is, therefore, increasingly difficult to justify the present procedure.[10]

A national survey showed that many foster parents were having difficulty, especially in meeting educational and medical expenses, and that some had cancelled their custodianship as a result.[11] In September 1942 foster parents were offered 7/6 a week,[12] to be paid quarterly and retrospectively from 1 January 1942. At the same time a central fund was set up in the United Kingdom to assist with expenses 'which may be outside the ability of the custodian to meet, but which may be considered necessary in the interests of the child'.[13] Foster parents could access this fund through their state child welfare department. While ordinary medical and dental expenses were readily reimbursed, the London committee of CORB had to approve non-urgent medical treatment and other exceptional expenses.[14]

Phyllis and Eric Ward received a warm welcome from foster parents, Mr and Mrs Bridge, of Yass. Mr Bridge was the local stock and station agent and gave the children many memorable experiences in rural Australia. His wife died of cancer in April 1945, but the bonds between him and the children were so strong that there was no thought of their moving to another foster home. (Phyllis Thatcher)

Families generally welcomed this assistance, although some opted for the money to be held in trust by the child welfare department of the state. Apart from the money, some children remember being recipients of clothing and other items from CORB. Peggy McLeish remembered her foster family receiving a letter from CORB once a year, asking if there was anything they needed. One year they had no pyjamas, so these were sent. Playsuits were sent another year. Peter Barnard remembered receiving a chemistry set through the Child

Welfare Department when they found out he was interested in his cousin's chemistry books. 'I made a total nuisance of myself with it by making hydrogen sulphide in the train.' Holidays were also arranged for children, often through voluntary associations such as the YMCA, and usually at the request of foster parents to give them some respite from the children.

Absorbing the children into their families cannot have been easy for foster parents, regardless of their financial circumstances. On the one hand they were advised that most of all the children needed a home and love[15]; on the other they were warned about 'the danger of setting up a deep emotional relationship which is not intended to be permanent.'[16] One foster parent expressed the confusion: 'The Department has us a little puzzled. They said we gave too much and on another occasion that we were trying to treat the girls as if they were our own.'[17]

As a reminder of the temporary nature of the relationship, foster parents were advised to have the children call them uncle and auntie, never mother and father. They were also expected to help the children 'remember their loved ones in their evening prayers ... and see that the children regularly write home ... and possibly send snapshots to show how well they are getting on'.[18] With the best of intentions, some people were overwhelmed by the responsibility of caring for someone else's child. John Hare, for example, recalled one of his sisters never being let out of the house by herself. Others, while they provided well for the children's physical care, withheld any demonstration of affection, particularly towards older children. Many interviewees lamented the lack of physical contact — hugs and cuddles — although often commented that other children in the family received the same distant affection.

For the children, adjustment to life in foster families was overshadowed by separation from their natural families. Self-confident children, who had already developed a degree of independence from their parents, seem to have adjusted relatively easily. These children had the ability to thrive in situations that were not always perfect, but where at least their physical needs were met. They could find fulfilment outside the immediate family, with other people or interests. Many of these children have no recollection of being homesick. On the contrary, children who had never before been away from their families, regardless of their age, frequently pined for a long time.

More than half the children stayed in their first placements for the duration of the war; others moved on, some many times. The tendency to assess the scheme according to

Child Welfare often arranged holidays for evacuee children, usually at the request of foster parents. Ken Gregory was having a holiday at the Manse in Toronto, New South Wales, when this photo was taken. He is pictured (on left) with an Australian boy and J. P. Baillie, the Methodist minister. (Ken Gregory)

the number of moves obscures the fact that some children stayed in unhappy and uncaring situations when a move was desirable. Many children, unhappy or mismatched in their first placement, settled well with their second families. Others moved through a series of homes, generally settling in one.

Joan Hodgson stayed in a miserable situation the whole time. Her memory is one of such intense unhappiness that any positive experience has been blotted out. She was eight when she arrived with her older sister, Margaret, to live with relatives. It was a disastrous placement from the beginning. To this day they are considered the English relatives who arrived without anyone knowing they were coming. She claims her relatives refused to take the government contribution, seeing it as charity, yet failed themselves to provide the girls with certain basic necessities. Joan went barefoot all the time she was in Australia, returning to England with badly infected feet. She and her sister were constantly made to feel unwanted, an attitude passed on to friends of the family. 'Other people in town were constantly putting us down, saying such things as "Do you know how lucky you are?"' Joan was also given a hard time at school. 'I was often bashed up by the other children and had to be let out of school ten minutes before them.' Her aunt was unsympathetic, telling Joan she should fight back. She refused to let the girls move to other relatives who would gladly have taken them. 'The attitude was one of "What will people think if I send you away?"' A thread of cruelty and meanness seems to have pervaded this relationship right to the end. When Joan was packing her few personal belongings to take home, amongst them was a treasured fur koala given to her by another relative. Her aunt immediately intervened: '"Where do you think you're taking that? It's not yours." I was flabbergasted and very upset.'

Ken Gregory also encountered an aunt with a mean and spiteful streak. Although not physically abusive, she made his life miserable by her behaviour and words. In retrospect Ken considers she was mentally unbalanced — 'a nut case'. Nevertheless, her treatment of him remains a disturbing memory. Ironically, in April 1943 *Pix* magazine chose Ken and his foster family for a feature story on evacuees. The captioned photographs provide a story of family bliss, a stark contrast to the life described by Ken.

Child welfare departments were responsible for monitoring the placements. In some states, officials visited the homes regularly and wrote comprehensive reports on the children. The quality of supervision varied within, as well as between, states, with reports on country children being done by sparsely placed country staff. Most children remember visits by the welfare department. Some also remember Cyril Bavin visiting their homes. All too often, interviews excluded the children or were conducted in the presence of foster parents, giving the children no opportunity to express any grievances. Theoretically, older children, especially those in cities, could contact the Child Welfare Department or CORB office themselves. Many did. Ken Gregory visited the Sydney office fairly regularly in later years: 'The lady in the Child Welfare Department was like oil on troubled waters. She was a real diplomat. She had all sorts of kids going in there; now I realise there were some that must have been in a bad way.'

Younger children and children in isolated areas rarely had an opportunity to initiate contact. Joan Hodgson remarked that even when her sister was working she was employed in the same office as their cousin. 'Any attempt to use the phone was met with rebuke.' Furthermore, the girls' aunt censored their letters, making it impossible for them to write home about their situation. Joan's unhappiness welled over during a two-way radio broadcast with her family in Manchester. 'When I heard my mother's voice I just cried.'

When an undesirable placement was discovered, prompt action often followed. Jean Schultz recalled commenting to some other Jewish evacuees about her unhappiness and asking if their foster mother would take her. Word was passed to Cyril Bavin, who came from Sydney to see Jean. A move soon followed — to an elderly couple with four adult sons. 'They were wonderful people. I was the kid sister and I was indulged.' Unfortunately for some children, their unhappiness was never discovered. Most endured the situation in silence, feeling powerless to do anything about it. A few took the situation into their own hands and ran away. John Templeton wrote tersely of his plight: 'I'm not much different to the other kids who came out. I was bashed stupid — worked like a horse and eventually ran away to a sheep station — caught and sent to a boys' home, from there to nice people at Clyde.'

Cases of excessive physical cruelty or abuse seem to have been rare, but they did exist. They are difficult to trace, as details were frequently omitted from the records. Maureen Greening, who was seven when she arrived in Australia, talked about her ill-treatment, yet her case was never documented. She was from a family of five children evacuated to Australia. After six months together with an aunt and uncle, the children were separated. Maureen recalled being taken to the Child Welfare Department where she was paraded as at a cattle auction. 'I remember walking down the stairs and people sitting there. You had to walk in front of them.' In the following years, Maureen was moved from one abusive situation to another — 'I was pushed from pillar to post' — ending up in later years with a woman who belted her mercilessly. For Maureen there was no happy home in all the moves.

John Hare, on the other hand, claimed he was happy in all his homes, bar the first. There were eight of them, a record amongst evacuees to Australia. His extraordinary case illustrates many issues surrounding the placement and movement of children. After spending about a week at the Travellers' Aid Society hostel, John was reunited briefly with his sisters. He vividly remembers the day he was taken to his first home:

> I can remember being picked up at that hostel ... the car was driven by someone in a uniform ... my sisters were in the car and we were all being taken to this home where an elderly couple, an old couple, came out. I met them outside with my suitcase, said 'good bye' to the girls, then they got in the car and drove off. I can remember chasing the car down the road. I was in a panic. But the car just went too fast for me.

Old they may have been, but this couple, like many other Australian families, had applied to adopt a British war orphan. An incontinent child for the duration was no substitute and the placement broke down within days. From there, John moved to another family in Melbourne, one with a young child. It was a good arrangement all round and one in which he would probably have stayed had his father not, with the best of intentions, intervened. In November Walter Hare wrote to the Child Welfare Department requesting that his four children be placed close to their uncle in Bendigo. John remembered having a wonderful Christmas before moving: 'I remember that Christmas because it was the first time I'd received a dozen pennies rolled up in newspaper. A dozen pennies! I'd never had so much cash in my hand. I wrapped and unwrapped those pennies so many times.'

Then came the move to Bendigo, at first to a temporary home, then to one which he shared with his youngest sister. Reasons for moving from that and subsequent homes read like a litany: foster mother went into hospital for a heart operation, foster mother developed shingles in the back and went into hospital, foster father called into the reserve army so foster mother sold the shop where they were living and went to live with relations, foster mother had another baby and invalid mother came to live with her. By the time John went to his eighth family at the end of 1943 he had become accustomed to living out of a suitcase. 'After I'd been there a few weeks she said. "John, that is your chest of drawers to put your clothes in." I think I said I didn't know how long I was staying. At that she broke down.' It was a happy ending. John stayed there till the end of 1945 when his father requested the children's return to England.

Next to changing circumstances in foster families, children's behaviour caused most moves. Sometimes it was the inability of foster parents, often elderly or childless, to handle a young child. Rosalie Schultz, five years old on arrival, believes she was too active for her aunt. 'She couldn't handle me. My brother was a bit quieter, so he stayed. I was sent to boarding school.' While Rosalie's uncle provided well for her, sending her to Frensham, an exclusive boarding school, Rosalie had little family life during her stay in Australia. During the holidays she went to a friend of her uncle's rather than to her relatives.

More often foster parents were unable to persevere with certain behaviour or to endure the impact it was having on the rest of the family. By the time they arrived, many children were displaying a range of undesirable behaviours, reactions often to their unsettled lives — bed wetting, throwing things, hitting, stealing. Some also came with family practices quite at odds with those of their host families. Dorothy Brunt, whose family absorbed two evacuees, spoke of another evacuee, 'a nice kid', who came to her home town: 'They had a great problem getting him to take his singlet off. After a while they had to introduce him to the bathroom and ask for his washing.' With patience and understanding children could make these lifestyle adjustments and move through this emotional phase. Unfortunately for some, further disturbing influences, such as the death or divorce of natural parents, complicated the adjustment, frequently causing deeper psychological disturbances, ones more difficult for foster parents to handle.[19]

Anne Vincent pictured with her aunt in Adelaide. (Anne Lowden)

Ingratitude and selfishness were common complaints against children. 'The girls took everything as if it was their right to get it and never thought to give thanks for anything,' wrote one foster mother after returning her two charges to the Child Welfare Department.[20] While such behaviour was obviously upsetting, in the context of the children's unsettled lives, it was understandable. By the time they reached Australia many had become unquestioning recipients of whatever life offered. Furthermore, from the point of view of some children, usually teenagers, there was no reason to be grateful. They resented

Left: Recording a message to send home to England, Christmas 1940. Rosalie Schultz is in centre front behind the microphone; her brother Phillip is behind in the striped vest. (Sandra Jacobsohn)

Opposite: Near tears as they hear their mother's voice over the radio telephone are Margaret (left) and sister Joan Hodgson. With them is ABC announcer Richard Parry. (*Pix*, 17 April 1943)

being evacuated, being sent often to care for younger siblings from whom they were then usually separated. While their attitude may have been justified, it endeared them to noone and compounded other problems related to adolescence.

Adolescence, seldom a smooth passage, tested many relationships. Children described as 'nice', 'quiet', 'no trouble' at twelve years of age were within a year or so being labelled 'selfish', 'lazy' and 'retiring'. Their behaviour often became irksome to their hosts, just as the hosts' treatment of them frequently roused rebellion and hostility. 'Feels custodian does not understand her', 'resents not having more freedom', 'feels she is not trusted' were common entries in files for this age group. Foster parents were in an unenviable position, being responsible for pubescent children not their own. Peggy McLeish, who was fourteen on arrival, believes the responsibility made her uncle overly strict. She was never allowed out by herself. 'He wanted to keep me under lock and key. All I ever did was read or do homework.' 'Many of the kids became rebellious,' commented Alan Timmins. 'It would have been so easy to take off or run away.' That he did not may reflect the fortitude of his aunt who single-handedly was raising him, providing him with strict but fair treatment in a home and community where he was accepted as an equal. Unfortunately many foster parents reneged on providing sexual instruction during this time, but there is no reason to believe their own children fared any better. 'You're a big girl now', one evacuee was told when her periods started. 'I had chickenpox at the time and didn't know what was going on.' While many foster parents and children weathered these difficult years, for others it was a time of parting.

Finding new placements for older children became increasingly difficult as the war progressed. In February 1942 Geoffrey Shakespeare acknowledged this fact: 'It is becoming more difficult to replace children in fresh homes where this is necessary. As the war continues, conditions become more stringent, elderly people feel the prolonged strain of vigorous war guests, and older boys and girls are a bigger expense and responsibility than little children.'[21]

New placements were constantly being sought. People who had originally applied for children received a form letter: 'There is [a girl of — years] available and I wondered if

PIX Saturday, April 17, 1943 Vol. 11, No. 16

Radio Phone Talk
EVACUEE CHILDREN CALL HOME

you are still willing to care for an evacuee child.' The letter included a time when someone from the Child Welfare Department would visit to discuss the matter. In this way homes were found for many children, but not for all. A newspaper and radio appeal in August 1944 shows homes still being needed for children who were not permanently placed.

Institutions were occasionally used as a last resort. Victorian records show only a few children in that state entering institutions. In New South Wales, the situation was considered 'acute' in 1944 when there were six children housed in institutions. Efforts were made to find at least temporary homes for, as Cyril Bavin pointed out, 'difficulties might arise when reports of these children's placement reached England'.[22] Elsie Harding's (now Sutherland) experience shows that these efforts were not always successful: 'My aunty took us in, but she didn't want us. I went to a girls' home at Guildford and my brother went to a home for boys in Glebe. But I was lucky. I was picked out by a lady to do domestic work for them, which I did until I went back to England with my brother. My brother stayed all those years in a home.'

Group homes were occasionally used although, as Ernest Lowe's case suggests, the care provided was questionable: 'I was placed in a foster home with nine other boys, all orphans and Australians. I was never happy there and was always hungry.'

Peter Barnard might have shared this institutional fate had a family not intervened at the eleventh hour. At thirteen Peter left what he described as 'a messy family'. Having arrived in Australia, he and his younger sister Winsland went to live with an uncle and aunt on their thousand-acre farm at Melrose. The spacious environment appealed to Peter, as did life generally with his rather eccentric uncle, an electrical engineer turned farmer. 'He was an artistic chap — played the violin. He turned himself into a farmer who just wore an old black shirt, old pair of black trousers with a strap around the middle, and boots, and a pipe with a lid on it to stop sparks from coming out, for bushfires.' Peter recounted one of his many unusual experiences with the Grahams: 'My uncle used to kill a sheep now and then by putting it in a wheelbarrow and cutting its throat, then skinning it. This was quite foreign to someone from a town, but it was all part of quite an amazing experience.'

A year later the experience came to an abrupt end when the illness of his aunt prompted the sale of the farm. The two children were moved to a wealthy family in Adelaide, people 'with a totally different background from mine. When we arrived they had a gardener, a parlour maid, a house maid and a cook. They quickly disappeared thereafter, and I was taught useful things like how to wash up the proper way.' It was a troubled placement for Peter:

> There was always something. I'd see him do something and think, 'That's a good idea.' He

Peter Barnard, front row, third from left, at King's College, Adelaide.

was syphoning out something one day. So I thought I'd clean out his pond, only to get it in the neck because he kept his fish in the bloody thing. On another occasion I saw him casting aluminium in a little pot. I thought I'd like to caste something, so I started a collection of bits of metal from railway carriages, which he discovered in a drawer. He wasn't very happy about that, and I didn't give him any explanation as to why I should have this cache of stuff.

Peter was not surprised when he received his marching orders: 'Teenagers can be pretty terrible and I think I was. One day I was in the garden and he said I was leaving the next day. I don't remember thinking anything but "Oh". I can remember plodding down the road with my rucksack on my back.'

Phil Drabsch had succeeded with many difficult teenagers at the Magill Reformatory in Adelaide. Surely he could help this boy, child welfare thought. Phil and his wife, Dorryn, agreed to try. Phil immediately recognised Peter's superior intelligence and responded to it. 'He had a staggeringly high IQ. That was his trouble. His mental age was well above that of a lot of adults.' After years of being pushed around — nine schools and several evacuations by that time — Peter was finally expected to make decisions about his own life, and was accepted for the reserved, intelligent English boy that he was. A relationship of friendship and mutual respect developed. 'We had a couple of cows,' commented Phil, 'and we would talk as we milked the cows — about everything.' Peter added, 'Phil and I would do things like plastering a ceiling while talking Latin.' It was a relationship many teenagers might have envied.

Through his own ability, and the encouragement of his foster parents, Peter overcame his chequered early schooling and went on to graduate in medicine at Adelaide University. Many other children received generous educational support and encouragement from foster parents, including payment of fees at private day and boarding schools. A number of private schools subsidised fees for evacuees, including children from the Pacific region.[23] Andrea Wilson, the eleven-year-old escapee from the Solomon Islands, attended Frensham at Mittagong, near Sydney, as did Rosalie Schultz. Andrea also recalled some Dutch evacuees at Frensham. It was a very progressive school run by Winifred West from England, and for Andrea a wonderful social experience. 'Everyone was marvellous to me. The headmistress was really inspired ... I didn't find the separation horrific. I thought it was rather fun really because I had lots of children to play with and that to me was a picnic. I must have been starved. I must have been starved for childhood.'

Not all children were as enthusiastic about their schools. Beryl Minter found the Methodist Ladies College in Adelaide 'a bit of a hoot' and very conservative: 'There were sixty of us in the boarding school ... There was a great mixture of teachers there, some of them were not qualified, some of them were awful and some of them absolutely first class. I think during the war a lot of teachers went off and they had difficulty replacing them.'

Peter Barnard also commented on the curious array of teachers at King's College, Adelaide, during the war: 'There was a man who had a voice as low as I could sing my lowest note, who sort of floated in from the Northern Territory ... Another chap had a brain tumour, then there was a dwarf ... But it was a nice school.' For Philip Robinson, boarding school was an unwelcome disruption. He was two years into a wonderful life in the sugarcane country of Queensland when he was bundled off to school in Brisbane. 'I hated every minute of it.'

The majority of children attended state schools, where their fortunes varied. Many 'started behind the eight ball', as Ken Gregory noted, having had major disruptions to their schooling before leaving Britain. Further moves in Australia, together with the transition to a different school system, inevitably caused some difficulties and disgruntlement. Peggy McLeish, previously attending a Catholic girls' school in England, commented, 'When I came out here I had to go to a co-educational school. That nearly killed me. I used to blush and get embarrassed. I just dropped my bundle at school.' Having moved homes several times in Bendigo, John Hare found he knew everyone by the time he entered Bendigo High School. In 1942, with civilian evacuation and air raids high on the agenda in Australia, John became something of a celebrity: '"Could you bring your gas mask to school", I was asked. I took it to every school in Bendigo — showed them what it looked like and how to put it on. Then I had to get on the teacher's table and show them how we were taught to lie down with our hands over our heads.'

Some older evacuees never returned to school after arriving in Australia. Many others left school when they turned fourteen or after completing the Intermediate Certificate. Being children from Britain's grant-aided schools, this is not surprising. Many had parents whose expectations and means for providing schooling beyond the compulsory years were limited. For the average Australian working-class family, leaving school at fourteen was also the norm. Even with the government contribution, maintaining foster children's schooling was a financial burden many Australian families could not afford. Those willing to support further schooling could have the children sit for government scholarships, which provided assistance at state and private high schools, and at technical and other institutions. British children, unlike their foreign counterparts, could also apply through the Australian Universities Commission for financial assistance for university, although a statutory declaration of natural parents' income had to be provided. Very few children applied for this assistance.

The reluctance of Britain to recognise overseas training and awards possibly discouraged some children from entering apprenticeships and higher education. The British Ministry of Labour indicated that years served in Australia in an apprenticeship would not be recognised in the United Kingdom. In response, an agreement was reached in 1944 that, at the end of the war, children could remain to complete studies and retain their right of a free passage home, as long as they returned at the earliest opportunity after completion of their training.

CORB never seriously considered returning children before the end of the war, but as the war dragged on, steps were taken to allow special cases to go home early. In September 1944 the option of release from CORB was given to certain older children: boys of at least seventeen and a half years who wished to enlist in the United Kingdom and Indian armies; boys seventeen and over who wished to return to the United Kingdom for national service other than the army; girls of at least nineteen who wished to return to their parents. The latter category was justified on the grounds that these girls 'had reached an age where they should have the protection and advice of their mothers'. It followed a request in which some girls explained to Cyril Bavin, 'We are afraid that we may meet our opposite number in this country and that would stop us going home altogether'.[24] Having gained their parents' permission, ninety evacuees returned home before the end of the war, including some who were allowed to return for compassionate reasons and some boys who returned to join the merchant navy. No explanation is given as to why children who had not found permanent placements by then were not included.

Only a small number of the almost six hundred evacuees came of military age during the war. Nor was there any opportunity for putting up one's age given the tight rein CORB kept on the children. John Templeton may have found the one loophole. He returned to England in 1944 because his mother was dying. Free of CORB, he then put up his age and joined the RAF. Of those eligible to enlist, thirty-six joined the Australian forces, having gained the necessary parental permission. Patricia Greening recalled 'sweating tears of blood' in case her father refused her permission to join the air force. Having received it, her rather troubled life improved immensely — meeting different people, making friends and enjoying a social life in Melbourne during leave from Point Cook base. Peggy McLeish also found joining up a liberating experience. She had moved by then from the heat and loneliness of Paxton to a machinist's job in Newcastle: 'As soon as I could I joined up. It was the best time of my life. You had discipline and chores and learned to be independent — and you had plenty of friends.'

For many, like Philip Robinson, the romance of flying fighter planes remained a dream:

> I joined the RAAF. I had dreams of returning to England as a fully blown pilot and flying Spitfires or Hurricanes against the Luftwaffe, but this was not to be! I learnt to fly in Tiger Moths, but the war was almost over so my career was cut short. In 1945 I was discharged and went back to Childers to work in the sugar cane.

Repatriation became a major issue in Australia from late 1943. The Department of the Interior began considering legal and financial issues related to evacuees remaining in Australia at the end of the war.[25] As these discussions occurred amidst planning for postwar child migration, interest in retaining CORB children was high. The Department of the Interior stated the case bluntly: 'From a child migration point of view we would be getting a very desirable class of migrant at a very cheap price'.[26]

In 1944 surveys were conducted of preferences in regard to children staying, leaving or having parents join them at the end of the war. The head of the Child Welfare Department in Victoria criticised the survey, declaring that it was unsettling for children and parents, and scarcely an accurate indication of their desires and intentions when general repatriation became possible.[27]

It was a matter which must have played on the minds of all evacuees, parents and foster parents. 'There was always somebody saying, "I guess you'll be going home one day",' commented John Hare. While some children longed for the reunion, the years in Australia and away from their families left many with divided loyalties. As relationships in Australia developed, relationships with natural families often went into abeyance. Although CORB had been strict about children maintaining regular contact with their families,[28] the letters and cables were often fragile threads over such distance and time. For many children, communication was reduced to the monthly cable with its preset, numbered messages. 'The postmaster would ask, "Which one's it going to be, Johnny boy?" and I'd call out the number, "Number nineteen, happy birthday mum," or something like that.'

A system of radio broadcasts, managed jointly by the BBC and the ABC, supplemented the cables, but was a rare treat. At first a two-way program, 'Children Calling Home' was broadcast every six weeks. Children and parents were often so overwhelmed with emotion on hearing each other that the broadcasts were changed to one-way prerecorded sessions, aired in Australia as 'Hello Children' and in Britain as 'Hello Parents'.[29]

In ideal situations parents wrote regularly to their children as well as corresponding with foster parents and occasionally exchanging photographs. Where this happened, children were kept informed of events at home, although it was often left to foster parents to convey detailed information. In May 1941, for example, Freda Morgan received the following letter from her father, a grim reminder of the reason she and her brothers were in Australia:

My dear Freda,

I am so glad to hear you have received our letters and photos. Glad you liked them. You say 'glad our house is safe'. No doubt you will know by now it is not and we are now living with Auntie Flora ... Well dear, don't worry. We are safe and have got over it. I bet you are glad I sent you to Australia now. It was hard to part with you but I thought I was doing the best for you all. Now I know I'm right and I'm very happy you are with such lovely people. You are very lucky children.

A letter to Freda's foster parents was more explicit:

I suppose you have read about Liverpool being bombed for seven days. On the first night a land mine dropped behind the house gutted the place. Every door, window, ceiling and wall ... everything just blown away. I picked myself up and looked for my wife and Olga. Found them among the dishes and furniture, soot, glass, plaster and all the rest of the junk that falls at a time like that ... Cyril was in bed with the bedroom ceiling on top of him. The shock was so great ... but he was not hurt ... Tell Freda three houses opposite are flat to the ground ... It is hard to say where to go as almost everywhere has been hit or blasted ... Please tell the children not to worry ... We don't mind what we go through knowing our dear ones are safe in a happy home.

For children who received no such reassurances of love, redirecting their feelings to affectionate foster parents was a matter of course. It was a risk all parents had taken, perhaps unwittingly, to protect their children. As Jean Schultz commented: 'If you send a child away you have to take the risk of losing the affection of your child, no matter how good the home. My parents were not so good so it was quite easy for my feelings to get channelled to my foster parents who showed love and affection. They were my parents as far as I was concerned.'

Attachments to Australia also formed over the years, leaving many children ambivalent about going home. Regardless of their personal situations, through living with Australian

Thirty-six CORB children joined the Australian forces. Permission had first to be gained from parents. Patricia Greening (left) recalled 'sweating tears of blood' as she waited for her father's permission to join the air force. Peggy McLeish (right) joined the army in 1944. For her it was a very liberating experience, 'the best time of my life'.

families they had experienced an Australian childhood and often developed a deep attachment to the country — or at least to its climate, relaxed lifestyle and space. Ultimately, it would be the country more than personal relationships that would entice many to return.

Despite these attachments, as the war drew to a close foster parents were more likely than children to be distressed over the pending separation. For the children there was the excitement of another sea journey and thoughts of seeing families again. For Australian families who had formed strong attachments to the children, the future looked bleak. CORB received many letters requesting permission for children to stay. One letter, for example, claimed the child was terrified of ships and planes and included a doctor's certificate recommending that she stay till her parents could join her. The plea of John Hare's foster mother is particularly touching. After moving through so many placements, John now had a foster mother who desperately wanted to keep him. The reply from CORB suggests there were many similar cases: 'I am very sorry that both you and John are upset. Indeed it is a very great break to part with anybody who has lived as your own child in your home. There are many people who are dreading the news of the children's departure.'

Eric and Phyllis Ward's parting scene portrays vividly the deep relationships that developed between some British evacuees and their borrowed families. They had had five happy years in Yass, being inducted into country life by their stock and station agent foster father.

'I had a wonderful opportunity to learn about the real Australia,' commented Eric, who often accompanied his foster father on inspections of livestock and properties in the bush. Only months before leaving, their foster mother died of cancer. Eric recalled leaving a very lonely foster father: 'He'd lost his wife in April and was really devastated. One of the most terrible scenes I can remember was standing on the quay as we left to go back to England in December 1945. He was standing there with his daughter and he had tears running down his face, waving to Phyl and I.'

Meanwhile, twelve thousand miles away, parents prepared for the return of their distant children.

The main party of South Australian evacuees leaving for home on the *Empire Grace*, 15 November 1945. Thirty-one British evacuees went to South Australia through the Overseas Children's Scheme.

9

No Time for Childhood

The hardships of their early lives prepared the Polish boys for Australia. Although on arrival most regarded themselves as children, or 'not quite grown up', their childhoods as eastern Jews had been tough, making them both resourceful and independent. 'We were battlers from the word go,' commented Werner Teitel. 'We had hurdles to jump all the way. We had to look forward and watch our backsides at the same time. We were not liked. And our only trouble was that we were Jews ... I went to work at eleven. School was from eight till one, and from one till dinnertime I worked.' In this respect, the Polish boys differed from British evacuees and from many German and Austrian youth who came to Australia. German youths later commented, 'Polish Jews were better prepared for life ... They had been brought up as Jews, were always exposed as Jews and had to struggle ... They knew how to make a living, while we were muffs and just did what we were told.'[1] Hans Eisler, who arrived from Austria at fourteen, confirmed that nothing in his pampered early life prepared him for the hardships and loneliness of life in Australia. Regardless of one's past, Jack Garbasz reflected, 'being on your own at fourteen is quite a blow. You feel extremely insecure.' Fortunately for Jack and the other Polish boys, their care had been well considered. When they disembarked in Melbourne on 29 May 1939 they were received by a very welcoming Jewish committee.

For two years the Polish Jewish Relief Fund had awaited their arrival. The twenty men who had volunteered to be their guardians had formed a committee, headed by Jonas Pushett.[2]

Many were at Station Pier to greet the boys. Some had photos of their boys, to whom they had been matched by lottery. Max Goldberg recalled their arrival: 'Mr Pushett and all his friends were waiting there at the port. I can vividly remember Mr Pushett and Mr Arthur Rose running around yelling, "Boys, boys, boys". We were on the ship and they were on the wharf.'

Alwin Spiegel's first impression was more monetary: 'There was something to pay for one boy. So one of these men pulled out a big wad and started to peel off money. 'Oh God', I thought, "this is a terrific country".' Alwin later discovered that it was not unusual for people to flash wads padded with newspaper.

They had few expectations, as Jack Garbasz explained:

> We didn't know what to expect and we weren't disappointed. I wasn't disappointed with whatever I got ... I didn't know I was getting a guardian. Already when I arrived on the boat somebody called me and that was my guardian. That is the first time I began to understand that I would have somebody that would take an interest in me.

Later that day, the boys officially met their guardians at the Kadimah, the Jewish community centre in Carlton, an inner suburb of Melbourne where most eastern Jews settled on arrival.[3] According to Jonas Pushett, the idea was 'to have a home — not to live in — but someone to keep an eye on them.' For Alwin Spiegel, problems began immediately. 'I was the only mug whose big brother never turned up ... At the Kadimah each boy got up and then they called the big brother. When it came

Aleck Katz (left), Szymon Klitenik and Jack Schwartz tending a crop of beans at Kuitpo Colony, South Australia, 1939. Kuitpo was run by the Central Mission, Adelaide and attracted many young refugees who went there to learn basic farming skills. Werner Teitel, missing from the photo, also went to Kuitpo soon after arriving in Australia. Szymon Klitenik was killed in New Guinea in 1942. (Aleck Katz)

my turn it was a bloke by the name of Ted Newton. He never turned up. Mr Pushett took me on as an honorary one, so he finished off with two.'

Accommodation had been arranged in north Carlton. The boys were divided into groups of four to six and placed in boarding houses within walking distance of each other. It was a business arrangement, but the families with whom they boarded, also recent arrivals, provided the boys with a familiar environment, as well as some guidance and support in their new lives. Norman Schindler commented of his family:

> They had rented this double-storey terrace house ... It had four bedrooms ... and they used two of the bedrooms to accommodate six boys — three beds and a cupboard in a room. The mother was a very kindly soul and when she had time she listened to us telling her a few of our problems. But she was mainly involved in giving us food and washing our clothes, for which she was paid.

Complemented by guardian support, it was a sound arrangement for parentless children of this age. The boys had each other, they were in a family environment, with families of similar backgrounds, and they were relatively independent.

As chairman of the committee, Jonas Pushett assumed major responsibility for the boys. Following their arrival, he took them to meet Frances Barkman, secretary of the Australian Jewish Welfare Society. She performed her infamous name-changing act: 'Some of them had names she did not like so she changed the names for them. One was named Garbasz. She didn't like it ... He became Best instead of Garbasz. One was Poczter, so she changed it to Porter.' Jack Garbasz recalled the occasion:

> She said, 'Your names are impossible. Australians can never pronounce such foreign names and they are not suitable for people who want to be Australians ... We will fix it.'

She said to me, 'Jankiel Garbasz is a terrible name. We will make it Jack Best.' Until I got discharged from the army I was Jankiel Garbasz, known as Jack Best. When I got out of the army I said, 'I have nothing to do with Jack Best. Garbasz is my name. My family's all Garbasz. Let it be Garbasz.' She wanted to make us instant Australians. You lose your identity ... and while you are very young you don't realise it.

Foreign clothing and behaviour were also scrutinised. Alwin Spiegel recalled the fate of two pairs of new knickerbockers: 'That was the fashion in Germany. I was so proud of them, but the committee said, "You can't wear them. Nobody wears them. We'll get them altered and made into long pants for you." They made a hell of a mess of them.'

As time passed they began to understand the soundness of this practical advice. George Perl commented:

When we came to Australia you couldn't walk in the street and talk another language. We did occasionally, but people started looking at you. It was not pleasant. To sit in a tram and read a Jewish or foreign paper was impossible. I understand exactly what happened. It was not because of racism. It just didn't enter Australians' heads that there was any language except English.

Confronted with their foreignness, differences between the Polish- and German-born boys soon disappeared. 'When we got to Australia we found out it didn't matter who we were or what we were,' according to Werner Teitel. 'We were all foreigners and that gave us a common bond.'

Within days of their arrival the boys started work. Plans to provide six months intensive schooling to learn English had been scrapped. Only Max Goldberg was given the opportunity to return to school. His guardian offered to adopt him and send him to school, but Max declined: 'I came from a very poor home and when I discovered I could earn a shilling to send home to my parents ... I thought I should do that'. The first jobs were often menial and temporary — organised by the committee to get them started. Aleck Katz recalled his first job, in fabric dyeing: 'I was at it three weeks and didn't like it. The ammonia and the chemicals! Being right from the village I thought, "Oh God, it will kill me, all the fumes".' Others went to various clothing factories or, in a few cases, found work immediately in their trades. Different practices and equipment generally made the latter unsatisfactory. George Perl, who had almost completed a three-year carpentry course in Poland, found furniture making in Australia quite different: 'In Poland we were taught to make furniture without nails — just gluing and joining. It was a different class of work.' Werner Teitel returned to butchering, but only briefly. 'Coming from a country without mutton, the smell of mutton offended me.' Their work environments generally determined how well the boys settled into these jobs. Communication was often a problem, even when employers were Jewish. In George Perl's case, 'The owner was a Jew from England. He tried to explain the work to me in Yiddish, but I couldn't understand his Yiddish. I didn't know any English. So I felt very awkward there. I couldn't ask any questions. I felt very isolated.' Jack Garbasz, on the other hand, worked for a Polish Jew in a hosiery factory and found the environment very friendly and informal. 'He was an old Bundist, from the Jewish socialist movement in Poland, and we used to have arguments [about politics]. We were on an equal footing socially ... We went to the same club. His daughter and I used to meet there and we used to go to various functions.'

Content or not, the boys saw these early jobs as a first step. Despite a lack of English, most enrolled almost immediately at night school, in either the Intermediate Certificate or in various trade courses. Bully Taylor and another teacher from Melbourne Grammar provided English classes. 'It was one of those wonderful things,' according to Jack Garbasz:

> He was a gentile and he devoted his time every Saturday night ... He would come to Carlton where we lived ... they used to give us a room at the Kadimah and we would study English. That was wonderful ... He was a very good teacher ... of course we were very receptive; we wanted to learn. Only later did it dawn on me how much a sacrifice it meant to him. But I was always extremely grateful to him.

Ever ready for an engagement on politics, Jack commented that the two men were from the Henry George movement. 'They believed all the world's troubles would be solved by making the land public and not private. I used to have in my broken English discussions about politics. But it was such fun.'

Thoughts of home were never far away, particularly in the early period. Norman Schindler commented, 'After I had been here about three or four weeks and started to get into a routine it was then I became terribly homesick. I missed my family very much.' Letters helped fill the gap. Through letters, parents frequently offered guidance and advice. Max Nagel's father wrote weekly before war was declared. Amidst family news, he regularly admonished Max for errors in his German: 'I must unfortunately point out a few small errors, because German is your mother tongue, and if one does not know one's mother tongue one cannot learn any other ... I correct your German mistakes so that you will take more care with English.' He offered other fatherly advice:

> I beg you should behave very well and learn your job well, so that hopefully with time you will get to know people and will perhaps be able to do something for us so that we can all come over there. Dear boy there is another great request we have of you. You should not waste your free time with nonsense, but conscientiously learn education and also read Jewish newspapers and magazines. In Melbourne there are many of these kinds of publications.

Werner Teitel's mother wrote a similar letter on 2 July 1939, the eve of his fifteenth birthday:

> My beloved Werner.
>
> I was very happy to hear from you d boy. Above all to know you're healthy and lively and that you've settled in well at your new apprenticeship. If you have to cut that amount of meat there in one day instead of fourteen days that's something you have to get used to. You have been without work for eight months and in foreign countries one has to work harder than in Germany. Everyone says so ...
>
> My d Werner enjoy your free time without playing cards for you have seen the passion of your father and what became of it. Do me a favour and promise me, your mother, my d Werner, for you are on your own in the world. Go instead to the cinema or read good books then you can learn something. You write that you are in good hands which gives me great comfort, knowing that you'll be encouraged to do good. For you my good boy turn fifteen tomorrow and already have been torn far away from a mother's heart. Yes d child maybe it is our fortune that you'll get us out of Poland one day as d Kurt has done with his parents.
>
> Tomorrow we'll drink a good cup of coffee to you on your birthday and our thoughts will be with you my d Werner ... Thus beloved Werner once again all my best wishes for your birthday, together with hearty regards and kisses from your loving mum and children.

The support network organised by the committee gradually took effect. 'Things started working out,' Jack Garbasz recalled. 'We could see that the committee was taking care of us financially and really looking after our needs. I started losing my insecurity. I was really beginning to feel that I had somewhere to get support. That made me feel good.'

Having a caring guardian contributed greatly to Jack's feeling. 'I really enjoyed my guardian and his wife. They were very kind to me. They lived close by and I used to go there every Friday night and every Sunday for lunch. They also used to take me for outings.' The situation for the other boys varied. Jonas Pushett commented that hardly any of the guardians looked after the boys in the way intended. 'They were too busy with their own lives. Too busy! Too busy!' Nevertheless, a number of the boys, apart from Jack Garbasz, recalled having good relationships with their guardians and spoke of continuing friendships with their families. As Norman Schindler pointed out, 'it was a matter of luck who was allocated to each boy and how they handled the situation and how much time and effort they devoted to the boy in their charge.' Having a wealthy guardian was not necessarily an advantage, he discovered. Even though his guardian stood by him, Norman felt a social distance that was a barrier for a young boy needing a family environment.

> I saw him perhaps once a week or once a fortnight. He would come in his big American Buick, take me to his home, which was very sumptuous and luxurious, and I had an evening meal with them. I felt a bit uncomfortable. Then I would come back to this place which was very basic. It didn't help my morale terribly much. I saw the two extremes and I couldn't quite picture myself in any role.

Other boys had considerably less involvement with their guardians, although this was sometimes by choice. 'My guardian was a nice fellow,' commented George Perl, 'but I never came to him with problems. If I had problems I solved them myself... It was all right. He did the job when he needed to.'

As guardians drifted away, the Pushetts stepped in. Within a short time, they became the mainstay for many boys.

One day I had a family of three little children, and overnight my wife had not only three children, but twenty-three, and she really put all her effort into satisfying them. They used to come in of a Sunday morning and they used to give away their earnings ... and she gave them two and sixpence pocket money and whatever they needed — socks, repaired or new shoes, pants, underwear, shirts.

Max Goldberg recalled the Sunday ritual:

> We used to turn up with our torn socks and underpants and Mrs Pushett used to give us new things. It was an experience — a beautiful story. Sunday we got our little parcels and our pocket money and away we went ... Mrs Pushett used to make jam and we used to have this every Sunday with biscuits and tea. It was a wonderful support.

Even those who had attentive guardians or felt independent would make the Sunday visit. According to George Perl, 'I didn't have any worries or complaints. I didn't want anyone to do anything for me. I tried to do it myself. But I used to go because they were lovely people, Mrs Pushett especially ... She was really marvellous. She was the support for all of us.'

Having received the boys' earnings, Mr Pushett went around each Sunday paying their board. With weekly earnings generally below the twenty-five shillings required for board, the Australian Jewish Welfare Society paid a regular subsidy to the Polish Jewish Relief Fund. The annual report for 1939 shows a donation of £546 13s. 6d. for the first year. The Welfare Society, believing the Polish committee had its own funds, was irritated by this continuing expense. In January 1940, the directors resolved that 'no further contributions should be made towards the maintenance of the Polish youths until Polish funds, available in Melbourne, were transferred to the Society ... and the control of the Polish youths was transferred to some person other than Mr A. S. Rose.' In fact, although Arthur Rose remained chairman of the Melbourne branch of the Polish Jewish Relief Fund, he had little involvement with the boys. Having secured their admission to Australia, he withdrew to pursue schemes for bringing other Polish refugees to Australia, in particular those stranded in Japan.[4] As for money, any funds were held by the Sydney branch and had been collected to help refugees enter Australia. They were not available for maintaining refugees already in Australia.

The financial situation came to a head over the hospitalisation of Norman Schindler about six months after his arrival. As Norman explained, 'One night I went to night school and was going across Flinders Street when a car came down without any lights and I got hit.' Norman received a severe knock to his knee, an injury which led to three long, lonely years in hospital. To fill the time he 'started reading all the newspapers. Any words I didn't know I looked up. I became quite proficient in English.' He completed the Intermediate by correspondence in about six months. 'Then I became a bit more ambitious and decided to do matriculation. So while I was in hospital I was doing the work and sending it in and they were sending it back, and so on. By the time I left hospital I had matriculated.' Norman's guardian then paid for him to study commerce at university.

Payment of the hospital accounts caused quite a stir. The Department of the Interior and the Commonwealth Investigations Branch were both involved, aiming to ensure that the committee honoured its pledge not to allow any of the boys to become a charge on public funds.[5] Eventually the Polish Jewish Relief Fund paid £126 3s. 4d. owing to Prince Henry's hospital, and the Austin hospital, to which Norman was transferred, accepted ten shillings a week from the Australian Jewish Welfare Society for Norman's care. Despite its objections to the activities of the Polish committee, the Welfare Society continued to subsidise the boys for as long as necessary.

Information provided to the Immigration and Passports office in October 1941 suggests that, apart from Norman, only two boys, both apprentices, were not by then self-supporting.

The boys were oblivious to this friction. As Jack Garbasz commented, they all longed to be self-supporting. 'We felt we were getting charity and we wanted to get over with the charity as soon as we could.' Till that became possible, they continued each week to hand over their earnings and collect two and sixpence pocket money. When asked how he managed on this amount, Werner Teitel replied: 'It was sufficient. A glass of lemonade — twopence, a piece of cake — twopence, a newspaper — twopence, a pound of grapes — a penny.' Some boys even managed to save a small amount, either to send home or to help their families at a later date. In Poland, two and sixpence was a small fortune. 'I remember sending two and sixpence and I felt they will have a wonderful life out of this,' recalled Max Goldberg. 'That was my great ambition.'

Helping their families migrate was foremost in their minds.

> The thing which kept them going was the memory of their families back home who didn't have this fantastic opportunity in a marvellous sunny land. You know, if you took your finger out and you went to work you could make something of your life. They all had in the beginning this hope in their hearts that they could bring their parents and their family out.[6]

Norman Schindler recalled discussing the matter with Frances Barkman at the Jewish Welfare Society office.

> I made an appointment and I went to see her ... I told her who I was and my family circumstances and so forth. I said I wanted to have a chance to bring them out and she said, 'Look, it's very difficult to get permits, but start with your sister and bring her out first'. She took her particulars and so on. I felt very

happy about that, but then, within a month or two, the war started and of course that was the end of that.

Farming offered the best opportunity for saving. Within weeks of their arrival at least five boys had chosen that option. Max Nagel went to a farm in Victoria, while four others went to Kuitpo colony in South Australia. Kuitpo, run by Adelaide Central Mission, was a drawcard for many refugees and unemployed people. It provided basic farm training and the opportunity for employment on farms. Samuel Wynn, a guardian and a prominent member of the Australian Jewish Welfare Society in Melbourne, organised for the Adelaide Welfare Society to sponsor the four boys for a period of training at Kuitpo. Werner Teitel, one of the four, reflected on their experiences at Kuitpo: 'We worked as farm hands. We cleared the bush, and there were days we spent felling trees.' His fortune began to take off. 'We got full board and lodging, plus working clothes ... old railway uniforms which the government supplied. And instead of two and sixpence we got five shillings.' Farmers came regularly to Kuitpo to hire farm hands. Not wanting to be alone, the boys insisted on going at least in twos. 'We didn't want to lose our identity and be lonely,' explained Aleck Katz. 'A lot of farmers didn't like it, naturally.' After five months Werner Teitel decided to try his luck alone and went to work for Italians in Piccadilly, in the Adelaide Hills. 'That was very good ... I got ten shillings a week! That was a hell of an increase, from two and sixpence to five shillings to ten shillings. And board — as much as you could eat.' At the end of 1939, Werner and the other boys who had gone farming, returned to Melbourne. Concerned that they were losing their identity, Jonas Pushett readily supported their request to return and helped them find jobs in the city. For Werner the draw to country life, and its earning potential, remained strong. Soon he was again on a farm, this time a dairy farm in Gippsland where he worked ten months for thirty shillings a week.

I came back a millionaire! I saved up £120. Once again you had nothing to spend it on and you had all the food you wanted. They worked you hard ... from four in the morning till eight at night. We had Sundays off, from ten in the morning after we'd done the milking and the cleaning of the sheds ... until four o'clock, then we did the milking again.

Werner lived with an elderly English woman and her two adult children. He recalled her kindness and the help she gave him with his English: 'She made me write letters and used to correct them for me. She used to make me read books. She was a nice lady.' In this small rural community, Sunday church service was the social event of the week. 'It was non-denominational and you had wandering minstrels of all denominations coming through. Nobody cared. It was an outing — a meeting place. It had nothing to do with church. On Tuesday night you could go to the same hall and play euchre and five hundred.' Nevertheless, it took courage for the fifteen-year-old Jewish boy to begin attending the Sunday gatherings. When invited by the neighbouring young people to join them, he found many excuses:

> The first week I had to write a letter ... the second week I had to do my washing, which was an outright lie because the lady of the house did my washing; the third week I had to do some mending, and the fourth week they said to me, 'Is something wrong? Don't you like us?' I said, 'Yes, I like you.' 'Come on, won't you come with us?' And I said, 'I can't come because I am a Jew.' They stepped five paces backwards and said, 'You can't be!' I said, 'Why can't I be?' They said, 'You're just like us.' I said, 'What do you mean "just like us"?' 'Well, our fathers told us that Jews have horns and a tail and look like the devil. But you are just like us, so come along.' So eventually the

fifth week I went and for the rest of the ten months I went with them.

On Sundays Werner often met two of the other boys, Max Nagel and Max Loftus, who were working on nearby farms. 'We would get on the horse and meet somewhere in between.' It was a good life according to Werner, but 'there came a time ... I went back to town' — back to the communal life of Carlton.

Formed in 1911 to promote Yiddish culture, the Kadimah was the hub of Jewish life in Carlton. 'It was like a home away from home,' explained George Perl. 'You would go there to borrow books, to listen to a lecture, to see a play. You'd meet some people there. Jewish life was concentrated there at that time.' For young people from poverty-stricken villages in Poland it opened up the world. 'It was marvellous,' commented Yossel Birstein, another young emigre and friend of George Perl. He had never before seen Yiddish theatre nor had access to such an array of Yiddish literature. Boys who had grown up in eastern European families in Germany were drawn into this communal life; in time many spoke fluent Yiddish.

Most young Polish refugees were not religious. According to Betty Doari, who married one of them, 'They wanted to go dancing, not to synagogues'. Zionism remained a driving force for most of the twenty who arrived in May 1939. In 1940 they formed a Zionist youth movement, the Habonim, a movement which spread during the war years to Sydney, Brisbane and Perth.[7] The movement, together with activities at the Kadimah, occupied any spare time and confined all social life and friendships to the Jewish community around Carlton. Consequently, there was little socialising with Australians. This included Australian Jews unless they lived around Carlton or frequented the Kadimah or Habonim, which some young people did.[8]

Boys who went farming were both alienated from Jewish cultural life and forced to interact with Australians. It could be very lonely. Even where people were friendly, there was often a social distance between locals and foreigners. Despite experiencing much kindness in the country, Werner Teitel found Australians generally unaccepting of foreigners:

Australians were a funny people ... We would gladly have mixed, but they wouldn't let us in. They kept us out. They tolerated us, but didn't accept us, right from the word 'go' ... They didn't disagree with you. They fought you. You had a fight. Once he knocked you down or you knocked him down you shook hands and you had another drink.

Social isolation rather than any dislike for the land frequently caused the drift back to the cities. Aleck Katz commented that he 'would have stayed on a farm, with somebody as company, had it not been for the war'. His dream was to find a farmer to sponsor his family to Australia. 'Father, mother, everybody had experience on the farm ... I'm sure I would have been one of the earliest to bring my parents out ... but with the war all our ideas were shattered.'

German and Austrian youths admitted through various schemes had no choice about going on the land. Although girls often stayed in the cities as domestics, boys 'had to go on the land. That was understood,' remarked Keith Muenz. The twenty Welfare Guardian Society boys who arrived in May 1939 were no exception, but being given twelve months farm training was unusual. On arrival they were taken to Dookie and Wangaratta in rural Victoria. There they boarded with farmers and attended either Dookie Agricultural College or Wangaratta Technical College. Manfred Anson recalled going to 'the technical school every day mostly by bus, sometimes by bike. There we mixed for the first time with Australian boys and girls who looked upon us as total strangers from another planet.'[9] When they were not at school they helped on the farms. Charlie Trainor described his life: 'I worked very hard for nothing. Every morning I was milking cows in the dark, then had breakfast and got ready quickly for the bus. Went in the bus to Wangaratta, stayed till about three thirty, went back on the bus to Everton and then milked the cows and helped on the farm.'

The Welfare Guardian Society paid the farmers ten shillings a week for board and gave the boys two and sixpence a week pocket money. It also paid their school fees and bus fares, and provided clothing and other necessities; for example, when Charlie Trainor needed a bicycle, the Guardian Society sent him a second-hand one. These German and Austrian youths also had guardians — mostly Anglo-Australian Jews living in Melbourne. Although the guardians and the Society provided materially for the boys, there was generally little contact between the boys and their guardians. Charlie Trainor commented that his guardian was very good to him, yet, between visiting Melbourne in October 1939 for a Jewish holiday, and 1942, he never saw him. According to Charlie, Fred Lester, now deceased, fared better: 'Freddy Lester had a very very good guardian ... They had no children and they treated him as their own. They'd come up to Wangaratta in the car and look after him. He was sports mad; if he needed cricket bats or soccer balls or anything they'd take care of it.'

As the boys completed their training and dispersed to other farms, many lost touch with each other and with the Jewish community.[10] One of the guardians later commented to Jonas Pushett: 'Pushett, you brought out twenty boys. You've got your hands on them. We brought out boys. They went to the country and they disappeared. We don't know anything about them.'

Young people without organised support had a much harder time. On arrival they were dispersed to farm and domestic positions without any consideration for their youth. One woman described her reception by the Jewish Welfare Society as like going to a slave market. In Sydney she and other girls were distributed amongst waiting employers: 'You go up there. You take her. You take her. Bye.' Of the seven girls who arrived together in 1938, 'four committed suicide. Two went into prostitution, because we didn't have any money. We didn't have anything.'[11] The Gross-Breeseners received similar treatment: 'After arrival in Australia we were split into various groups. Some of us proceeded to Sydney, others disembarked in Melbourne, where a few stayed, and the rest of us were sent to Adelaide.' Wherever they went, they were 'processed' by the Welfare Society and dispersed to farms. 'There was no red-carpet reception by the Welfare Society in Sydney in the Maccabean Hall. In fact it was rather like a slave market. There were some tall Australian farmers waiting for us, and they would point and say, 'I take you and you and you'.[12]

Treatment on farms varied enormously, from outright cruelty to genuine friendship. Herco Cohn, who went to a dairy farm in Foster, said he was treated very well, but confirmed that many other Gross-Breeseners had a hard time. Hans Eisler, the fourteen-year-old from Austria, received both extremes of treatment. The YMCA met his group in Sydney and, after a couple of days, dispersed them to farms across New South Wales.[13] Hans went to a government experimental farm at Wagga Wagga. After the kindness he had received in England, his treatment by Australian boys was a shock:

> They were rather cruel, particularly to me because I was younger. It was bastardisation exercises — having to shove peas with your nose through cow dung. I remember very distinctly the day war was declared — I'd only been there about a month. It was a Sunday

night, the fire was going, and Menzies declared war on Germany. And I felt so good. They played the national anthem, 'God save the King'. I stood up and they all laughed at me. Then, when I sat down, they removed the chair and I fell ... They had a lot of fun at my expense, and that hurt at the time ... Then came the Jewish holidays and I remember asking to be excused ... and that sort of set me aside from the rest. Overall I had one very good friend, a Scottish boy. He used to stick up for me the way I used to stick up for others in Vienna. Unfortunately he had an accident — lost an eye. A pitchfork went through his eye at the farm.

After about six months Hans left Wagga and was placed by the YMCA on a farm near Wollongong:

> That's probably the worst four months of my life because the people I worked for on the poultry farm were very cruel. They made me sleep in the barn. I was bitten by rats ... They gave me food once or twice a day and if I asked for more they refused it. No meat. One egg ... jam on Sundays was the big treat. They were the meanest people I've ever met. They were supposed to pay me five shillings a week. I did get it a few times, but certainly not weekly. I was completely dependent on them. I couldn't speak English. I didn't know what to do.

Hans took the matter into his own hands:

> On the King's birthday weekend there was a game of soccer at Corrimal. I went and didn't go back. Left all my things there. I felt very free ... When I went back and reported to the YMCA they sent me to a farm in Turramurra. It was called the New Zealand farm. The owner was a one-armed New Zealander. Now he was just the opposite. He was kind and co-operative. I loved working for him. He gave me ten shillings a week, and extra occasionally ... and made me feel important. He was wonderful.

When the farm was sold in December 1940 Hans moved to Sydney, and got a job on the metal presses doing war work. As an enemy alien turned sixteen, he was obliged to report regularly to the police — for him more of a social occasion than a burden: 'It was good fun going to the police station. "Here I am again!" They treated me like a good old friend.' Like most young refugees from Nazism, Hans was 'busting to join the army to fight Hitler. I was a youngster. I thought I'd be able to win the war by myself ... I tried to join the navy and spent a couple of days in navy quarters until they found out firstly, I was too young and secondly, I was an enemy alien.' Still sixteen, he joined the army in May 1941. 'Again they found out I was an enemy alien.' He was allowed to stay, but was transferred to ordnance. 'I was one of the first to start the labour companies. They were companies that at first dug and emptied latrines, cleaned up the showground after the troops — ordnance in general.'

As allies, the Polish boys were eligible to enlist in the armed services, although at first 'they didn't know what to do with us', commented George Perl. Most were under age before 1942, although this did not necessarily deter them. Max Nagel tried persistently to join the army. He recalled visits to recruiting offices in both Melbourne and Mirboo, where he was farming:

> I got an old recruiting sergeant and the minute I walked in he used to say, 'Not yet'. I kept doing this every month or so. I was making my normal visitation and the sergeant had a smile on his face and he said to me, 'I think I can do something for you'. So we sat down and we started filling out the forms. I was sixteen years old then. He asked me my age. I said, 'I'm eighteen'. And he said, 'Max, you are making a mistake. You had better make it twenty.' And this is exactly what he did. When I got discharged ... I had only aged sixty-three days, though I had served thousands.

Jack Garbasz proudly displaying his new RAAF wings, 1944. (Jack Garbasz)

Alwin Spiegel, 'fighting the war very hard, single handed.' Alwin was with the AIF in both the Middle East and New Guinea. (Alwin Spiegel)

At seventeen years and three months, Alwin Spiegel went to the Melbourne Town Hall to enlist. When the recruiting officer queried his age, Alwin replied, '"Eighteen." "You got to have your parents' permission." I said, "I got no parents." He said, "What about your guardian?" I said, "I got no guardian". So he looked at me and said, "Right, you're twenty-one." From then on I was twenty-one.' For Jack Garbasz it was not as easy. 'The sergeant took one look at me and said, "Listen sonny, we don't take children. Go to the air force." So I went to the air force. But in the air force they were much more strict about age, so I joined up just around my eighteenth birthday.' By then, Australia was also under attack and Jack had mixed feelings about his involvement. 'I felt that besides wanting to fight against Nazi Germany, I wanted to fight for Australia, the country that could give me a future.'

Manpower regulations interfered with the attempts of some Polish boys to enlist. Having passed the air force exam, Aleck Katz had his dream quashed by an employer who complained to the recruiting office: '"You can't have the boy. He's on protected industry." So they rejected me.' Disappointed, Aleck left his employment and moved to a farm, also a protected industry. About two months later the army conscripted him and, after basic training, sent him to Sydney for engineering training. Manpower regulations would have exempted many from the armed services, but, among the Polish boys, only Sigi Jaffe, for religious reasons, chose this option, staying in a woollen mill throughout the war.[14]

Early in 1942 allied aliens not in protected industry, who had not volunteered, were conscripted, mostly into the AMF, the Australian Military Forces, otherwise known as the militia. Many of the Polish boys who volunteered about that time also found themselves in the AMF. Werner Teitel was among them. 'We applied to join the AIF and they stuck us in the AMF and ultimately into the Labour Corps.' Based in Albury, where the different railway gauges met, they were mainly involved in unloading and loading ammunition and supplies onto railway carriages. Apart from Australian officers, the employment units were made up of foreigners. 'We were all foreigners,' explained Werner. 'We moved in clusters ... Italians, Greeks, Yugoslavs, Macedonians, Bulgarians ... we were all in one heap. When you picked one you picked the lot.' The employment units also included many German and Austrian refugees who in 1942 were reclassified as friendly enemy aliens and allowed to volunteer. Many who did not volunteer were conscripted into the Civil Aliens Corps.[15]

Being denied combat duty was a bitter disappointment but, Werner Teitel rationalised, the civilian work 'had to be done and I made the most of it'. As leader of his unit, Werner took pride in his work and negotiated concessions for his men. 'We were a good-performing unit. We were the strongest team and took all the hard jobs. We did our work in record time ... didn't knock off for smoko ... The deal was we could leave when we were finished. We were free by one o'clock and had the afternoon in town.'

After twenty-one months in the army Werner was reclaimed by the butcher to make smallgoods for the American army. By that time he had learnt a lesson about volunteering. 'We had a good old sergeant major who gave us a lecture. He said, "You volunteer once. After that you volunteer no more. You do as you're told and you do a good job. You don't disobey, but you don't volunteer. You don't step forward." Something registered.'

Not everyone heeded this message. When a change of policy in late 1942 provided the opportunity to transfer to the AIF, Szymon Klitenik, one of the twenty Polish boys, volunteered. Six weeks later he was killed in action in New Guinea.[16]

The other Polish boys who went overseas — Max Nagel to Malaya, Alwin Spiegel to the Middle East and New Guinea, and Max Juni to Borneo — survived the war, although Max Nagel was aptly described as 'the greatest survivor of them all'.[17] He was barely seventeen when he left for Malaya with the signal corps of the Eighth Division. It was a memorable occasion:

> We were on our way overseas to Malaya and the last call in Australia was Perth ... We disembarked and a lot of the boys decided to see the girls. In Perth in those days you had special streets set aside ... I only need one hand to tell you how many times I had it previous to that ... They took me along and after we were done it came time to pay. I don't remember how much it was but whatever the amount was I only took out half the amount. The young lady looked at me, like I am going off my rocker, and she said more or less, 'What is this?' I said something to the effect that 'I'm under age and under age you only pay half price. So I go along with that'.

On 16 February 1942 Max was captured by the Japanese. It was his eighteenth birthday. He remained a Japanese prisoner of war until 1945 and was in Nagasaki when the atomic bomb was dropped. Shortly afterwards, the plane on which he was being flown back to Australia crashed on take-off. Max was one of the few survivors, a fact he attributes to his curiosity as much as to luck. He was ensconced in the plane's gun turret when the crash occurred.

Being in the air force or the army was not necessarily a ticket for overseas. In frustration, Max Goldberg tried to transfer from the air force to the navy: 'I wanted to join the navy so that I could get closer to the Germans. I was a great hero in those days.' Based in Queensland much of the time, Max at least saw some of Australia through the air force. George Perl lamented that even this opportunity was denied him. After twelve months doing mechanical and electrical courses, he was sent to Tocumwal on the New South Wales–Victorian border. 'It was a huge air force base — thousands of people there. We were repairing aircraft. I got sick and tired of being there. I applied several times to go somewhere else ... "No! No! You're wanted here". I was discharged from there. So I didn't see Australia through the air force.'

Through the services, George did meet many Australians. 'When I was in the air force I met some lovely Australians, especially country people — really decent, straight, honest, you couldn't better them — and we were good friends'. The other Polish boys also spoke of good mates and close friendships, some of which survived the war. As Jews and foreigners, most encountered their share of ignorance and harassment. Aleck Katz' experiences in the AIF were not unusual, although being ruffled by swearing may have increased provocation. 'I couldn't get used to their swearing. Every time they swore I thought they'd mean me, but when I learnt to swear back I sort of neutralised myself.' Nevertheless, he experienced some ugly incidents: 'We were on a rifle range once. I happened to be a good shot and one of them got jealous of me because I beat him in points. He came up and wrecked my rifle.'

Being incited to fight was common. 'We used to get hidings.' Some of the non-commissioned officers were particularly bad. 'I didn't like the NCOs. They read the wrong literature — that's what I hated. I didn't mind having skirmishes with them, but they read anti-Jewish propaganda books and articles ... One NCO was maniacal. I always used to skirmish with him.'

Hans Eisler was court-martialled for fighting a non-commissioned officer: 'One of the sergeants made an anti-semitic remark. He was stone drunk. I gave him a bit of a hiding.' The slate was cleared shortly afterwards when Hans prevented a bushfire from destroying an ammunition dump. 'That made me a hero.' It also changed his life. Hans was promoted to corporal and put in charge of the gardens at Concord Repatriation Hospital in Sydney. His platoon of seven Greeks 'kept the garden in immaculate fashion', while he reaped all the praise.

> All I had to do was to pay them every Thursday ... They grew vegetables on the side. It gave them extra pocket money. Nobody cared. I didn't care. They were happy. They were able to go to their wives each night — legally or illegally I don't know. There were tents attached. It was a wonderful sweetheart deal we had. Everybody was happy.

Hans passed his time with soldiers returning from the war. 'I met Australians. I played chess and bridge and euchre. I read books. Particularly, I started studying — for the Intermediate. From then on I've never looked back.'

Some acts of discrimination were greeted with a shrug. Mandatory church attendance was one of them. Non-attendance generally meant being relegated to kitchen or latrine duties. Aleck Katz chose the latter till his friends persuaded him to attend church. Jack Garbasz turned the issue into quite a fiasco:

> There was a parade. You walk around and somebody is drumming. The officers leave and the sergeant major takes over. As usual, he says, 'Catholics to the left and Church of England to the right'. I spoilt his parade and he was very upset. He gives me a shout, 'On the double!' So I doubled up to him and he said, 'What's the matter with you?' 'Well, I'm Jewish.' So he sent me to clean the latrines ... The following Sunday he was already smart ... so he says, 'Catholics to the right, Jews to the left, Church of England to the rear'. And another guy was left out. He doesn't understand what is happening, so he says, 'Who the hell are you?' The other guy replied, 'I'm agnostic'. He was upset because we were giving him a hard time.

Following this, Jack studied the King's

regulations regarding Jews in the services.

> There it said you were entitled to Jewish holidays plus travelling time to the nearest synagogue. So I explained to my commanding officer that my nearest synagogue was Melbourne, two days travel by train from Queensland. So for Yom Kippur I used to get two days travelling time to Melbourne and two days back.

Never one for religion, Jack spent the time in Brisbane, much to the envy of his friends. 'Some guys came and said, "Jack, is it difficult to convert?" I was nearly in the conversion business.'

Despite Jack's good humour, a personal attack by a stranger had a shattering effect:

> I'd just got my wings, which was a big thing in the air force, and I was on a tram going home. There was one vagrant Australian and he was drunk. He looked at me, and I was in uniform with my wings proudly displayed, and he said, 'Heh, Jew boy, why don't you go to Palestine.' All my dreams were dashed right there and then, and I said to myself, 'I will never bring up my children in a country like this. Never!

Comments from friends also hurt. 'The thing that always hurt most was when people I was getting friendly with would say, "You're okay. It's the other Jews".' Based in Palestine with the Australian forces, Alwin Spiegel experienced this regularly.

> You'd go into Tel Aviv and the others would be saying, 'Bloody Jews. The bastards. They took me down from this.' I said, 'I'm one.' They said, 'No, you're not a bloody Jew. You're all right. But them.' I always had this sort of thing. Just normal. But I had no trouble. The 'bloody Jew' came into it every now and then, but personally I had no hassles.

While in Palestine, Alwin had the opportunity to visit relatives. It was his first family contact since war began. After leaving Zbonszyn, his family, like many, had not had

Werner Teitel, 1942. Werner applied to join the AIF but, like many refugees, was put in the AMF, the militia, and ultimately into the Labour Corps, where he was assigned to non-combat duties. (Werner Teitel)

Max Nagel in Lahore, Malaya, at the end of 1941 (Max Nagel)

time to send a forwarding address before war severed links between Australia and German-occupied Europe. Werner Teitel and his parents were also in this predicament. Although Werner received none of his mother's letters until after the war, her letters are a poignant testimony of both the general situation in Poland and of a mother's private grief for her family. When it became apparent her letters were not reaching him, Werner's mother tried writing via relatives in South America. In May 1940 she wrote from Dabrowa, in Poland: 'We still haven't heard from our dear Werner. Therefore we enclose a letter for him and a picture that you can send to him so that the poor boy at least knows where we are.' The situation was by then grave: 'Only one thing will save us, that is to get away from here quickly. But the big question is, "Who will help us?" ... I have only one wish, that is to see our beloved Werner once more, for we now belong to Germany again.'

In a letter sent in August 1940, also via South America, Werner's mother revealed the deteriorating situation in Poland and her deep sadness over the separation from her son:

My beloved Werner.

I haven't had any mail from you since 10.8.39. This has been a long time and hard for us, but we are burdened with so many things these days, one gets used to everything ... Arnold Zeger [a friend] has sent us a picture of himself ... As I now opened the letter the picture fell out. Our Isilein stood next to me, picked it up and said, 'Werner! Werner!' and he kissed the picture and didn't let go of it. I was so moved by the child that I wept ... our Isilein doesn't know his big brother. You have been torn from us so quickly ... May the almighty father in heaven guide and protect you my dear child wherever you go, and stand by you so you'll grow up to be a good honest human being. This is the holiest wish of your dear parents ... We thought last year that we would be redeemed, and now once again ... your dear daddy again has no work. It is prohibited for us. 6000 men are without income. Yes, that's how it's going in this foreign country. In the meantime you, dear Werner, have surely become a big farmer. My good Werner keep enjoying well-being and for now hearty greetings and kisses. Loving you, your mother, father and children, and always thinking of you.

In desperation Werner's father finally made contact through the International Red Cross: 'Parents and siblings are healthy. Son Werner should send a sign of life. We haven't heard from him since the outbreak of war.' After that, they exchanged a few brief messages through the Red Cross. These twenty-five word messages were indeed 'signs of life', giving hope to recipients at both ends. Usually they ended abruptly, with no hint of the encroaching doom. The final message from Werner's father in February 1943 was no exception: 'We are all healthy and still here. We are happy that you're well too. Write more often. Many kisses, father, mother and siblings.'

Letters between Australia and Russian-occupied Poland continued, with difficulty, until the German occupation in June 1941. In January 1941 Max Nagel's father wrote:

My dear son Maxi

Unfortunately the war prevents us from corresponding but today I would like to try all the same to write you a few lines. Perhaps we will be lucky and you will be able to receive a letter from us via Moscow. We have been under Soviet rule for over three months, and we are all getting on very well here. Your grandparents and all the relatives are well. We are very concerned about you and imagine that you are the same about us. How are you? Hopefully very well. Otherwise nothing new. We greet and kiss you and wish you all the best. Your father.

Censorship occurred at both ends. Aleck Katz had a number of letters stamped 'opened by censor', and returned. Undeterred, he

Hans Eisler in his AMF uniform, Sydney Botanic Gardens, 1942. (Hans Eisler)

Charlie Trainor, one of the Welfare Guardian 'boys' (Charlie Trainor)

continued to write regularly, finding open cards more likely than letters to get through. 'People who had experience in World War I said, "Keep writing. Keep writing. Maybe one in ten will get there. As long as something gets there".' Letters that arrived via Russia were carefully worded and frequently required reading between the lines. Aleck interpreted one from his brother:

Dear brother Ela

We have received your card, for which we are thankful. We are all in very good health. We are working. ('He puts work because under the Russian regime you had to work.') I work in a glass factory and dad is a book-keeper for the accountant in the village co-operative. ('All the land must have gone under the village co-operative. I think they had jurisdiction only around the house.') We don't live badly. ('He didn't say 'good', but he didn't say 'bad'.') Thank God for what we have. ('I wonder why he said 'God'. It was unusual to say 'God'.') How are things with you? How's your health? Dear brother, do not worry about us. So long as you write to us we'll be happy. Regards from all your friends. Stay well and happy. Regards from the whole family. Aaron Katz.[18]

There were no Red Cross messages, no 'signs of life', from these small Polish villages after the German onslaught. Only those who braved the march into Russia with the retreating Russian army then had any chance of communicating with Australia. In this way George Perl retained links with two sisters and a brother, but of the family still in the village, nobody heard any more.

As the war ended, another phase opened in the lives of all these by now young adults. Wartime service had generally promoted a sense of belonging to their new country. Max Goldberg's comment was not unusual: 'When I came out of the air force I felt part of Australia'. Australia acknowledged their contribution and, on discharge, offered them Australian citizenship. However, the immediate future was determined not so much by affiliations to Australia as by events in Europe. News of families was all that mattered now. During the years of silence there had always been hope of family reunions. Even as the liberating armies revealed the horror of Nazi atrocities there was still hope. Until letters or survivor lists proved otherwise, always there was hope.

10

GOING HOME

As Australia celebrated the end of the war, Jewish refugees pored over lists of survivors, trying to trace their families. Among them were those whose parents had had the courage and foresight to send them to safety. Usually it was a futile search. 'I was at Larino as the lists came out,' commented Ursula Kaye. 'The Welfare held them. I went to the Welfare Society and looked through the lists. Nothing!' Dr Tuesley from UNRRA, the United Nations Relief and Rehabilitation Administration, went to Europe to find out what had happened to the Larino children's parents. In time, some received details of deportation dates and destinations of their families. This information usually confirmed earlier fears that when the Red Cross messages ended so had their parents' lives. At that point, generally early in 1943, their families had been rounded up and transported east, mostly to Auschwitz.

Ellen Lewinski discovered that her father, sister and step mother 'were arrested on 19 February 1943 and were transported east, and that they died in Auschwitz'. Her eldest sister in Palestine later filled in some of the gaps:

> My middle sister was in hiding. My father had managed to find a place for her with a non-Jewish family whose bone structure and colouring was similar to my sister's ... She insisted on breaking cover to see if my father was all right. She sensed something was wrong. She arrived together with the Gestapo and got arrested with them. It must have hurt my father terribly because he had had the opportunity to save all his children and now, because of this love, this bond — the bond was so strong she had sensed he was in trouble.

Laurie Badrian learned that his mother Kathe was deported in 1943 but that his father, Walter, died earlier. Jo Lehmann and her sister, Edna, know that their mother died at age thirty-two in Auschwitz. Margot Goldstein's father, unable to raise the money for Shanghai, died in Sachsenhausen concentration camp some time before the 1943 Berlin round-up. After the war a cousin found an official letter informing Margot's mother of her husband's death. Margot's mother, brother and sister were taken 'some place else ... not Auschwitz ... probably Riga'.[1]

Betty Abrahamson heard that her parents were sent east on 27 February 1943. In September 1945 Betty received a remarkable letter from her brother Zvi. He was twelve when Betty left for Australia and was amongst a handful of Jews who survived underground in Berlin. In this first letter to Betty after the war he described briefly what had happened to the family and to Berlin Jews after her departure:

> After you left us in June 1939, life went on. Dad went to work and I diligently went to school. But there was always a tension in us, when will the girl write again, and we did receive regular mail from you till the war broke out. Despite the war we also received your Red Cross letters and we always replied.
>
> By the outbreak of the war we were still left unmolested ... New vexations from the Nazis came soon as all Jews were forced into compulsory labour work ... I had to work nights in a factory which of course made me sour. Mum had to work at Siemens and A.E.G. and Dad remained at his old working place in

his craft. In this way we were robbed of our harmonious family life ... In 1941 every Jew had to wear a star, then the food rations were cut short ... Despite all this our family stood like a tree whom nothing could bring to fall. Relatives would be visited as much as time allowed it ... [but] quite often one was far too tired to leave home after a day's work. So passed time week after week, and weeks became months, our feeling for time was almost lost ... Day after day we had to deal with new harassments.

When the deportations started in 1942 we believed the Nazis had reached their highest point. But later it should become even worse. Up till 1942 our family had always been together, but then we were forced apart. Grandpa was first to go. He was displaced to Theresienstadt, and we never got news from him again. It was a terrible time. We assembled daily to be sure that no-one else was removed ... Then a hard blow hit us. Aunt Erna and uncle Hermann were deported. You can imagine what a mood our family was in. Everyone had the absolute feeling we'd come to an end.

And so it happened. The Jews in Berlin were fewer day after day. To humiliate us, the Nazis ... used synagogues and other Jewish community buildings as assembly camps for Jews awaiting transport to the eastern region. Then on the 27 February the remaining Berlin Jews were seized in a mass campaign and sent off to the concentration camps in cattle carriages. This mass campaign was the most terrible thing I experienced in Berlin. The SS and the Gestapo, the Party and the Police, even the Military, all had been mobilised to make Berlin free of Jews within a few days. They tore children from mothers, the people wearing only their working clothes were taken out of factories, all Jews. Since all of them had to go branded it was very easy. All Jews in trams, subways, trains, on the streets, no matter where they happened to be, all were seized and put into a deportation camp ... By this mass campaign all our beloved ones were sent to the east. Also Mum and Dad. Bear in mind the 27 February. We will determine this day as the anniversary of our beloved parents' death ... With the death of our beloved parents we have lost much ... something which nobody will be able to substitute for us ... Mum always spoke a lot of her little Betty and was so proud when she spoke of you. She wanted so much to see you again. She always said if she could see you once more then she could die in peace. But unfortunately it happened differently.

Through the support of a non-Jewish aunt and an underground Zionist group, which received money from Switzerland, Zvi evaded capture and remained hidden in Berlin throughout the war. Between two and three thousand Jews escaped the 27 February campaign. Most were later captured and sent to concentration camps. Zvi was picked up twice by the Gestapo. The first time he escaped, the second time, shortly before the end of the war, he was taken to a concentration camp but was released by the Red Army.

Details about the fates of Polish families were often not available. The Germans slaughtered entire Jewish communities during their push through Poland into Russia. Only much later were some of the Polish youths able to piece together what happened to their families. Some never did. Postwar refugees who knew Werner Teitel's family told him how his mother had helped many people survive in the ghetto of Dabrowa before being shipped to Auschwitz. He learnt that his sister, Waltraut, 'was shot at the railway station when they were shipping them out for prostitution. She stepped out of line — spoke — they shot her. They couldn't have been more than fourteen-year-old girls.' When George Perl's sisters and brother returned to their village from Russia they heard and saw for themselves the devastation to Jewish life in the area bordering Russia. 'It was very difficult to believe.' Around Sarny, where George had attended technical school, Jews had been herded into ghettos and

Leaving Larino for a rare and last holiday together at Dromana on the Mornington Peninsula, 24 December 1945. Left to right: Herman Gold, Jo Lehmann, Edna Lehmann, Ellen Schaechter (holding parcel), Betty Abrahamson, Hermann Levy (behind Betty), Alfred Stocks, Laurie Badrian, Ellen Lewinski. (Marion Paul)

forced into slave labour. For the price of a bag of salt, the local Ukrainian population collaborated with the Nazis to hunt down escapees.[2] Jack Garbasz described what happened when 400 women escaped from Sarny in 1942:

> They were working in a factory making uniforms for the German army when they escaped. They were scattered all over the countryside. The Germans didn't bother running after them, but they put out a notice saying, 'Anybody bringing back one of these women gets four pounds of rough cooking salt.' They brought back all of them.

The Sarny ghetto was liquidated on 28 August 1942. Aleck Katz talked of his father's escape:

> The Germans used to take the Jewish people to a place in front of the railway yards for roll call ... and work allocation. One day when they took them to this place there were machine-guns positioned around the marketplace. A local fellow seeing this, shouted out, 'Jewish people save yourselves.' The machine guns started blazing. People were running in every direction. My father escaped. He got into the forest and joined the Russian partisans.

Aleck's father survived — the only parent from the twenty Polish boys to do so. The war over, he emerged from the forest into a world of continuing hostility towards Jews.[3] Warned that the Ukrainians occupying his property would kill him if he returned, he went to a displaced persons' camp in western Germany. Aleck organised an Australian permit for him, but his father died before it could be used.

Of the Larino children, three had families in Shanghai; two had a father in Palestine. Ellen Rothschild's mother was the only parent to survive in Germany. She acquired false papers and lived underground in Berlin. 'She did a lot of nursing in private homes during the war, with false papers. At the end it became too dangerous, but she was lucky. She was hidden by friends in Berlin. They hid her during the day and she would go out in the evening a bit. But they were risking their lives.'

It was a matter of luck and timing that she was not arrested. 'One day,' reported Ellen, 'she went to the Red Cross to look for messages from me and she met the postman coming down. He warned her, "Don't go there today. They're waiting".' Ellen attributed her mother's survival largely to her own departure. 'As far as I'm concerned my mother would not have survived if I had not left.' Her mother later told her that knowing she was safe gave her something to live for. Being alone also enhanced her mother's opportunities to remain hidden. From the Larino children and the Polish boys a few siblings also survived — invariably older and mostly through escaping to Palestine or Russia before the war or ahead of German occupation.

In August 1945 Arthur Calwell, Minister for the recently created Department of Immigration, announced that a limited number of permits would be issued to close relatives of Jewish residents in Australia.[4] Through arrangements made with the Executive Council of Australian Jewry, permits were available to a wide range of relatives:

> Parents (wherever they are located), adult children and (if married) their wives and children, grandparents, brothers and sisters, uncles, aunts, nephews, nieces, first cousins and fiances provided they are of the Jewish faith and that during the war years of Europe they:
>
> a) were in concentration or forced labour camps,
> b) were deported from their usual place of residence,
> c) carried on a clandestine existence in occupied Europe.

> The arrangement covers Jews in Shanghai, Manila and the Far Eastern areas, provided they were in concentration camps etc. Conditions a), b) and c) do not apply in the case of parents.[5]

The irony of the situation is inescapable. Before the war Australia had refused entry to unaccompanied Jewish children whose parents were alive, the grounds being they would begin a chain of migration. The handful who escaped these restrictions were now mostly orphans and generally unable to take up Arthur Calwell's offer of family reunion. A few surviving parents and siblings did come to Australia, although shipping restrictions delayed reunions. Parents from Shanghai arrived in 1946, but those from Europe came later; it was 1949 before Ellen Rothschild's mother and stepfather arrived from Germany.

Robbed of both family and homeland, adults and children cast around for direction and purpose for their lives. Aleck Katz commented on the difficulty of settling down, and on the wandering that became a pattern of life for many who had lost their families. He stayed with his guardian for a while, contemplating his options. 'I didn't know what to do — go to America, stay here and marry'. Aleck stayed, as did the majority from the Polish group. Leaving was not a consideration for Alwin Spiegel. 'This was my home by that time.' Werner Teitel, who had married in 1944, added: 'I had no desire to go. I was one of the greatest Australian ambassadors that ever lived. Talked Australia, Australia.' Hans Eisler, whose parents were both murdered, felt likewise. Australia had become home, a place where he felt comfortable and could pursue the life he desired. Union activities, rugby union and cricket were central to that life and ensured Hans' acceptance in mainstream Australia.

A few from the Polish group joined relatives overseas. While Max Nagel was a prisoner of the Japanese, a cousin had arrived in Australia with the American army. Having heard Max had immigrated to Australia, he searched for

Marion Ehrlich (left) and Ellen Rothschild at the Melbourne Zoo, September 1945. All twelve of the girls stayed at Larino until 1946, some until 1948. (Ellen Shafer)

Edna Lehmann left to join her father in Palestine in June 1947. She pursued a nursing career, first in Israel then in England, where she met her husband, Aubrey, and settled. (Jo Weinreb)

him by advertising in all the Jewish papers. Jonas Pushett saw the advertisement and responded. After the war the family organised Max's migration to America. 'Up to that time,' said Max, 'I had never thought of going back to Europe or leaving Australia. The only reason I decided to leave — when I found out what happened during the war in Europe and that I did have family in America then I did need a little family togetherness if for no other reason than that I thought we could put the pieces together.'

Others looked to Palestine to fill the void. Even before hearing of his family's fate Michael Porter had decided 'no more wandering. I am going to the Jewish homeland. I am going to bring my family to Palestine.' Through the Habonim, the Zionist youth organisation, Michael underwent farm training in preparation for migration to Palestine. In 1946 he was among the first group of five young people from Australia to settle in Palestine. After initially settling on the Habonim kibbutz in the Galilee, they established Kfar Hanassi, the first Australian kibbutz in Israel.[6]

The declaration of the state of Israel in 1948, followed by the Arab–Israeli war, prompted Jack Garbasz to head for Israel. By that time Jack said he felt 'quite Australian ... I had tried to assimilate an Australian life ... I was involved very heavily in the trade union movement ... [through that] I probably had a lot more contact with Australians than the other boys did.' Nevertheless, 'the moment the state was declared and I heard about Arab armies invading Israel I didn't feel I could sit back and not help ... considering what happened to my family — all murdered, all my family ... I didn't really come here to settle down ... I just came to help. Once the war was over I decided to stay.' Jack served in the Israeli air force until 1953, after which he became a navigator with El Al.

As minors and wards of the Australian Jewish Welfare Society, Larino children had fewer immediate options. In preparation for the arrival of postwar refugee children, the Welfare Society was interested in having the original group move on, but there seems to have been no urgency. During the summer of 1945 they were together for a fortnight's holiday at Dromana, which Ellen Lewinski described in her diary as 'such a gorgeous holiday' — sleeping on the verandah of their little white cottage, swimming, dancing, having sing-songs. It was one of their few, and certainly their last holiday together. In 1946 the group began dispersing. The remaining boys left Larino — Alfred to join his parents who arrived in Sydney from Shanghai, Laurie to live with his aunt and uncle, Hermann Levy to board with his Hebrew teacher, Mrs Hertz and her husband, and Herman Gold to board. Their matron, Ursula Kaye, also moved that year. With Frances Barkman's sudden death on 28 September 1946, a chapter at Larino closed. The name was changed to the Frances Barkman Home, a fitting tribute to the woman responsible for bringing to Australia the only group of young refugee children.

There was less pressure on the girls to leave. Although Ingrid and Marion Ehrlich left in 1946 when their parents arrived from Shanghai, some of the other girls stayed at the home till 1948. Ellen Rothschild found these later years 'pretty awful because we felt like boarders there. We weren't really wanted because they had the new influx from Europe — all different ages, all different stages.' Nevertheless, as they left school and began work, new opportunities and friendships emerged, helping them come to terms with a future in which most knew their parents would be absent.

The Welfare Society continued to direct their futures as long as the girls remained in its custody. When Jo and Edna Lehmann's father requested that his daughters join him in Palestine, the Welfare Society sent Samuel Wynn to investigate the situation. On his return he advised that the girls were better off staying in Australia and finishing their education.

However, their father insisted, so they left in mid-1947. 'The Australian Jewish Welfare Society didn't want us to go there,' Edna recalled. 'They'd subsidised us all these years. They wanted Australian citizens … and I suppose in their own way they wanted to do what was right for us.' For Edna, the upheaval was more emotional than her departure from Germany. 'The first move I didn't realise what was going on, but this move I did. I really cried because I realised I wasn't coming back to Australia … the Zionist Youth came and danced the horrah, the dance of the pioneer young people when they emigrate to Israel.'

In 1948, Margot Goldstein also left for overseas, to join relatives in the United States, but when Ellen Lewinski's sister asked for Ellen to join her in Israel, the committee refused. 'The committee wouldn't let me go because the war in Israel had broken out. I was very very hurt by that. I'd thought of Australia as a transit camp. I'd never thought that I would do anything but end up in Israel with my sister.' Had she gone, Ellen would have found living in Israel vastly different from Melbourne, where her social life was blossoming.[7]

The political unrest, the curfews, the economic hardships and unbearable heat made the move to Palestine extremely difficult for Jo and Edna. 'Australia seemed heavenly in comparison to life in Palestine at that time, just before the outbreak of the Arab–Israeli war in 1948,' Jo commented. Once again, as Edna explained, they found themselves the enemy:

> We always seemed to be the enemy wherever we went. In Australia we were the enemy because we were Germans and in Palestine because of British [connections]. Everyone who had lost someone because of British action couldn't bear the thought of anyone speaking English. So when they heard us speaking English we were put in our places pretty severely. 'How dare you speak English in our country. This is a Jewish land. We don't want this enemy.'

Rejoining their father after ten years apart was even more stressful. They had never been close. Edna recalled being 'a bit in awe of him. I very much respected him … .but I couldn't get close to him emotionally because I didn't remember him as a father.' 'He remembered us as being six years old and four years old, and not as adolescents,' Jo added. 'Of course he thought he was doing the best thing for us. He had married again and was offering us a home.' That home was a small apartment in Haifa, which they shared with their father, his wife and young daughter. Living space was so cramped their father would leave each evening and allow his wife and the two girls to sleep in the one double bed. Nothing had prepared them for this austerity, neither their former lives at Larino nor their memories of their father's affluent life in Germany. Nor had their father written of his changed circumstances. Relationships with their stepmother were very strained, although in retrospect they realise how difficult the situation was for her. Although the reunion was a big disappointment, both Jo and Edna found happiness and fulfilment elsewhere. As they learnt Hebrew and made friends, Israel became home and Australia receded into the past. Against her father's wishes, Jo joined the army. She married and settled in Israel and later pursued an academic career. After nursing in Israel for a few years, Edna went to England in 1955 to study midwifery. There she met her husband and made her home.

Reunions in Australia were generally no easier, although in these cases it was the parents who had the added stress of adjusting to a new country. It was probably harder for the old than the young. Marion Ehrlich recalled meeting her parents after seven years apart: 'We went with Ursula to the boat to collect my parents. We expected them to be tall … but they looked so small and so yellow … they didn't feel like our parents.' A different language and a different way of life separated them. 'They couldn't speak any English and we had to try and speak German,' added Marion. 'We were pretty assimilated … I felt almost like an Australian child.' It was painful for the parents too. Ursula Kaye recalled the girls' mother saying to her in German, 'I want my little dolls back'. This thinking set the tone for many post-reunion relationships — parents clinging to their children, trying to regain the lost years.

Parents arrived from Europe and Shanghai with nothing. The emotional stress of trying

Frances (left) and Paula Kochen (centre) went to Melbourne with their mother and an older sister in 1939. Unable to keep three children in her live-in position at the home of Samuel Wynn, Mrs Kochen placed her two younger daughters at Larino. Although she visited them regularly, the girls grew up as part of the Larino group. After the war they rejoined their mother. Betty Abrahamson (right) went to live with them while she considered her move to Israel. Elizabeth Street, Melbourne, December 1948. (Betty Midalia)

to rekindle a relationship was exacerbated by living in cramped conditions and working in menial jobs. 'We lived in this awful place in St Kilda,' recalled Marion Ehrlich. 'We shared a bathroom with several other people on the same floor. There was no kitchen. We had to wash up in a little basin in the hall.' Factory work was too strenuous for Ellen Rothschild's aged and ailing mother and stepfather. Her stepfather wanted to return to Germany and to take Ellen with him. Although Ellen had a good relationship with her mother, she was 'very unhappy with that idea ... I really didn't want to leave.' Having lived so much of her young life in Australia, Ellen, like most of the Larino children, considered Australia home. Her stepfather died in 1950, after which her mother returned to Germany where she could receive a pension. She returned to Australia two years later, by which time Ellen had married and begun her own family.

Reunions of other separated children, both in Australia and overseas, tended to follow the pattern of the Larino children. When Inge Sadan, who went on a kindertransport to England in 1939, described her reunion with her parents, she could have been writing a page in a Larino notebook:

> When I met them they'd become old ... they didn't seem like my parents ... I had forgotten my German; all I could say was 'mutti' and 'papa'. I'd never seen a man cry before. My father cried. It was the climax of five years waiting. It was shattering ... My mother had left a little girl of nine and thought she still had to help me dress. I was shocked ... I was fourteen by then. There was such a tremendous gap, and they were foreigners. I was English already.

Through her involvement with kindertransport reunions, Inge has heard hundreds of similar stories — about dreams of happy reunions shattered by the effect of years of separation. It was the same for many British evacuees who returned home after the war.

* * *

Child evacuees from Britain were in an enviable position at the end of the war. Despite widespread destruction and loss of life in Britain, most of the children evacuated to Australia were able to return to both their homeland and their families. Their repatriation was delayed by the many thousands of others clamouring for priority shipping — servicemen and women, private evacuees from Britain, families from Malaya, Hong Kong and the Pacific region, internees and prisoners of war. In September Cyril Bavin, CORB's representative in Australia, voiced his concern: 'I am getting desperate with all the children clamouring to be sent home, the custodians who are anxious to finish their war service and get rid of the children, and the parents who are crying out for the return of the children'.[8]

In October Cyril Bavin strongly supported a suggestion that the Prime Minister send a thankyou letter to all custodians. He felt 'this might do something to mitigate the ruffled feelings of so many custodians regarding the return of children home'.[9] Bavin deeply regretted the end of the scheme. He continued to view it as 'the soundest form of juvenile immigration ever thought of' and believed, 'if only it were possible to perpetuate it, it would result in a very valuable addition to Australia's under-population'.[10] Friction over shipping delays was not a fitting end. 'It seems to me such a crying shame that such a wonderful patriotic gesture on the part of the Australian people and a scheme that has been so pre-eminently successful should come to such a sad end.'[11] The secretary of the Victorian Children's Welfare Department viewed the return of the children in 'dribs and drabs' as a waste of a grand opportunity for propaganda: 'From the Commonwealth's point of view the propaganda possibilities in the delivery of the children to Britain in one party are so great

John Hare, thirteen, with his sisters (from left) Betty, seventeen, Peggy, nineteen and Joan, fifteen during a reception at Melbourne Town Hall on the day of their departure, 5 December 1945. Melbourne's lord mayor, Mr (later Sir) Raymond Connelly looks on. (John Hare, from the *Melbourne Herald*)

that I am sure, if it were put to them in the right way, the War Transport people could have set aside one vessel for the job. "The Singing Ship Returns" and all that sort of thing!'[12]

Given the shipping situation, it is remarkable that by December 1945 all CORB children wishing to return home had left Australia. About 20 per cent opted to stay in Australia, either indefinitely, to complete courses, or to await the arrival of parents. Some of these returned to Britain the following year, when courses were completed or parents failed to immigrate because of delays in shipping. As the children left they were presented with a souvenir booklet — 'a memento of [their] stay in Australia and ... a publicity vehicle for migration purposes'.[13] There were hopes all round that many would return, either alone or with their families. In the meantime, the weeks at sea generally provided a happy transition back to their former lives.

Phil and Dorryn Drabsch escorted seventy-two evacuees back to Britain on the *Andes*. Built to carry 1000 passengers, it had been converted to a troop ship and carried about 4000 passengers on that journey. Before leaving Sydney, CORB informed Phil and Dorryn that a girl had been raped on an earlier journey. They were instructed to supervise their charges closely. The rules were strict, but there remained scope for flirtation and friendship.

At one meeting between the girls and the escorts, the girls asked if they could talk to the flight sub-lieuies. I agreed this was all right.

All they could do was talk and walk around the top deck with the young men. One girl somehow contacted one of the servicemen on the lower deck. She wanted to know if she could go and talk to him. So Bessy (another escort) and Dorryn went down with her. She asked, 'Can I kiss him?' They turned their backs while she kissed him ... We learned later that they married. Another became engaged to a sub-lieuie.

John Hare confirmed from his sister's diary that escorts were also very strict on their ship, the *Aquitania*, especially with the older girls. He has more vivid memories of the many returning ex prisoners-of-war. 'They got up to all kinds of things — anything to make a bob, to buy cigarettes and so on. They'd make games and set them up around the deck.' Amongst these POWs were a few who had sailed on the *Batory* to Singapore in 1940.

Anxiety overwhelmed some children as they neared home. Freda Morgan, returning on the *Empire Grace*, was 'absolutely over the moon about going home' until the ship reached Gibraltar. The engineer found her on deck one night 'sobbing [her] heart out.' "What's the matter?" he asked. I said, "I have changed so much. Will they still love me? ... I know I love them but will they still love me?"' Through long and frequent letters, Freda and her parents had remained close during the years of separation. Her foster parents had also written regularly. These letters and photos relayed changes that had occurred and helped ensure a happy homecoming and reunion. 'It was a wonderful homecoming,' recalled Freda. 'Of course lots of tears. Lots and lots. We wanted to say everything at once ... and of course a home I had never seen before' (her original home was destroyed by bombing). Joan Hodgson, so unhappy in Australia, was also overjoyed to be home. She arrived on her thirteenth birthday. To celebrate, her mother had saved her rations for a birthday cake. 'It was so small but it meant more to me than all the sponge cakes and other food we had had at our aunt's place, where the tables were laden.'

Neighbours frequently joined the homecoming revels. Phyllis and Eric Ward's father met them at Liverpool station, from where they took a taxi home. 'Mum and my sister were waiting at the front gate and half the people in the street were watching ... Next day they had a street party for the kids that had come back from the Antipodes, so again we were the centre of attention and were very aware that people were looking at us.'

John Hare and his three sisters also received a hearty communal welcome. 'It was marvellous getting home. There were banners across the street saying, "Welcome home Peggy, Betty, Joan and John". Then there was a bit of a party.' The reception did not sway their determination to return to Australia. 'We got home on a Thursday and we were in Australia House on the Monday.' The *Sun* reported the incident:

> Three girls and a boy — teenage evacuees who returned on the *Aquitania* two days ago from Australia — marched into the Immigration Office of Australia House yesterday. As they lined the counter, four others trooped in and stood behind the youngsters — they were the parents and two small sons. The four in front chorused, 'We want to go back to Australia' ... The eight faces fell when an harassed official handing out forms told them it would be two years before a boat would be available.[14]

Arriving home was an anti-climax for some evacuees. One of the three returning Greening children, Maureen, recalled staring at a woman and a girl amongst the milling crowd on the railway station. 'I said to Shaun, "Do you think that's our sister and our mum?" and he said, "I don't know".' There were kisses and greetings when they recognised each other, but on the train going home their sister, Patricia, was already thinking, 'Oh God, what have I come back to — this horrible dark, dirty country?'

As he alighted at Newcastle station two days before Christmas, Alan Timmins had similar thoughts:

> 'What have I come to?' I arrived about 10 p.m. at night at Newcastle station. The station was dark and dismal. I recognised my father there. He didn't know it was me ... We got a taxi and went home. It was a novelty for about a fortnight. The hardest part was Christmas day and I'm having a chop with my father. My mother was away with friends. She informed me later she and my father were separating.

The nostalgia of homecoming was often fleeting, even in the best of family circumstances. The winter of 1945 was grim. With coal rationed, the houses were particularly cold. Within days of her arrival Freda Morgan was in bed with pneumonia. 'The doctor gave us a docket for coal for the bedroom. You couldn't afford to have a fire in the bedroom but it was necessary for me.' Although her health improved, her outlook did not. 'The snow came up the walls. It was very very high. It was very very cold, and then we found that it was dark in the morning and dark at night. When you went to work it was in the dark ... I loved being home. I loved being with the family, but I just found it very dreary.' The following year Freda made a gracious exit by joining the WRNS. She remained close to her family, but independent; she was thus free from the stresses that blighted many family reunions, including that of her younger brother. He was six when evacuated and later became very bitter towards his father over the evacuation.

As they settled into their daily routines, parents and children felt the impact of the years apart. Weeks after their arrival, Phil Drabsch visited the homes of the children he had escorted on the *Andes*. He found parents reluctant to talk. 'They felt — I can't explain it — their children had been away ... and when they came back they appeared not to be their children. They'd changed so ... the parents were pleased to have their kids back again, but were resentful.' Patricia Greening voiced similar sentiments about her parents: 'I couldn't say my family were my family any more'.

Many parents were neither prepared for, nor able to handle, the changes. 'Quite honestly I think my father thought I was going to be a ten-year-old boy again and continue from where we left off,' commented Ken Gregory. It was all too much for John Hare's father.

> Before we went away nobody except father spoke when we sat down for a meal. If you wanted something you indicated where it was. When we went back there was a girl nineteen, seventeen, fifteen and a boy thirteen — all had lived the free life in Australia ... When you got to the table everyone talked ... that was the first time you'd seen each other for the day ... when we got home we were talking and getting up when we wanted to get up ... my dad couldn't control us ... it wasn't long before he left home.

Although his father returned some months later, family tension continued and added to what was already a difficult adjustment for John. Like many evacuees, he had experienced comfort and spacious living in his Australian foster homes. Back home there was neither space nor privacy, and little money. 'There was always a crowd in the house.' At fourteen he was forced to leave school and take a job as an office boy in London. 'I hated working. I hated being back ... there were lots of buildings and houses down all around ... the rationing ... we didn't see fruit or vegetables for months.' As occurred in many families, another child had been born during the war, usurping John's position in the family, and further adding to his discontent.

While children tried to bridge the gap, they often found, as did Cliff Humphreys, that 'family ties were strained beyond their limits'.

Reflecting on his family relationships, Peter Barnard, who did not return to England until 1949, commented: 'Most of these people I had not known for many years ... these people found it difficult to get used to me — and I suppose I found it difficult to get used to them.' Although Phyllis Ward was pleased 'to be home and be with the family and catch up on things ... I felt like I was treading on eggs all the time. You didn't want to say the wrong thing and upset dad. We had far broader minds than our parents had.' 'Religion was one of the big things,' added her brother, Eric. 'Out of consideration for them we would go to church on Sunday with dad ... but of course in the afternoon you were expected to go for a walk or something and when we told them we played tennis on a Sunday afternoon in Yass — despite the fact it was a church club we were playing for — that caused arguments.' The workplace added to Eric's discontent. Shortly after his return, he began work as an office boy in Liverpool. The social stratification shocked him. 'It was "Sir this" and "Sir that", to anyone who had any authority over you. When you're sixteen or seventeen that's everyone.' He recalled an office boy being fired for calling the boss 'Mr Winter' and not 'Sir' on a train. Ken Gregory also commented on workplace relationships as a major adjustment he faced on his return. 'Australia was God's own country, because it was hell on earth working in those sorts of conditions after you had been used to the relative freedom between people in Australia'.

Religion aggravated a prickly relationship between Beryl Minter and her parents. 'My parents were very church oriented — Methodist ... my mother tried to include me in various church activities, but some of the people were so prudish and bigoted ... Unbelievable! I resented it ... so I went off and joined the Anglican church. Through years of living with an uncommunicative aunt, then being in boarding school, Beryl had become very 'self-contained'. She resented having a mother who now treated her as a little girl and pried into her life. She married 'to get away from the family'. The marriage was not successful, a fact Beryl attributed to her separation. 'I was a deprived child. I think that I had no concept of proper relationships and I think that was due to the business of being evacuated ... that was a fact of being on my own and having a substitute mother who was herself rather reserved.'

The inability to rekindle close relationships with their families was devastating to children deprived of love during their separation. Maureen Greening tried to find the love she had been denied in Australia.

> I wanted to get close with my mother. My mother had long hair. I can remember she would be in the chair and I would brush it ... I would try to do this when I returned and she would say, 'Oh, Carol is brushing my hair.' I tried to get close to her but ... we were strangers and we weren't accepted. I never felt part of the family. Our way of life was different from what their way was.

Not wanted at home, abused in Australia, the pain runs deep in Maureen — a feeling of being hurt by everyone. Her sister Patricia found the reunion equally, though predictably, traumatic. Her father had always been domineering, often drunken, but in Australia Patricia had romanticised about a different life and 'kidded herself' she could change things at home. 'When things are bad children cope by imagining. Coming back it was not as I had imagined. That's when reality crept in ... I went back to a very bad life. A very bad life.' Her father's abusive, threatening behaviour continued. 'I finally married someone I went to school with just to get away from home.'

Anne Vincent found the reunion so stressful she developed agoraphobia. Having adapted to a working-class life with her Australian relatives, Anne returned to a mother who taunted her for her Australian accent and mannerisms. 'She didn't want to know what it was like while I was away.' Instead of the love she sought, Anne was the butt of hurtful remarks such as, 'I couldn't introduce you to my friends'. 'I wanted her affection so I put up with it.' Reflecting on the experience, Anne articulated the thoughts of many separated children: 'It was easier to go than to come back'.

Rosalie Schultz wondered if she ever had close bonds with her family — there were so many other young children. Certainly on her return at ten years of age there was little relationship with either parent. 'I never really got to know my family again ... I felt out of place when I got back because the sister who was only a year younger felt put out by no longer being the eldest of the family.' Rosalie returned to a very busy Jewish household after years in an exclusive Christian boarding school. There were now five younger children, as well as a one-year-older brother with whom she had been evacuated. The family lived in the residence attached to the local library, where her father was the librarian. 'My joy in life was helping in the library after school ... I also had an eighteen-month-old sister and I attached myself to her and didn't really have much to do with any of the other sisters.' The library and the baby sister gave Rosalie such pleasure that the other things seemed unimportant. Nevertheless, there was considerable fall-out from the evacuation. Her parents decided they would emigrate to Australia and, in preparation, her father went to university to become a teacher. Eventually Rosalie married outside the Jewish faith, a long-term effect she thinks of the evacuation and of living those years outside a Jewish environment. If Rosalie has any regrets they concern her father who disowned her as a result of her marriage. Only since moving in his later life to the Montefiore Home in Sydney has he made amends. For Rosalie it has meant a reconciliation with a father she lost many years ago.

Remaining Jewish was never an issue for Jean Schultz. Returning from a loving foster family in Caulfield to her unaffectionate family in the East End of London was her concern. Jean had no illusions about the reunion and delayed it as long as she could. She remembered both the vibrancy and the squalor of market life: 'The stench, the mildew and the decaying food that piles up before the rubbish man comes ... people telling jokes and yelling out ... "Come and buy my onions. Your husband won't go near you for a week." I used to remember that.' There were also images of her father: 'I remember my father trudging through the snow pushing a barrow of cakes and biscuits ... I can see him now slipping in the snow, trying to push this barrow through the slush. It was a hard life.' In 1946 Jean returned to this ghetto environment, to her parents' one-bedroom tenement flat. She shared a bed with her mother. There was no bathroom, 'only a public bath across the road where you paid a penny'. All around were reminders of the blitz — physical devastation, school friends killed in direct hits, a father who as an air raid warden had been there to pull out the bodies and the limbs. There also, people were searching the lists for survivors of the Holocaust. All were grim reminders of fates that might have been.

The dearth of shipping interrupted many plans to return to Australia. It also delayed family reunions for children waiting in Australia for families to emigrate. In February 1946 Arthur Calwell placed parents of these children next on the priority list behind returning Australians and wives and children of Australian servicemen, but pointed out that 'even then owing to the number of high priority cases and the dearth of shipping it may be some time before parents of overseas children are able to secure passages to Australia'.[15] The few parents who did arrive in 1946 came as full paying passengers. During that year the United Kingdom and Australian governments agreed upon free and assisted passage schemes to Australia and in December Calwell 'promised that the highest possible priority of travel under these schemes, as well as for ordinary travel, will be accorded to parents of British evacuee children now in Australia and to evacuee children who have been repatriated to the United Kingdom and now wish to return here'.[16] True to his word, when the United Kingdom–Australia Free and Assisted Passage Agreements began operating on 31 March 1947, evacuees and their families were given priority. Evacuees received a letter offering them a free or assisted passage. The offer prompted further emotional turmoil for many evacuees and their families.

Phyllis and Eric Ward anguished over the decision before returning to their foster father in Yass.

> We were getting letters from him saying, 'If you want to come back I would love to nominate you' ... and we were busting to get back ... We knew that whatever we did we were going to hurt someone. We were going to hurt Mum and Dad if we went; we were going to hurt Mr Bridge if we didn't. So it was an agony for some weeks.

Jean Schultz returned alone in 1947 following her parents' indecision about migration. She was unconcerned; her Australian foster family had her love and it was to them she returned. Her parents followed in 1950. Although it was rare for children under sixteen to emigrate alone, Maureen Greening did. At fourteen she returned to the custody of her Australian foster parents, where the abuse continued.

John Hare would readily have accepted the offer had it not been for his mother. His foster parents had been regularly sending letters and food parcels. 'A year or so after I was back they wrote to father offering to look after me. My father asked me but I declined when I saw the look on my mother's face. I would love to have gone.' The loss of her children was a source of continued grief for John's mother. John recalled how upset she became at his writing 'home' under a photo taken in Australia. In later years she would blank out when their father discussed the past with them. Family plans to emigrate never materialised; in 1949, aged sixteen, John returned alone to Australia, against his mother's wishes. Other evacuees declined the offer, claiming 'it would have broken their mother's hearts' if they had left again.[17] Braham Glass' parents even threatened to drop dead.

Audrey Dickenson, who had a very close relationship with her mother, accepted the offer on condition her mother accompanied her. They migrated in 1947. The Australian government's hope that evacuees would be 'ground bait for parents'[18] materialised to some extent. Many parents did migrate to Australia as a result of the evacuation scheme. Some, like Audrey's mother, settled, while others returned to Britain, unable or unwilling to make the necessary adjustments.

By 1947 relationships and other commitments, including national service, kept many evacuees in Britain. For Alan Timmins national service was a welcome relief from the loneliness of being home. On his return Alan had to deal not only with the divorce of his parents, but also with the fact that he had no friends. He was so lonely he would go to the pictures twice on Saturday nights for something to do. When he was called up he volunteered for the navy, and joined the mercantile marine, a career which took him around the world and eventually, in 1964, back to Australia. In 1947 Ken Gregory was locked into an apprenticeship in engineering and had no immediate prospect of emigrating to Australia. 'I saw it as not an urgent thing I had to do, but something in the back of my mind that I would do in the future.' He returned in 1957.

The drift to Australia continued over the years. Derek Simpson recalled the exact moment he made the decision:

The Schultz family fulfilled the hopes of the Australian government that British evacuees would stay in Australia or return to Australia with their families. Mr and Mrs Schultz and their seven children arrived in Sydney on the *Chitral* in September 1949. Rear, left to right: Freda, Rosalie (now Rosalie Schultz, former evacuee), Phillip (also a former evacuee). Middle row, left to right: Elissa, Mr Sidney Schultz, Mrs Kitty Schultz holding Hinda, Sandra (at end). In front, with her father's hand on her shoulder, is Leonie. (Sandra Jacobsohn, from *Sydney Sun*, 8 September 1949)

It was the shortest day of the year ... and this funny round little white thing was just above the horizon and I looked at it and thought, 'Oh yuck!' I was shivering with an overcoat, gloves and things around my ears, trudging through the snow and thinking if I was back in Australia I'd be lying on the beach today.

Australia became home for at least one-third of the evacuees.[19] The others mostly stayed in Britain, although a small number settled elsewhere. Having weathered the initial adjustment they found in Britain the opportunities and lifestyles of their choice, or else became anchored in Britain by relationships or lack of money. Peter Barnard felt that even at thirteen he was rather set in his ways. 'There's something about me that's British and I don't think I'd wanted to change.' Influenced by his educated English foster parents, Donald Mitchell left Australia in 1944 with a stronger appreciation of British culture than when he arrived. After service with the British navy he took advantage of the Atlee Government's generosity to ex-servicemen and studied English at Oxford. Anne Vincent also remained in England. Having readjusted to life there, she said she 'couldn't make the transition again', even if she had wanted to.

Some evacuees wanted no reminders of Australia. Elsie Harding wrote of her brother who spent most of the evacuation years in a boys' home in Sydney: 'My brother would not come back to Australia even for a holiday'. These individuals remain a hidden casualty of the evacuation scheme, their numbers unknown. There are others who, although scarred by ill-treatment, have been able to put the experience behind them and build new lives in Australia. John Templeton who returned in 1949 wrote: 'At that time in history I think this country was the very best in making boys into men one way or the other. I caught a heart bug for Australia and have never been able to get rid of it.' For years Maureen Greening resisted becoming an Australian citizen or calling Australia home. After the way she had been treated as a child she thought, 'Who wants to become an Australian?' Returning from a visit to England in 1980, she remarked to her husband, '"It's lovely to be home." He asked me whether I realised what I had said. I said, "Yes. It's lovely to be home." He said that that was the first time I had ever called Australia home.'

A small number of evacuees opted not to return to Britain. At the end of the war Peggy McLeish was engaged and her wedding organised. Her father's health had deteriorated greatly and through lengthy correspondence her parents advised her to stay: 'There was nothing to go back to'. It was a self-sacrificing suggestion on their part and one she always regretted following.[20] Ted Flowers had no regrets. A student at Sydney University at the end of the war, he saw Australia as home and had no wish to return to England. Ernest Lowe may have been one of the few who neither returned nor saw his family again. His case is surely one of the most pathetic. In 1990 he wrote:

> I have only just found out that all the children had to go home. I was never contacted and I feel very hurt that through someone's neglect I was deprived of the love and home life with my family after the war ended ... I am trying to find out the reason I was overlooked and who is responsible as to this day I have never had anyone come to check why I was still here. I could not afford to pay my own fare home nor could my family.

Child evacuees from the Pacific sometimes joined returning CORB evacuees. Others were reunited in Australia. Andrea Wilson, from the Solomon Islands, was reunited with her parents in Sydney. She found the postwar years with them more difficult than the separation. Her parents had lost everything. Between them, the Japanese and the Americans had flattened the home in Tulagi and destroyed the family's possessions.

> After the war we were always pushed for money because father was over retirement age and the reparations never came through ... I remember the first house we rented for a year. We had no furniture and were sitting on orange boxes and eating off other orange boxes ... I found all that rather difficult, whereas I hadn't found the war difficult ... I didn't find the separation horrific. I thought it was rather fun really, because I had lots of little girls to play with and that to me was a picnic.

Cut off from their gracious colonial life, her parents were lost. 'I suppose we were a rather pathetic family after the war. Father running around sort of cut off, not in his prime — sort of past his prime — and mother making rather heavy weather of being a housewife.' Unable to return to her home in the Solomons, Andrea moved to Denmark, where relatives 'fed [her] on the history of the family's life in the East.' In the late 1940s her parents returned to England where they 'meandered along in bad health, very bad health ... the end was fairly sad ... they never received what they felt they should have received — recognition or reparation ... the old timers still talk about reparations'.[21]

* * *

Being separated from their families and uprooted from their homelands had a lasting effect on all these children. For a small number that effect was overwhelmingly positive; they found in foster families loving relationships they had never experienced in their natural families. The remainder paid various prices for their removal to safety. Being reunited did not wipe out the impact of separation. Reunions rarely fulfilled expectations. More commonly they caused further upheaval and created additional stress. Addressing a conference on Jewish child survivors, historian Martin Gilbert expressed the belief that the problems of children reunited with their families have not been recognised.[22] The stories of children in this book support that belief. There is a myth that reunions lead to 'happy ever after' endings. Reality shows otherwise. In the case of reunited Jewish children the endings were invariably overshadowed by the Holocaust.

Children who were never reunited bear a different burden. For children of Holocaust victims, that burden is intensified by the knowledge that their families were murdered in an horrific act of genocide. Bruno Bettelheim wrote about the difficulty these children had resolving their grief after the Holocaust. Without tangible evidence — even through facts printed in a book — many were never able to give up hope and accept their parents' death. The result has been permanent grieving and the inability to live a normal life.[23] 'The Holocaust pursues us daily,' commented Hermann Levy, a classic example of Bettelheim's finding. 'It is like having a flea in your head.' Although he was told in June 1942 that he was an orphan, Hermann did not know until 1988 how his father had died. The information came through a newspaper article written by an historian in his home town, Rostock.[24] 'My preoccupation with the fate of my sister and parents continued over the decades. I just could not accept the bare statement that they were no longer alive, but needed to know more.' He knew his sister Hannah arrived in Theresienstadt on 25 June 1943 and was transferred to Auschwitz on 19 October 1944 where 'she presumably died on 27 October 1944'. In 1972, through the International Red Cross, Hermann obtained documentary evidence of Hannah's fate and in 1991, through the Rostock archives, discovered she had been adopted by the head of the Rostock Jewish community after his father's death: she was later shipped to Theresienstadt with the remaining 150 Rostock Jews.

Others have learnt to live with the past, focusing on 'the cup that is half full instead of the half empty one'. Yet, more than fifty years later, the wounds still bleed when touched. One interviewee told of how another in later life would phone him daily and cry. '"I've got to release my sorrow somewhere", he would say.' Inge Sadan talked of the 'dividing line between those whose parents did survive and those whose parents didn't. There's a big pain in them — those who didn't know how their parents died. There's a terrible, terrible despair inside them ... I don't think I could have survived mentally not knowing what had happened to my parents ... It's coming home to roost now somehow ... they've got more time now to think and reflect.'[25]

Home remained an elusive place for many former child refugees to Australia. None of the non-British interviewees returned permanently to the countries of their birth, although many have visited, often only in recent years. Israel has continued to attract some. Margot Goldstein believes her identity remained primarily Jewish despite the years in Australia, and later America. She thus felt at home in Israel after her move there in 1955. It also gave purpose to her life. 'As long as you have been saved you want to make your life meaningful.' Betty Abrahamson said she always felt very comfortable about being Australian, but at the same time held to Zionist ideals. After hearing from her brother at the end of the war her resolve to move to Israel strengthened. Betty was the one Larinoite to join the Habonim, and in 1950–51 went on hahsharah, preparation for settlement on a kibbutz in Israel. She made the move in 1952 with her husband, but returned a year later due to his disquiet with kibbutz life. Betty then settled in Perth.

The 1967 war prompted a worldwide movement to Israel. Till then Hermann Levy had felt 'impregnated by everything Australian and British. I was so emotionally involved that I cried at the beautiful ceremony of the coronation of the queen. Being Australian was an anchor in my life ... The turning point was June 1967. At that moment both my wife and I realised that Australia no longer "pulls" us, that our natural place is Israel.' George Perl also moved to Israel about that time, but found 'it was too hard ... I didn't like the way they were doing things there — business, relationships ... I was used to Australian life. So I came back and started again.'

Australia remained home for many who found refuge here as children. Others consider it a second home. Having migrated from America to Israel in the 1980s, Max Nagel said, 'nostalgically after forty-odd years I still feel closer to Australia than to America'. Jack Garbasz agreed: 'When I came here everyone called me an Australian ... Today I consider myself an Israeli, but I have a very fond memory of Australia. I feel a closeness to Australia.' Margot Goldstein is not as enthusiastic. She cannot divorce Australia from her unhappiness at Larino. 'I never thought that I wanted to go back to Australia ... when I talk about Australia I really talk about the home. Actually, that is Australia for me ... I don't have any happy recollections.'[26] Other Larinoites, who broadened their horizons and developed interests beyond the home, do have happy memories and continuing friendships with Australians. Ellen Schaechter, who moved to New York in 1961, remains staunchly Australian. 'I won't give up my citizenship because I feel Australia was there for me when I needed it. It gave me a good education and a sense of fairness and freedom I could not have felt anywhere else.'

It is a tragedy that Ellen was one of so few European children to whom Australia extended such hospitality.

Conclusion

A visit to the Children's Memorial Hall at Yad Vashem is a chilling experience. After descending into a room where three-dimensional photos of children are exhibited, the visitor enters the memorial hall. Five candles give way to an infinite number, symbolising the souls of children who died during the Holocaust. One and a half million Jewish children died during the Nazi regime of terror, victims of the genocidal war against the Jews.[1] The Jewish child survival rate in Poland is staggering — 0.5 per cent of the prewar population.[2] After liberation, child survivors emerged from their hiding places, from the forests, from convents and gentile homes, from spaces where only a child could hide. Most had been orphaned and found neither security nor understanding in the postwar world. 'We were not like others,' wrote one child, who hid for two and a half years in a hay loft. 'No-one else could understand our past. We the children of the Holocaust have been overlooked, our words too faint to be heard. Invisible, we carried our burden in silence and alone.'[3]

Inhumanity towards children during the Second World War was not confined to Jewish children. Gypsy children were also marked for extermination by the Nazis, as were the disabled.[4] Other children became victims of their parents' circumstances — deported from their homelands, abandoned when parents were removed to labour camps, orphaned and interned. Many others were forcibly removed from their families for germanisation. A countless number also became civilian casualties of the war.

Underground networks in Europe worked courageously on behalf of children during the war, although Deborah Dwork claims that most children who survived were helped by personal, familial contacts rather than by organised networks. Since its establishment Yad Vashem has honoured about 10 000 people as 'righteous gentiles' — 'high-minded Gentiles who risked their lives to save Jews during the Holocaust'. These were ordinary men and women who had the strength and moral fortitude to act rightly in the face of Nazi evil. Tragically, they were few, but their deeds are models of human behaviour and their personal qualities deserving of attention. Generally they were 'individualists, independently minded, strong in their sense of selfhood, clear in the moral principles — be they Christian, or humanist, or anti-Nazi, or simply anti-authority. They had the strength to perform great deeds usually against the greatest odds.'[5] The citizens of several European nations — for example, Belgium, Denmark, Bulgaria, Italy — were prominent for helping their Jewish populations. As a gesture for the rescue of Danish Jews, the entire Danish population was included amongst the righteous.

The extent to which the global community could have contributed to rescuing European Jews has been laboriously debated since the Holocaust. Mass extermination began with the German invasion of Russia on 22 June 1941. Judgment of efforts to save Jews from extermination has to be reserved to action after that time, when 'the final solution' became Nazi policy and public knowledge.

Rescue from persecution not extermination

should be central to analysis of responses in the 1930s and early war period. Pressure for refuge mounted during that period. With it came increased efforts to gain permits for children and youth, those who were primarily but not exclusively Jewish. The 1935 Nuremberg laws stripped Jews of civil rights; they also removed education and career opportunities for Jewish youth. Jewish organisations accepted that removal from Germany had become the only viable solution, also that Palestine alone could not solve the problem. A worldwide search for refuge for young people began in earnest. Events of 1938, culminating in Kristallnacht, increased the tempo dramatically. Although the Holocaust was still inconceivable, parents now feared for their children's safety to the extent many became desperate to send away even their very young children. Parents' readiness to give up their children may be the most accurate gauge of the gravity of the situation by 1938. In ignoring their pleas, the nations of the world reneged on any moral responsibility they had to children.

John Fox argues that there is no international morality or 'imperative responsibility' that obliges groups or governments to respond to the fate of specific minority groups in other societies. There is only humanitarianism, which depends on what is politically and practically feasible at the time.[6] Nevertheless, fifty-four nations endorsed the 1924 Declaration of the Rights of the Child, thereby accepting in principle that all children should receive relief and shelter in times of distress. The League of Nations reaffirmed this charter in 1934 and from 1936 the protection of children was the subject of various international meetings and conferences.[7] The distressed situation of European children was well known by 1938, but Britain alone honoured the international agreement by admitting almost 10 000 German and Austrian children between December 1938 and September 1939.

Australia's contribution was dismal — seventeen children under twelve, twenty to thirty fourteen- and fifteen-year-olds. No consideration was given to providing temporary refuge to non-British children. As happened for adults, the Australian government sized them up as immigrants and responded accordingly. Only later, in the face of the Pacific crisis, did the Australian government relax its entry requirements for those in need of refuge. Humanitarianism and morality aside, the response to foreign children seems extremely short-sighted in view of Australia's perceived population needs at the time and the widespread support for child migration. The crisis for European children coincided with a period of intense activity in British child and youth migration to Australia. Paradoxically, while non-British parents were clamouring for refuge for their children, organisations involved with British child and youth migrants were unable to fill their quotas. None apart from the YMCA gave serious consideration to including the persecuted children or youth of continental Europe in their schemes. Nor did the Australian government encourage them to do so.

The response of the Australian government to foreign children illuminates its attitude to refugees generally. Arguments against the admission of large numbers of refugees centred firstly on the economic disadvantage they would impose on Australian workers, and secondly on the undesirability of allowing group settlement. Neither argument held true for children. Children posed little threat to the Australian workforce; furthermore, if large numbers had entered they would almost certainly have been dispersed across Australia into families or group homes. Opposition to children was primarily on the grounds of their potential to begin a chain of unwanted foreign migration.

The churches and voluntary organisations share the responsibility for Australia admitting so few children. Among them, the Australian Jewish Welfare Society was by far the most active and powerful lobby group. Having been formed at the request of the Commonwealth government, it worked closely with government officials and helped shape government policy toward refugees. While much criticism has been levelled at the Welfare Society and the established Jewish community for their attitudes towards refugees, far less attention has been paid to the inertia of other religious groups.

Fear of anti-semitism and the threat to their social and economic status prevented the majority of established Jews, especially the highly anglicised Sydney community, from agitating for the admission of large numbers of refugees. Nevertheless, as Hilary Rubinstein points out, through its cautious and conservative position the Welfare Society retained the trust of the Commonwealth government. A more radical approach may have undermined that trust and the cooperation it generated.[8] Paul Cullen rationalised the situation, claiming that, as Australians, established Jews did not understand what was happening in Nazi Europe.[9] Despite regular visitors representing refugee organisations in London and numerous first-hand accounts from refugees, Australian Jews seem to have grasped neither the urgency nor the magnitude of the crisis. As he campaigned for the Kimberley scheme, Isaac Steinberg remarked on the apparent apathy of the Jewish community:

> Do not millions of our nearest and dearest, our parents and our children, face at present dire danger in Europe? Is not the world wide press filled with descriptions of their fears and sufferings? Is not each issue of every Jewish paper or magazine wet with hot blood and tears of our own kith and kin whom from afar address to us heart-rending cries for pity? And yet, Jewish life in this country goes on complacently and undisturbed. What is the explanation? It seems to me that the reason of it is that the Australian Jew has not yet grasped two important things. He does not yet grasp the magnitude of the disaster in Europe and he does not yet feel how great could be his own help for his tortured brethren.[10]

Failure to understand the situation and its urgency characterised the Welfare Society's response to unaccompanied children. When finally they began negotiating with the government for a child quota, Welfare Society officials talked in terms of orphans. They had not grasped that children going to England in kindertransports were not orphans, but children whose parents were so desperate to find refuge they were willing to send them away alone. The government weighed this factor heavily. When it agreed in March 1939 to include 750 children in the 15 000 quota for refugees, it insisted the children be orphans. This restriction, together with an age limit of seven to twelve years, made filling the quota impossible. While there were orphans in Germany and Austria, it was the action of parents which secured children a place on a kindertransport. Who else had the time or commitment to organise the many documents required by children leaving Germany or entering Australia?

Only when it realised young orphans were not available did the Welfare Society try to negotiate some flexibility into the government offer. In the meantime, there was no urgent attempt to fill the 1939 quota for 250 children. Having been informed of its quota, the Sydney branch of the Welfare Society embarked on a building program rather than a rescue mission. Nor did any of the branches attempt to find guarantors or foster homes, an essential move if large numbers of children were to be admitted.

The outbreak of war interrupted attempts to remove children from Germany and German-occupied Europe, yet negotiations conducted during 1940 suggest that, even if war had been averted for another six or twelve months, few children would have entered Australia. With strict adherence to children under twelve, preferably younger, to children who were fully Jewish and to children without parents, it is unlikely that even siblings of the Larino children would have followed.

During the war, when it did grasp the magnitude of the disaster in Europe, the Jewish community became more committed and united in its efforts to help.[11] When the opportunity arose in 1944 to rescue Hungarian Jews, the Jewish Advisory Board of Australia, representing a cross-section of the Jewish community, urged the government to issue permits for 3000 adults and 5000 children.[12] The Australian Jewish Welfare Society had also by then indicated its readiness to care for thousands of children if only the government would help financially.[13] The Australian government, unlike many others, offered no financial support for refugees, children or adults. This had a crippling effect on the efforts of all Australian refugee organisations.

Although plans for postwar child migration included both British and non-British children, the Australian government continued to distance itself from child rescue during the war. It granted the Australian Jewish Welfare Society 150 permits in 1943, and another 150 in 1944, but there was little compassion in the offer. All children had to be guaranteed by the Welfare Society, which launched a massive fund-raising appeal to support the admission of the children. The 300 permits were used by OSE-ORT to guarantee the entry of children into Switzerland until transport could be arranged. Although none of the children came to Australia,[14] the availability of the permits was a definite contribution to child rescue. Nevertheless, given that the Australian government knew by then of Nazi atrocities, the offer seems to have been more a cautious gesture of goodwill toward the Welfare Society than a serious attempt to help children. The official response to admitting 700 Polish Catholic children in 1944 further reflects the government's indifference to the plight of non-British children, regardless of religion and despite a growing interest in them as future immigrants. Although the request was for temporary refuge, fully funded by the Polish government, the Australian government refused to admit the children on the grounds a new Polish government might not honour the agreement; furthermore, Australian officials were concerned over implications if the children later applied to stay but were deemed unsuitable as immigrants.

Nicolas Winton commented that for Australia to have become involved in child rescue there needed to be an organisation to arrange the movement, with an agent to arrange the European end, agreement that Australia would take the children, arrangements for their welfare when they arrived, and money to pay for transport and maintenance. All these mechanisms were put in place for British children in 1940.

The government response to British children in 1940 provides a stark contrast to that given non-British children. Despite the temporary nature of overseas evacuation, the Australian government saw the evacuation scheme as potentially a migration scheme. It hoped many of the children would stay in Australia and that families would join them. This was in direct opposition to the stance taken on parents of non-British children whose very existence led to those children being excluded. In its enthusiasm, the Australian government offered to fund the entire overseas evacuation scheme — passages and maintenance, initially for 5000 children but ultimately for as many as the British government could send.

The Australian public rallied, genuinely wanting to help children and seeing the fostering of an evacuee as a useful contribution

A fifty year reunion in Melbourne, 1989, for some of the twenty men who came to Australia through the Polish Jewish Relief Fund. Seated, left to right: Aleck Katz, Jack Schwartz, Jonas Pushett, Alwin Spiegel. Standing, left to right: Norman Schindler, George Perl, Max Goldberg, Werner Teitel, Syd Miller, Max Juni. Jonas Pushett, who was instrumental in arranging for the boys to come to Australia, died in Melbourne in 1994. Jack Schwartz died in 1990. (Jonas Pushett)

to the war effort. Many offers indicated a willingness to take a child regardless of nationality. This supports the belief that, given the opportunity, many Australians would have responded compassionately to refugee children needing asylum. They were never asked. The Commonwealth government and the Australian Jewish Welfare Society had a stranglehold on decisions about refugee children; neither consulted the Australian public. Recent refugees, those who had greatest understanding of the situation in Europe, were also refused a voice and the opportunity to receive refugee children into their homes. Although attitudes of Australians toward refugees were generally lukewarm, Isaac Steinberg showed the extent to which public sympathy for foreign refugees could be aroused. Through tireless work and his dynamic personality, Steinberg drummed up support for the Kimberley scheme across Australia, amongst politicians, church leaders, unionists, agriculturalists and the general public. Support spread across all sectors of the Christian churches, at the highest levels. Ironically, both the Jewish establishment and Zionists condemned and lobbied against the scheme, a stance which probably influenced the Commonwealth government's decision not to approve it.[15] Had someone with Steinberg's commitment and magnetic appeal campaigned on behalf of children it is probable he could have harnessed the support of powerbrokers in all sectors of the community and developed a non-denominational committee along the lines of that formed in England. There is every reason to believe Australians would have responded, as had the British, to an appeal to help children and would have guaranteed children or absorbed them into their homes. There is less reason to believe either the Jewish establishment or the Commonwealth government would have supported such a movement. Even in later years the Welfare Society was opposed to placing children in refugees' homes. Placement in gentile homes was never considered. In England, the Refugee Children's Movement regularly placed Jewish children with gentile families. The priority was rescue. Many children survived as a result, although their spiritual lives often suffered.

Although the Children's Overseas Reception Board made efforts to include a cross-section of British children in the overseas evacuation scheme, that cross-section related only to the socio-economic status of families. Children who were not white, Anglo-Saxon and able-bodied were not included. Jews and Catholics were also restricted to a percentage of the total number of evacuees. Those most in danger from an invading German army were either excluded or given no priority — Jewish children, black children, disabled children and children of political activists opposed to Nazism.

Only 577 British children arrived in Australia before Britain suspended the evacuation scheme in September 1940. Australia hoped for a resumption and clamoured for this even after the *City of Benares*' disaster and the later loss of many escorts returning from Australia to Britain.[16] Australia's readiness to place children's lives at risk supports the belief that the interests of children were not foremost in the minds of government officials who promoted the scheme. Gaining British immigrants and cementing Empire ties were the priorities. Acknowledging that many evacuees would be only temporary guests, a deal was made that future sailings would include a quota of children for Fairbridge Farm schools. The political motives of Britain in setting up CORB later received considerable attention. The political motives of Australia were never examined.

The motives of parents were a different matter. With few exceptions, British parents in 1940, like those in Germany, Austria and elsewhere before the war, sent their children away to protect them. The decision was not made lightly. It was brave, well-intentioned and certainly not absurd.[17] There is a tendency for former British evacuees to ignore the context within which parents made that decision and to pass a superficial and subjective judgment on overseas evacuation. Many question the wisdom of the scheme and their parents' motives. This is surely a case of being wise after the fact. The threat of invasion should be central to any judgment of overseas evacuation. This was the context within which British parents made their decision. Had the invasion occurred, evacuees' assessment would almost certainly be quite different.

Removal overseas spared children suffering and saved lives, but it was not without a price. Despite their various backgrounds, the loss of family emerged as a unifying theme in the stories of these children, even of those reunited with their families. More than fifty years after leaving their families, interviewees spoke of the immediate and lingering effects of their separation and after-care. The two are finely interwoven, the nature and quality of substitute care invariably affecting the overall experience. Age and maturity at separation, previous family experiences and trauma, and individual temperament also greatly influenced how each child responded to the situation. Separation from family was complicated by other separations — from homeland, from familiar cultural and social worlds and sometimes from foster families and other attachments formed after leaving home.

Although the moment of parting left an indelible image in the memories of many children, it was frequently more stressful for parents than for children. Many children had little warning or understanding of what was happening. They believed they were going on a short holiday, an adventure. It was a time for fun, and they puzzled over displays of emotion by parents and better informed older siblings. Both British and German parents tended to confide in their older children, regardless of age, and withhold information from younger children. Eight-year-old Joan Hodgson had no idea she was going to Australia and chastised her older sister for crying. Edna Lehmann recalled asking her nine-year-old sister, "'Why's mummy crying? We're going on a picnic." I was sort of laughing and she said, "Shut up, Edna!"' A relative later told Betty Abrahamson that at the Berlin railway station "You just wanted to go off and play with the other children. Even in those last few minutes you didn't want to stay with your mum.' From Betty's point of view there was no reason to be upset. 'My mother had said, "You're going on a holiday to Australia" ... I thought that was terrific ... I was pretty happy.' Betty compared her naivety to that of another nine-year-old, Margot Goldstein:

> I remember as clear as anything ... when we left Bremen we were in the same cabin ... I remember we looked through the porthole and everyone was waving. And she was crying and crying. I was smiling and happy. I said, 'Why are you crying? We're going on a big adventure.' She had been told ... perhaps she was just more aware than I.

Margot's letters, included in earlier chapters, confirm her maturity and level of understanding. Children like her, in whom parents had confided, and those who had been exposed to Nazi brutality, especially the humiliation or removal of family members, had more cause to worry. Even so, they were often comforted by the promise that siblings and parents would follow them to Australia.

Adolescents generally were better informed of circumstances surrounding their departure. Many of the fourteen- and fifteen-year-old Polish boys initiated their own emigration. Partings were emotional, but hopeful. Emigration offered them a unique opportunity and a chance to help their families escape from poverty and oppression. Many British adolescents, on the other hand, did not choose to leave. They saw no purpose in their evacuation, other than to care for younger siblings or relatives, and resented their parents' decision.

While some children remained buoyed by the prospect of adventure, homesickness subdued much of the initial excitement. A day out from Liverpool ten-year-old Ken Gregory, an only child, recalled how alone he felt amongst the hundreds of children on the *Batory*. 'I remember sitting there at the concert ... in a big crowd on my own and thinking about what my mother and father would be doing at home.' Crying and bed-wetting were common as young children faced daily life without the physical presence and comfort of parents. Peer pressure sometimes encouraged self-control in older children. Ellen Schaechter recalled telling another child on the *Orama* to stop crying. 'I told her to be quiet because we all missed our families. It was considered cruel of me, but I thought it made sense to let her know she was not alone.' Despite these anxieties, parents had not been wrong when they described the journeys as picnics and holidays. New experiences and adventures were plentiful, treats were laid on and children, especially the British, were accorded celebrity status at ports of call. Overall, the journeys were happy occasions, albeit long and tiring, and the children arrived in Australia excited about what would happen next.

Having arrived at their destinations they went into a variety of care arrangements — foster care, group homes, independent living with or without guardians, and boarding schools. With few exceptions, the 577 British evacuees went into the homes of Australian families. It was a well-conceived, though quickly executed, plan and acknowledged the importance of family to children's well-being. While thousands of Australians had offered their homes to evacuees, only 27 per cent of the children went initially to those families. The remainder were placed with relatives. The fact that many of those placements broke down cannot be blamed entirely on the Australian relatives. Only 4 per cent of those relatives formally applied to take the children. Most of the children were unofficially nominated — parents had provided the names of relatives but not necessarily confirmed their readiness to receive the children. In many cases, cables were exchanged and agreements reached. Even so, decisions were made hastily at the Australian end. Some relatives heard through child welfare officials, usually only weeks before the children's arrival, that they had been nominated. While many relatives welcomed the opportunity, others refused or took the children under duress. Many had neither the financial means nor space to accommodate an extra child or, in many cases, several children. Children moved on quickly from some of these homes; others stayed unhappily with uncaring relatives for the duration of the war.

About 60 per cent of evacuees stayed in their first placements for the duration of the war. Pressures of war and changing circumstances of families caused many moves. Children's behaviour caused others. Mismatches were inevitable but most children settled down when moved to another family. Sheila Hammond, who went first to relatives, was typical of many.

> It was not a good association and I became somewhat unruly after a few months. I was eventually thrown back into the pool and allotted to an English couple doing their 'war duty'. They had two older daughters, one only thirteen months older than I. The following four years were the happiest of my then life. I ended up calling them Mum and Dad and

Jack and Shulamith Garbasz in Israel, 1990. Jack went to Israel in 1948. Shulamith was already in Palestine when the state of Israel was declared. Having survived three Nazi concentration camps, she moved to Palestine and joined the infant state's army. In the independence war against the Arabs she was the only female 'rifleman' among those who held the hills around Jerusalem. Jack died in 1995. (Jack Garbasz)

Hans Eisler at home in Sydney, 1994. With his passion for rugby, cricket and trade unions, Hans quickly made Australia home. (Bob Anderson)

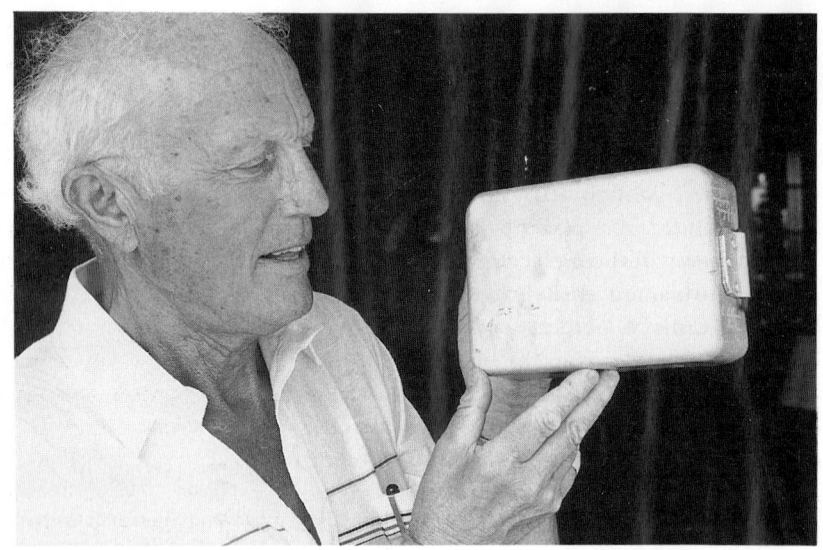

Max Nagel in Israel, 1993. Max left Australia for America in 1946, rejoining what remnants of his family remained after the Holocaust. He and his wife, Nita, moved to Israel in 1983. The mess kit Max is holding was engraved and decorated for him by other POWs in Japan. (Bob Anderson)

loved them till their deaths many years later. My foster father even paid for my fare back to them after my twenty-month return to England.

Some evacuees went through many moves, but a move was unquestionably better than leaving a child in an unhappy environment. Children who eventually found a happy placement seem not to have experienced any long-term harmful effects from their moves whereas those who stayed in unhappy placements are filled with sad, sometimes bitter, memories.

The most successful placements were those where children were wanted and were absorbed into the family. Children generally reciprocated by forming new attachments. These were often at the expense of former bonds, but that was the price parents paid for their children's safety. As Jean Schultz commented, 'If you send a child away in the formative years you take the risk of losing the affection of your child'. That risk cannot justify the withholding of love. Studies of unaccompanied children conducted during World War Two found children under four could not retain emotional links to their parents beyond a one or two month period.[18] The period increased with age, yet even in school-aged children intellectual memory and affectively charged images of parents often became vague and shadowy within about a year.[19] Young children not able to form new attachments were thus left in an emotional limbo, clinging to fading memories of family and sometimes recreating an idealised image of the family to whom they longed to return.

In contrast, adolescents were more able to divide their loyalties, developing new relationships while retaining the old. At the same time, many had no wish for new family attachments. As Max Nagel commented, 'I knew in my mind that I had plenty of family support, though they were not around ... I couldn't see when I had parents and brothers, even though they weren't close by, that I wanted somebody else to become a substitute parent.'

The guardian scheme was a very successful model of care for Max and the other Polish boys. These fourteen- and fifteen-year-olds arrived with few expectations but with a strong resolve to be self-supporting and to help their families. The support they received matched their needs and aspirations. It gave them security while allowing them to develop independence. While living in the Jewish community of Carlton the Polish adolescents were also able to maintain a link with the past. Regular letters from home during the early period also helped in this regard. Adolescents in the Welfare Guardian Society's scheme had less emotional support. Located in rural Victoria, most had infrequent contact with both their guardians and the Jewish community. Nevertheless, the Australian Jewish Welfare Society devoted considerable time and money to the education and care of these adolescents, especially in their first twelve months in Australia.

A variety of studies collated by Ressler, Boothby and Steinbock found that adolescents often react to family separation by becoming depressed, moody, withdrawn, more aggressive and by developing psychosomatic problems such as headaches and stomach aches.[20] These descriptors apply more to British evacuees than they do to the non-British adolescents who came to Australia. The stress of living in foster care may have contributed to this.

British adolescents often had a difficult time settling into foster homes. Geoffrey Bilson also found this among evacuees in Canada,[21] Kathryn Close in America[22] and Susan Isaacs within Britain.[23] The problem extended to many other evacuees as they reached puberty and struggled through adolescence with foster parents whose standards and expectations sometimes differed greatly from those of their natural parents.

Conflict with family is normal in early adolescence. In families that weather the storm well, parents have a sympathetic understanding of their child established over years of living together; the adolescent in the relationship has a clearly defined set of parental standards, values and beliefs to challenge. Without a shared past, foster relationships that begin in adolescence are likely to be difficult for both foster parents and children. Successful relationships for British adolescent evacuees in Australia occurred when foster parents set limits and offered guidance, but allowed adolescents to make decisions affecting their lives. Mutual trust and friendship often followed. Unfortunately, many foster parents took their duty of care so seriously and exerted such strict control over their adolescent charges that relationships were fractious. Life for adolescent evacuees in caring but excessively strict homes improved as they joined the work force or the armed services. Relationships with their foster parents also tended to improve after that, sometimes becoming quite close.

Group homes or boarding schools may be preferable alternatives for adolescents over fourteen who cannot settle with foster families. Susan Isaacs found the behaviour of older adolescents within England improved when they were placed in group settings, especially when accompanied by other siblings, friends or familiar teachers.[24] Kathryn Close found a similar outcome among older adolescent evacuees in America when they went to boarding school and were provided with a 'sponsor' family whom they visited during holidays and at weekends. The success of the Polish scheme also supports this arrangement. All these examples emphasise the continued need for support and protection throughout adolescence, but the importance of making that support relevant to the needs and maturity of young people. Unaccompanied adolescents who had no support after their arrival in Australia were extremely vulnerable to abuse and exploitation. Some like Hans Eisler were able to remove themselves to safety. Others, even those over sixteen, sometimes suffered years of hardship and loneliness.

Group care did not provide the sustained individual care required by the young German children who came to Australia. Although children who grew up in the Larino home received adequate physical care, overall their social and emotional needs were not met. Ellen

Lewinski summarised the situation described by many of the children: 'We were fed adequately. We were dressed, sure, in second-hand clothes, but we were dressed. We were educated. We were looked after if we were sick. And yet there was a desolation because there was no love. There couldn't be'. In times of stress all children, even adults, reach out for the physical comfort and closeness of family. Despite the kindness and efforts of staff, the Larino children had to adapt to life without this support.

> At times when you weren't feeling well you'd think it would be nice to go to mummy and say, 'I've got a tummy ache' and cry on somebody's shoulder, but there was really nobody to go to. You just had to say, 'I've got a tummy ache', and wait for the doctor to come. There was no mollycoddling ... We got used to being on our own.[25]

Jo Lehmann expressed their common need: 'We wanted someone to hug us and kiss us.' In time they learnt to hide their worries and sadness about absent parents, but in the quiet of night many poured out their grief privately.

Without the support of families, the self-esteem and self-confidence of many children suffered. Being German, Jewish and a refugee was cause for any child's self-esteem to take a battering in the 1930s and '40s. Massive doses of positive reassurance were needed to counteract the negative messages bombarding them both in Germany and Australia. The warm and supportive environments provided by the Fixels and Mr Carter, the principal of Balwyn State School, were important buffers in the early days. The emphasis placed on Jewish education must also have reassured the children that some aspects of their identity at least were valued. Nevertheless, the overwhelming message they received was one which devalued their past and admonished them to assume a new identity, one which encompassed Judaism, but demanded that they be 100 per cent Australian. The Australian Jewish Welfare Society and the women's committee which controlled Larino were insensitive to the children's needs in their pursuit of this goal. Expectations of gratitude and frequent reminders to the children of their refugee status exacerbated the situation and left many Larinoites with bitter and unhappy memories of their days at the home. As adults, most concede the Jewish community was well-intentioned, but ignorant of their needs as children and adolescents.

As a result some children developed behaviours related to low self-esteem and self-confidence — blushing, stammering, excessive embarrassment when asked to perform in front of others, shyness. Misbehaviour was a not uncommon response of older boys. The Larino girls recalled adolescence as a particularly difficult period, a time when they were extremely self-conscious. Ellen Lewinski commented:

> We stood out in a crowd and we didn't stand out as fashion models. We stood out as the orphanage children ... it's not a high status, it's a low status, and I think it affected us all ... It would have been better if they'd made less effort to involve us in social functions in those sensitive teenage years. The committee had us mix with their children who were beautifully dressed ... and we were in second-hand clothes that looked it ... We had to go to synagogue looking drab, and then to be taken to social functions without the proper clothes made us the butt of teasing ... It would have been better to arrange social functions with people more like us ... I used to be so shy I'd spend all my time with the mothers helping to get the supper ready ... At the end of every function we were given food to take home. That singled us out too.

Adolescence marked the end of school and the beginning of work. In many cases, especially for the boys, the Larino adolescents

CONCLUSION

Larinoites came from around the world to attend a fifty-year reunion in Melbourne in 1989. Men in back row, left to right: Richard Dreyfus, Alfred Stocks, George Dreyfus, Hermann Levy, Laurie Badrian, Harry Bader. Women in middle row, left to right: Ellen Rothschild Shafer, Ellen Schaechter Ostrower, Jo Lehmann Weinreb, Ingrid Ehrlich Naumberger, Margot Goldstein Herschenbaum, Ursula Kaye Meyerstein, Marion Ehrlich Paul (behind Ursula), Ellen Lewinski Anderson. Women in front: Paula Kochen Boltman, Betty Abrahamson Midalia, Frances Kochen Rothschild, Ilse Frank Saunders. Missing: Edna Lehmann Samson, Herman Gold (now Larry Gould) and Hedi Fixel. (Ellen Lewinski Anderson died in 1992, Alfred Stocks in 1996.) (Hedi Fixel)

were forced into careers not of their choosing. Many left their options open by attending night classes, and later pursued tertiary studies and careers related to earlier aspirations and expectations. A few closed off their options and live with regret. This seems not to have been a particular problem amongst other adolescent evacuees and refugees. Most of the British evacuees felt their career opportunities were enhanced by coming to Australia; many also expected and wanted to leave school at fourteen. Poles, Germans and Austrians who arrived as adolescents generally saw themselves as responsible for making their own way. The Polish adolescents, for example, happily accepted menial jobs at first, but only as stepping stones to something better. They kept all their options open, grasping opportunities as they presented. Military service opened up further opportunities for most of them.

The Larino children developed various strategies for coping with the stresses of separation and life at the home — absorbing themselves in school work and reading, finding support from available adults — the matron, the cook, the Hebrew teacher. Strong bonds also developed among the children, especially among the girls. These bonds have withstood the test of time, providing friendship and support not available to children who went into foster care.

Temperament was an important factor in determining how all children coped with separation and other stressful experiences. Outgoing, extroverted children were better equipped to handle less than ideal care

George Dreyfus, at home in Melbourne. George is well known as a musician and composer. (Bob Anderson)

Hedi Fixel whose intellect, good humour and wisdom remain impressive despite her physical frailty. Hedi lives in Hobart where she moved with her husband, Ferry, in 1941. Ferry died in his nineties in 1990. (Bob Anderson)

arrangements; they were more likely to have the social skills required to form friendships and interests beyond the care situation. They found outlets in sport, school and other people. Shy and difficult children generally lacked these skills and were more vulnerable to the effects of inadequate care. Through interviews, letters and documents it was possible to see the dispositions and personalities of many children at the time of leaving home. Invariably the withdrawn, the extroverted, the happy, the worried child who emerged through these was present in the adult I interviewed. Although basic temperaments seem not to have changed, insensitive treatment had a profound effect on the lives of more vulnerable children.

Previous family practices and experiences also continued to influence children after their arrival in Australia. Children who were secure but independent at the time of separation were better equipped to handle life without their parents. These findings are consistent with other research on separated children. At a conference of directors of children's villages, held in Switzerland after the Second World War, D. Rey commented on how older children who had once enjoyed family warmth and whose parents had encouraged independence, possessed qualities which helped their recovery from family loss:

> A child's past history plays an important part in his adjustment. Certain fundamental aspects of character and personality are formed in infancy. A child who has had ideal parents and a long history of family affection, will suffer a great deal for a certain length of time from the disorganisation caused by war, but nevertheless possesses values and habits that in the long run will facilitate his adjustment, especially if his early upbringing has taught him to rely on himself.[26]

Young children, and often younger siblings, generally had less opportunity and potential to develop buffers such as independence and a strong sense of self before being separated. Inadequate aftercare had a profound and lasting effect on many of them, especially where it was compounded by other stressful experiences.

The end of the war brought new stresses to most children, many of whom were by then young adults. For many Jewish children the loss of immediate family was total. The devastation of the Holocaust becomes comprehensible when its effect is seen on the lives of this small number of children. Its effect lingers in their daily lives — the absence of extended family, for some unresolved grief and guilt, for others a deep sadness beneath a calm and controlled demeanour.

Loss of a different nature occurred for many children reunited with their families. The excitement of the homecoming or reunion was often shattered as children and parents faced each other over an abyss of five, sometimes eight or more, years apart. 'Eight years for a grown-up is nothing,' commented Jo Lehmann, 'but for a child it is. I was almost nine when I got to Australia and I was seventeen when I came here [to Israel]. I was a different person'. Parents and children had both changed in the years apart. Parents seemed old and small. Harsh wartime experiences had wrought other scars. Patricia Greening expressed the views of many when she said, 'I couldn't say my family were my family any more'. Parents experienced the same feeling as they tried to resume relationships with children who no longer behaved like their children. Many parents could not make the adjustment and treated their adolescents like the young children who had left home many years before. Many were overbearing and intrusive, wanting to regain the lost years. Not all reunions failed but, across the range of refugee and evacuee children who came to Australia, this was the most common scenario. The reunions were often more stressful than the initial parting and separation. They were complicated by attachments to people and places which had developed during the years in Australia.

Successful reunions occurred where natural bonds were strong, especially where friendship and interdependence existed between child and parent; these were more likely to be mother and daughter relationships and seem often to have been forged in the absence of a husband and father. Because of their strong bonds, separation had been hard for these children, though many seem to have endured it stoically. Regular communication also helped with later reunions. Letters and occasional photos enabled children to retain links with their past and enabled both parties to adjust to the changes of ageing and development. Older children had an advantage in this regard, being able to read and write comprehensive letters. Young children lacked the skills, and often interest, to engage in regular correspondence and were dependent on adults or older siblings to retain this link with home. Children from Germany and German-occupied Europe generally had no opportunity to exchange information with parents after war was declared. Letters and Red Cross messages told little; they were mainly signs of life and expressions of love and hope.

The question of separation remains vexed. It is an extreme measure and can only be recommended in extreme circumstances. Those circumstances existed in prewar Nazi Germany and in many neighbouring countries. The need intensified and extended to many other children during the war years. Australia could have provided a haven to many European children but, while it flung its doors wide open for British children, it refused entry to all but a handful of non-British children. Nevertheless, Australia's official response should not detract from the well-intentioned efforts of the many individuals who helped unaccompanied children who did arrive in Australia in this period. Nor should any ill-effects of separation

At home in England, 1993. Above: Peter Barnard. Below: Anne Vincent Lowden. (Bob Anderson)

and inadequate after-care detract from the courageous behaviour of parents in sending away their children. In making this decision parents generally put their children's interests before their own. Surviving letters reveal the anguish of parents in making that decision, and their grief over their lost children. Freda Morgan, one of three children from her family evacuated to Australia, summarised the position: 'My father was doing what was right for us. He was not doing what was right for him'.

The principle of placing children's rights and interests above those of parents should guide decisions on separation. Where separation is warranted, providing appropriate alternative care becomes the critical issue. The experiences of these children show that when supportive and nurturing substitute care is provided, children can survive separation remarkably well. Some even benefit from it. On the contrary, separation without good after-care can be disastrous. Ideally, that care should be in a family environment, although for older adolescents other arrangements may be preferable. In emergencies, group care may also be inevitable. The reflections of these former child refugees suggest group care can be successful if it strives to replicate home life as closely as possible — small child-staff ratios; competent, caring male and female staff; opportunities for children to have regular social contact with children and adults outside the group home, including links with families who will provide each child with satisfying family experiences. Regardless of the nature of the care, regular monitoring of placements, and children's involvement in that process, are essential.

The rights of children seeking refugee status, and those of all children temporarily or permanently deprived of their families, are now enshrined in Article 22 of the United Nations Convention on the Rights of the Child, adopted in November 1989:

1. States Parties shall take appropriate measures to ensure that a child who is seeking refugee status or who is a refugee in accordance with applicable international or domestic law and procedures shall, whether unaccompanied or accompanied by his or her parents or by any other person, receives appropriate protection and humanitarian assistance in the enjoyment of applicable rights set forth in the present Convention and in other international human rights or humanitarian instruments to which the said States are Parties.

2. For this purpose, States Parties shall provide, as they consider appropriate, co-operation in any efforts by the United Nations and other competent intergovernmental organizations or non-governmental organizations co-operating with the United Nations to protect and assist such a child and to trace the parents or other members of the family of any refugee child in order to obtain information necessary for reunification with his or her family. In cases where no parents or other members of the family can be found, the child shall be accorded the same protection as any other child permanently or temporarily deprived of his or her family environment for any reason, as set forth in the present Convention.

Although the Convention has more clout than the 1924 Declaration of Geneva, it remains for governments to enact it through legislation. Guidelines on the entry of unaccompanied children to Australia are vague. The now-defunct Comprehensive Plan of Action (CPA) endorsed by Australia in 1989 has largely dictated Australia's response to unaccompanied children in recent years. This action plan was developed through international collaboration to resolve the flow of refugees from Vietnam and Laos. Through the CPA, the Australian Department of Immigration and Ethnic Affairs discouraged the entry of unaccompanied minors, many of whom since the 1960s have died in horrific circumstances while fleeing their countries or have been severely traumatised by witnessing horrific events. Special cases are admitted where a committee has determined 'resettlement in Australia is in the minor's best interests'.[27] This nebulous rider, used constantly throughout the Convention on the Rights of the Child, inevitably paves the way for subjective decision making, usually by adults about what they consider are the best interests of the child.

Fear that children will be used as anchors for family migration seems to underpin the Department of Immigration's response to unaccompanied children. This position bears remarkable similarity to 1930s regulations which barred unaccompanied refugee children with living parents. For those children, Australia's refusal to admit them was a death sentence.

Immigration in the 1990s is vastly more complex than it was in the 1930s and '40s, but it is hoped that lessons learned from the Second World War will be heeded in the development and implementation of future regulations. Children continue to be victims of ethnic and political violence; many also become perpetrators. So much so that aid agencies such as Save the Children have refocused on 'children at war' as a priority. Reuniting separated children with their families and caring for those orphaned by war have become central to their work. The appalling situations of so many children in former Yugoslavia, Rwanda and other theatres of war have refocused debate also on the voluntary removal of children in emergencies.

The separation of children from their families is now widely regarded as abhorrent. The unjustified removal of many children, including Aboriginal children and British child migrants, has left many people in Australia with a bitter legacy. But has the pendulum swung too far? This study reaffirms that family is central to children's well-being, but claims removal from natural families is at times both necessary and desirable. It acknowledges that children can be deeply and adversely affected by the experience, but stresses that separation alone is not the cause. What precedes and follows separation are equally important. The final word is reserved for those whose coming to Australia as unaccompanied children meant survival. Unanimously they agree that Australia acted rightly in admitting them, not only on a personal level, but in terms of Jewish survival. They lament the fact that so few children, including their siblings, had that opportunity.

SUMMARY INFORMATION ON ARRIVALS OF CHILDREN AND YOUTH

Port of Arrival	Date	From	Number in Group	Number Under 16	Details
Sydney Melbourne	Various April to Dec. 1938	Germany	44	?	31 Jewish boys and 13 Jewish girls, 15-17 years, who arrived in small groups
Melbourne	15 May 1939	Germany & Austria	20	5	Jewish boys, 15-19 years, sponsored by the Welfare Guardian Society, Melbourne
Melbourne	28 May 1939	Poland	20	17	Jewish boys, 14-16 years, sponsored by the Polish Jewish Relief Fund, Melbourne
Sydney	19 July 1939	Germany	21	1	Jewish boys/youths and girls, 15-28 years, from Gross-Breesen farm in Germany, sponsored by the Australian Jewish Welfare Society, Sydney
Melbourne	23 July 1939	Germany	17	17	Jewish children, 7-12 years, sponsored by the Australian Jewish Welfare Society, Melbourne
Sydney	26 July 1939	Germany & Austria	16	1	Boys/youths of various denominations, 14-22 years, sponsored by the German Emergency Fellowship Committee (Society of Friends)
Fremantle Melbourne Sydney	9 October 1940 14 October 1940 16 October 1940	England, Scotland & Wales	477	477	British children, 5-15 years, evacuated though the Children's Overseas Reception Board (CORB), a government scheme, arrived on the *Batory*
Fremantle Melbourne Sydney	13 October 1940 20 October 1940 24 October 1940	England & Wales	82	82	Second group of British evacuees, arrived on the *Nestor*
Fremantle Adelaide	13 November 1940	England	18	18	Third group of British evacuees, all boys, 10-14 years, arrived on the *Diomed*

German and Austrian boys sponsored by the Jewish Welfare Guardian Society, Melbourne.
Arrived in Melbourne on the *Jervis Bay*, 15 May 1939

The Australian Jewish Welfare Society regularly changed the names of refugees when they arrived in Australia. The new name is given in brackets. Fifteen of these boys came from Germany, five from Austria.

* indicates brother follows in list

Name	(New name)	Age	Name	(New name)	Age
Ansbacher, Manfred	(Anson)	17	Jachmann, Hans	(Harry Jackman)	17
Apt, Gunther	(Upton)	16	Kahn, Alfred	(Cann)	17
Bacharach, Paul	(Baxter)	17	Kammermann, Egon	(Edgar Kasmer)	15
Baron, Werner	(Barton)	15	Lustig, Fritz	(Fred Lester)	16
Bauer, Fritz	(Bower)	15	Neumann, Rudolf	(Robert Newman)	19
Bernstein, Manfred*	(Berns)	15	Reiner, Heinz	(Raynor)	17
Bernstein, Rudolf	(Berns)	16	Riese, Gunter	(George Rees)	17
Dreifus, Otto	(Drayton)	15	Schustick, Otto	(Sherwin)	17
Elsoffer, Werner	(Eltham)	19	Simon, Hans		16
Halberstadt, Rudolf	(Robert Halbert)	16	Trangott, Kurt	(Charlie Trainor)	17

Sources: Inward passenger lists – ships, AA (Vic) CRS B4 397/X3.

Boys from Poland, sponsored by the Polish Jewish Relief Fund, Melbourne.
Arrived in Melbourne on the *Oronsay*, 28 May 1939

Name on arrival		Age	Home
Bialostocki, Izrael	(Bill Baker)	15	Baranovicz, nr Brest, Poland
Ball, Stanislaw	(Stanley Ball)	15	Borislav, SE Poland
Eitinger, Zygmunt	(Sigmund Ettinger)	14	Dortmund, nr Essen, Germany
Garbasz, Jankiel	(Jack Garbasz)	14	Sarny, Poland
Getzler, Leopold	(Leon Getzler)	15	Berlin, Germany
Goldberg, Mejev	(Max Goldberg)	14	Brest, Poland
Jaffe, Siegfried	(Sigi Jaffe)	16	Berlin, Germany
Juni, Maksymilian	(Max Juni)	15	Dortmund, nr Essen, Germany
Kac, Ela	(Aleck Katz)	15	Rokitno, nr Sarny, Poland
Klitenik, Szymon		15	Telechan, nr Brest, Poland
Laffelholz, Marcus	(Max Loftus)	15	Cologne, Germany
Midler, Israel	(Syd Miller)	15	Brest, Poland
Nagelberg, Max	(Max Nagel)	15	Hamburg, Germany
Perelsztejn, Gdala	(George Perl)	16	Milacze, nr Sarny, Poland
Poczter, Michael	(Michael Porter)	14	Brest, Poland
Schindler, Norbert	(Norman Schindler)	15	Essen, Germany

Spiegel, Alwin		16	Wattenschied, nr Essen, Germany
Szejnfeld, Edward	(Max Sheinfeld)	14	Hamburg, Germany
Szwarc, Icko	(Jack Schwartz)	15	Wytkowicze, nr Berezno, Poland
Teitel, Werner		14	Herne, nr Essen, Germany

Note: All boys from Germany were born in Germany, but were Polish nationals by virtue of their fathers' nationality. All had been deported to Zbonszyn in Poland at the time of leaving for Australia. Age relates to age on arrival in Australia. All boys were under sixteen when their Australian permits were issued in February 1939. Nine were then fourteen.

Sources: Inward passenger lists - ships, AA (Vic) CRS B4397/X3; also A434: 41/3/1039. Aleck Katz assisted with name changes and home locations. Note that Brest is also known as Brzesc-on-Bug (Polish), Brisk (Yiddish) and Brest-Litovsk.

YOUNG REFUGEES FROM THE GROSS-BREESEN FARM IN GERMANY. ARRIVED IN SYDNEY ON THE *STRATHALLAN*, 19 JULY 1939

		Age	
Auerbach, Rudi		19	
Bacharach, Erick	(Eric Baker)	16	
Born, Herbert		15	
Cohn, Hans		17	
Cohn, Herbert	(Herco Cohn)	17	
Cohn, Siegbert	(Robert Cohen)	18	
Czollek, Franz	(Frank Shelley)	19	
Danziger, Kurt	(Fred Danby)	19	disembarked Melbourne
Flaschner, Hanna		19	
Gasiorowski, Klaus	(Frank Jenner)	19	disembarked Melbourne
Hanf, Peter		17	
Immerwahr, Fritz		17	disembarked Melbourne
Jonas, Siegbert	(John Siegbert)	28	
Kaminsky, Herbert		18	disembarked Melbourne
Pikarski, Werner		17	
Pollnow, Hermann	(Harry Peters)	18	disembarked Melbourne
Radinowski, Erwin	(Erwin Radd)	16	
Rosenbaum, Inge		16	
Schiftan, Leo		16	disembarked Melbourne ★
Stranz, Guenther	(George Strong)	17	disembarked Melbourne
Wachsmann, Gerhard	(Harold Winston)	17	

At least six other Gross-Breeseners, all aged over sixteen, arrived in Australia before the outbreak of war:

Sabine Fertig
Hans Goldman (Clive Hastings)
Ilse Redlich (Ilse Howard)
Heinz Leschinsky (Henry Liner)
Peter Wolf (Peter Wilmont)
Gert Zussmann

RELUCTANT REFUGE

Fred Fabian, a young teacher at the Gross-Breesen farm, also arrived before the outbreak of war. Several other Gross-Breeseners, who went to Kenya before the war, migrated to Australia in the 1950s.

★ According to Herco Cohn, Leo Schiftan remained one of the New South Wales group. If he disembarked in Melbourne it was to visit relatives.

Sources: Herco Cohn; K269/6 Perth passenger lists and C1115/6 Sydney passenger lists 1923-1964. Wolfgang Matsdorf, *No Time to Grow*, p. 81, gives the total number who arrived before the end of 1939 as thirty-three.

GERMAN JEWISH CHILDREN SPONSORED BY THE AUSTRALIAN JEWISH WELFARE SOCIETY, MELBOURNE.
ARRIVED IN MELBOURNE ON THE *ORAMA*, 23 JULY 1939

★ indicates brother or sister follows in list

		Age	Home†
Abrahamson, Betty	(Betty Midalia)	9	Berlin
Badrian, Lothar	(Laurie Badrian)	7	Berlin
Dreyfus, George ★		10	Berlin
Dreyfus, Richard		12	Berlin
Ehrlich, Ingrid ★	(Ingrid Naumberger)	10	Muhlhausen
Ehrlich, Marion	(Marion Paul)	9	Muhlhausen
Frank, Ilse	(Ilse Saunders)	10	Berlin
Goldwasser, Herman	(Larry Gold)	11	Berlin
Goldstein, Margot	(Margot Herschenbaum)	9	Berlin
Lehmann, Traute ★	(Jo Weinreb)	9	Berlin
Lehmann, Edna	(Edna Samson)	7	Berlin
Lewinski, Ellen	(Ellen Anderson)	9	Berlin
Levy, Hermann		10	Rostock
Rohrstock, Alfred	(Alfred Stocks)	7	Berlin
Rothschild, Ellen	(Ellen Shafer)	9	Kassel
Schneider, Rolfe	(Rolf Taylor)	8	Berlin
Schaechter, Ellen	(Ellen Ostrower)	10	Berlin

† where family lived at the time child emigrated. As a result of Nazi persecution, some families had moved to these larger centres during the 1930s.

Sources: Inward passenger lists - ships, AA (Vic) CRS B4397/X3. Laurie Badrian, Paula Boltman, Ursula Meyerstein and Ellen Shafer also contributed information for this list.

APPENDICES

GERMAN EMERGENCY FELLOWSHIP COMMITTEE GROUP.
ARRIVED IN SYDNEY ON THE *ORAMA*, 26 JULY 1939

Fifteen of the group were classified as non-Aryan Christian and were nominated by the German Emergency Fellowship Committee (Society of Friends). The other, Hans Eisler, was a Jewish boy whose older brother in England may have organised his inclusion in the group.

	Age	Home Country		Age	Home Country
Adler, George	19	Austria★	Merz, Kurt	18	Austria
Alter, Charles	19	Austria	Muenz, Kurt (Kieth)	18	Austria
Broh, Heinz	18	Germany	Marx, Ullrich	22	Germany
Englander, Godfrey	17	Austria	Nossal, Tommy	18	Austria
Eisler, Hans	14	Austria	Rieger, Gert	16	Austria
Kranz, Raoul	17	Austria	Schussler, Kurt	19	Austria†
Kornfeld, Jodok	17	Austria	Stein, Ernst	16	Austria
Lang, Franz	16	Austria	Ulmer, Herbert	18	Austria

★ Formerly from Czechoslovakia   †Italian nationality

BRITISH CHILDREN EVACUATED FROM BRITAIN TO AUSTRALIA IN 1940

The children arrived in three parties – 477 on the *Batory*, 82 on the *Nestor* and 18 on the *Diomed*. Before embarking, each child received a numbered disc, to be worn at all times. The children's names are set out below in order of these numbers. Where an evacuee participating in the research has changed his or her name, the current name appears in brackets.
★ indicates brother or sister follows in list.

Children arriving on the *Batory*

87 HARRIS, Eleanor, 15, Barry ★
88 HARRIS, Melvin, 13, Barry ★
89 HARRIS, Reginald, 10, Barry ★
90 HARRIS, Ruby, 7, Barry
91 MATTHEWS, Margaret, 15, Barry
92 DAVIDSON, Frederick, ?, Bridlington
93 SCHULTZ, Phillip, 6, Hull ★
94 SCHULTZ, Hester, 5, Hull
    (Rosalie Tobin)
95 BROWN, Joan, 11, Birmingham
97 DEELEY, Betty, 12, Birmingham ★
98 DEELEY, Philip, 14, Birmingham
99 JONES, Sheila, 7, Swinton
100 HAWLEY, Anthony, 10, Barnoldswick
101 SALT, Albert, 12, Birmingham
102 SPINKS, Iris, 9, Birmingham ★
103 SPINKS, George, 7, Birmingham ★
104 SPINKS, Joan, 5, Birmingham

106 BRENNAND, Anthony, 13, Blyth
107 BROWN, Evelyn, 11, Blyth
110 PATTERSON, Elsie, 9, Blyth ★
111 PATTERSON, Jean, 13, Blyth
112 PATTERSON, Rita, 8, Blyth
113 WOODS, Francis, 12, Blyth
114 WOODS, Isabella, 11, Blyth
    (Isabella Summerbell)
115 BULLEN, Donald, 9, Liverpool
118 DUFFY, Francis, 13, Bradford
119 FAREY, Doreen, 12, Bradford
120 FETHNEY, John, 13, Bradford ★
121 FETHNEY, Michael, 9, Bradford
122 FIELD, May, 14, Bradford
123 HARDISTY, Helen, 13, Bradford ★
124 HARDISTY, Ian, 10, Bradford
125 LANGDALE, Keith, 15, Bradford
126 LEE, Allan, 12, Bradford

127 METCALFE, Kenneth, 15, Bradford
128 RUSSELL, Jack, 13, Bradford
129 STANWAY, Robert, 14, Bradford
130 WEBSTER, Derric, 9, Bradford *
131 WEBSTER, Catherine, 7, Bradford
134 LITTLE, Phyllis, 14, Cardiff *
135 LITTLE, Isobel, 11, Cardiff
136 JONES, Lewis, 12, Cardiff *
137 JONES, Lillian, 7, Cardiff
140 THOMAS, Denis, 12, Cardiff
141 WILLIAMS, Dorothy, 11, Cardiff
142 COLE, Jean, 15, Grays
143 CORNISH, Patricia, 10, Loughton
144 COX, Gerald, 9, Chelmsford *
145 COX, David, 8, Chelmsford
146 DIXON, Joan, 11, Chelmsford
147 LAMBLEY, Winifred, 10, South Benfleet*
148 LAMBLEY, James, 5, South Benfleet
149 SOLE, Kathleen, 12, South Benfleet
150 BOWCOCK, Arnold, 13, Colchester
151 BURRELL, Dennis, 14, Colchester *
152 BURRELL, Trevor, 10, Colchester
153 CAPPS, Victor, 13, Colchester
154 GRAY, Michael, 9, Colchester
155 HADDOCK, Vernon, 7, Colchester
156 WARD, Michael, 15, Colchester
157 WIGHT, Richard, 12, Colchester *
158 WIGHT, Rex, 10, Colchester
159 WHITTEN, David, 13, Southall
160 WILKINSON, Sidney, 12, Colchester *
161 WILKINSON, Philip, 12, Colchester
166 BAKER, Dulcie, 14, Darlington *
167 BAKER, Arthur, 10, Darlington
168 BELL, Margaret, 8, Darlington
169 COOPER, Launa, 9, Darlington
173 WILLIAMS, Doreen, 10, Manchester
174 KERSHAW, Evelyn, 11, Darlington
175 LUPTON, Nora, 9, Darlington
176 McLEISH, Margaret, 14, Darlington
 (Peggy Cox)
177 SIMPSON, Jean, 12, Darlington
178 SNAITH, Sheila, 13, Darlington *
179 SNAITH, Noreen, 12, Darlington
180 THOMPSON, Sylvia, 8, Darlington
181 ANSELL, John, 11, Doncaster *
182 ANSELL, Julie, 9, Doncaster
183 HIGGINBOTTOM, Geoffey, 8, Doncaster

184 HOGARTH, Stanley, 10, Doncaster *
185 HOGARTH, Betty, 9, Doncaster
186 HOWARTH, Brenda, 13, Doncaster
187 LOXTON, Joan, 7, Doncaster
188 SMITH, Geoffrey, 9, Doncaster
189 WARD, Eric, 11, Liverpool *
193 WARD, Phyllis, 13, Liverpool
 (Phyllis Thatcher)
190 FLOWERS, Edward, Edward, 13,
 Chester-le-Street
191 HOLMES, Violet, 12, Newcastle-on-Tyne
192 ROBINSON, Rosemary, 13, Middlesborough*
194 ROBINSON, Lilian, 8, Middlesborough
195 TEMPLETON, John, 11, Hartlepool
196 WILLIAMS, Marie, 13, Newcastle-on-Tyne
197 ASCOTT, Kenneth, 12, Greenford
198 BERNARD, Robert, 10, Hanwell
199 BYFORD, Iris, 12, Hanwell *
200 BYFORD, Lawrence, 7, Hanwell *
201 BYFORD, Maureen, 7, Hanwell
202 COLES, Richard, 13, Greenford
203 GIBSON, Janet, 9, Wycombe Marsh *
204 GIBSON, Robert, 9, Wycombe Marsh
205 GRANT, Olive, 13, Northolt *
206 GRANT, Roy, 10, Northolt
207 GREENING, Patricia, 13, Northolt *
 (Patricia Duffy)
208 GREENING, Terence, 14, Northolt *
209 GREENING, Shaun, 9, Northolt *
210 GREENING, Maureen, 7, Northolt *
 (Maureen Norling)
211 GREENING, Dominic, 6, Northolt
213 HILL, Patricia, 8, W. Ealing
214 HILLIER, Frank, 13, Hanwell *
215 HILLIER, John, 12, Hanwell
216 JOHNSON, Robert, 12, Greenford
219 OWEN, Roderick, 8, Greenford
220 ROSS, Gordon, 13, Hanwell
221 SAUNDERS, Stella, 8, Ealing
222 WOOLLEY, John, 11, Hanwell
225 BARKER, Derek, 9, Enfield
226 HARKNESS, Deirdre, 12, Enfield
227 HENRY, John, 7, Enfield *
228 HENRY, Pamela, 6, Enfield
235 BERTRAM, Doreen, 13, Durham *
236 BERTRAM, Robert, 10, Durham
237 CLOUGH, Greta, 10, Gateshead

APPENDICES

239 LAIDLER, Margaret, 13, Felling
240 SIMPSON, Derek, 13, Gateshead
241 STONE, Lillian, 13, Felling
242 TIMMINS, Alan, 11, Gateshead
243 WAUGH, Wilfred, 13, Gateshead
244 WEATHERBURN, Peter, 7, Gateshead
247 BRYDGES, Mary, 12, Grimsby
248 BUDDERY, Leonard, 10, Grimsby
249 CORMACK, Kenneth, 11, Grimsby
250 CUCKSON, Peggy, 13, Grimsby
252 SMITH, Iris, 13, Grimsby
253 SMITH, Nan, 14, Grimsby *
254 SMITH, Sheila, 14, Grimsby
261 BARRETT, Edward, 13, Hull
262 BORRILL, Herbert, 10, Hull
263 CRAWFORD, Brenda, 10, Doncaster
264 FARROW, John, 12, Hull
265 GOODFELLOW, Rita, 12, Hull *
266 GOODFELLOW, Barbara, 10, Hull
267 SCARBOROUGH, Jean, 9, Hull
268 TAYLOR, Maurice, 13, Hull
271 WHYTE, Cynthia, 10, Ilford
272 BARTON, Patricia, 11, Carisbrooke
273 EEDLE, Donald, 12, Sandown
274 KENCHINGTON, Agnes, 12, Newport
275 PENNY, Michael, 14, Undercliffe *
276 PENNY, David, 12, Undercliffe *
277 PENNY, Margaret, 9, Undercliffe
278 PIGGOTT, Bernard, 8, Freshwater
279 TOWNSEND, Norman, 13, Newport
280 WHILLIER, Jean, 14, Gatcombe *
281 WHILLIER, Joan, 12, Gatcombe
282 ALEXANDER, Joseph, 11, Canterbury
283 ANDREWS, Elizabeth, 12, Leeds *
284 ANDREWS, Audrey, 13, Leeds
285 BELMAR, Leon, 15, Eltham
286 BOWMAN, Terence, 8, Welling
287 BRIANT, Joyce, 14, Ashford
288 CLOUT, Jacqueline, 12, Ashford *
289 CLOUT, Yvonne, 10, Ashford *
290 CLOUT, Alan, 9, Ashford
291 COLEMAN, John, 12, Bexley *
292 COLEMAN, Frederice, 10, Bexley *
293 COLEMAN, Anthony, 8, Bexley
294 PERREN, Doreen, 12
295 DEACON, Joan, 7
296 EDNEY, Frank, 14, Tonbridge

297 GALE, Audrey, 9, Edenbridge *
298 GALE, Shirley, 9, Edenbridge
299 GOLLOP, Joyce, 11, Bexley
300 HADAWAY, Bernard, 13, Sittingbourne
301 HANSON, Frederick, 12 *
302 HANSON, Richard, 10 (* 304)
303 WALSHAM, Doris, 11, Liverpool
304 HANSON, Derek, 5
305 HARRIS, Geoffrey, 5, Bexley Heath *
306 HARRIS, David, 11, Bexley Heath
307 LLOYD, Verna, 13, Bromley *
308 LLOYD, Clarice, 11, Bromley
309 LOFT, Dorothy, 15, Bromley *
310 LOFT, Reginald, 13, Bromley
311 PACKMAN, Betty, 13, Ashford
312 PARRETT, Joan, 15, Sevenoaks
313 PEMBERTON, Leo, 11, Bromley
314 PUXTED, Robert, 14, Tenterden
315 ROACH, Yvonne, 9, Welling
316 ROSE, Arthur, 12, Dartford *
317 ROSE, Jean, 6, Dartford
318 SMITH, Anthony, 13, Glasgow
319 WASTELL, George, 14, Mottingham *
320 WASTELL, Alan, 13, Mottingham *
321 WASTELL, Edna, 11, Mottingham *
322 WASTELL, Colin, 7, Mottingham
323 SHARP, Joan, 6, Pendlebury
324 WHITTAKER, Patricia, 13, Orpington
335 COATES, Alan, 11, Leeds *
336 COATES, Dorothy, 13, Leeds
337 JONES, Magaret, 13, Manchester
338 CLARKE, Patricia, 14, Liverpool *
339 CLARKE, Billie Diana, 11, Liverpool
340 HARDCASTLE, Shirley, 7, Leeds
341 HARDCASTLE, Harry, 11, Leeds
342 HELLIWELL, Barbara, 9, Leeds
343 MACDONALD, Jessie, 15, Leeds
344 MORRIS, Irene, 8, Leeds
345 RATCLIFFE, Annie, 9, Leeds *
346 RATCLIFFE, Phyllis, 14, Leeds
    (Phyllis Holdsworth)
347 CARTHEW, Roland, 13, Peckham
348 COHEN, Sidney, 14, Hackney *
349 COHEN, Ralph, 12, Hackney
350 DICKENSON, Audrey, 12, Charlton
    (Audrey Watson)
351 GLASS, Essie, 13, E1 *

352 GLASS, Braham, 7, E1
353 GOLDRING, Pamela, 6, E5
354 HOUGHTON, May, 13, E3
355 McGINTY, Patricia, 8, Liverpool
356 JEFFREY, Alan, 10, SE9 ★
357 JEFFREY, Brenda, 9, SE9
358 KEEN, William, 5, N16
359 LEWIS, John, 6, W. Kensington
363 MILLS, Teresa, 13, Blackwall
364 NOAH, Rachel, 12, W. Kensington
365 PALLIS, Elsie, 11, Dalston, E8 ★
366 PALLIS, Patricia, 9, Dalston, E8
367 POTTER, Theresa, 14, SE18
368 RANDALL, June, 13, N16 ★
369 RANDALL, Howard, 10, N16
371 SCHULTZ, Jean, 10, E1 (Jean Saltzman)
372 STEVENSON, Cyril, 14, W6
373 STROUD, Joan, 10, SW7
374 WATERS, Kenneth, 8, SW1
377 AUSTIN, Laura, 13, Newcastle-on-Tyne
378 GRAHAM, Dorothy, 13, Newcastle-on-Tyne
379 HUDSON, Valerie, 5, Newcastle-on-Tyne
380 QUINN, Robert, 13, Newcastle-on-Tyne
381 SMITH, Joan, 6, Newcastle-on-Tyne
382 STEPHENSON, Robert, 9, Belford, Northumberland
383 TRIGG, Charles, 13, Newcastle-on-Tyne★
384 TRIGG, William, 12, Newcastle-on-Tyne
385 BARRETT, George, 13, Dereham ★
386 BARRETT, John, 12, Dereham
394 BROWNE, Ann, 8, Norwich
395 KNIGHTS, Ronald, 12, Norwich
396 POWELL, Elizabeth, 11, Merthyr Tydfil
397 BARRETT, Norman, 13, Plymouth
401 HOOK, Laura, 13, Port Talbot ★
402 HOOK, Trevor, 11, Port Talbot
403 DWYER, Patrick, 11, Romford
404 KERSHAW, Rosemary, 7, Romford ★
405 KERSHAW, Judith, 6, Romford ★
406 KERSHAW, Anna, 5, Romford
407 PROCTOR, Elizabeth, 13, Gidea Park, Essex ★
408 PROCTOR, Andrew, 5, Gidea Park, Essex
413 DINGWALL, George, 14, Sheffield ★
414 DINGWALL, Audrey, 12, Sheffield ★
415 DINGWALL, Kenneth, 8, Sheffield ★
416 DINGWALL, Yvonne, 6, Sheffield
417 LOWE, Kathleen, 11, Sheffield
418 SLINGSBY, Joseph, 9, Sheffield ★
419 SLINGSBY, Sheila, 6, Sheffield
420 STACEY, Jack, 14, Sheffield
421 STEVENS, Geoffrey, 11, Sheffield
423 FUDGE, Judith, 6, Southampton
424 HOLWAY, Eileen, 10, Portsmouth
427 WILLIAMS, John, 9, Southampton ★
428 WILLIAMS, Jean, 7, Southampton
430 DUFF, Irene, 14, South Shields ★
431 DUFF, Laura, 12, South Shields
432 STAFF, Denis, 11, South Shields ★
433 STAFF, Heather, 9, South Shields
434 THOMPSON, Godon, 14, South Shields
435 CLAMPS, Stanley, 11, Stockton
436 COLLINS, George, 15, Stockton
437 DAWSON, Theresa, 8, Stockton ★
438 DAWSON, Marie, 7, Stockton ★
439 DAWSON, Peter, 6, Stockton
441 WALTERS, Vera, 10, Liverpool
442 HANDYSIDE, Sylvia, 10, Stockton
443 HARVEY, Ronald, 15, Stockton
444 MACAULAY, John, 12, Stockton
445 RILEY, William, 8, Stockton
446 SHUTE, Charles, 9, Sheffield
451 BOARD, Joyce, 13, Swansea
452 BUDGEN, Gerald, 12, London
456 PERKINS, Rosina, 12, Tottenham ★
457 PERKINS, Albert, 10, Tottenham
458 WHEATLEY, Eileen, 8, Tottenham
459 GREGORY, Kenneth, 10, Willesden
460 TWEED, Leonard, 11, NW10
461 ASH, Douglas, 14, Wimbledon
462 HEATH, Patricia, 13, Wimbledon ★
463 HEATH, Derek, 12, Wimbledon
464 JUDD, Arthur, 8, Wimbledon ★
465 JUDD, Douglas, 10, Wimbledon
466 McCAPPIN, Joan, 14, Wimbledon
467 SHARPE, David, 12, Wimbledon
470 LOCKWOOD, Roger, 12, York
471 RICHARDSON, Terence, 11, York
472 VARLEY, Robert, 10, York
473 EVANS, Muriel, 10, York
474 SPELLER, John, 8, York
475 STOUT, Freda, 13, York
476 YOUNG, Raymond, 14, Hessle ★
477 YOUNG, Julia, 12, Hessle ★
478 YOUNG, Albert, 7, Hessle

480 PAGE, Jean, 14, Middlesborough
481 RUSSON, Christine, 11, Redcar ★
482 RUSSON, Doreen, 7, Redcar
483 SKINNER, James, 13, Thornaby ★
484 SKINNER, Rhoda, 11, Thornaby ★
485 SKINNER, William, 9, Thornaby
486 WILSON, Ruth, 13, Sunderland
487 FOGGAN, Blanche, 12, Blyth ★
488 FOGGAN, Joseph, 10, Blyth ★
489 FOGGAN, June, 8, Blyth
490 LAST, Henry, 12, Brightlingsea
491 DOMMERSON, Kenneth, 13, Rayleigh
492 CHAMBERS, Kathleen, 12, Liverpool
493 STONE, Geoffrey, 14, Manningtree ★
494 STONE, Michael, 12, Manningtree ★
495 STONE, Philip, 9, Manningtree
496 BISHOP, Ronald, 10, Hornchurch
497 DRAKE, Pauline, 15, Tollesbury
498 HUMBER, Leslie, 13, Romford ★
499 HUMBER, Geoffrey, 10, Romford
500 HARE, Peggy, 13, Hornchurch ★
501 HARE, Betty, 12, Hornchurch ★
502 HARE, Joan, 10, Hornchuch ★
503 HARE, John, 7, Hornchurch
504 BUNDOCK, Trevor, 8, Thundersley
505 BLAKEMAN, Charles, 13, Birmingham
506 ROBINSON, Philip, 14, Birmingham
509 DONALD, George, 13, Bishop Auckland★
510 DONALD, Barbara, 11, Bishop Auckland★
511 DONALD, Harry, 10, Bishop Auckland (514)
512 HARDING, Elsie, 12, Billingham ★
513 HARDING, George, 10, Billingham
514 DONALD, Martha, 13, Bishop Auckland
515 WEEKS, Leslie, 14, Durham
516 RUDGE, Raymond, 13, Gateshead ★
517 RUDGE, Alan, 8, Gateshead
518 MUNRO, Joseph, 14, Tyneside ★
519 MUNRO, Charles, 9, Tyneside
520 WINDER, Terence, 10, Bristol
522 WALKER, David, 13, N21
524 HIBBERT, Edwin, 9, Teddington
525 LANG, Benedict, 12, Ashington
526 DIXON, Charles, 12, Whitton, Middlesex
527 LE GROS, Daphne, 14, Teddington
528 EDWARDS, Eileen, 12, Hampton
529 VINCENT, Anne, 11, Hampton
(Anne Lowden)
531 RUMENS, Terence, 10, Wembley ★
532 RUMENS, Geoffrey, 10, Wembley
533 EDKINS, Peter, 11, Hayes, Middlesex
534 DOUGHTY, John, 15, Holloway
535 URSELL, Marjory, 11, Hampton
536 PALMER, Pamela, 14, Harrow
537 BURROW, Enid, 7, Salford (see 552)
538 TONGE, James, 13, Wembley ★
539 TONGE, Anthony, 10, Wembley ★
540 TONGE, Michael, 6, Wembley
541 PLENTY, Anthony, 7, Wembley
542 BULLARD, Robert, 8, Wembley
544 WIX, Dennis, 13, Teddington
545 STOREY, Roy, 15, Teddington ★
547 STOREY, Michael, 8, Teddington
548 TOFT, Philip, 6, Ruislip
549 FARQUHARSON, Paul, 12, Ashford ★
550 FARQUHARSON, Reginald, 10, Ashford
552 BURROW, Marion, 11, Salford
554 PIPER, Kenneth, 9, Edgeware
555 ROGERS, Anthony, 9, Twickenham ★
556 ROGERS, David, 6, Twickenham
563 DAVIES, Cyril, 12, Walsall ★
564 DAVIES, Philip, 10, Walsall
565 COOPER, Douglas, 11, Walsall
566 MITCHELL, Albert, 13, Walsall
567 COCKER, Donald, 9, Oldham
733 MALLETT, Brenda, 9, Raynes Park
3501 FERN, Lloyd, 12, Dundee
3502 HERD, Ian, 11, Methil ★
3503 HERD, Andrew, 9, Methil
3504 KILPATRICK, George, 10, Burnbank ★
3505 KILPATRICK, Emerson, 8, Burnbank (see 3563)
3506 LAUGHLAN, Samuel, 11, Bellshill ★
3507 LAUGHLAN, Duncan, 8, Bellshill
3510 RUNDLE, Douglas, 8, Motherwell ★
3511 RUNDLE, Gregor, 12, Motherwell
3512 SCOTT, John, 14, Ayr
3513 BARCLAY, Robert, 13, Edinburgh
3514 BRALSFORD, David, 7, Edinburgh
3515 CRUDDAS, John, 13, Enfield
3516 GLASIER, William, 8, Edinburgh (see 3545)
3517 MACKIE, David, 8, Edinburgh ★
3518 MACKIE, Walter, 9, Edinburgh
3519 McINTYE, Peter, 13, Edinburgh
3520 NICHOLSON, William, 13, Edinburgh

3521 ROBERTSON, George, 12, Edinburgh ★
3522 ROBERTSON, William, 10, Edinburgh
3523 ROBERTSON, William, 10, Leith (see 3553)
3524 SMITH, David, 12, Edinburgh
3525 VALVONA, Ralph, 9, Edinburgh
3526 AITCHISON, Thomas, 14, Dumbarton
3530 HILL, Ian, 9, Glasgow
3531 HOOPER, Brian, 9, Johnstone
3532 LAIRD, John, 8, Glasgow
3533 MILLAN, William, 11, Glasgow
3534 McDONALD, Ramsay, 10, Glasgow (see 3578, 3579)
3535 McNEIL, Thomas, 11, Glasgow
3536 PATERSON, Samuel, 12, Baillieston
3537 TIERNEY, Albert, 11, Glasgow
3538 TURNBULL, Robert, 12, Glasgow
3539 WIGG, Arthur, 9, Glasgow (see 3599)
3540 YOUNG, Andrew, 10, Glasgow
3541 BLANCHE, Adina, 11, Edinburgh ★
3542 BLANCHE, William, 7, Edinburgh
3543 CAMERON, Sheila, 14, Edinburgh
3545 GLASIER, Dorothy, 11, Edinburgh
3546 LAW, Annie, 14, West Calder
3547 PATERSON, John, 5, Glasgow ★
3548 PATERSON, Margaret, 9, Glasgow
3549 RENNY, Mabel, 7, Arbroath ★
3550 RENNY, Maureen, 8, Arbroath
3551 RICHARDSON, Elizabeth, Edinburgh
3552 ROBERTSON, Constance, 12, Edinburgh ★
3553 ROBERTSON, George D, 5, Leith
3554 SINCLAIR, Margaret, 7, Edinburgh
3555 TROTTER, Margaret, 11, Edinburgh
3556 CUTHBERT, Helen, 9, Glasgow ★
3557 CUTHBERT, Katherine, 7, Glasgow
3558 FARMAN, Harriet, 12, Bridge of Don
3559 GOUGH, Christopher, 6, Edinburgh
3560 HOOPER, Kathleen, 11, Johnstone ★
3561 HOOPER, Winifred, 5, Johnstone (see 3531)
3562 HOWE, Ethel, 12, Glasgow
3563 KILPATRICK, Margaret, 7, Bunbank
3564 LOW, Helen, 5, Dundee
3566 MILLAN, Terence, 7, Glasgow (see 3533)
3568 SOMERVILLE, Isabella, 12, Rutherglen
3569 TIERNEY, Joseph, 6, Glasgow (see 3537)
3570 WYLLIE, Jessie, 10, Mauchline
3578 McDONALD, Mary, 14, Glasgow
3579 McDONALD, Margaret, 12, Glasgow
3580 McINTYRE, Mary 11, Edinburgh (see 3519)
3581 SWAN, Ruby, 9, Leith
3583 VALVONA, Caroline, 6, Edinburgh (see 3525) ★
3584 VALVONA, Doreen, 13, Edinburgh
3585 WALKER, Janet, 8, Edinburgh
3586 BARTON, Roberta, Glasgow
3587 CUNNINGHAM, Annie, 10, Glasgow ★
3588 CUNNINGHAM, Esther, 7, Glasgow ★
3589 CUNNINGHAM, Isabella, 12, Glasgow
3590 LAUGHLAN, Jeanie, 10, Bellshill (see 3506, 3507) ★
3591 LAUGHLAN, Jessie, 14, Bellshill
3592 MACKIE, Lois, 10, Glasgow
3593 MILLER, Mary, 13, Glasgow
3595 McINTYRE, Rachel, 10, Glasgow
3596 McNEIL, Jessie, 12, Glasgow (see 3535)
3597 ROSS, Irene, 12, Cambuslang
3598 TIERNEY, Agnes, 12, Glasgow (see 3537, 3569)
3599 WIGG, Elizabeth, 7, Glasgow
3600 WILLIAMSON, Nessie, 11, Glasgow
3601 WHITE, Margaret, 10, Bonnybridge
3602 FULLERTON, Jack, 9, Glasgow ★
3603 FULLERTON, Marion, 14, Glasgow ★
3605 DAVIDSON, Annie, 13, Glasgow ★
3606 DAVIDSON, Margaret, ?, Glasgow
3607 GAIRDNER, William, 12, Glasgow
3610 OSWALD, John, 6, Edinburgh
3611 YOUNG, Grace, 11, Edinburgh
3612 CREEVY, Charles, 8, Glasgow ★
3613 CREEVY, Mary, 11, Glasgow
3614 GRAVIL, Sydney, 14, Glasgow
3720 BOYD, Ross, 12, High Burnside

Children arriving on the *Nestor*

138 RICHARDS, Ruth, 12, Cardiff ★
139 RICHARDS, Barbara, 11, Cardiff
1982 VOS, Kenneth, 12, Harrow ★
1983 VOS, Theodora, 14, Harrow
1984 FREEBORN, Mary, 13, Wimbledon ★
1985 FREEBORN, John, 9, Wimbledon
1986 GUTHRIE, Donald, 13, Liverpool
1987 MACLAGAN, Robert, 9, Chertsey ★
1988 MACLAGAN, Ian, 10, Chertsey ★
1989 MACLAGAN, Catherine, 12, Chertsey ★
1990 MACLAGAN, Sheila, 14, Chertsey.
1991 BIRTWISTLE, Shirley, 5, Stockport
1992 HIGGINS, John, 8, Stockport
1993 FAGEN, William, 8, Cheadle Hulme ★
1994 FAGEN, Arthur, 5, Cheadle Hulme
1995 HUME, Peter, 11, Manchester
1996 CHADWICK, David, 10, Stockport
1997 WILLIS, John, 13, Stockport
1998 GARNER, Jack, 12, Manchester ★
1999 GARNER, Ann, 6, Manchester
2000 KENYON, Charles, 10, Stockport
2001 SCOTT, Florence, 13, Stockport
2002 ELLIS, Leonard, 13, Manchester ★
2003 ELLIS, Alan, 9, Manchester
2004 ORWIN, Joan, 11, Cheadle
2005 JAMES, Geoffrey, 9, Stockport
2006 ECCLES, George, 12, Stockport
2007 JONES, Janet, 6, Stockport
2008 EMBLING, Barbara, 15, Stockton
2010 MANNING, Dulcie, 9, London
2011 VICKERY, John, 5, Tiverton
2012 BESWICK, Audrey, 14, Oldham
2013 BARNARD, Ernest, 13, Ealing ★
 (Peter Barnard)
2014 BARNARD, Margaret, 9, Ealing
2016 JENKINS, Gwyneth, 12, Bury St Edmunds
2017 BOOCOCK, Joan, 10, Bradford ★
2018 BOOCOCK, Clarice, 13, Bradford
2021 WATKINSON, Roger, 10, Thornton Heath
2022 REED, Martin, 11, Banstead ★
2023 REED, Derek, 9, Banstead
2024 O'DOWD, Pamela, 15, Surbiton
2025 CLEWES, Mary, 13, Orpington
2027 HAMMOND, Sheila, 11, Tolworth
 (Sheila Slight)
2028 TILLMAN, Robert, 13, Mortlake
2029 STANDAGE, Brenda, 12, N. Cheam ★
2030 STANDAGE, Norman, 9, N. Cheam
2031 MINTER, Beryl, 10, Purley (Beryl Smith)
2032 EDWARDS, Derek, 11, Worcester Park
2033 LOWE, Ernest, 13, Coulsdon
2035 PAWSEY, Derek, 8, N. Cheam ★
2036 PAWSEY, Sylvia, 12, N. Cheam ★
2037 PAWSEY, Peter, 6, N. Cheam
2039 WATTS, Hilary, 13, Epsom
2040 MORAN, John, 10, Mitcham
2041 HEDGECOE, Kathleen, 12, Cheam
2044 DUBERY, Mervyn, 13, Epsom
2045 BOLING, Michael, 11, Surbiton ★
2046 BOLING, John, 6, Surbiton ★
2047 BOLING, Geraldine, 13, Surbiton
2048 LONGWORTH, Joan, 14, Sutton ★
2049 LONGWORTH, Iris, 6, Sutton
2050 ROGERS, Janet, 10, Bristol
2051 JARRITT, Frieda, 14, Bristol
2052 CASTLE, Pauline, 14, Bristol
2550 MORGAN, Maurice, 7, Liverpool ★
2551 MORGAN, Freda, 12, Liverpool ★
 (Freda Welsh)
2552 MORGAN, Percy, 14, Liverpool
2553 FLETCHER, John, 7, Liverpool ★
2554 FLETCHER, Geraldine, 8, Liverpool
2555 CLARKE, Thomas, 12, Liverpool ★
2556 CLARKE, Gladys, 10, Liverpool ★
2557 CLARKE, John, 5, Liverpool
2564 HACKETT, John, 12, Liverpool ★
2565 HACKETT, Sheilagh, 9, Liverpool
2566 DUFF, Gordon, 13, Bolton
2567 GARDNER, Beryl, 9, Manchester ★
2568 GARDNER, William, 6, Manchester
2569 PRINCE, Marjorie, 5, Manchester
2570 HODGSON, Margaret, 13, Prestwich ★
2571 HODGSON, Joan, 8, Prestwich (Joan Sullivan)
2572 CLIPSTONE, Patricia, 11, Nottingham
2573 CRAWSHAW, Nellie, 12, Bolton

RELUCTANT REFUGE

Children arriving on the *Diomed*

3129 MILLINGTON, Kenneth, 12, Warrington
3130 HOUGHTON, Tony, 14, Warrington ★
3131 HOUGHTON, Donald, 11, Warrington
3132 NAYLOR, Stuart, 11, Warrington
3133 SMITH, Gordon, 12, Southport
3134 RIMMER, Henry, 13, Southport
3137 WILSON, Harry, 13, Rochdale
3138 GARFAT, Frank, 12, Rochdale
3140 RILEY, Leslie, 11, Manchester
3141 THOMPSON, Gordon, 13, Manchester
3142 MASSEY, David, 11, Liverpool
3143 CARDY, John, 12, Lancaster
3144 BEECH, Arthur, 13, Oldham
3145 HUMPHREYS, Clifford, 12, Oldham
3146 TOMLINSON, Jess, 12, Blackburn
3148 EASTHAM, Alan, 13, Foulridge
3149 MITCHELL, Donald, 13, Colne
3150 PHILLIPS, Anthony, 13, Colne

Sources: Michael Fethney, *The Absurd and the Brave*, The Book Guild, Sussex, 1990, pp. 304-33; A659/1: 40/1/6582 and A659/1: 40/1/6584.

Chapter Notes

INTRODUCTION

1 Kathleen Freeman, *If Any Man Build: The History of the Save the Children Fund*, p. 39.

2 Martin Gilbert, 'Not to Forget', keynote address, The Hidden Child Second International Gathering, Jerusalem, 12–15 July.

3 Paul Thompson, *The Voice of the Past*, pp. 113, 137.

4 ibid, p. 131.

CHAPTER 1

1 Extract from a poem written by a child who went to England, cited in Karen Gershon, *We Came as Children*, p. 173.

2 From a speech to party district leaders, April 1937. Reprinted in J. Noakes and G. Pridham (eds), *Nazism : A History in Documents and Eyewitness Account, 1919–1945*, Vol. 1, p. 550.

3 Yitzhak Arad, Yisrael Gutman and Abraham Margaliot (eds), *Documents on the Holocaust*, pp. 39–41.

4 Council for German Jewry, Annual Report of the British Section for 1937, p. 7, file 34, reel 5, Archives of the CBF.

5 Activities of the Zentralausschuss of the Reichsvertretung der Juden in Deutschland, October 1937, p. 29, 553/1, Leo Baeck Institute, Jerusalem.

6 ibid., p. 32.

7 Abraham Margaliot, 'The Problem of the Rescue of German Jewry During the Years 1933–1939; The Reasons for the Delay in their Emigration from the Third Reich', in *Rescue Attempts During the Holocaust*, p. 259.

8 Activities of the Zentralausschuss, op. cit., October 1937, p. 25.

9 Anita Lasker-Wallfisch, unpublished autobiography, 1925–46, p. 5, 92/31/1, Imperial War Museum, London. The family was typical of many — an optimistic father who believed Nazism was a passing phase, until Kristallnacht. Attempts after that to obtain a family permit for America were futile. The children were consequently sent to homes in England and France; the parents remained in Germany and died in a concentration camp.

10 Interview, name withheld.

11 Interview with Alwin Spiegel.

12 Interview, name withheld.

13 *The World's Children*, November 1936, p. 22. Archives of SCF, London.

14 L13/165, Central Zionist Archives, Jerusalem.

15 Interview with Peter Praeger, cited in Barry Turner, *And the Policeman Smiled*, p. 13.

16 Kiryl Sosnowski, *The Tragedy of Children under Nazi Rule*, 1962, p. 12.

17 Reprinted in Macardle, op. cit., p. 31.

18 ibid.

19 Reported in 'Fuhrer: Seduction of a Nation', *True Stories*, ABC television, 14 August 1994.

20 Richard Grunberger, *A Social History of the Third Reich*, p. 282.

21 Noakes and Pridham, op. cit., Vol. 1, pp. 428–9.

22 R. d'Harcourt, 'L'autriche sous si regime Hitlerien', *Revue de deux mondes*, 1 September 1939.

23 Translation of document NG-1889, Office of the Chief of Counsel for War Crimes. The document is from the Reich Foreign Office, dated 23 July 1938. M-9/37(1a), Archives of Yad Vashem, Jerusalem.

24 Margaliot, p. 265.

25 Lucy Dawidowicz, *The War against the Jews*, p. 190.

26 First Annual Report of the Council for German Jewry, 1936, pp. 12–13, file 34, reel 5, Archives of the CBF. A detailed description of Youth Aliyah is provided in Norman Bentwich, *Jewish Youth Comes Home: The Story of the Youth Aliyah 1933–1943*.

27 The situation was described as 'hopeless' by the Executive Council of German Jewry in minutes of 16 March 1937, file 2, reel 1, Archives of the CBF.

28 This arrangement avoided the boycott on transmitting sterling to Germany.

29 Anthony Read and David Fisher, *Kristallnacht: Unleashing the Holocaust*, pp. 28–9.

30 ibid., p. 47.

31 Minutes of the Council of Save the Children Fund, 21 July 1938, Archives of SCF, London.

32 From 'SS Views on the Solution of the Jewish Question', reprinted in Arad, Gutman and Margaliot, op. cit., p. 119.

33 From 'Extract from the Speech by Hitler, January 30, 1939', reprinted in ibid., p. 132.

34 Read and Fisher, op. cit., p. 31.

35 Memo from Elsley Zeitlyn, Polish Jewish Relief Fund, London, 14 February 1940. Records of the Jewish Board of Deputies, C11/12/88, Greater London Record Office, London.

36 Jewish Telegraphic Agency, *Daily News Bulletin*, 22 February 1939, Weiner Library, London.

37 Report by Ida Whitworth on a visit to Berlin, January 1939, FRCA/18/2, Library of the Religious Society of Friends, London.

38 'Letters of a twelve-year-old girl from Vienna', 02/476, Archives of Yad Vashem, Jerusalem.

39 M. Mitzman, 'A visit to Germany, Austria and Poland in 1939', 02/151,

Archives of Yad Vashem, Jerusalem. Berner, 'Children in Vienna', *Jewish Frontier*, Vol. 7, 1939, p. 11 commented that 'in autumn 1938 the starvation of the Jewish and non-Aryan children of Vienna began'.

40 Jewish Telegraphic Agency, *Daily News Bulletin*, 15 December 1938, Weiner Library, London.

41 Norman Bentwich was at the forefront of many refugee organisations in Britain, including the Council for German Jewry. He was a former professor of international relations at the Hebrew University in Jerusalem, Attorney-General in Palestine from 1921 to 1931, and later the High Commissioner of Refugees. He and his wife played a pivotal role in attempts to emigrate children and youth to Australia.

42 John Presland, 'A great adventure', file 156, reel 28, Archives of the CBF. On 1 March 1939 the age was reduced to sixteen.

43 Movement for the Care of Children from Germany, First Annual Report, November 1938–December 1939, file 153, reel 28, Archives of the CBF.

44 Report on visits by W. R. Hughes from the German Emergency Committee, 26 November to 14 December 1938, FCRA/18/2, Library of the Religious Society of Friends, London.

45 German Emergency Committee papers 1933–1946, FCRA/18/2, Library of the Religious Society of Friends, London.

46 *The Times*, 9 December 1938.

47 *The Times*, 29 December 1938.

48 *The Times*, 2 May 1939.

49 *The Times*, 24 August 1939.

50 Director of a Frankfurt orphanage to the Council for German Jewry, 22 November 1938. Document file 608, Weiner Library, London.

51 Movement for the Care of Children from Germany, First Annual Report, November 1938–December 1939, op. cit.

52 Nicholas Winton, a young English stockbroker, and Trevor Chadwick, a teacher, took it upon themselves to organise a number of kindertransports from Czechoslovakia to England, the first by plane and thereafter by train and boat. In Prague they worked through the British Committee for Refugees from Czechoslovakia, an organisation run by the Society of Friends and other volunteers. For a description by Trevor Chadwick see Karen Gershon, op. cit., pp. 22–5. Comments by Nicholas Winton appear in Turner, op. cit., pp. 92–5. Work in Czechoslovakia was funded largely by an appeal made by the Lord Mayor of London.

53 Between February and August 1939 the Polish Refugees' Fund in London removed to England three groups of children (154 altogether) who had been deported to Zbonszyn on the Polish border. Jewish Telegraphic Agency, *Daily News Bulletin*, 20 February and 28 July 1939, Weiner Library, London.

54 Judith Tydor-Baumel, *Unfulfilled Promise*, p. 141.

55 Letter from Nicholas Winton, 5 January 1994.

56 Letter from Norbert Wollheim, 11 October 1993. Norbert Wollheim removed neither himself nor his family from Germany. He, his wife and son were all deported to a concentration camp; only he survived.

57 Annual report of the Fairbridge Farm Schools 1940, PRO series: DO35/703 (AJCP reel PRO 5420).

CHAPTER 2

1 From the autobiography of Kingsley Fairbridge, cited in Women's Group on Public Welfare, *Child Emigration: A Study Made in 1948–50 by a Committee of the Women's Group on Public Welfare*, p. 15.

2 Cited in Gillian Wagner, *Children of the Empire*, p. 205. The full text of the speech appears in *Express and Telegraph*, Adelaide, 13 October 1921. Dr Barnardo's work with destitute children began in England in the 1870s. In 1886 he introduced a boarding out system, whereby children gathered into his refuge were fostered into families in the country. The growing number of children in his care led him also to consider emigration as a way of providing a future for his children. In 1882 the first party of Barnardo's children went to Canada. Barnardo died in 1905, before migration from the Barnardo's Homes extended to Australia. By the outbreak of the Second World War 2 342 Barnardo's children had emigrated to Australia and 28 689 to Canada. See A. E. Williams, *Barnardo of Stepney*.

3 Correspondence with the Northcote Trust. M series: Fairbridge Society Records 1912–1976 (AJCP reel M1843).

4 Barry Coldrey, *Child Migration, the Australian Government and the Catholic Church 1925–1966*, pp. 22–33. Coldrey claims that children selected for emigration in the 1930s were considered the 'cream' of the orphanages. This was not the situation after the Second World War.

5 Fairbridge Society Records 1912–1976 (AJCP reels M1843 and 1845). Records of the children who left on the *Orama* on 17 June 1939 show that their parents knew they were in Australia. Some corresponded, although often letters were irregular and petered out over the years. Their parents' consent had to be gained if, as minors, the children wished to marry or join the armed forces.

6 Margaret Humphreys, *Empty Cradles*. A general contention is that parents placed their children in orphanages on the understanding they would be adopted. Numerous child migrants claim they were told their parents were dead; many parents claim they were never told their children had been removed from Britain.

7 Memorandum on Australian immigration laws and practices and the present policy of His Majesty's Government regarding the reception of immigrants, Appendix C of Report on the Evian Conference by T. W. White, A461/1: M349/3/5 Part 1.

8 Comment by T. H. Garrett, Assistant Secretary of the Department of the Interior, cited in Paul Bartrop, *Australia and the Holocaust 1933–45*, p. 31. Bartrop examines attitudes within Australia to Jewish refugees and details the emergence and development of a refugee policy in the years 1933 to 1945.

9 Extract from policy speech delivered by Prime Minister Lyons on 28 September 1937, A461/1: A349/1/7 Part 1.

10 Paper from the Department of the Interior on decisions taken by Cabinet on 4 March 1938 with respect to immigration, 16 March 1938, A461/1: A349/1/2 Part 3.

11 Policy statement on white alien immigration, 16 March 1938, A461/1: A349/1/2 Part 3.

12 Paper presented at the British Commonwealth relations conference, 23 July 1936, A255/393, Central Zionist Archives, Jerusalem.

13 Notes on the migration of German Jewish refugees to the dominions, 11 November 1937, PRO series: DO35/705 (AJCP reel 5420).

14 Report of the Reichsvertretung for 1938, file 555, Leo Baeck Institute, Jerusalem. The report shows that intensive preparatory work began early in 1937. Learning English was an important part of that preparation. The London committee had a policy not to approve emigration unless a person had a command of the language of the country. The report points out the difficulties this created for people in small towns and for children for whom travelling to classes was unsafe.

15 Report of the Reichsvertretung for 1938, file 555, Leo Baeck Institute, Jerusalem. A few of the girls were eighteen and nineteen.

16 Telegram to Norman Bentwich, 10 September 1938, A255/301, Central Zionist Archives, Jerusalem. The N.S.W. Department of Agriculture later granted further places to refugee boys at Glen Innes and other farm schools.

17 Immigration of Jews into Australia, paper prepared for Cabinet by John McEwan, Minister for the Interior, 25 May 1938, A461/1: M349/3/5 Part 1.

18 Telegram from the Minister for the Interior to the High Commissioner, London, 23 June 1938, A461/1: M349/3/5 Part 1.

19 Cable from the Prime Minister to the High Commissioner in London, 14 October 1938, A461/1: M349/3/5 Part 1.

20 Speech by T. W. White to the Intergovernmental Committee at Evian, 6–15 July 1938, A461/1: M349/3/5 Part 1.

21 Extract from Cabinet minutes, 7 April 1938, shows the rejection of this proposal. Details of this scheme are in Chapter 4.

22 Memo on white alien immigration, July 1938, A461/1: A349/1/2 Part 3.

23 Charlotte Carr-Gregg and Pam Maclean, 'A Mouse Nibbling at a Mountain: The Problem of Australian Refugee Policy and the Work of Camilla Wedgwood', p. 54. Through the YMCA Cyril Bavin was involved in training British youth for land settlement in the dominions. During this visit to Australia he was also representing the Overseas League and the Church of England Advisory Council on Empire Settlement.

24 Camilla Wedgwood was the daughter of outspoken British parliamentarian, Colonel Josiah Wedgwood. She came to Australia in 1927 to take up a position in the Anthropology Department at Sydney University. In 1935 she became Principal of the Women's College at Sydney University.

25 Letter from Camilla Wedgwood to John McEwen, 6 December 1938, A1: 38/11509.

26 In November 1938 the London committee put forward a proposal for the admission of 300 lads, the first fifty to be selected immediately from those already in England. In March 1939, with no decision yet made on the 300, the London committee modified the request to one hundred.

27 Letter from Camilla Wedgwood to the London committee, minutes of the German Emergency Committee, 18 April 1939, FCRA/3, Library of the Religious Society of Friends, London.

28 Minutes of the German Emergency Committee, 16 May 1939, FCRA/3, Library of the Religious Society of Friends, London.

29 Several of the original sixteen did not pass the medical and were replaced by other boys.

30 The German Emergency Fellowship Committee sponsored this boy and paid the £50 landing money required. It took months for the government to approve the application, the boy arriving in Australia on the *Lahn* in August 1939. The NSW Department of Agriculture offered him a place at the Farm School at Glen Innes.

31 Movement for the Care of Children from Germany, First Annual Report, November 1938–December 1939, file 153, reel 28, Archives of the CBF.

32 ibid.

33 ibid.

34 Extract from *Hansard*, House of Representatives, 25 May 1938. A461/1: A349/1/7 Part 1.

35 Letter from R. H. Wheeler to the Department of the Interior, 19 April 1939, A659/1: 40/1/192.

36 Coldrey, op. cit., p. 30.

37 Letter on behalf of the secretary of the Department of the Interior to the secretary of the Public Works Department, Victoria, 6 June 1939, A445/1: 124/1/47.

38 W. D. Forsyth, *The Myth of Open Spaces*, pp. 188–9.

39 Letter from R. H. Wheeler, Australia House, London, to the Department of the Interior, 24 November 1938, A445/1: 124/1/47.

40 Letter from R. H. Wheeler to the Department of the Interior, 4 April 1939, A1/1: 38/11509.

41 ibid.

42 Minutes of the Australian Jewish Welfare Society, Western Australia branch, 6 December 1938. Archives of AJWS, Perth.

43 Conditions governing child migration from Malta to the Christian Brothers associated institution in Western Australia, 16 May 1938, A436/1: 49/5/1220. The scheme did not commence until after the war, but financial arrangements were as outlined in this 1938 report.

44 Report by T. W. White on the Evian Conference, A461/1: M349/3/5 Part 1.

45 Refugee Children's Movement, Third Annual Report, 1941–2, file 153, reel 28, Archives of the CBF. The British government also started funding the voluntary organisations on a pound for pound basis from the end of December, 1939; this amount was increased even further in 1940.

46 Letter from Camilla Wedgwood to her sister, Helen Pease, 30 November 1939, cited in David Wetherell and Charlotte Carr-Gregg, *Camilla: A Life*, p. 113. Wedgwood was referring to the announcement made in December 1938 that 15 000 refugees would be admitted over the next three years, a public announcement of the quota which was already operating. Wedgwood was largely instrumental in encouraging a breakdown of the annual quota into 4 000 Jews and 1 000 others.

47 Letter from Camilla Wedgwood to Helen Pease, 15 January 1939, cited in Wetherall and Carr-Gregg, op. cit., pp. 112–13.

48 A461/1: A349/1/7 Part 1.

49 Memo from the Department of the Interior to the Prime Minister, 8 May 1939, A461/1: A349/1/7 Part 1.

50 Department of the Interior memo, 24 November 1938, A433/1: 43/2/46.

51 All guarantors had to sign an agreement that the nominee would not become a charge on the state for five years. Although the Australian Jewish Welfare Society technically was not responsible for those it did not guarantee, it assumed responsibility when guarantees broke down or when people were in need of assistance.

52 Minutes of the Executive Council of AJWS, 30 November 1938, Archives of AJWS, Sydney.

53 Minutes of the Executive Council of AJWS, 22 January 1939, Archives of AJWS, Sydney. SS raided the Gross-Breesen farm on 10 November 1938 and sent many of the trainees to Buchenwald concentration camp. Wolfgang Matsdorf, who came to Australia in 1938, was largely instrumental in persuading the Welfare Society to support the Gross-Breesen application. According to Matsdorf, thirty-three young people, aged from fifteen years of age, came to Australia before the end of 1939. A group of twenty-one arrived in July.

54 Minutes of the Australian Jewish Welfare Society, Western Australian branch, 8 December 1938, Archives of AJWS, Perth.

55 Minutes of the Executive Council of AJWS, 10 January 1939, Archives of AJWS, Sydney.

56 Minutes of the Executive Council of AJWS, 29 December 1938, Archives of AJWS, Sydney. These minutes indicate that both Perth and Melbourne branches had written again to the executive, indicating their interest in a children's scheme.

57 Minutes of the Executive Council of AJWS, 22 January 1939, Archives of AJWS, Sydney.

58 Letter from Harry Lesnie, secretary of AJWS, to the Minister for the Interior, 6 February 1939, A434/1: 49/3/3.

59 Department of the Interior memo, Jewish refugee child migration, 22 August, 1939, A434/1: 49/3/3.

60 Letter from J. A. Carrodus, Department of the Interior, to H. Lesnie, Australian Jewish Welfare Society, 16 March 1939, A433/1: 43/2/46.

61 While nineteen permits were used, only seventeen refugee children went in the group to Melbourne. It is probable the other two permits were used by the children of Dr Falk who accompanied the seventeen children.

CHAPTER 3

1 Letter from Walter Badrian, 17 April 1939.

2 Movement for the Care of Children from Germany, First Annual Report, November 1938–December 1939, p. 5, file 153, reel 28, Archives of the CBF.

3 Interview with Herta Souhami, Institute for Oral Documentation, Hebrew University, Jerusalem, cited by Judith Baumel, *The Jewish Refugee Children in Great Britain 1938–1945*, 1981, p. 84.

4 Movement for the Care of Children from Germany, First Annual Report, November 1938–December 1939, op. cit., p. 6.

5 Working report of the Reichsvertretung for 1938 file 555. Leo Baeck Institute, Jerusalem.

6 Although all German Jews became stateless, there was a category of Polish Jews living in Germany who became stateless when Polish authorities in Germany confiscated or refused to renew their passports. They were constantly at risk of being sent over the border.

7 George Dreyfus, *The Last Frivolous Book*, p. 11.

8 Activities of the Zentralausschuss of the Reichsvertretung der Juden in Deutschland, October 1937, 553/1, Leo Baeck Institute, Jerusalem.

9 Internal memo from T. H. Garrett, Department of the Interior, 15 December 1939, A434/1: 49/3/3.

10 The usual route of children to England was through Holland, via the Hook of Holland to Harwich. A smaller number left from Hamburg, on ships bound for America via Southampton. I have heard of no other kindertransports leaving from Bremerhaven. None of the other Australia-bound children, nor any of the children headed for England, could throw any light on this matter. A search in the Public Record Office, London, enhanced the mystery surrounding the voyage. The incoming passenger lists for the *Europa* for June 1939 (BT 26/1184) include no record of these three hundred or so children.

11 Letter from R. H. Wheeler, Australia House, London, to T. H. Garrett, Department of the Interior, 5 December 1939, A434/1: 49/3/3.

12 Interview with Hedi Fixel. Other people who helped in an unofficial capacity with the children were Kitty Solomons, who had been working in the Overseas Department at Woburn House and was moving to Australia to assist the Australian Jewish Welfare Society with its refugee work; also, seventeen-year-old Ilse Howard.

13 H. Hurwitz, 'I Bought out a Ship's Load of Refugees', *Sun News-Pictorial*, 1939 (exact date unknown).

14 Letters from Margot Goldstein to her family, 20 June to 16 July 1939.

15 *Hebrew Standard*, 25 May 1939.

16 Minutes of the Executive Council of the Australian Jewish Welfare Society, 22 January 1939, Archives of AJWS, Sydney.

17 Interview with Alfred Stricker. Having arrived in Australia with his mother, Alfred was placed in various foster homes and boarding schools and eventually in the Isabella Lazarus Home. The Home was taken over by the army in 1942, at which time the children were moved to a large private home at Killara. A fictional story of life at the Isabella Lazarus Home is told in Alan Collins, *The Boys from Bondi*, 1987.

18 Minutes of the executive of the Western Australian branch of the Australian Jewish Welfare Society, 4 May 1939, Archives of AJWS, Perth.

19 Minutes of meeting of Directors of the Australian Jewish Welfare Society, Melbourne, 30 August 1939, Archives of AJWS, Melbourne.

20 Letter from Frank Silverman, general secretary of the Australian Jewish Welfare Society, to A. R. Peters, Department of the Interior, 17 August 1939, A434/1: 49/3/3.

21 Department of the Interior, memo on Jewish refugee child migration, 22 August 1939, A434/1: 49/3/3.

22 Decree issued by Himmler, German document on the emigration of Jews, 1 November 1941, M1/DN/25/1822, Archives of Yad Vashem, Jerusalem.

23 Cablegram from the Prime Minister's Department to the High Commissioner's Office, London, 27 November 1939, AA(Victoria) B741/3:V4281.

24 Letter from Australia House, London, to T. H. Garrett, 5 December 1939, A434/1: 49/3/3.

25 Letter from the general secretary of the Australian Jewish Welfare Society, Sydney, 21 November 1939, op. cit.

26 Press statement, 16 April 1940, AA(Victoria) B741/3:V4281.

27 Department of the Interior memos, 15 December 1939 and 21 December 1939, A434/1: 49/3/3.

28 Extract of a letter from the Australian Jewish Welfare Society to the Overseas Settlement Department, London, submitted to the Department of the Interior, 22 December 1939, A434/1: 49/3/3.

29 Extract of a letter from the Australian Jewish Welfare Society to the Overseas Settlement Department, London, submitted to the Department of the Interior, 22 December 1939, A434/1: 49/3/3.

30 Letter from the Australian Jewish Welfare Society to the Department of the Interior, 23 May 1940, A434/1: 49/3/3.

31 Minutes of a meeting of directors of the Australian Jewish Welfare Society, Melbourne, 22 May 1940, Archives of AJWS, Melbourne.

32 Press statement by the Minister for the Interior, 16 April 1940, AA(Vic.) B741/3:V4281.

33 Memo from T. H. Garrett to J. A. Carrodus, Department of the Interior, 28 May 1940. Garrett recommended approval for 500 children, but Carrodus, who made recommendations to the Minister, changed this to one hundred. The Minister, H. S. Foll, approved one hundred. A434/1: 49/3/3.

34 Letter from the Overseas Settlement Department, London, to the Australian Jewish Welfare Society, 15 August 1940. Reference is made in this letter to the Overseas Settlement Department having written to the AJWS about this restriction on 29 July 1940. A434/1: 49/3/3.

35 Handwritten note by the Minister for the Interior on a Department of the Interior memo on Jewish refugee children, 16 October 1940, A433/1: 49/3/3.

CHAPTER 4

1 Celia Heller, *On the Edge of Destruction: Jews of Poland Between the Two World Wars*, expands on the concept of caste in relation to Polish Jews, and the persistent, discrediting stigma of being Jewish in Poland.

2 Heller, op. cit., p. 77.

3 According to 1931 census data, seventy-six per cent of Polish Jews were urban.

4 Heller, op. cit., p. 225.

5 All the land except for that immediately around the house was on a ninety-nine year lease. Russian Jews were not allowed to build houses, even on leased land; police would demolish them before they were completed. Nevertheless, the law stated that once the roof was on, the house could not be demolished, so Aleck's grandfather outsmarted the system by building his house overnight — even to the point of getting the roof on.

6 Australia put up many obstacles to the entry of eastern European Jews, including a language test. Nevertheless, Suzanne Rutland records that 2 000 entered in the peak years of 1926 to 1928. Rutland, *Edge of the Diaspora*, p. 147.

7 Governments defined refugees in terms of those under Nazi rule: 'the term "refugee" at present is understood to apply to persons of German nationality, or former German, Austrian, or Czechoslovakian nationality, against whom there is political discrimination. It applies particularly to Jews and non-Aryan Christians (i.e. persons of Jewish or partly Jewish extraction, but of Christian faith).' Department of the Interior memo, 27 April 1939, A433/1: 43/2/46.

8 Hilary Rubinstein, in examining Polish migration to Australia in the 1920s, discusses the formation of earlier support groups — the Kadimah (1922) and the Welcome Society (1926). Rubinstein, *The Jews in Australia*, Vol. 1, p. 151.

9 Polish Jewish Relief Fund, *An Appeal for Help*. The brochure is undated, but is with materials dated 1934 to 1937. Papers of Melech Ravitch, the Hebrew University, Jerusalem.

10 Letter from the Polish Jewish Relief Fund to the Department of the Interior, 21 September 1937, A434/1: 41/3/1039.

11 Letter to Melech Ravitch, 20 May 1937, papers of Melech Ravitch, the Hebrew University, Jerusalem. Melech Ravitch was a Polish writer who came to Australia in 1933. He collected money for Jewish Folk Schools in Poland and was generally active in matters to do with Polish refugees, including the scheme proposed for settling 30 000 Jewish people in the Kimberley region of Western Australia.

12 Letter to Commonwealth Investigation Branch, Canberra, from Inspector Roland Browne of the Melbourne Branch, 23 September 1937, A434/1: 41/3/1039.

13 Letter from the Polish Jewish Relief Fund to the Department of the Interior, 21 September 1937, A434/1: 41/3/1039.

14 Department of the Interior memo, 5 October 1937, A434/1: 41/3/1039.

15 Handwritten note on the memo of 5 October 1937, ibid. Thomas White was Australia's spokesperson at the Evian conference in July 1938.

16 Memo from the Minister for the Interior to Cabinet, 1 November 1937, A434/1: 41/3/1039. In this, Interior recommended that 'the Jewish Relief Fund be advised that the Government does not approve of the proposal submitted by them'.

17 A Cabinet minister wrote 'approved' on the Department of Interior's memo to Cabinet, next to the recommendation that 'the Jewish Relief Fund be advised that the Government does not approve of the proposal submitted by them'. A handwritten note by J. A. Carrodus to the Minister for the Interior, 11 April 1938, indicates he and his staff interpreted this to mean Cabinet accepted Interior's recommendation. 'Apparently that is not correct,' Carrodus added. A434/1: 41/3/1039. Cabinet minutes cited in the previous note definitely stated that approval was not given.

18 Memo on white alien immigration, July 1938. The memo provides details of approvals given for certain classes and groups of white aliens, and dates approved. A461/1: M349/3/5 Part 1. The only fee charged by the government was £1 for each landing permit.

19 Organisation and Rehabilitation through Training (ORT) was the education arm of JEAS, an organisation founded in Russia in the late 1800s. ORT's work included running vocational schools in eastern European countries. During the Second World War it merged with another former Russian organisation, OSE (Jewish Health Society) and became known as OSE-ORT. OSE-ORT was heavily involved in child rescue during the war.

20 An extract of the instructions sent to ORT, included in a letter from the Polish Jewish Relief Fund to the Department of the Interior, 27 June 1938, A434/1: 41/3/1039.

21 Benschen, or NeuBenschen as it was correctly called, was the German border town; Zbonszyn was the Polish town. They were separated by a no man's land.

22 By German law a child took the citizenship of its father; by Polish law the country of birth determined citizenship.

23 Interview with Michael Poczter, known in Australia as Michael Porter, cited in *Jerusalem Post*, 13 June 1989.

24 Letter from JEAS to Jojna Kac, 16 March 1939. Translated from Yiddish by Aleck Katz. Three hundred zlotys were then equivalent to about £50 sterling, about the amount required for travel from Poland to Australia; the passage from England to Australia cost £39 pounds sterling.

25 Letter to Werner Teitel from his mother, 9 April 1939. Werner's mother, sister and baby brother were still in Germany when he left for Australia.

26 Dr Maurycy Lebenson, previously a manager of Hicem in Danzig, and his wife, accompanied the boys to Australia. They were originally given approval to remain in Australia for twelve months. Permanent residence

was granted in January 1940. A434/1: 41/3/1039.

27 Letter to Max Nagel from his father, 23 April 1939.

28 Max Nagel's father frequently refers to the expense of sending letters airmail; yet he wrote to his son at each port and, on his brief return to Germany, even sent Max an international coupon for a reply airmail letter.

29 J. M. Machover, 'Towards Rescue', p. 7. Machover travelled to Australia on the *Ceramic*, which collided with a British freighter off Cape Town on 13 August 1940. No lives were lost, but the accident may have influenced his opinion on the safety of sea travel. The sinking of the *City of Benares* a month later — discussed in Chapter 5 — no doubt confirmed this opinion.

30 Martin Gilbert says more than a quarter of a million Polish Jews fled eastwards between the end of September and mid-November 1939. Gilbert, *The Holocaust: a History of the Jews of Europe during the Second World War*, p. 92.

CHAPTER 5

1 Richard Titmuss provides the following statistics for child evacuees in September 1939: 797 000 unaccompanied children, 524 000 mothers and children, 7 400 children under five evacuated to nurseries. He estimates that, apart from the government scheme, another 2 000 000 people were evacuated privately. Titmuss, *Problems of Social Policy*, pp. 563, 102. Other major government-organised evacuations occurred in August 1940 and in 1944, in response to the 'flying bombs'. There were numerous re-evacuations within these periods as people drifted in and out of danger areas according to the threat at the time.

2 *Sydney Morning Herald*, 27 September 1939.

3 E. D. Darby, 'Wartime Migration: British Children for Australia', p. 45, notes that about 2 000 children were being adopted annually in Australia by 1940, with insufficient children available to meet requirements.

4 Despite the Australian government's wish to continue assisted migration during the war, the British government discontinued the scheme in September 1939. All government grants to voluntary societies were subsequently withdrawn except for maintenance grants for children in Farm schools, including after-care grants to Dr Barnardo Homes.

5 Transfer of young children from the United Kingdom to Australia during the war, report by J. H. Honeysett, 23 May 1940, A659/1: 50/1/2053.

6 Proposal for the transfer of young children from the United Kingdom to Australia during the war, submitted by Senator Foll, Minister for the Interior, to Cabinet, 29 May 1940, A659/1: 50/1/2053.

7 *Sydney Morning Herald*, 27 May 1940.

8 Cable from Menzies to the Australian High Commissioner in London, 29 May 1940, A659/1: 41/1/1261. It is frequently cited that offers were received from the Canadian government on 31 May and from the governments of Australia, New Zealand, South Africa and the United States several days later. In fact, the Canadian offer was made in the Dominions Office on Friday 31 May, at a meeting called by the High Commissioner for Canada. After the representatives for Canada House had left the meeting, R. Wiseman of the Dominions Office read a letter from Australia House regarding Australia's offer. Clearly this offer had been received by, if not before, 31 May.

9 Press statement, 31 May 1940, A659/1: 50/1/2053.

10 Statement prepared for the Department of Information for use in a short-wave broadcast, no date but around 20 June 1940, A659/1: 50/1/2053.

11 Letters and telegrams to the Prime Minister, A1608/1: D39/1/3.

12 Letter to the Prime Minister from the Refugee Council of Tasmania, 7 June 1940, A1608/1: D39/1/3.

13 Letter to the Minister of the Interior from the Migrants' Consultative Committee, 3 June 1940, A434/1: 49/3/3.

14 Attached to a memo from Thomas Garrett to Senator Foll, 7 June 1940, in which Garrett asks why the cable has not been dispatched. He points out that, in view of the many requests for particularly French and Dutch children, it is highly desirable that the scheme should embrace them. A659/1: 50/1/2053.

15 Geoffrey Shakespeare, 'History of the Children's Overseas Reception Board, 1940–1944', p. 2, DO131/43, Public Record Office, London.

16 In late August the age limit for boys was dropped to fourteen. Cable from Secretary of State for Dominion Affairs, 23 August 1940, A1608/1: C39/1/3 Part 1.

17 Shakespeare, op. cit., p. 4.

18 Winston Churchill in the House of Commons, 18 July 1940. PRO series DO35/712 (AJCP reel 5423).

19 Records of the Cabinet Office, 17 June 1940, CAB 65/7, Public Record Office, London.

20 Cable from the High Commissioner to Prime Minister Menzies, 18 June 1940, A1608/1: C39/1/3 Part 1.

21 Cable from the High Commissioner to Prime Minister Menzies, n.d. but 18 or 19 June, 1940, A1608/1: C39/1/3 Part 1.

22 Cable from the Prime Minister Menzies to the High Commissioner in London, 20 June 1940, A1608/1: C39/1/3 Part 1.

23 *Sydney Morning Herald*, 4 June 1940.

24 *Sydney Morning Herald*, 18 June 1940.

25 Parents had been advised to apply through the local school authority

unless their children were attending schools that were not grant-aided.

26 Geoffrey Shakespeare, *Let Candles Be Brought In*, p. 254. To counteract criticism that the scheme would favour the wealthy, a quota was established for the two kinds of schools: in England, 75 per cent of children were to come from grant-aided schools, in Scotland, forty-nine out of fifty children from what were termed local education authority schools. See House of Commons debate for 2 July 1940. PRO series DO35/713. (AJCP reel 5424).

27 Cabinet minutes, 22 June 1940, CAB 65/7, 174(40). Public Record Office, London.

28 Broadcast talk by Geoffrey Shakespeare, Sunday 23 June 1940, DO131/43, Public Record Office, London.

29 *The Times*, 25 May 1940.

30 'Imminence of a German invasion of Great Britain', report by the Joint Intelligence Sub-Committee, 4 July 1940, CAB 66/9, Public Record Office, London.

31 Richard Collier, *1940: The World in Flames*, p. 128.

32 Mass Observation was founded in 1937 by a group of young English intellectuals, chief of whom were Tom Harrison, Charles Madge and Humphrey Jennings. They were inspired by a desire to create an anthropological record of the British, and recruited thousands of volunteers for this purpose. Volunteers became observers, regularly completing thematic questionnaires, keeping diaries, conducting interviews and surveys, and writing. The rich store of primary source material was used for many publications and reports during the war. In 1940 Mass Observation was feeding reports on morale to the Ministry of Information.

33 Cable from the Department of the Interior to the High Commissioner, 1 July 1940, A659/1: 46/1/4515.

34 Conference of Commonwealth and state government representatives, Canberra, 27 June 1940, A659/1: 41/1/1261.

35 A659/1: 46/1/4515.

36 Item 371, A2697 Vol. 4B.

37 Letters to various consuls, 17 June 1940, FO371/25250, Public Record Office, London. British parents were expected to pay at least six shillings sterling a week, the amount contributed for maintenance of children evacuated within Britain.

38 Note from Thomas Dunlop to the Foreign Office, 2 July 1940, FO371/25250, Public Record Office, London.

39 Comment written on a Foreign Office memo from T. M. Snow, 5 July 1940, FO371/25250, Public Record Office, London.

40 War Cabinet minutes, 10 July 1940, CAB65/8, 199(40), Public Record Office, London.

41 Minutes of the Executive of the Central Council for Jewish Refugees, 26 June 1940, file 6, reel 2, Archives of the CBF.

42 Minutes of the Advisory Council of CORB, 2 July 1940, PRO series DO35/713 (AJCP reel 5424).

43 Letter from W. Brand to the Department of the Interior, 21 June 1940, A434/1: 49/3/3.

44 Minutes of the executive of the Jewish Welfare Guardian Society, 18 July 1940, Archives of the AJWS, Melbourne. See Chapter 2 for other information on the Welfare Guardian Society.

45 Minutes of the Advisory Council of CORB, 16 July 1940, PRO series DO35/712 (AJCP reel 5423).

46 A659/1: 46/1/4515.

47 Comment by Churchill on CORB, 11 July 1940, PREM 4: 99/1, Public Record Office, London.

48 House of Commons, 16 July 1940, PRO series DO35/712 (AJCP reel 5423).

49 Minutes of a meeting of the Civil Defence Executive Sub-Committee, held on 1 August 1940 to discuss the future of the Children's Overseas Reception Scheme, FO371/25251, Public Record Office, London.

50 Cable from the Prime Minister to the High Commissioner, 1 August 1940, A1608/1: C39/1/3 Part 1.

51 A659/1: 40/1/6582. This in fact was an error; the *Diomed* was delayed until 17 September.

52 Memo from the Department of the Interior, 31 July 1940, A659/1: 40/1/6582.

53 A nominal roll for each of the ships evacuating children to Australia is in A659/1: 46/1/4518; included is a roll for the *Largs Bay*, due to sail on 25 September 1940 with 155 children.

54 VPRS 10093/7. Public Record Office, Melbourne.

55 Cable from the Department of the Interior to the High Commissioner, 18 September 1940, A659/1: 40/1/6590.

56 VPRS 10093/3, Public Record Office, Melbourne. The last sentence of her letter was underlined in red by the Victorian committee.

57 Cable to the Department of the Interior, 21 September 1940, A659/1: 40/1/6590.

58 Letter from Walter Hare to his brother Claude, 18 August 1940, VPRS 10093/5, Public Record Office, Melbourne. This and other items from this closed file have been used with permission from John Hare. This was Walter's first communication with his brother about the children. In his letter he said the application form asked him to supply the name of a friend or relative, 'the idea being for those responsible for the evacuation to get in touch with them'. He and other parents probably assumed this would happen before the children sailed, but it did not. Unless parents took the initiative to cable Australian relatives and friends, the children were at sea before relatives and friends heard they had been nominated.

59 Memo sent airmail from London to the Premier of South Australia, 31 July 1940. It explains that the carriage of the children was regarded as a secondary consideration by the Ministry of Transport. A1608/1: C39/1/3 Part 1.

60 Donald Mitchell, 'A Wartime Voyage to Australia: Durban — Adelaide', *Sea Breezes*, Vol. 65, No. 542, 1991, pp. 831–3. A deck steward on the *Diomed* later told Donald Mitchell that on the afternoon of 12 September the captain returned from the commodore's conference and instructed his personal steward to make up a berth for the commodore in the pilot's cabin behind the wheelhouse.

61 Ralph Barker, *Children of the Benares*, tells the story of the sinking of the *City of Benares* and the inquiry which followed.

62 Geoffrey Shakespeare's report to CORB on the sinking of the *City of Benares* on 17 September 1940, report dated 22 September 1940, FO371/25252, Public Record Office, London.

63 Minutes of the Board of CORB, 1 October 1940, PRO series DO35/713 (AJCP reel 5424).

64 Memo by R. A. Wiseman, the Dominions Office, 4 September 1940, PRO series DO35/703 (AJCP reel 5420).

65 Address by Geoffrey Shakespeare to the Victoria League, 15 July 1941, p. 21, DO131/28, Public Record Office, London.

66 Letter from the Prime Minister's Department to the High Commissioner of the United Kingdom, 3 October 1940, A659/1: 46/1/4515.

67 Australia received 577 CORB children, Canada 1 532, New Zealand 202 and South Africa 353. From June 1940 to December 1942, 829 children were evacuated privately to Australia, 669 in the months of August and September 1940, when CORB children were being evacuated. DO131/27, Public Record Office, London.

68 Diary of A. Frazer-Allen, nurse escort on the *Batory*, 84/2/1, Imperial War Museum, London.

CHAPTER 6

1 Letter to Betty Abrahamson from her brother Zvi in Germany, 15 September 1945.

2 Marvin Tokayer and Mary Swartz, *The Fugu Plan*, tell of the difficulties Polish refugees had gaining exit visas from Russian-occupied territory. Through the goodwill of Senpo Sugiharo, the Japanese consul in Lithuania, and the Dutch ambassador in Latvia, about 6 000 mostly Polish refugees received temporary visas for Japan, though only 1 300 left Lithuania. Dutch consuls were instructed to stamp refugees' passports or papers with 'No visa to Curacao is required'. On sighting this, the Japanese consul provided the temporary visas which allowed refugees to travel across Russia and enter Japan. From Japan they hoped to gain permits for America or other countries. Few did, and in September 1941 the Japanese moved all remaining anti-Axis refugees to Shanghai.

3 Irena Grudzinska-Gross and Jan Tomasz Gross, *War through Children's Eyes: The Soviet Occupation of Poland and the Deportations 1939–1941*, pp. xxii—xxiii.

4 Martin Gilbert, *Atlas of the Holocaust*, documents the acts of terror and the expulsions the invading German army inflicted on both Jews and non-Jews throughout Poland and other European countries from 1 September 1939. Azriel Eisenberg, *The Lost Generation: Children in the Holocaust*, pp. 172–183, also describes the Einsatzgruppen, or killer squads, each consisting of 500 to 600 men, which accompanied the advancing German army. Eisenberg includes an extract from the Nuremberg record of Otto Ohlendorf, commander of a squad that killed 90 000 Jews and gypsies in the area bordering Poland and White Russia. In 1942 Eichmann provided decorated gas vans to spare the assassins unnecessary trauma when murdering children and women.

5 Kyril Sosnowski, *The Tragedy of Children under Nazi Rule*, p. 62ff, describes the deportations from the Zamosc region in the Lublin province. In 1942 110 000 Poles, including 30 000 children, were evicted, to be replaced by German settlers. Following deportations such as this, people were sent to forced labour camps in Germany or to concentration camps. The old, the sick and unwanted children were often abandoned.

6 Memo from the state police, 1 November 1941, M1/DN/25/1822, Archives of Yad Vashem, Jerusalem. The document indicates that the order was effective from 23 October 1941.

7 In November 1941 leading SS personnel were invited to a conference to discuss the 'final solution'. At this conference, the Wannsee conference, held in Berlin in January 1942, Heydrich informed participants that the policy of emigration was being replaced by the evacuation of Jews to eastern Europe. This plan was to include English Jewry. What would happen in the east was not spelt out, although those at the top had determined that the 'final solution' meant extermination, and it was only a matter of months before the death camps were in operation. In *Atlas of the Holocaust*, p. 64, Martin Gilbert claims that Hitler's plan to exterminate at least the eastern Jews had been made by May 1941 when he set up the mobile killing squads.

8 Cable from Bruce to Menzies, 23 December 1940, A1608/1: F19/1/1. The Polish government in exile in England would have funded the scheme.

9 Cable from the Department of External Affairs, London, to the Prime Minister, 25 January 1941, A1608/1: F19/1/1.

10 Report by the Dominions Office on efforts by the dominions to help allied refugees from the continent, 18 June 1941, PRO series DO35/1002 (AJCP reel 5550).

11 Foreign Office response to a suggestion that Australia be thanked for its offer, 19 February 1941, PRO series DO35/1002 (AJCP reel 5550).

12 Cable from the Secretary of State for Dominion Affairs, London, to Southern Rhodesia, 15 January 1943. It contains details of the cable sent to the British Ambassador in Washington regarding United States co-operation in solving the refugee problem, A1608/1:Y19/1/1.

13 Isaac Chomski, 'Children in Exile', pp. 522–8. For details on these camps see David Lowrie, *The Hunted Children*, Chapters 12 and 13.

14 Cited in Judith Tydor-Baumel, *Unfulfilled Promise*, p. 86.

15 M. Marrus and R. Paxton, *Vichy France and the Jews*, discuss the deportation of Jewish children from France. They maintain French authorities encouraged the inclusion of children, although at first the Germans gave parents in Vichy France the option of leaving behind children over five years old.

16 According to Tydor-Baumel, op. cit., pp. 83–8, about three hundred, mostly Jewish, children reached the United States before the German occupation of the free zone. Chomski, op. cit., describes the wretched state of most of these children who were either orphaned or whose parents were interned. Ernst Papenek, *Out of the Fire*, pp. 217–28, discusses the bureaucratic barriers he encountered in the United States in acquiring visas for these children.

17 'Fighting fund for the rescue of persecuted Jewish refugee children from war devastated Europe to Australia', n.d. [1944 or 1945]. Pamphlet published by the Australian Jewish Welfare Society, Sydney. File 169, Australian Jewish Historical Society, Sydney.

18 In May 1943 the Sydney branch of the AJWS launched a Save the Children appeal to raise £50 000 for fares and maintenance of the children. The Melbourne branch declined to become involved until it could be assured that transport was available.

19 Meeting of the subcommittee on child migration, Department of the Interior, 24 January 1944, A989/1: 44/43/554/2/5.

20 Minutes of a meeting of the directors of the AJWS, 31 July 1944, Archives of the AJWS, Melbourne. For this reason New South Wales branch of the AJWS launched the Rescue the Children appeal in May 1943. Victoria launched its appeal early in 1945.

21 Letters from various organisations to the Department of the Interior, A1608/1: Y19/1/1. Also, Bureau of Jewish Affairs newsletter 964. *Smith's Weekly*, notorious for its anti-foreigner stance, appealed to Australians on 14 and 21 November 1942 to consider how they could offer asylum to Hitler's child victims.

22 On 6 December 1944 Cabinet approved a postwar scheme for British and non-British child migrants that would operate alongside schemes of the voluntary organisations. The proposal was for 51 000 children — 17 000 a year over three years.

23 Krstyna Skwarko, *The Invited*, p. 15.

24 Britain, Canada and the American Red Cross had agreed to help resettle 50 000 orphaned or lost children from the Soviet Union but, on 12 June 1942, Stalin rejected the request, allowing only 15 000 to 20 000 to leave for Iran (Persia).

25 Skwarko, op. cit., p. 20. She was put in charge of an orphanage which travelled with the Polish army to Iran.

26 ibid, pp. 42–3.

27 Department of the Interior memo, 11 April 1945, stated they were 'all Catholics, no Jews'. A1608/1:AU39/1/3. Several letters in this file indicate the involvement of Archbishop Mannix in this representation.

28 The Department of Defence advised that accommodation could be provided at Puckapunyal military camp in Victoria. Telegram from the Department of Defence to the Department of the Interior, 8 January 1945, A433/1: 44/2/5976.

29 Department of the Interior memo, 9 January 1945, A433/1: 44/2/5976.

30 Translation of document NG-1794, Office of Chief of Counsel for war crimes, M-9/50(17), Archives of Yad Vashem, Jerusalem. The request was made at the end of 1943. Negotiations were carried on via the Swiss ambassador in Berlin, Feldscher; it became known as the Feldscher affair.

31 ibid.

32 Cable to the Prime Minister, 8 September 1944, A461/1: MA349/3/5 Part 2. Various related letters and cables are in B36, Archive of Australian Judaica, Sydney.

33 Report to Cabinet from the Minister of the Interior, 23 October 1944, A461/1: MA349/3/5 Part 2.

34 The Prime Minister of New Zealand intervened on behalf of these children. While visiting London he discussed the matter with the British Minister of War Transport and on his return to New Zealand sent a formal request for assistance to the Secretary of State for Dominion Affairs. An early opportunity arose to move the children by a British ship from Bombay, but difficulties occurred in moving them to Bombay in time. United States authorities then agreed to carry the children on a troopship from India, with a returning furlough draft. Statement from Department of External Affairs, 16 November 1944, and cable from same department, 11 November 1944, A434/1: 47/3/4316.

35 The British government was concerned that should the Nazis release the surviving Hungarian Jews the United States government would not assume its fair share of the burden. The draft report was sent to the

Commonwealth government for comment on 4 January 1945. The reply of 20 March 1945 amended the statistics and emphasised the number and categories of people evacuated from Malaya (7 000), Netherlands East India (2 000), China and Hong Kong (2 000) and the territories of Papua, New Guinea and Nauru (5 000). A1608/1:Y19/1/1.

36 *Sun*, 18 February 1941. The evacuation from Hong Kong involved women and children. *Sydney Morning Herald*, 7 August 1940, states that at that stage all children were accompanied by a parent or guardian.

37 At the beginning of January 1942 the Immigration Officer in Singapore was authorised to issue visas to 200 alien European women and children who were in a position to maintain themselves for at least twelve months. A433/1: 42/2/236.

38 Department of the Interior memo, 6 January 1942, A433/1: 42/2/236.

39 Press statement by Prime Minister Curtin, *The Times* (London), 14 January 1942.

40 The group consisted of seventeen British children, one Dutch and one Czech, all aged between six and twelve. According to the British Consul in Medan, the alien children did not require permission to enter Australia because they were under the guardianship of the headmaster's wife. Attempts were made by him to contact parents, with the result that many of the children were reunited with their mothers soon after their arrival in Australia on 4 February 1942. The others, some whose parents could not be traced, settled on a farm near Geelong with staff from the school and some other women from Sumatra. A433/1: 49/2/5251.

41 Letter from Arthur McEvoy in Penang to his in-laws in England, 27 June 1940.

CHAPTER 7

1 Letter from Margot Goldstein to her family in Germany, 23 July 1939.

2 *Westralian Judean*, 1 August 1939.

3 ibid.

4 Although the overall responsibility for the children was vested in the Melbourne branch of the Australian Jewish Welfare Society, the Ladies' Auxiliary of the Society assumed much of the responsibility. From their ranks a House Committee was formed, with responsibility for the day to day running of the home where the children lived. An Education Committee was also formed in August 1939.

5 *Woman*, 27 November 1939.

6 *Australian Jewish Herald*, 3 August 1939.

7 Paula Kochen, cited in *Australian Jewish News*, 11 August 1989.

8 The parents of these children were interned, but permission had been given for children up to fifteen years to leave the camp. This was raised to seventeen years by the end of April 1941.

9 The film was taken at Dr Jona's home at Montrose. Also shown in the film is Dr Steinberg, known for his involvement in the Kimberley scheme. A video copy of the film is in the George Dreyfus collection at the National Film and Sound Archives, Canberra. The original is held by Dr Walter Jona, Melbourne.

10 Minutes of meeting of Board of Directors of the Australian Jewish Welfare Society, 12 March 1941, Archives of AJWS, Melbourne.

11 Cited by Suzanne Rutland in 'Australian Responses to Jewish Refugee Migration Before and After World War II', pp. 38–9.

12 David Wetherell and Charlotte Carr-Gregg, *Camilla: A Life*, pp. 119–120.

13 Minutes of meeting of Board of Directors of the Australian Jewish Welfare Society, 3 September 1941, Archives of AJWS, Melbourne.

14 At meetings of of the Board of Directors of the Australian Jewish Welfare Society, held in February 1944, the following arrangements were proposed: 'H. Gold to board; L. Badrian to live with uncle; A. Stocks likewise; H. Bader to be taken into parents' home as soon as possible; R. Taylor to be boarded with his sister with an allowance to her'. The remaining boy, Hermann Levy, was presumably to stay at Larino. Qualms about placing children in the homes of refugees, also discussed in these meetings, probably prevented the boys from being moved till after the war.

15 The Welfare Guardian Society was a committee of the Jewish Welfare Society, interested in the migration of Jewish youth for agricultural training. In 1939 a group of twenty youths arrived in Australia under the auspices of the Welfare Guardian Society. The boys were placed at agricultural schools in Dookie and Wangaratta, and lived on surrounding farms.

16 Minutes of meeting of The Jewish Welfare Guardian Society, 27 June 1943, Archives of AJWS, Melbourne.

17 Minutes of meeting of The Jewish Welfare Guardian Society, 10 February 1944, Archives of AJWS, Melbourne.

18 Minutes of meeting of Board of Directors of the Australian Jewish Welfare Society, 9 December 1942, Archives of AJWS, Melbourne.

19 *The Marvellous World of George Dreyfus*, compact disc or audio-tape MD3129, Move Record Company, Melbourne.

20 Jo's father was in Palestine. Ellen Lewinski and Betty Abrahamson were also outgoing; neither had a surviving parent.

CHAPTER 8

1 *Sydney Morning Herald*, 17 October 1940.

2 Comment by Joe Honeysett in a report to the Department of the Interior, 12 October 1940, A659/1: 40/1/6590.

3 Editorial, *Australian Women's Weekly*, 2 November 1940.

4 *Courier-Mail*, 18 October 1940. There had been an AIF march in the morning and many people, according to the *Courier-Mail*, had stayed on from that to welcome the children.

5 Memo from Joe Honeysett, 22 October 1940, A659/1: 40/1/6590.

6 Statement by the chairman of the New South Wales Overseas Children Citizen's Committee, *Sydney Morning Herald*, 2 November 1940.

7 Report by Cyril Bavin, 15 September 1943, VPRS 10093/8, Public Record Office, Melbourne.

8 Case files include comments from children such as 'don't fit in', 'stuck up', VPRS 10093/1–7, Public Record Office, Melbourne. Numerous interviewees supported this. These findings are consistent with those from my interviews with other unaccompanied youth and children.

9 Cases cited in VPRS 10093/3, Public Record Office, Melbourne. Many interviewees also believed that their foster families were receiving this money.

10 Letter from the High Commissioner for the United Kingdom, Canberra, to the Prime Minister, 22 December 1941, A1608/1: S39/1/3.

11 Letters from premiers of Queensland and Western Australia, A1608/1: S39/1/3; also Victorian case files, VPRS 10093, Public Record Office, Melbourne.

12 The Australian equivalent of six shillings sterling. Where parents were unable to make a contribution the amount came from the United Kingdom Treasury. A letter from CORB to the Department of the Interior, 26 June 1944, shows that the majority of parents were paying the full amount. Of the 389 children who were not then self-supporting, 339 had parents who paid six shillings sterling a week, 44 less than six shillings, and only six who paid nothing. A659/1: 46/1/613 Part 4.

13 Memo from Cyril Bavin, CORB's representative in Australia, to the Department of the Interior, September 1942, A679/1: 46/1/609. Correspondence shows that this money did not come from parents' contributions.

14 Letter from Cyril Bavin to the Department of the Interior, 25 July 1944, shows that by then custodians could claim £2 10s a year for school books and equipment and £7 10d a year for clothing. Bavin had authority to approve amounts in excess of these if the requests were strongly supported by the child welfare department. For other expenditure he had to gain approval from CORB in London. A679/1: 46/1/609.

15 Letter to foster parents from the chairman of the New South Wales Overseas Children's Committee, 15 October 1940, SZ73, Archive Office of New South Wales.

16 'Borrowed Children', *Sydney Morning Herald*, Women's Supplement, 8 October 1940.

17 Letter from B. Whigham to Isabella Brown, 1 January 1941.

18 Letter to foster parents, 15 October 1940, op. cit.

19 There are several cases of children displaying severe emotional disorders, including perverse sexual behaviour, after hearing of the death or separation of parents. If parents stopped writing this also sometimes caused serious emotional reactions.

20 Letter from a foster parent to her daughter's escort, Isabella Brown, 6 January 1941.

21 Speech by Geoffrey Shakespeare at the Kinsmen luncheon, 17 February 1942, DO131/28: XC1143, Public Record Office, London.

22 Letter from Cyril Bavin to the Department of the Interior, 27 April 1944, A659/1: 46/1/613.

23 The British government contributed at least a proportion of the fees for British evacuees from the Pacific. The Netherlands East Indies government and the Portuguese government did the same for their nationals. A1608/1: Y19/1/1.

24 Letter from Cyril Bavin to the Department of the Interior, 19 May 1944, A659/1: 46/1/613. Records show three marriages and seven engagements by the end of the war, CP815/1/1: BUN24/21/5 Part 1.

25 In September 1944 Cabinet gave approval for CORB children to stay in Australia, provided they were acceptable from a migration point of view, in cases where the parents intended to settle in Australia and where the children wished to remain and had their parents' consent to do so. A2684/1: 1366.

26 Letter to Treasury from the Department of the Interior, 8 September 1944, A659/1: 46/1/613.

27 Letter from the Children's Welfare Department, Victoria, to the Department of the Interior, 22 November 1944, A659/1: 46/1/613.

28 The child welfare departments were informed each month of children who had not sent their monthly cable. VPRS 10093/8, Public Record Office, Melbourne. The cable service for both parents and children was provided free of charge by Cable and Wireless Limited and operated throughout the dominions. Soon after arrival, children were given a card with a selection of numbered texts. Sending a cable required going to the post office and requesting a particular numbered message be sent.

29 In Australia records were made with usually four children at a time. These were then sent by surface mail to Britain and, three to four months after being recorded, were played over the radio in a regular 'Hello Parents' broadcast. 183 children (and 348 parents) sent messages this way. 94 two-way conversations were held before the 'Children Calling Home' program was stopped. VPRS 10093/8, Public Record Office, Melbourne.

CHAPTER 9

1 Wolfgang Matsdorf, *No Time to Grow*, p. 106. Although half the boys had been born in Germany, they were

the children of eastern Jews, who had a considerably lower socio-economic status in Germany than did German Jews. All are referred to here as Polish Jews as that was their legal status in Australia.

2 Letter from Arthur Rose to the Immigration and Passports Office, 15 October 1941, A434/1: 41/3/1039. Jonas Pushett arrived penniless from Poland in 1926. Like many contemporaries, by 1939 he was of comfortable means and well established in the Melbourne Jewish community.

3 Jewish immigrants from eastern Europe began settling in Carlton in the 1870s. See Hilary Rubinstein, *The Jews in Australia*, Vol. 1, p. 157. The Polish immigrants who arrived in the 1920s strengthened the Jewish connection with Carlton, so that by the 1930s eastern Jews arriving in Melbourne automatically went first to Carlton. German and Austrian Jews generally settled across the river, around the more prestigious area of St Kilda.

4 Through collaboration with Hicem, Arthur Rose raised money and gained entry permits to Australia for 166 Polish families stranded in Kobe. Discussion of these arrangements appear in minutes of meetings of the directors of the Australian Jewish Welfare Society, 9 and 16 July, 13, 19 and 25 August 1941. Arthur Rose's commitment to rescuing refugees never ceased to upset the Australian Jewish Welfare Society. In a meeting on 25 August 1941 the directors resolved to inform Canberra that the Australian Jewish Welfare Society would no longer 'recognise any financial obligation with regard to such Jewish immigrants whose permits are obtained by the Polish Jewish Relief Committee unless the Society is fully consulted before an application is lodged for such permits'. Archives of AJWS, Melbourne.

5 Commonwealth Investigations Branch memo, 25 November 1941, A434/1: 41/3/1039.

6 Interview with Betty Doari.

7 The first Zionist youth movement, Shomrim, was established by young refugees in Sydney in 1939. The Habonim focussed on younger people. It became the channel through which many young people later went to Palestine/Israel.

8 Interview with Francie Spiegel. Francie, wife of Alwin Spiegel, was from an Anglo-Jewish family living in St Kilda, and regularly attended functions at the Kadimah and Habonim. This seems to have been rare among older Australian Jews and among German refugees who regarded Carlton as inferior.

9 'Farmboy Refugees', *Australian Jewish Times*, 19 May 1989.

10 Manfred Anson believes fourteen of the group intermarried. He has lost touch with everyone. *Australian Jewish Times*, 19 May 1989. Charlie Trainor confirmed that very few married Jewish girls.

11 They were among the forty-four young people who arrived in small groups in 1938 after vigorous campaigning by Norman Bentwich. The interviewee was sixteen on arrival.

12 Matsdorf, op. cit., p. 101. Matsdorf, pp. 97–105, provides accounts from many of these young settlers of their farming experiences in Australia.

13 This was the group that came under the auspices of the German Emergency Fellowship Committee. A letter from the European Emergency Committee, Sydney, to the German Emergency Committee, London, 20 September 1939, provides details of placements of all sixteen boys, A659/1: 39/1/4451. Camilla Wedgwood was responsible for finding them positions.

14 *Jerusalem Post*, 13 June 1989. Sigi Jaffe was the only orthodox boy in the group.

15 Kate Darian-Smith, *On the Home Front: Melbourne in Wartime 1939–1945*, p. 74. The Civil Alien Corps (CAC) was a section of the Civil Construction Corps, which contained mostly older men, but also about four thousand young alien men who were not regarded as a threat to national security.

16 According to Aleck Katz, Rabbi Goldberg, a chaplain in New Guinea, later found Szymon Klitenik's grave and replaced the cross with the Star of David.

17 *Jerusalem Post*, 13 June 1989.

18 Letter to Aleck Katz from his brother in Poland, 16 October 1940. The final letter was dated 5 March 1941.

CHAPTER 10

1 After the war, Margot's cousin recovered this and other letters from a neighbour. Margot's letters to her family, cited throughout this book, were among them.

2 Interview with Aleck Katz.

3 Alan Dershowitz, *Chutzpah*, p. 146, describes the postwar pogroms in Poland. He states that 1 500 Jewish survivors of the Holocaust were murdered in Poland in 1945 and 1946. The most infamous of these pogroms was in Kielce on 4 July 1946 when local Poles murdered forty Jews and wounded another sixty.

4 *Sydney Jewish News*, 31 August 1945. Calwell was sworn in as the first Minister for Immigration on 13 July 1945. In his autobiography, *Be Just and Fear Not*, pp. 101–2, Calwell describes how in his first weeks in office he worked with Jewish leaders trying to expedite the arrival of surviving 'fathers and mothers, brothers and sisters, and sons and daughters of members of the Jewish community already in Australia...I automatically approved of each list because I trusted my Jewish friends and they trusted me.'

5 Memo from A. R. Peters, acting secretary, Department of Immigration, 5 November 1945, AA(Vic) B741/3:V/4069.

6 Betty Doari was one of the original five. She married Michael Porter a couple of years after their settlement in Palestine. He had by then Hebraicised his name to Doari. In 1993 I visited Kibbutz Hanassi, where Betty still lives, as did Michael till his death in 1991. With its many gum-trees and Australian occupants, Hanassi retains an Australian aura, but its days as an Australian kibbutz seem numbered as there are no young Australians replacing the now ageing pioneers.

7 Diary entries for 1946 are filled with the prattle of a sixteen-year-old girl about weekends with friends, dances, boys, clothes. There is no mention of her family, nor of going to Israel, although her sister's request may not have been conveyed to her at this stage.

8 Letter from Cyril Bavin to the Department of Immigration, 4 September 1945, A659/1: 46/1/830.

9 ibid., 9 October 1945.

10 Statement by Cyril Bavin to a conference of welfare departments held in Melbourne, 17 June 1945, A659/1: 46/1/830.

11 Letter from Cyril Bavin to the Department of Immigration, 9 October 1945, A659/1: 46/1/830. Through the YMCA Cyril Bavin had a long involvement with child and youth migration before the war.

12 Letter from E. J. Pittard, secretary of the Children's Welfare Department, Melbourne, to Cyril Bavin, 15 May 1945. A659/1: 46/1/830.

13 Letter from the Department of Immigration to the Department of Information, 27 July 1945, A659/1: 46/1/830. Details on the booklet are in CP815/1/1: BUN24/21/5. In 1946 the booklet was reprinted, with the children's names omitted, under the title *Australia: A Home and a Future for British Youth*. It was distributed to promote migration to Australia.

14 *Sun*, 15 January 1946.

15 Letter from Arthur Calwell, Minister of Immigration, to Prime Minister Chifley, 28 February 1946, A461/1: Q349/1/7.

16 Memo from the Department of Immigration to Ben Chifley, 11 December 1946, A461/1: Q349/1/7.

17 Comments such as this were made on a number of the 154 questionnaires gathered for research purposes by Patricia Lin. The questionnaires are in 91/32/2, Imperial War Museum, London.

18 Letter from Marjorie Maxse, Director of CORB, 10 August 1943, DO131/35, Public Record Office, London.

19 Edward Stokes, *Innocents Abroad: The Story of British Child Evacuees in Australia, 1940-45*, p. 205, provides this figure. I believe it is higher, given the number of evacuees I have identified who are neither part of the reunion network nor had contact with other evacuees. Of the 577 evacuees who came to Australia a large number remain unaccounted for.

20 Peggy could never afford the fare to England, but after her father died the parishioners at her mother's church raised the money to send her mother to Australia. When Peggy's mother was dying Peggy's children paid her fare to England. These two brief encounters were her only family contact after leaving England in 1940.

21 Andrea now lives in England. The British government never gave reparations to colonial families uprooted by the Japanese war.

22 Martin Gilbert, 'Never To Forget', keynote address, The Hidden Child Second International Gathering, Jerusalem, 12–15 July 1993.

23 Bruno Bettelheim in Claudine Vegh, *I Didn't Say Goodbye*, pp. 161–79.

24 Frank Schroder, 'What Happened to Martin Levy?', 17 October 1980, source unknown. This article reached Hermann through a third person in 1988. It states that his mother died of tuberculosis on 4 November 1939. Exactly two years later, his father jumped from a window of their apartment block in Rostock — 'another citizen driven to death by the brown criminals', commented Frank Schroder.

25 Many former British child migrants who were denied information on their families share this pain, their unresolved pasts causing a lifetime of grieving.

26 The phenomenon of unhappy children becoming anti-Australian may not be uncommon. Some British evacuees also responded this way. A Perth Child Welfare Department letter, written on 11 August 1947, and referring to British children who migrated to Catholic institutions in the 1930s, states: 'The 1938–39 scheme in many ways was disastrous. Children brought out under this scheme became anti-social, anti-Australian and anti-Christ.'

CONCLUSION

1 Deborah Dwork, *Children with a Star*, note 27 on p. xxxiii, cites various sources on Jewish child survivor statistics. One source, Jacques Bloch, gives 1.6 million as the prewar population of Jews under sixteen 'living in what became the theatre of war'; the postwar population was 175 000. This included 30 000 children repatriated from the Soviet Union to Poland and Romania.

2 ibid.

3 Quoted by Martin Gilbert, 'Never to forget', keynote address The Hidden Child Second International Gathering, Jerusalem, 12–15 July 1993.

4 J. Noakes and G. Pridham, (eds), *Nazism: A History in Documents and Eyewitness Accounts, 1919–1945*, Vol. 2, pp. 997–1048, describe the Nazi 'euthanasia' program, which began before the war. Through it, mentally and physically disabled patients were transferred from hospitals and asylums to gas chambers. Children were taken to special paediatric clinics established in hospitals throughout the Reich. There they were 'either effectively starved to death, often dying of

diseases provoked by malnutrition, or given lethal injections or doses'.

5 Jewish Museum of Australia, *Courage to Care: Rescuers of Jews during the Holocaust*, p. 9. The exhibition acknowledged rescuers and the rescued who now live in Australia. At Yad Vashem in Jerusalem there is a an avenue of the righteous, where a tree is planted in memory of every 'righteous gentile'; a plaque on the tree tells about the person in whose memory the tree was planted.

6 John Fox, 'German and European Jewish Refugees, 1933–1945: Reflections on the Jewish Condition under Hitler and the Western World's Response to their Expulsion and Flight', in Anna Bramwell, (ed.), *Refugees in the Age of Total War*, p. 80.

7 Minutes of various Geneva meetings are in the file 'Children and war: miscellaneous notes and reports', Archives of SCF, London.

8 Hilary Rubinstein, *The Jews in Australia*, Vol. 1, p. 169.

9 Interview with Paul Cullen, cited in Suzanne Rutland, 'Australian Responses to Jewish Refugee Migration Before and After World War II', p. 38. Paul Cullen was the son of Sir Samuel Cohen, first president of the Australian Jewish Welfare Society.

10 Isaac Steinberg, *Plain Words to Australian Jews*, cited in Leon Gettler, *An Unpromised Land*, p. 102.

11 Following the Australian government's public denouncement of Nazi atrocities on 18 December 1942, the United Emergency Committee for European Jewry came into being, with Dr Machover as its chairman. Konrad Kwiet claims that with this the monopoly on leadership traditionally held by the establishment was finally broken. Representatives from both the Zionist camp and the refugee community now shared the power. Konrad Kwiet, 'Responses of Australian Jewry's Leadership to the Holocaust', in William Rubinstein, (ed.), *Jews in the Sixth Continent*, pp. 209–10.

12 Cable from Mr Symonds and Mr Masel to the Prime Minister, 5 September 1944, file B36, Archive of Australian Judaica, Sydney.

13 Meeting of the subcommittee on child migration, Department of the Interior, 24 January 1944, A989/1: 44/43/554/2/5.

14 These children went mostly to Israel or America after the war. The 300 permits, plus one hundred for the Welfare Guardian Society, went to other orphaned children and youth, small groups of whom began arriving in Australia in February 1948. The aim of the Australian government to admit 51 000 British and foreign child migrants never materialised. Non-British children were generally not available, Israel being the preferred option for Jewish orphans. The focus then switched to British children, with the voluntary organisations and churches resuming their prewar activity.

15 Steinberg later won over a few from both camps, but he remained on the fringe of the Jewish community.

16 Six CORB escorts including Australian escort, Doris Beeston, died on 27 November 1940 when a German raider sank the *Rangitane* on which they were returning to England. Eight other escorts were among eighty-one survivors picked up by another German raider after it sank the *Port Wellington* on 30 November 1940. They were taken to Europe as prisoners of war. Joan Fieldgate died from illness while in captivity; the others were released and repatriated to Britain in January 1943 through an exchange of prisoners organised by the Red Cross.

17 Michael Fethney, *The Absurd and the Brave*, frequently describes the CORB scheme as absurd.

18 Anna Freud and Dorothy Burlington, *War and Children*, pp. 60–4.

19 Susan Isaacs, *The Cambridge Evacuation Survey*, cited in Everett Ressler, Neil Boothby and Daniel Steinbeck, *Unaccompanied Children*, p. 175.

20 Ressler and others, ibid., pp. 155–6.

21 Geoffrey Bilson, *The Guest Children*.

22 Kathryn Close, *Transplanted Children: A History*.

23 Susan Isaacs, *The Cambridge Evacuation Survey*, pp. 54–5. This survey was conducted in 1940 and focussed on children evacuated to Cambridge.

24 Older children interviewed by Susan Isaacs also commented that it would have been better to go straight to work than to have to adjust to school life for a short time.

25 Interview with Edna Lehman.

26 D. Rey, cited in Ressler et al., op. cit., pp. 163–4.

27 Information provided by Tony Hamilton-Smith, Department of Immigration and Ethnic Affairs, Adelaide, December 1994. Relevant guidelines are in DIEA, *Procedures Advice Manual*, Pam3, Commonwealth of Australia, Canberra, 1994, Generic Guidelines B2, pp. 5–18.

SELECT BIBLIOGRAPHY

PUBLIC ARCHIVES

ARCHIVE OF AUSTRALIAN JUDAICA, SYDNEY

B series: N.S.W. Jewish Board of Deputies
B36 Persecutions; *Hebrew Standard* cuttings 1941
B37 Protest re mass Jewish migration to Australia; Shanghai; Nazi persecution of children
E series: Executive Council of Australian Jewry
E18 Correspondence file 21/2/46–31/10/46
Max Joseph Collection
Box 8 Association of Jewish Refugees 1939–42
Box 11 Publicity material
Subject Files
Australia and the refugee
Internment of Jewish refugees

ARCHIVES OFFICE OF NEW SOUTH WALES

Department: Education
SZ73 Unregistered correspondence 1933–51; includes children evacuated from Great Britain to New South Wales 1940
Department: Child Welfare
7/4621 Miscellaneous files
7/4622 Miscellaneous files

ARCHIVES OF THE CATHOLIC DIOCESAN CENTRE, ADELAIDE

Immigration 1 Various letters, reports etc. on child migration, from 1946, with reference to earlier activities
Immigration 2 Child migration, from 1948

AUSTRALIAN ARCHIVES, CANBERRA

Series number: A1/1
Department: Attorney General
37/16847 Australian National Travel Association. Admission boys from India
38/7083 Conference on migration for settlement, Geneva 1938
38/11509 German Emergency Fellowship Committee. Admission of non-Aryan Christians of Jewish extraction
38/11516 Migration statistics 1933–36
38/23138 AJWS. Proposal re control of Jewish migration
38/25491 Catholic refugees from Europe
38/32877 Council for Civil Liberties. Inquiry re refugees
38/33259 German democratic refugees from Sudeten area. Question of admission to Australia
38/3606 New South Wales: resumption of assisted migration
Series number: A373/1
Department: Security Service, Army
890 Jewish refugees in Australia
1680 Refugees from the Pacific area

Series number: A432/57
Department: Attorney-General
1938 League of Nations
1938/1184 Convention concerning the status of refugees coming from Germany: Geneva
1939/329 Support for Spanish refugee children
Series number: A433/1
Department: Interior
39/2/174 Spanish refugees: admission
39/2/664 United Kingdom. Statement on alien refugees
40/2/3030 Migrants Consultative Committee. Re Jewish refugees
41/2/222 Admission of 180 Polish boys for the duration of the war, question of
42/2/236 European women and children from Malaysia
43/2/46 Refugees (Jewish and other). General policy file
44/2/1703 Society of Friends (Quakers). Admission of youths, non-Aryan Christian refugees for farming
44/2/5976 Polish refugee children in Iran
49/2/5251 Evacuation of school children from Sumatra
49/2/5422 Evacuations to South Australia from abroad - policy and general questions
Series number: A434/1
Department: Interior
40/3/3266 Victorian International Refugee Emergency Committee. First Annual Report
41/3/1039 Polish Jewish Relief Fund — migration of children
44/3/1272 AJWS. Report re condition of Jewish children in Europe
46/3/265 Continental Catholic Migrants Welfare Committee. Re refugees (migrants)
47/3/2642 Polish Relief Committee (Victoria), Admission of limited number of male Jewish orphans to Australia
47/3/4316 Polish refugee children — admission to New Zealand
48/3/4074 Refugees in UK. 1. Admission to Australia; 2. Plans for resettlement
48/3/9033 Europe's children, by Zelda Popkin
49/3/3 AJWS. Scheme for admission of 300 refugee children. Part 1
49/3/7286 Australian Refugee Immigration Committee 1938–48
50/3/1145 Unaccompanied youths and children: Part 1 1948–50
Series number: A436/1
Department: Interior
49/5/1220 Catholic Episcopal Migration and Welfare Association. Request for Maltese children from Malta
Series number: A445/1
Department: Immigration
124/1/47 Assisted migration. General policy
133/2/8 Catholic Episcopal Migration and Welfare Association — Perth. Child migration
133/2/90 Catholic Episcopal Migration and Welfare Association - request for Maltese children from Malta
255/1/8 Admission of Polish refugee children in India to Australia
Series number: A446/1
Department: Immigration
62/67352 IRO. Intergovernmental Committee for Refugees 1943–1946
Series number: A461/1
Department: Prime Minister
A349/1/2 Part 1 Immig. Policy. Part 1, 1934–5
A349/1/2 Part 2 Immig. Policy. Part 2, 1935–6
A349/1/2 Part 3 Immig. Policy. Part 3, 1937–8
A349/1/2 Part 4 Immig. Policy. Part 4, 1939–44
A349/1/7 Part 1 Child migration. General, 1937–44
A349/1/7 Part 2 Child migration. General. Part 2, 1944–50
A349/3/1 Part 1A Immigration restriction. Australian policy. Main file, 1920–25
A349/3/1 Part 2 Foreign Immig. Policy, 1937–40
A349/3/1 Part 3 Foreign Immig. Policy, 1940–48
D349/1/2 Part 2 Immigration. Unofficial schemes, 1925–38
I349/1/3 Empire Migration and Development Conference, October 1937
M349/1/7 Child migration to Catholic institutions. Western Australia
M349/3/5 Part 1 Jews - policy. Part 1
MA349/3/5 Part 1 Jews. General. Part 1, 1933–38
MA349/3/5 Part 2 Jews. General. Part 2
N349/1/7 Child migration. Methodist homes for children. Western Australia
P349/1/5 Immigration encourgement. Government scheme. South Australia. Settlement of 6,000 boys, 1922–24
Q349/1/7 Admission to Australia of British and refugee children
Y349/3/5 European refugees. Admission to Australia
Series number: A659/1
Department: Interior
39/1/818 Publicity abroad. Assisted migration
39/1/1551 Austro-Australian Jewish Relief Committee, purpose of
39/1/4451 Refugees (Emergency Council). Organisation in N.S.W. for their absorption
40/1/192 Burnside children. Group nomination
40/1/645 Overseas Children Scheme. Nominations forwarded to London. New South Wales
40/1/4919 Consul General of the Netherlands re Netherland children coming to Australia
40/1/5431 Overseas Children Scheme. Victorian police
40/1/6335 Overseas Children Scheme. Group school children to Victoria
40/1/6453 Overseas Children Scheme. Nominations forwarded to London. Queensland
40/1/6454 Overseas Children Scheme. Nominations forwarded to London. South Australia

BIBLIOGRPAHY

40/1/6452 Overseas Children Scheme. Nominations forwarded to London. Victoria
40/1/6582 Overseas Children Scheme. MV *Batory*
40/1/6583 Overseas Children Scheme. Publicity
40/1/6584 Overseas Children Scheme. SS *Nestor*
40/1/6585 Overseas Children Scheme. Financial arrangements and provision of funds
40/1/6587 Overseas Children Scheme. Allocation to states on population basis
40/1/6590 Overseas Children Scheme. Visit of J. H. Honeysett to Perth
40/1/7621 Overseas Children Scheme. Report on arrangements in Queensland for reception and placement of children from MV *Batory*
40/1/7825 Queensland Master Printers & Allied Traders Association. Information re British child evacuees
40/1/7831 Overseas Children Scheme. Evacuation of physically defective children overseas
40/1/7963 Overseas Children Scheme. Fund for evacuee children
40/1/8157 Overseas Children Scheme. Expenses paid in connection with examination of children by Dr W. A. Park
41/1/75 Overseas Children Scheme. Queensland reimbursement claims
41/1/597 Overseas Children Scheme. Evacuation scheme for school children
41/1/1261 Overseas Children Scheme. Transfer of war orphans
41/1/1373 Arrivals and departures of assisted migrants. Statistics for 1932–1940
41/1/1554 Overseas Children Scheme. Discharge of D. A. Manning from scheme
41/1/1670 J. Alexander. CORB 282. Circumstances under which above was evacuated
41/1/1771 Salvation Army policy file, 1929–42
41/1/2707 Overseas Children Scheme. Maintenance of escorts while in Australia
41/1/2724 Overseas Children Scheme. Reimbursement claims. Victoria
41/1/2756 Overseas Children Scheme. Reimbursements claims. Western Australia
41/1/3157 Transfer of British and refugee children to Australia. Offers of assistance from organisations
41/1/5012 Priority bookings. Travel between Australia and U.K. (via U.S.A.)
41/1/7821 Evacuation of women and children from Darwin, Papua and New Guinea by SS *Zealandia* December 1941
41/1/7822 Evacuation of women and children from Darwin and New Guinea by SS *Koolinda* January 1942
43/1/3278 Fairbridge Farm Schools. Migration during war
43/1/4124 Overseas Children Scheme. Audrey Beswick: transfer to Darwin
43/1/4703 Overseas Children Scheme. Financial assistance from the Australian Universities' Commission
44/1/846 46/1/609 Overseas Children Scheme: Question of employment of girls in army in India
44/1/863 Overseas children. Regulations under the National Security Regulations
44/1/1134 Overseas Children Scheme. Record of children and custodians (Queensland) Part 2
44/1/3895 Overseas Children Scheme. Record of children and custodians (Queensland) Part 1
45/1/125 Overseas children. Enlistment of English born boys in UK or Indian army
45/1/510 Assisted migration. Policy during state of war, 1939
45/1/511 Agreements. Empire Settlement Act
46/1/609 Overseas Children Scheme. Establishment of fund to meet special expenditures
46/1/613 Overseas Children Scheme. Policy. Part 4
46/1/782 Overseas children. Letters from, describing impressions of Australia
46/1/830 Overseas children. Return of main body to U.K. Arrangements
46/1/831 Marriages in Australia: Overseas children
46/1/839 United Nations Relief and Rehabilitation Administration. Agreement between various governments including Australia
46/1/4515 Overseas Children Scheme. Policy. Part 2
46/1/4518 Overseas Children Scheme. Nominal rolls
50/1/689 Overseas children remaining in Australia. Part 5
50/1/690 Overseas children remaining in Australia (after return of main body). Part 6
50/1/2053 Overseas Children Scheme. Policy file. Part 1
Series number: A679/1
Department: Interior
44/1/3313 Overseas Children Scheme: release from scheme to return to the UK, 1944
46/1/609 Overseas Children Scheme: special fund
46/1/839 United Nations Relief and Rehabilitation Administration
Series number: A989/1
Department: Foreign Affairs
43/755/6 Evacuation of Jewish refugees from Vichy France
44/43/554/2/5 Migration - Australia. Child migration
44/43/554/2/5/1 Child migration - Polish child migration to Australia
44/735/753/11 Relief representations: European Children's Relief Fund
Series number: A1066/1
Department: External Affairs
M45/17/2 United Emergency Committee for European Jewry: Mauritius internees
Series number: A1608/1
Department: Prime Minister
AU39/1/3 Polish children from Iran
B61/1/1 Control of passenger traffic in time of war
C39/1/3Part 1 Admission to Australia of British and refugee children. Policy. Part 1
C39/1/3Part 2 Admission to Australia of British and refugee children. Policy. Part 2
D39/1/3 Admission to Australia of British children. General representations
E39/1/3 Transfer of children to Australia: nominations (cables)
F19/1/1 Assistance to Poland. Migration of refugees
S39/1/3 British children from UK - financial
X39/1/3 Admission to Australia of war orphans from UK
Y19/1/1 War refugees - policy
Series number: A1838/265
Department: External Affairs
1531/71/1 Immigration. Migration Australia. Interdepartmental Committee
Series number: A1928
Department: Health
520/35 Section 1 Hong Kong evacuees
520/35 Section 2 British refugee children
Series number: A2671
Department: War Cabinet
294/1942 Evacuee children from the external territories. Child endowment
Series number: A2673
Department: War Cabinet and Advisory War Council, minutes
3/357 19 June 1940
3/383 2 July 1940
4/455 Internal evacuation: Australia
Series number: A2684
Department: War Cabinet and Advisory War Council, minutes and files
716 Evacuation of children from vulnerable areas
1167 Shipping position 1943–46
1366 Post war migration
Series number: A2697
Department: War Cabinet, minutes and submissions
4A/371 Transfer of overseas children to Australia
4A/374 Reference to agenda item 371
4B/371 Transfer of overseas children to Australia
Series number: A2697 XR1
Department: War Cabinet
Volume 4/371 Transfer of children from UK to Australia during the war
Series number: A2698 XR1
Department: War Cabinet, numerical index cards
Volume 1/371 Transfer of young children from UK to Australia during the war
Series number: A2699
Department: War Cabinet, index book 1939–41
550 Admission of 180 Polish boys
Series number: A2937/1
Department: External Affairs, London
NN Evian Conference
221 Refugees. General, 1938–45
Series number: A6006/1
Department: Prime Minister
2nd Lyons Ministry 7 November-December
Series number: A3258 XM
Department: War Cabinet
5/215 Jews (British subjects) resident in UK - question as to whether they should be granted assisted passage
5/284 Relief of suffering in Spain
Series number: CP815/1/1
Department: Information
BUN24/21/5 Part 1 Migration - Booklet for evacuee children

BUN24/21/5 Part 2 CORB children in Victoria (compiled 18/9/45)
BUN 25/21/19 Migration. Child migration, 1943–49
Series number: SP109/1
Department: Information
78/12/27 Films of evacuee children 1941
78/16/2 Cinema films, photographs and broadcast recordings of evacuee children travelling to Australia
Series number: SP109/3/1
Department: Information
382/3 Box 63 *Women's Weekly* relating to evacuees
386/8 Box 63 *News*, Adelaide. Articles re evacuees
Series number: SP112/1/1
Department: Information
263/1/1 Suggestions for the welfare of child refugees in Australia, 1940
265/15/7 Questions relating to refugee children

AUSTRALIAN ARCHIVES, NEW SOUTH WALES

Series number: C1115/6
Department: Immigration
Passenger lists. Inward ships, Sydney
Series number: C3458
Department: Immigration
Aircraft papers, Inward passenger lists, Sydney
Series number: SP1084
Department: Customs
Aliens' arrival January to December 1940
Series number: SPC1
Department: Information: State Publicity Censorship
104 Censorship of interviews with persons arriving from the Far East
122 Arrival of vessels carrying British children
124 Departure of vessels carrying British children
153 Sinking of *SS Rangitane*
386 Evacuation and evacuees

AUSTRALIAN ARCHIVES, SOUTH AUSTRALIA

Series number: AP570/1
Department: Social Services
F081 Child endowment
F0213 Chinese evacuated from Nauru and Ocean Island
Series number: AP570/2
Department: Social Services
A448 Evacuee children from overseas
A449 Evacuation of children (in case of emergency)
Series number: D1915/0
Department: Commonwealth Police, Investigation Branch, S.A.
22320 Association of Jewish Refugees
Series number: D2248
Department: Immigration
Inward passenger lists, Adelaide, 1941–48

AUSTRALIAN ARCHIVES, VICTORIA

Series number: B4397/X3
Department: Immigration
Inward passenger lists 1924–1964
Series number: B741/3
Department: Commonwealth Investigation Service
V/161 Immigration problems
V/4069 Permits to enter Australia
V/4281 Alien communities in Victoria (1936–50)
V/5164 Jewish Welfare Society
Series number: MP508/1
Department: Army
82/713/233 Evacuation of children
115/701/78 Memo from societies working among refugees

AUSTRALIAN ARCHIVES, WESTERN AUSTRALIA

Series number: K269
Department: Customs
Inward passenger lists, Perth

AUSTRALIAN JEWISH HISTORICAL SOCIETY, MELBOURNE

Letter from Mr and Mrs Taft to the Department of Child Welfare, Melbourne, 1940.
Welfare Guardian Society

AUSTRALIAN JEWISH HISTORICAL SOCIETY, SYDNEY

66 Australian Jewish Welfare Society
169 *Dunera* and refugees; includes AJWS pamphlet, 'Fighting Fund for the Rescue of Persecuted Jewish Refugee Children from War Devastated Europe to Australia
655 Immigration and emigration
533 Isabella Lazarus Children's Home
832 Letters to Rabbi I. A. Falk from refugees, 1938–40
C2 Australian Jewish Welfare Society, Annual Reports 1938–78

AUSTRALIAN JEWISH WELFARE SOCIETY, MELBOURNE

Annual reports of the AJWS
Exercise book on Larino Home, 1947–53
Guardian reports and other old files
Minutes of meetings of the Directors of the AJWS, from July 1939
Minutes of Executive meetings of the Jewish Welfare Guardian Society, March 1939 to October 1945

AUSTRALIAN JEWISH WELFARE SOCIETY, PERTH

Minutes of the Executive of the W.A. branch
Minutes of the General Committee of W.A. branch of AJWS

AUSTRALIAN JEWISH WELFARE SOCIETY, SYDNEY

Minutes of Annual General Meetings 1939–89
Minutes of Executive Committee meetings, November 1938 to April 1939
Minutes of Rota committee meetings, January 1938 to June 1939
Scrapbook showing children selected by OSE (Geneva) for Australia, post war

AUSTRALIAN WAR MEMORIAL

PRMF 0021 Mass observation file reports 1937–49:
87 What children think of war, April 1940
174 Refugees — change in attitude, June 1940
284 What is likely to have happened to Britain by the end of the year — a survey of public opinion, July 1940
299 Children and the war, July 1940
454 Photograph of woman and child; propaganda picture, October 1940
467 The official side of evacuation, October 1940
544 Attitudes to invasion, January 1941
594 The invasion leaflet, February 1941

CENTRAL ZIONIST ARCHIVES, JERUSALEM

Series: L13 Central Bureau for the Settlement of German Jews in Palestine, London
56 Central welfare organisation for German Jews
57/1 Child migration and Youth Aliyah
74 Reports on various countries
146 Jewish Refugees Committee - German Jewish Aid Committee
147 Council for German Jewry 1936–39
149 Central British Fund for German Jewry 1933–34
165 The Jewish situation in Germany
171 Norman Bentwich: report on a visit to Berlin, November 1933
Series: A255 Personal archives of Norman Bentwich
301 British Commonwealth Relations Conference 1938
325 High Commissioner for Refugees (Jewish and other) coming from Germany
388 High Commissioner for Refugees: duplicated documents 1936
390 British Commonwealth Relations Conference 1938
393 British Commonwealth Relations Conference 1938, 1937, 1936
397 Racial persecution in Germany 1933–39
400 Evian Conference
402 Various papers by Norman Bentwich on Austrian and German refugees
422 Refugees in England
440 Central British Fund for German Jewry
764 'The Problem of the Refugees in Europe', paper written by Norman Bentwich for *Contemporary Review*, undated but about 1941
Series: S6 Executive of the Zionist Organisation and the Jewish Agency for Palestine in Jerusalem, Tel-Aviv and Haifa, Immigration Department
3865 Immigration of internees from Australia to Palestine

BIBLIOGRAPHY

3868–9 Letters from internees in Australia re immigration to Palestine
Series: S75 Executive of the Zionist Organisation and the Jewish Agency for Palestine in Jerusalem, Tel-Aviv and Haifa, Youth Aliyah Department 1933–71
661 Correspondence on release of boys from internment in Australia, 1941
662 Report on release of six Youth Aliyah boys from internment in Australia
1361 Report from Tatura
1975 Australia and New Zealand: correspondence 1940–43
1979 Australia and New Zealand: correspondence 1946

FILM AUSTRALIA, SYDNEY

Notes on interviews conducted by Avivah Ziegler, 1991.

GREATER LONDON RECORD OFFICE

Records of the Board of Deputies of British Jews 1939–1966:
B4/CON23 Conference on emigration
E1/37 Council for German Jewry
B4/EM32 Emigration - settlement of German Jewish refugees in Australia
C11/12/12 France
E3/532/1 German Jewish Aid Committee
C11/12/88 Poland. Refugees
E3/109 Poland. 1937
C9/1/c6 Refugee Children's Movement
C11/7/3d/5 Relief and reconstruction

HEBREW UNIVERSITY, JERUSALEM

Papers of Melech Ravitch

IMPERIAL WAR MUSEUM, LONDON

79/22/1 J. D. Layton, miscellaneous letters and reports
80/39/1 Mrs Burkill - Refugee Children's Movement
84/2/1 Diary of A. Frazer-Allen
91/6/1 William Kahle, 'What would you have done?', unpublished manuscript
92/31/1 Autobiography of Anita Lasker-Wallfisch
Misc. 593 Report on SS *Benares'* sinking
Misc. 818 Mrs Burkill's experiences with the Cambridge Refugee Children's Movement
Misc. 1768 Inquiry into sinking of the *Rangitane*
Mrs B. Hoops - evacuation from Penang
Captain W. E. H. Lang - children escaping to Java

LEO BAECK INSTITUTE, JERUSALEM

409/1 Council for German Jewry
553/1 Jewish welfare organisations in Germany
555/1 Reports of the Reichsvertretung der Juden in Deutschland

LIBRARY OF THE RELIGIOUS SOCIETY OF FRIENDS, LONDON

FCRA/2 8 German Emergency Committee: minutes 1936–193

FCRA/3 German Emergency Committee: minutes 1939
FCRA/13 German Emergency Committee. Executive Committee minutes 1938–1939
FCRA/18 German Emergency Committee papers 1933–1946
FCRA/25 Correspondence of Movement for the Care of Children from Germany
MS volume 54 Australia and New Zealand Committee

MITCHELL LIBRARY, SYDNEY

A4118 NSW Department of Education, Record of service in two world wars, part 2
CY1165/A4993 Dreadnought Trust N.S.W.
CY1165/A4995 Dreadnought Trust N.S.W.
MSS3842 Society of Friends N.S.W. Records 1867–1978

MORTLOCK LIBRARY, ADELAIDE

Z Pam: 325.9423/S726 South Australia: the wheat and garden state; opportunities for boys to become farmers, n.d., possibly 1920s

NATIONAL LIBRARY, CANBERRA

Australian Joint Copying Project, PRO series:
DO35/529 reel 5373; DO35/674 reel 5409;
DO35/703 reel 5420; DO35/705 reel 5420;
DO35/711 reel 5423; DO35/712 reel 5423;
DO35/713 reel 5424; DO35/717 reel 5426;
DO35/718 reel 5426; DO35/720 reel 5426;
DO35/1002 reel 5550; DO35/1139 reel 5619;
DO35/1140 reel 5619; DO57/152 reel 6742;
DO114/74 reel 6004
Australian Joint Copying Project, M series:
M1841–5 Fairbridge Society Records 1912–1976
Religious Society of Friends (Quakers) in Australia, 1900–1969 - MS 4953:
Papers of Brian Fitzpatrick - MS 4965
1a Correspondence
1b Agenda, minutes and reports
1g Scrap books and press cuttings

PUBLIC RECORD OFFICE, LONDON

Series number: BT26/1184
Department: Customs
Incoming passenger lists
Series number: DO131
Department: Dominions Office
11 Guardianship: general. 1941–1942
27 Statistics of children leaving the UK
28 Children's Overseas Reception scheme. Speeches and general surveys
35 Settlement overseas of CORB children. General
42 Awards for services
43 History of CORB 1940–1944
56 Use of parents' contributions
58 Financial basis of CORB scheme 1940
59 Transport (shipping)
68 Policies and responsibilities of the board in general
69 Children's trust accounts
70 CORB. Proposed investigation of results of scheme

74 Confidential report to CORB by Roland Cartwright, escort to CORB children
80 Michael Rennie, escort. Died in *City of Benares*.
106 Children's Overseas Reception Board: Australia
Series number: FO371
Department: Foreign Office
24086 Admission of refugees to various countries
25250 1940. Evacuation overseas
25251 1940. Evacuation overseas
25252 1940. Evacuation overseas
25253 Emigration of aliens
Series number: HO213
Department: Home Office
993 Adoption of children who are not British subjects
994 Refusal of exit permits to aliens contributing to war effort
995 Spanish refugee children
Series number: CAB65
Department: War Cabinet
65/7 Cabinet conclusions May-June 1940
65/8 Cabinet conclusions July-August 1940
65/13 Confidential annexes 1 May–30 June 1940
65/14 Confidential annexes 1 July–30 August 1940
Series number: CAB66
Department: War Cabinet
66/9 Cabinet papers 1940
Series number: PREM4
Department: Prime Minister
39/3 Advisory Council on Aliens July 1940-February 1941
42/1 Migration 1942–45
98/3 Relief for children in occupied Europe 1942–44
99/1 Evacuation 1940–44

PUBLIC RECORD OFFICE, VICTORIA

Series number: VPRS10093
Department: Child Welfare
1–9 Children's Overseas Reception Board files (closed)

SAVE THE CHILDREN FUND, LONDON

M1/7 Minutes of the Council of Save the Children Fund 1929–35
M3/1 Minutes of the Executive Committee 1938–42
Minutes and agendas of the board of officers January 1939-August 1940
Annual reports
Children and war: miscellaneous notes and reports

STATE RECORDS, SOUTH AUSTRALIA

Series number: GRG7
Department: Immigration, Publicity and Tourist Bureau
76 Miscellaneous immigration records
Series number: GRG29
Department: Social Welfare
1 Annual reports of the State Children's Council and the Children's Welfare and Public Relief Department, 1887–1955

93 Reports and correspondence concerning foster mothers and applicants
95 Reports and correspondence on war evacuees from the UK, 1940–45 (closed)
122 Release order under Immigration (Guardianship of Children) Act
125/1 Conference papers and correspondence on immigration of minors 1948
129 Case histories of children in the care of the department 1938–62

Series number: GRG41/34
Department: Immigration
Incoming passenger lists 1940

Series number: GRG69
Department: Kindergarten Union of South Australia
8/2 Correspondence of the Secretary 1936
8/16 Correspondence on the appointment of Secretary and office staff
8/28 Annual meeting correspondence
9/10 Files of the Secretary 1941–75
17 Annual Reports

UNIVERSITY OF MELBOURNE

Archives of the Central British Fund for World Jewish Relief:
File 2, reel 1 Council for German Jewry
File 5, reel 2 Central Council for Jewish Refugees
File 6, reel 2 Executive of the Central Council for Jewish Refugees, October 1938-May 1944
File 15, reel 4 Anglo-Jewish Conference 1936
File 25, reel 4 Norman Bentwich: report on a visit to Vienna, 17 August 1939
File 34, reel 5 CBF Annual Reports, 1934–1962
File 35, reel 6 International Conference for the Relief of German Jewry, London, 1933
File 39, reel 7 Domestic Bureau of Council for German Jewry
File 53, reel 10 Austria: reports on visits by Norman Bentwich 1938–1939
File 56, reel 11 Australia: correspondence United Jewish Overseas Relief Fund 1944–50
File 61, reel 12 France: reports and correspondence 1944–56
File 63, reel 12 Germany: pre-war reports
File 84, reel 16 Dominions: minutes, memoranda and correspondence re emigration
File 96, reel 19 Czechoslovakia: Czech Refugee Trust Fund
File 146, reel 26 Excerpts from children's letters - undated
Files 153–166, reel 28 Refugee Chldren's Movement
File 174, reel 32 Jewish Refugees Committee (German Jewish Aid Committee): Executive Committee minutes November 1934-January 1938
File 175, reel 32 Jewish Refugees Committee (German Jewish Aid Committee): Executive Board minutes February-August 1939
File 176, reel 32 Jewish Refugees Committee (German Jewish Aid Committee): Minutes March 1944-November 1946

WEINER LIBRARY, LONDON

Document 606 Correspondence of the Reichsvertretung with the Council for German Jewry; correspondence of the Council for German Jewry with the Dominions Office
Document 608 Council for German Jewry
Document 683 Portugal
Document 744 Emigration from Germany
Document 1044 The Rescue Movement (London)
Press archives, reel 17 Invasion of Britain
Press archives, reel 148/215D Aliens and refugees - migration and settlement. This includes the *Daily News Bulletin* issued by the Jewish Telegraphic Agency.

WIZO STATE COUNCIL OF VICTORIA

ADAR 5746 The Jews and Japan

YAD VASHEM, JERUSALEM

M–9/37(1a) Office of the Chief Counsel for War Crimes. Emigration to Palestine
M–9/50(17) Office of the Chief Counsel for War Crimes. France, children, emigration to Australia
MF–12(47) Microfiche records of the Reichsvertretung der Juden in Deutschland (originals badly damaged before filming). In German.
MI/DN/25/1822 Re Jewish refugees leaving from German ports. In German.
P–14/2 Bureau of Jewish Affairs
P–14/10 Australia and the refugee
02/151 M. Mitzman: a visit to Germany, Austria and Poland in 1939
12/177 Experiences of a 'Mischling' in Frankfurt
02/340 Captain Foley: bribery of Nazi officials
02/476 Letters of a 12 year old girl from Vienna, winter 1938/39. In German.
02/501 Interview at Bergen-Belsen, anonymous

PRIVATE ARCHIVES

Diaries
Ellen Anderson (in possession of her daughter, Binky Henderson)
Ferry Fixel (in possession of his wife, Hedi Fixel)
Isabella Lupton
Pat McEvoy
Sheila Slight

Personal documents and letters
Laurie Badrian, Margot Herschenbaum, Aleck Katz, Hermann Levy, Isabella Lupton, Pat McEvoy, Betty Midalia, Max Nagel, Ellen Shafer, Werner Teitel, Charlie Trainor, Joyce Turnbull, Freda Welsh

INTERVIEWS AND CORRESPONDENCE

Interviews
Ellen Anderson, Laurie Badrian, Andrea Bannantyne, Peter Barnard, Yossel Birstein, Paula Boltman, Dorothy Brunt, Herco Cohn, Peggy Cox, Beryl Daley, Anne Dawkins, Betty Doari, Millie Donald, Alf Downes, Dorryn Drabsch, Phil Drabsch, George Dreyfus, Richard Dreyfus, Patricia Duffy, Hans Eisler, Mollie Elvish, Hedi Fixel, Ted Flowers, Helmut Graf, Jack Garbasz, Shulamit Garbasz, Max Goldberg, Ken Gregory, John Hare, Margot Herschenbaum, Aleck Katz, Hermann Levy, Anne Lowden, Isabella Lupton, Ursula Meyerstein, Gisella Michelson, Betty Midalia, Keith Muenz, Max Nagel, Ingrid Naumberger, Maureen Norling, Bill Oats, Ian Paterson, Marion Paul, George Perl, Jonas Pushett, Frances Rothschild, Inge Sadan, Jean Saltzman, Edna Samson, Norman Schindler, Ellen Shafer, Derek Simpson, Beryl Smith, Alwin Spiegel, Francie Spiegel, Alfred Stocks, Jules Stocky, Alfred Stricker, Joan Sullivan, Werner Teitel, Phyllis Thatcher, Alan Timmins, Rosalie Tobin, Charlie Trainor, Joyce Turnbull, Charles Wallis, Eric Ward, Audrey Watson, Jo Weinreb, Freda Welsh

Correspondence
Rodney Breen, Hazel Browne, Anne Dawkins, Braham Glass, Phyllis Holdsworth, Ilse Howard, Cliff Humphreys, Helmut Kallman, Helga Leslie, Hermann Levy, Pat McEvoy, Donald Mitchell, Lutz Noack, Ellen Ostrower, Bob Payne, Philip Robinson, Harry Schwersenz, Sheila Slight, Ernest Stein, Isabella Summerbell, Elsie Sutherland, John Templeton, Peter Tikotin, Alan Timmins, Jo Weinreb, Else Weiss, Freda Welsh, Nicholas Winton, Norbert Wollheim

NEWSPAPERS AND MAGAZINES

Advertiser (Adelaide)
Argus (Melbourne)
Australian Jewish Herald (Melbourne)
Australian Jewish News
Australian Jewish Times
Australian Women's Weekly
Bulletin
Canberra Times
Cape Times (Capetown)
Courier–Mail (Brisbane)
Daily Telegraph (Sydney)
Express and Telegraph (Adelaide)
Hebrew Standard
Hebrew Times
Herald (Melbourne)
Jerusalem Post
Jewish Chronicle (London)
Mail (Adelaide)
News (Adelaide)
Pix
Smith's Weekly (Sydney)
Sun (Sydney)
Sun News-Pictorial (Melbourne)
Sydney Jewish News
Sydney Morning Herald
The Times (London)
The World's Children (Save the Children Fund, London)
Transcontinental (Port Augusta)
Westralian Judean
Woman

PARLIAMENTARY PAPERS

Commonwealth of Australia, Parliamentary Debates, volume 163, 17 April to 31 May 1940

BOOKS AND ARTICLES

Andgel, Anne. *Fifty Years of Caring: the History of the Australian Jewish Welfare Society 1936–1986*, The Australian Jewish Welfare Society and the Australian Jewish Historical Society, Sydney, 1988

Arad, Yitzhak, Yisrael, Gutman, and Abraham, Margaliot. *Documents on the Holocaust*, Yad Vashem, Jerusalem, 1981

Australian Association of Jewish Holocaust Survivors. *The Gift of Life*, self published, Sydney, 1985

Barker, Ralph, *Children of the Benares*, Grafton Books, London, 1987.

Bartrop, Paul and Eisen, Gabrielle (Eds), *The Dunera Affair: A Documentary Resource Book*, Jewish Museum of Australia and Schwartz & Wilkinson, Melbourne, 1990.

Bartrop, Paul, *Australia and the Holocaust 1933–45*, Australian Scholarly Publishing, Melbourne, 1994.

Benjamin, Alison, *Children at War*, Save the Children, London, 1994.

Bentwich, Norman, *Jewish Youth Comes Home: the Story of the Youth Aliyah, 1933–1943*, Victor Gollancz Ltd, London, 1944.

Bentwich, Norman, *They Found Refuge*, The Crescent Press, London, 1956.

Berger, George, 'Australia and the refugees', part 1, *Australian Quarterly*, vol. 13, 1941.

Berner, George, 'Children in Vienna', *Jewish Frontier*, vol. 7, 1939.

Bilson, Geoffrey, *The Guest Children*, Fifth House, Saskatoon, 1988.

Blakeney, Michael, *Australia and the Jewish Refugees 1933–1938*, Croom Helm Australia, London, 1985.

Bramwell, Anna (Ed.), *Refugees in the Age of Total War*, Unwin Hyman, London, 1988.

Bullock, Alan, *Hitler: a Study in Tyranny*, Pelican Books, London, 1962.

Calwell, Arthur, *Be Just and Fear Not*, Rigby Limited, Adelaide, 1978.

Carr-Gregg, Charlotte and Maclean, Pam, 'A mouse nibbling at a mountain': the problem of Australian refugee policy and the work of Camilla Wedgewood, *Australian Journal of Politics and History*, vol. 31, 1985.

Carr-Gregg, Charlotte, The work of the German Emergency Fellowship Committee, 1938–1941. In W. D. Rubinstein (Ed.), *Jews in the Sixth continent*, Allen & Unwin, Sydney, 1987.

Castendyck, Elsa, 'Refugee children in Europe', *The Social Service Review*, vol. 13, 1939.

Chausse, Dorothy, 'The evacuation of refugee children our responsibility: notes and comment by the editor', *Social Service Review*, vol. 14, 1940.

Child Emigration Committee, *Child Emigration: a Study Made in 1948–50 by a Committee of the Women's Group on Public Welfare*, National Council of Social Service, London, 1951.

Chomski, Isaac, 'Children in exile', *Contemporary Jewish Record*, vol. 4, 1941.

Close, Kathryn, *Transplanted Children*, US Committee for the Care of European Children, New York, 1953.

Coldrey, Barry, *Child Migration, the Australian Government and the Catholic Church 1926–1966*, Tamanaraik Publishing, Melbourne, 1992.

Collier, Richard, *1940: The World in Flames*, Penguin Books, London, 1979.

Crosby, Travis, *The Impact of Civilian Evacuation in the Second World War*, Croom Helm, London, 1986.

Darby, E. D., 'Wartime migration: British children for Australia', *Australian Quarterly*, vol. 12, 1940.

Darby, E. D., *Orphans of the War*, British Orphans Adoption Society, Sydney, pamphlet no. 1, 1944.

Darian-Smith, Kate, *On the Home Front: Melbourne in Wartime 1939–1945*, Oxford University Press, Melbourne, 1990.

Darton, Lawrence, *An Account of the Work of the Friends Committee for Refugees and Aliens, First Known as the German Emergency Committee of the Society of Friends 1933–1950*, Friends Committee for Refugees and Aliens, London, 1954.

David, Kati, *A Child's War: World War 2 through the Eyes of Children*, Four Walls Eight Windows, New York, 1989.

Dawidowicz, Lucy, *The War against the Jews* (tenth anniversary edition), Seth Press, New York, 1975.

Dawidowicz, Lucy (Ed), *A Holocaust Reader*, Behrman House Inc, New Jersey, 1976.

Department of Immigration and Ethnic Affairs, *Procedures Advice Manual*, Commonwealth of Australia, Canberra, 1994.

Dershowitz, Alan, *Chutzpah*, Simon and Schuster, New York, 1991.

Detrick, Sharon (Ed.), *The United Nations Convention on the Rights of the Child*. Dordrecht, the Netherlands: Martinus Nijhoff Publishers, 1992.

Dreyfus, George, *The Last Frivolous Book*, Hale and Iremonger Pty Ltd, Sydney, 1984.

Dwork, Deborah, *Children with a Star: Jewish Youth in Nazi Europe*, Yale University Press, London, 1991.

Eisenberg, Azriel, *Witness to the Holocaust*, The Pilgrim Press, New York, 1981.

Eisenberg, Azriel, *The Lost Generation: Children in the Holocaust*, the Pilgrim Press, New York, 1982.

Feiglin, Risha, 'Jewish refugees from Hitler: the Australian experience as reflected in the literature', *Australian Historical Bibliography*, vol. 9, 1984.

Fethney, Michael, *The Absurd and the Brave*, The Book Guild Ltd, Sussex, 1990.

Forsyth, W. D., *The Myth of Open Spaces*, Melbourne University Press, Melbourne, 1942.

Fox, John, German and European Jewish refugees, 1933–1945: reflections on the Jewish condition under Hitler and the western world's response to their expulsion and flight. In Anna Bramwell (Ed.), *Refugees in the age of total war* (pp.69–85), Unwin Hyman, London, 1988.

Fox, Len, *Australia and the Jews*, League for Peace and Democracy, Melbourne, 1939.

Freeman, Kathleen, *If Any Man Build: the History of the Save the Children Fund*, Hodder and Stoughton, London, 1965.

Freud, Anna and Burlington, Dorothy, *War and Children*, Medical War Books, New York, 1943.

Friedlander, Albert (Ed.), *Out of the Whirlwind: a Reader of Holocaust Literature*, Schocken Books, New York, 1976.

Friedlander, Saul, *When Memory Comes*, Noonday Press, New York, 1991.

Fuller, E., *The Right of the Child*, Victor Gollancz Ltd, London, 1951.

German Government, *German-Occupied Great Britain: the Official Secret Document*. reprinted in Sussex by Scutt-Dand, Foord, 1941.

Gershon, Karen (Ed.), *We Came As Children*, Papermac, London, 1989.

Gettler, Leon, *An Unpromised Land*, Fremantle Arts Centre Press, Fremantle, 1993.

Geve, Thomas, *Youth in Chains* (2nd ed.), Rubin Mass, Jerusalem, 1981.

Gilbert, Martin, *Atlas of the Holocaust*, Macmillan Publishing Co. Inc, New York, 1982.

Gilbert, Martin, *The Holocaust: a History of the Jews of Europe during the Second World War*, Holt, Rinehart and Winston, New York, 1986.

Gilbert, Martin, *The Holocaust: the Jewish Tragedy*, Fontana, London, 1987.

Glas-Wiener, Sheva, *Children of the Ghetto*, Globe Press, Melbourne, 1974.

Golvan, Colin, *The Distant Exodus*, Australian Broadcasting Commission, Sydney, 1990.

Grudzinska-Gross, Irena and Tomasz Gross, Jan (Eds), *War through Children's Eyes: the Soviet Occupations of Poland and the Deportations, 1939–1941*, Hoover Institution Press, Stanford University, 1981.

Grunberger, Richard, *A Social History of the Third Reich*, Weidenfeld and Nicolson, London, 1971.

Haggerty, Robert, Sherrod, Lonnie, Garmezy, Norman and Rutter, Michael, *Stress, Risk and Resilience in Children and Adolescents: Processes, Mechanisms and Interventions*, Cambridge University Press, Cambridge, 1994.

Halls, W, *The Youth of Vichy France*, Clarendon Press, Oxford, 1981.

Hay, Ian, *Peaceful Invasion*, Hodder and Stoughton, London, 1946.

Heller, Celia, *On the Edge of Destruction.*: Schocken Books, New York, 1977.

Hilberg, Raul, *The Destruction of the European Jews* (revised and definitive edition), Holmes and Meier, New York, 1985.

Hitler, Adolf, *Mein Kampf*, Houghton Mifflin Company, Boston, 1971.

Hoffman, Louise and Masel, Shush (Eds), *Without Regret*, Centre for Migration and Development Studies, the University of Western Australia, Perth, 1994.

Humphreys, Margaret, *Empty Cradles*, Doubleday, London, 1994.

Inglis, Ruth, *The Children's War*, Fontana Collins, London, 1990.

Isaacs, Susan (Ed)., *The Cambridge Evacuation Survey*, Methuen, London, 1941.

Jewish Museum of Australia, *Courage to Care: Rescuers of Jews during the Holocaust*, catalogue of an exhibition at the Jewish Museum of Australia July 1992-January 1993, the Jewish Museum of Australia, Melbourne, 1992.

Johnson, B. S. (Ed.), *The Evacuees*, Victor Gollancz Ltd, London, 1969.

Kamenka, Eugene, 'A childhood in the 1930s and 1940s: the making of a Russian-German-Jewish Australian', *Australian Journal of Politics and History*, vol. 31, 1985.

Kennedy, J., *British Civilians and the Japanese War in Malaya and Singapore. 1941–1945*, Macmillan Press, London, 1987.

Klarsfeld, Serge, *The Children of Izieu: a Human Tragedy*, Harry N. Abrams Inc, New York, 1984.

Koch, H., *The Hitler Youth: Origins and Development 1922–45*, Macdonald and Jane's, London, 1975.

Kohler, Peter, 'Poland's pride', part 1, *Ships Monthly*, May 1986.

Kurek-Lesik, Ewa, 'The conditions of admittance and the social background of Jewish children saved by women's religious orders in Poland from 1939–1945', *Polin*, vol. 3, 1988.

Kwiet, Konrad, 'Be patient and reasonable! The internment of German-Jewish refugees in Australia', *Australian Journal of Politics and History*, vol. 31, 1985.

Kwiet, Konrad, Responses of Australian Jewry's leadership to the Holocaust. In W. D. Rubinstein (Ed.), *Jews in the Sixth Continent*, Allen & Unwin, Sydney, 1987.

Kwiet, Konrad, The persecution of non-Jews under Nazi rule. In Australian Association of Jewish Holocaust Survivors (Eds), *The gift of life* (pp. 43–8). Sydney: self published, 1989.

Lane, John, *Fairbridge Kid*, Fremantle Arts Centre Press, Fremantle, 1990.

'Let the children in', *New Republic*, vol. 98, 26 April 1939.

Leverton, Bertha and Lowensohn, Shmuel (Eds), *I Came Alone*, The Book Guild, Sussex, 1991.

Liffman, Herbert, 'In search of my identity', *Australian Journal of Politics and History*, vol. 31, 1985.

Lifton, Betty Jean, *The King of Children*, Pan Books Ltd, London, 1989.

Lowrie, Donald, *The Hunted Children*, WW Norton and Company Inc, New York, 1963.

Lucas, Richard, *The Forgotten Holocaust: the Poles under German Occupation 1939–1944*, University Press of Kentucky, Kentucky, 1986.

Macardle, Dorothy, *Children of Europe*, Victor Gollancz Ltd, London, 1949.

Machover, J. M., 'Towards rescue: the story of Australian Jewry's stand for the Jewish cause, 1940–1948', *Australian Jewish Historical Society Journal*, vol. 7, part 1, 1971.

Margaliot, Abraham, The problem of the rescue of German Jewry during the years 1933 - 1939; the reasons for the delay in their emigration from the Third Reich. In *Rescue attempts during the Holocaust: proceedings of the second Yad Vashem International Historical Conference*, Jerusalem, 8–11 April, 1974, Yad Vashem, Jerusalem, 1977.

Margolis, Laura, 'Race against time in Shanghai', *Survey Graphics*, no further details provided. Reprint available in file 37, New South Wales Jewish Board of Deputies, Archive of Australian Judaica, Sydney, 1944.

Markus, Andrew, 'Jewish migration to Australia 1938–49', *Journal of Australian Studies*, no. 13, 1983.

Marrus, M and Paxton, R., *Vichy France and the Jews*, Basic Books Inc, New York, 1981.

Matsdorf, Wolfgang, *No Time to Grow: the Story of the Gross-Breeseners in Australia* (reprint), Archive of Australian Judaica, Sydney, 1994.

Mazur, Betty, 'The German child transplanted', *Jewish Social Service Quarterly*, vol. 7, 1940.

Maclean, Meta, *The Singing Ship*, Angus and Robertson Ltd, Sydney, 1941.

Melander, Goran, The concept of the term 'refugee'. In Anna Bramwell (Ed.), *Refugees in the age of total war* (pp. 7–14), Unwin Hyman, London, 1988.

Mitchell, Donald, 'A wartime voyage to Australia *Sea Breezes*, vol. 65, no. 541 & 542, 1991.

Moss, John, *Child Migration to Australia*, Her Majesty's Stationery Office, London, 1953.

Newman, Jacob, *Kinder Transporte: a Study of Stresses and Traumas of Refugee Children*, 1992 (Available at Yad Vashem, Jerusalem).

Noakes, J and Pridham, G (Eds), *Nazism: a History in Documents and Eyewitness Accounts 1919–1945*, Volume 1, Schocken Books, New York, 1988.

Noakes, J and Pridham, G (Eds), *Nazism: a History in Documents and Eyewitness Accounts, 1919–1945*, Volume 2, Schocken Books, New York, 1988.

Oats, William, *Headmaster by Chance*, Aguerremendi Press, Sandy Bay, Tas., 1986.

Pack, Janet and Weis, Margaret, *Lost Childhoods: Children of World War 2*, Julian Messner, New York, 1986.

Papenek, Ernst, *Out of the Fire*, William Morrow and Company Ltd, New York, 1975.

Poliakov, Leon, *Harvest of Hate: the Nazi Program for the Destruction of the Jews of Europe*, Holocaust Library, New York, 1954.

Ramati, Alexander, *And the Violins Stopped Playing: a Story of the Gypsy Holocaust*, Hodder & Stoughton, London, 1985.

Read, Anthony and Fisher, David, *Kristallnacht: Unleashing the Holocaust*, Michael Joseph, London, 1989.

Ressler, Everett, Boothby, Neil and Steinbock, Daniel, *Unaccompanied Children*, Oxford University Press, New York, 1988.

Rich, Henry (Joe), *The Lochiel Apprentice: Memories of a Barwell Boy 1923–1934*, his son, R. Y. (Rich) Mulcahy, Adelaide, 1983.

Rosh White, Naomi, *From Darkness to Light: Surviving the Holocaust*, Collins Dove, Melbourne, 1988.

Rubinstein, Hilary, *Chosen: the Jews in Australia*, Allen & Unwin, Sydney, 1987.

Rubinstein, Hilary, *The Jews in Australia*, Volume 1, William Heinemann, Melbourne, 1991.

Rubinstein, W. D. (Ed.), *Jews in the Sixth Continent*, Allen and Unwin, Sydney, 1987.

Rutland, Suzanne, 'Australian government policies to refugee migration 1933–1939', *Journal of the Royal Australian Historical Society*, vol. 69, part 4, 1984.

Rutland, Suzanne, 'Australian responses to Jewish refugee migration before and after World War II', *Australian Journal of Politics and History*, vol. 31, 1985.

Rutland, Suzanne, *Edge of the Diaspora: Two Centuries of Jewish Settlement in Australia*, Collins Australia, Sydney, 1988.

Sandbach, Betsy and Edge, Geraldine, *Prison Life on a Pacific Raider*, Hodder and Stoughton Ltd, London, 1941.

Save the Children, *Putting Children First since 1919*, Save the Children, London, 1994.

Save the Children Fund, *Children in Bondage*, Longmans Green & Co, London, 1943.

Shakespeare, Geoffrey, *Let Candles Be Brought In*, Macdonald, London, 1949.

Sheridan, Dorothy, *Wartime Women*, Mandarin Paperbacks, London, 1990.

Shirer, William, *The Rise and Fall of the Third Reich*, Pan Books Ltd, London, 1972.

Shirer, William, *Berlin Diary: 1934–1941*, Sphere Books Limited, London, 1972.

Skwarko, Krstyna, *The Invited: the Story of 733 Polish Children Who Grew up in New Zealand*, Millwood Press, Wellington, 1974.

Sosnowski, Kiryl, *The Tragedy of Children under Nazi Rule*, Zachodnia Agencia Prasowa, Warsaw, 1962.

Stahl, Rudolph, 'Vocational retraining of Jews in Nazi Germany 1933–1938', *Jewish Social Studies*, vol. 1, 1939.

Stevens, Austin, *The Dispossessed*, Barrie & Jenkins Ltd, London, 1975.

Stokes, Edward, *Innocents Abroad: the Story of British Child Evacuees in Australia, 1940–45*, Allen and Unwin, Sydney, 1994.

Symonds, Saul, 'Australia and the refugees: a reply', *Australian Quarterly*, vol. 14, 1942.

Tatelbaum, Itzhak, *Through Our Eyes: Children Witness the Holocaust* (special edition for Yad Vashem bookshop), IBT Publishing Inc, Chicago, 1993.

Tatz, Colin, Racism: the role and responsibility of intellectuals. In *The gift of life*, Australian Association of Jewish Holocaust Survivors, Sydney, 1989.

Thalmann, Rita and Feinermann, Emmanuel, *Crystal Night: 9–10 November 1938*, Coward, McCann and Geoghegan Inc, New York, 1974.

Thompson, Paul, *The Voice of the Past*, Oxford University Press, Oxford, 1988.

Titmuss, R. M., *Problems of Social Policy*, His Majesty's Stationery Office and Longmans Green and Co. In W. K. Hancock (Ed.), *History of the Second World War*. United Kingdom Civil Series, London, 1950.

Tokayer, Marvin and Swartz, Mary, *The Fugu Plan: the Untold Story of the Japanese and the Jews during World War II*, Paddington Press Ltd, New York, 1979.

Towle, Charlotte, 'The effect of war upon children', *Social Service Review*, vol. 17, 1943.

Turner, Barry, *...And the Policeman Smiled: 10,000 Children Escape from Nazi Europe*, Bloomsbury Publishing Limited, London, 1990.

Turner, Barry, *The Long Horizon: 60 Years of CBF World Jewish Relief*, CBF World Jewish Relief, London, 1993.

Tydor Baumel, Judith, 'Twice a refugee: the Jewish refugee children in Great Britain during evacuation, 1939–1943', *Jewish Social Studies*, vol. 45, 1983.

Tydor Baumel, Judith, *Unfulfilled Promise: Rescue and Resettlement of Jewish Refugee Children in the United States 1934–1945*, The Denali Press, Juneau, 1990.

Vegh, Claudine, *I Didn't Say Good-bye*, E. P. Dutton Inc, New York, 1979.

Wagner, Gillian, *Children of the Empire*, Wiedenfeld and Nicolson, London, 1982.

Wetherell, David and Carr-Gregg, Charlotte, *Camilla: a Life*, New South Wales University Press, Sydney, 1990.

Wicks, Ben, *No Time to Wave Goodbye*, Bloomsbury Publishing Ltd, London, 1988.

Wicks, Ben, *The Day They Took the Children*, Bloomsbury, London, 1990.

Williams, A. E., *Barnado of Stepney*, George Allen and Unwin Ltd, London, 1943.

Women's British-Soviet Committee, *The Children Accuse Them*, self published, London, 1943.

Women's Group on Public Welfare, *Child Emigration: a Study Made in 1948–50 by a Committee of the Women's Group on Public Welfare*, National Council of Social Service, London, 1951.

Yahil, Leni, *The Holocaust: the Fate of European Jewry, 1932–1945*, Oxford University Press, New York, 1990.

THESES AND CONFERENCE PAPERS

Bartrop, Paul, *Indifference and Inconvenience: Australian Government Policy towards Refugees from Nazi Persecution, 1933–39*. PhD thesis, Monash University, Melbourne, 1988.

Baumel, Judith, *The Jewish Refugee Children in Great Britain 1938–1945*. MA thesis, Ramat-Gan University, Israel, 1981.

Gilbert, Martin, 'Not to Forget', keynote address at *The Hidden Child Second International Gathering*, Jerusalem, 12–15 July 1993.

Lin, Patricia, *Perils Awaiting Those Deemed to Rise above Their 'Alloted Status': the Social Impact of the Overseas Evacuation of British Children in the Second World War*. B.A. thesis, Princeton, New Jersey, 1991.

Palmer, Glen, *Determining Pre-School Children's Racial Attitudes from Their Responses to Books*, MA thesis, Flinders University of South Australia, Adelaide, 1986.

VIDEOS, FILMS AND SOUND RECORDINGS

Granada television, *Lost Children of the Empire*, released in England in 1989.

ABC television, *Fuhrer, Seduction of a Nation*, True Stories, 14 August 1994.

Polish Commission for the Investigation of Nazi Crimes, *The Stolen Child*, SBS television, 11 October 1993.

The Marvellous World of George Dreyfus, compact disc MD3129. Melbourne: Move Record Company.

INDEX

(SEE ALSO THE APPENDICES) NUMBERS IN ITALICS REFER TO PHOTOGRAPHS

Abrahamson, Betty 43, 46, 48, *53*, 103-106, 109-117, *116*, 123, 164-165, *166, 170*, 180-181, 188, *193*; Zvi 164-165, 180
abuse 18, 138, 177, 197
Adelaide 52, 103, 130-131, *139*, 141-143, *142, 149*, 154-158; Cheer-up hut 131
adoption 35, 38-39, 71, 72, 73, 75, 89-90, 138, 150
agriculture 20, 59, 96, 112, 155, 186
air force, Australian 144, *146, 158*, 158-161, 163; Israeli 168 ; RAF 144
Albury, NSW 159
aliens 8, 30-33, 52, 79-80, 97, 110, 155, 157-159; enemy 52, 79, 159
Andes (ship) 172, 174
Anschluss 20-22
Anson, Manfred 155
anti-semitism (see also Holocaust) 12-28, 55-59, 61-63, 67, 154, 160-161, 184
Aorangi (ship) 89
apprentices 16, 59, 62, 64, 124-125, 143, 151, 153, 177
Aquitania (ship) 173
Arandora Star (ship) 77, 81
army: American 167; Australian, (see also Australian Imperial Forces and Australian Military Forces) 99, 138, 144, *146*, 157-161, *161, 163, 158*; Australian Army Labour Corps 157-159, *161*; Austrian 23; British 98; German 12, 15, 20, 95-98, 165-166, 187; Indian *84, 133*; Israeli 170, *189*; Japanese 100, 159; Polish 98; Red Army 58, 68, 95, 163, 165
atomic bomb 159
atrocities (see also Holocaust) 7, 8, 19, 163, 185
Australia House, London 34, 36, 49, 52, 53, 173; see also Australian High Commission, Major Wheeler
Australian (commonwealth) government (see also Australian High Commission, parents) 29, *30*, 31, 35, 71, 97, 184, 186, 187; Commonwealth Investigations Branch 153; Department of Immigration 167, 197; Department of Information 129; Department of the Interior 33-34, 38-40, 49-54, 61, 64, 71-73, 78, 82-83, 89, 96-97, 144, 153;
Australian High Commission, London *30*, 73-80, 83, 96; see also Australia House, Stanley Bruce, Major Wheeler
Australian Imperial Force (AIF) 158-160, *158, 161*
Australian Jewry (see also Australian Jewish Welfare Society, Polish Jewish Relief Fund) 100, 127, 184-187; Adelaide community 52, 103, 154, 156; Melbourne (see also Larino) 38-40, 51-52, 54, 59, 80, 103-128, 138, 148-156, 164, 169, 180, 191-192; Perth 39-40, 51-52, 103, 155; Sydney 40, 50, 52-53, 73, 96, 155-156, 176
Australian Medical Association 78
Australian Military Forces (AMF) *146*, 158, *161, 163*
Australian Jewish Welfare Society (previously German Jewish Refugees Fund) 31-33, 37-61, 72-73, 76, 80, 83, 84, 94, 96-98, 103-104, 112-113, 118, 120, 125-126, 149, 152-156, 168-169, 184-186, 191-192, 200, 202
Australian Universities Commission 143
Austria 19-27, 39, 42, 184
Austrian: children 21, 25-27, 34, *35*; (see also refugee children and youth); refugees 12, 21, 25, 49, 52, 54, 59, 76-79, 120, 148, 155-157, 160, 193; Jews 20-24

Bader, Harry 126, 193
Badrian, Kathe 41, *46*, 47, 110, *128*, 164; Laurie *14*, 41, *42, 44, 46*, 47 and photo, *53, 108*, 110, *126, 128*, 164, *166*; Walter 41, 43, *46*, 47, 110, 164
Baeck, Leo 14, 20
Baker, Bill *69*
Baltrover (ship) 67
Ball, Stanley *69*
Balwyn, Vic 104-106, *105*, 118, 123, 192; Balwyn state school 104-107, *106*, 115-117, 123
Barkman, Frances 39, 52, 103-104, 112-113, 118, 121, 124, 149-150, 153, 169; Frances Barkman Home *105*, 169
Barnardo Home 29, 31, 35, 72
Barnard, Peter 35, 134-135, 141, *142*, 143, 175, 178, *196*
Barwell scheme 30
Batory (ship) (see also Singing Ship) 82-83, *85*, 86-87, *87, 90*, 90-94, 129 and photo, 131, 173, 188, 203
Bavin, Cyril 33-34, 134-144, 171
Beech, Arthur *92*
Beeston, Doris *90*, 92
Begin, Menachem 65
Belgium 27, 37, 53, 66, 71-72, 78, 182; Belgians 53-54, 72-74, 78
Bendigo, Vic 138, 143
Bentwich, Mami 26; Norman 26, 32, 36
Berlin 15, 22, 25, 27, 41-48, *42, 50*, 62, 164-167, 188
Bermuda Conference 97
Betar Zionist youth group 67
Bettelheim, Bruno 180
Big Brother Movement 30, 36
Birstein, Yossel 57, 155
Bishop of Chichester, UK 20
Bombay 93
Borneo 159
Boy Scout (see also Cyril Bavin) 72; Polish 95-96
Box Hill, Vic 116, 123, 124
Brecher, Herman 64
Bremen, Germany 48-49, 188
Bremerhaven, Germany 47-48
Brent, Heinz 39
Breslau, Germany 28
Brest-Litovsk, Poland 64-65
Brisbane 130, 143, 155, 161
Britain (see also England, Ireland, Scotland, Wales) 8-10, 20, 21, 26-29, 33, 35-38, 45, 52, 54, 71-84, 88, 95, 97, 99-101, 143, 145, 171, 172, 177-179, 183, 187, 191
British: Foreign Office 79, 96; government 8, 26, 29, *30*, 37, 74, 95-101 (see also Children's Overseas Reception Board); Ministry of Labour 143; restrictions of immigration to Palestine 26, 65, 99

235

British Orphans Adoption Society (BOAS) 71
Brown, Isabella 86, 88
Bruce, Stanley M 77, 96; see Australian High Commission
Brunt, Dorothy 139
Bulgaria 159, 182
Bundist 150
Calwell, Arthur 167, 176-177
Canada 75, 77, 79, 82, 88-89, 191
Cape Town 83, 90, 93
Carlton, Vic 133, 148-149, 151, 155, 191
Carrodus, Joseph A 52, 78
censorship 91, 130, 137, 162
Central British Fund 14, 28
Central Council of Jewish Refugees 79
Cessnock, NSW 131
child endowment 135
child migration 8, 28, 29-32, *30*, 35-37, 40, 49, 51, 71, 74-75, 89, 98, 99, 126, 144, 172, 183, 185, 187, 197; non-British 36-40, 49, 51-54, 59, 68, 98, 99, 183
Child Refugees Welfare League, Melbourne 38
child welfare departments, Australia 77, 83, 131, 134-141, 144
children: see refugee children and youth, child migration, parents, orphan and orphanages; destitute 16, 97; gypsy 182; homeless 98
Children's Inter-Aid Committee 20-21, 26, 33
Children's Overseas Reception Board (CORB) 70, 74-83, *85*, *87*, 88-89, 91, 92, 94 and photo, 101, 129-147, *146*, 171-179, 187, 203-210; inclusion of refugee children 72-80; British Jewish children (see also Schultz) 80, *85*, *129*
China 102; see evacuees
Christian Brothers, WA 35-37
Churchill, Winston 8, 74-77, 80-81
City of Benares (ship) 88, 89, 187
Civil Aliens Corps 159
Cohen, Sir Samuel 120
Cohn, Herco 156
Commissioner of Police, Victoria 78
concentration camps 9, 14, 16, 21-23, 27, 97, 123, 126, 164-165, 167; Auschwitz 164-165, 180; Buchenwald 23, 25; Dachau 23-24, 35; Muhlhausen 42, *46*; Riga 164; Sachsenhausen 23, 164; Theresienstadt 165, 180

CORB, see Children's Overseas Reception Board
corporal punishment 113, 160
Council for German Jewry, London 20, 26-27, 31-32, 42-43, 97
Country Party, WA 72
cruelty and brutality 18, 22, 23, 137, 138, 156, 188
Cullen, Paul 120, 184
Curtin, John 97
Czechoslovakia 27, 74, 78; Czechs 12, 52

Dabrowa, Poland 68, 162, 165
Danglow, Rabbi 118
Dawkins, Anne 94
Denmark 179, 182
deportation 19, 22, 62, 95, 97-98, 164-165
Dickenson, Audrey 83, 86, 177
Diomed (ship) 82-83, 86, 88-90, 93, 130, 203, 210
disembarkation 103, 129-130, 148; see embarkation
Doari, Betty 155
Dominions Office 8, 32, 74, 89
Dookie Agricultural College, Vic 155
Dovercourt, UK 39
Downes, Alf 134
Drabsch, Phil and Dorryn 142, 172, 174
Dreadnought Trust 30, 35
Dreyfus, George 9, 24, 45, 48, *53*, 109, *122*, 126, *193*, *194*; Richard *53*, 106, 109, *122*, 193
Dromana, Vic *166*, 169
Dunera (ship) *50*, 77
Dunkirk, France 77, 93
Dutch Refugees Committee 26

East Camberwell, Vic 123
Ehrlich, Ingrid 15, 42, 48-49, *44*, *53*, 103-128, *106*, *111*, 169-171, *193*; Marion 42, *46*, 48-49, *53*, 103-128, *168*, 169-171, *193*
Eichmann, Adolf 21, 22
Eisler, Hans 23, 26, 34 *and photo*, 35, 148, 156-157, 160, *163*, 167, *189*, 191
Elvish, Molly 121
embarkation 12, 48-49, 67, 86-87; see disembarkation

emigration: Germany 14-15, 19, 20, 22, 24, 32, 41-48, *47*, 95; Austria 21, 26; Australia 31, 168-170; Poland 55-56, 59, 64-68, 95, 188; wartime Europe 95-97
Empire Grace (ship) 173
Empire Settlement Act 29, 36, 37
England (see also Britain) 8, 10, 14, 20, 24-28, 33-45, 53, 67-68, 73, 82, 86, 94, 101, 120, 130, 133, 137-147, 150, 156, 160, 170-171, 175, 178-179, 184-187, 190-191, *196*
English (see also British): accents 132-134; identity 171, 178; language 26-27, 32, 34, 49, 59, 64, 67, 103, 106-107, 109, 115, 117, 150-151, 153-154, 157, 169-170, 178; people 48, 189; schools 20
escorts 47, 50, 67, 75, 86-93, *88*, *90*, *92*, *94*, 172-174, 187; ships 77, 89-90; see also Beeston, Brown, Kilby, Lebenson, Oats, Paterson
Essen, Germany 56, 62
Ettinger, Sigmund *69*
Europa (ship) 48
evacuation: within Britain 71; within Australia 143; from Britain 8, 71-94, 100-101; Penang 101; Solomon Islands 101-102
evacuees: from Britain (see Childrens Overseas Reception Board); Chinese 100, 102; from Solomon Islands 101-102, 142; Dutch 142; private from Britain 77, 81-82, 89, 93, 94, 171; from Hong Kong 100; to Burma 93-94; from New Guinea 100; from Sumatra 100; to/from Malaya 101
Evian Conference 21-22, 33, 37
Executive Council of Australian Jewry 167
Fairbridge children 28-31, 36-39, 49, 89, 187; Society 36, 71, 89
Falk, Dr Erna 44, 47, 49
family reunion (see also child migration, parents) 109, 163, 167-176, 195
farm training (also see Gross-Breesen) 20, 29-39, 89, *149*, 154-157, 168, 187, 201
Farquaharson, Paul and Reg *85*
First World War 7, 15, 23, 29, 55, 134, 163
Fixel, Ferry 49, 104, 106, *108*, *111*, 111-112, 114, 118, 192, *194*; Hedi 49, 104, 106, *108*, 109-114, *111*, *116*, 118, 121, 192, *193*, *194*

Flint Hall Farm, Hambleden, UK 34
Flowers, Ted 179
Foll, Senator Hattil Spencer (Minister for the Interior) 33-34, 40, 52, 72, 75, 77, 100
forced labour 64, 95, 164-166; camps 19, 98, 167, 182
Foster, NSW 156
foster families *133, 135, 139;* homes *132, 135;* parents 131, 135-142, 145-146, 173, 177-178, 191
France 21, 27, 37, 71, 74-79; see refugee children and youth; Dunkirk, France 77, 93; Gurs internment camp 97; Toulon 49; Vichy France 97
Frank, Ilse *53, 116, 193*
Frankfurt, Germany 27
Freedman, Rabbi 103
Fremantle, WA 67, 93, 103, 129
Frensham School, NSW 139, 142

Garbasz, Jack 56, 56-57, 65, 67, 69, 99 sisters, 148-153, 158 and photo, 160, 166, 168, 181, 189; Shulamith 189
Garrett, Thomas H 52, 73, 78
German (see also refugee children and youth, parents, army, emigration): attitudes to Germans 31, 107, 109, 150; culture and identity 107, 123, 150; government (see also Nazi) 12-13, 68, 95-97, 99; Jews 13-20, 22-28, 31, 41-48, 95, 120, 164-165, 184; language 11, 107, 109, 123, 151, 170-171; National Socialist (Nazi) Party 8, 13, 22; schools 15-18, *17, 35,* 43, *44,* 104
German Emergency (Fellowship) Committee 21, 25, 33-34, 37, 203; see also Society of Friends, YMCA
German Jewish Refugees Fund (see AJWS)
German-Soviet pact 68
Germany: (deportation from, see deportation; Polish emigration from, see emigration) emigration to 55-56; post war 171; pre war 7, 12-24, 41-48, 61-62, 151, 184; war years 1939-45 52, 95, 106, 122-123, 164-167
Gestapo 23-24, 44, *50,* 164, 165
Getzler, Leon *69*
ghettos 95, *99;* Germany 13; at university 59; East End, London 176; see also Dabrowa, Sarny
Glass, Braham 118, 177

Glen Innes, NSW 32, *35*
Goebbels, Josef 22
Gold, Herman *53, 106,* 118, 119, 124, *126, 166,* 169, *193*
Goldberg, Max *60,* 65, *69,* 148-153, 159, 163, *186;* family 60
Goldstein, Margot 10-11, 43, 47-50, *53,* 103-104, 107-110, *112, 116,* 117, 120-123, 164, 169, 180-181, 188, *193*
Gordon Highlanders 93
Gould, Larry (see Herman Gold)
Greeks 159-160
Greening, Patricia 83-84, 93, 144, *146,* 174, 195; Maureen 134, 138, 173, 175, 195
Gregory, Ken 10, 84, 92, 137, 143, 174-177, 188
Gross-Breesen, Germany 20, 39, 156, 201
Grynszpan, Herschel 22
guardians 29, 59, 77, 83, 100, 124, 148-158, 167, 188, 190-191; see Welfare Guardian Society
gypsies 13, 182

Haas, Elsa 107
Habonim Zionist youth movement 155, 168, 180
Hamburg, Germany 44, 47, *60,* 68, 118
Hamley Bridge, SA 133
Hammond, Sheila 87, 90, 189
Harding, Elsie 141, 178
Hare, John 93, 131, 136, 138, 143, 145, *172,* 173, 177; sisters *172;* Walter 83, 86
Havaara agreement 19
Henry George Movement 151
Herne, Germany 68
Hertz Mrs (see also Judd) 169
High Commissioner for the United Kingdom 72, 82, 135
Himmler, Heinrich 95
Hitler, Adolf 7, 12, 13, 16, 18-19, 22, 24, 46, 67, 71, 77, 107, 126, 157
Hitler Youth 16, 18-19, 46, *47*
Hobart, Tas, *194;* Hobart Rotary Club, 73
Hodgson, Joan *14,* 86, 87, 91, 137, 173, 188; Margaret 137, *141*
Holland, see Netherlands
Holocaust 7-10, 41, *46, 50,* 56, 58, *60,* 68, 95-97, 99-100, 126, 164-168, 176, 180-185, *190,* 195

homosexuals 13
Honeysett, Joe 71, 129-130
Hong Kong 100, 171
Horthy plan 99-100
Houghton, Tony *92*
Humphreys, Cliff 29, *92,* 174
immigration: (see also Australian [commonwealth] government, child migration, youth migration) Australia 30-38, 43-45, 52, 71, 74, 89, 98, 130, 144, 172-179, 185; non-British 30-33, 36, 52, 54, 59, 61, 100, 153, 167-168, 171, 183; assisted 61, 177; immigration, Palestine/Israel 21, 26, 59, 65, 168-170, 181
India 80, 93, 98, 144
internees 77, 82, 171
internment camps, Tatura 113, 126; Gurs, France 97
Iran (Persia) 98, 99, 100
Ireland 77, 90
Irish Free State 37
Isabella Lazarus home for children, Sydney 50-52
Israel (see also Palestine) 9-10, 22, 168-170, 180-181, *189, 190,* 195
Israelitische Kultusgemeinde 21, 26, 42
Istanbul 96
Italy 95, 182

Jaffe, Sigi 69, 158
Japan 8, 94-96, 100-102, 153, 159, 167, 179, *190*
JEAS (Polish Jewish immigration organisation) 61, 65
Jebb, Eglantyne 7
Jervis Bay (ship) 39
Jewish: Advisory Board 185; Agency for Palestine 26; see Australian Jewish Welfare Society; observances and holidays 118-119, 156-157, 160-161; quotas for Australia 33, 40, 52, 54; Refugees Committee 20; Welfare Guardian Society 39, 80, 98, 124, 155-156, *163,* 191, 200
Jews, see Australian Jewry, German, Polish, refugee children and youth
Joint Distribution Committee 14
Judd, Miss (see also Hertz) 118
judicial kidnapping 19
Judische Zentralwohlfahrtsstelle (Jewish social welfare department) 41-2

Juni, Max 69, 159, *186*

Kadimah Jewish community centre, Carlton, Vic 148, 151, 155

Kassel, Germany 42

Katz, Aleck 55, 56-59, *58*, 65, 67, *69*, *149*, 150, 154-155, 158-163, 166-167, *186*; Aaron *58*; family *58*

Kaye, Ursula 23, 114, 118-120, *119*, 124-127, *125*, 164, 169-170, *193*

Kilby, Chief Escort 92

Kimberley scheme 184, 186

Kinderauswanderung Abteilung (child welfare department) 42

kindergarten, Germany 42

kindertransports 27-8, 39, 41, 48, 51, 171, 184

Klitenik, Szymon *69*, *149*, 159

Kochen, Frances 107, 109, 121, *170*, *193*; Paula 109, *111*, 117, 121, *170*, *193*

kosher food 114-115, 118

Kristallnacht 22-24, 44, *50*, 183

Kuitpo colony, SA 149, 154

Lancashire, UK 88

landing money 30-34, 37, 39-40, 61

landing permit, Australia 30, 33, 39-40, 46, 52, 61

language (see English, German, Yiddish) 12, 33; foreign languages in Australia 150; French teacher 124; learning German in Australia 107, 109, 170

Largs Bay (ship) 89

Larino 104, *105*, 107, *108*, 109, 111-121, *113*, *116*, *119*, 124-128, *125*, *126*, 164, 166-171, *166*, *168*, *170*, 180-181, 185, 191-193, *193*

Latvia 99

League of Nations 7, 183

Lebenson, Dr 67

Lee Street School, North Carlton, Vic 133

Lehmann, Edna 15, 46-47, *53*, 104, 107, 114, 117, 164, *166*, *168*, 169, 188, 192, *193*, 195; Jo 45-49, *53*, 111, *112*, 114-115, 119, *166*, *193*

Lester, Freddie 156

Levi, Primo 10, 39, 65

Levy, Hannah 44, 47, 180; Hermann 23, 44, 47-48, 104, *106*, *108*, *111*, 118-124, *126*, *166*, 169, 180-181, *193*; Martin 44, 122, 180

Lewinski, Ellen 43, 47-48, *53*, 104, *106*, 111, *112*, 115-127, *127*, 164, *166*, 169, 192, *193*

Lisbon 95

Lithuania 99

Liverpool, UK *84*, *85*

Loftus, Max *69*, 155

London 7, 11-12, 16, 19, 21, 36, 39, 42, 45, 48-54, *53*, 67, 73-83, *85*, 88, 96-100, 135, 174, 176, 184

Lowe, Ernest 141, 179

Lyons, Joseph 31, 38

MacDonald, Malcolm 26

McEvoy, Arthur and Pat 101

McEwen, John 34

McLaren Vale, SA 131, 133

Maclean, Meta, The Singing Ship 91

McLeish, Peggy 86, 92-93, 131-135, *132*, 140, 143-144, *146*, 179

MacRobertson High School, Vic 124

Malaya 100-101, 159, *161*, 171

Manchester Regiment 93

Manila, Philippines 167

Manpower regulations 158

Mass Observation 77

Mein Kampf 16

Melbourne 10, 37, 40, 44, 47, 51-54, 59, 64-65, 73, 80, 103-104, 118, 120, 124, 130-133, 138, 144, 148, 151-161, 169, 200, 202

Melrose, SA 141

memory 9-10, 50, 66-67, 86, 91, 93, 131, 137, 153, 181, 190

Menzies Robert G 8, 72-80, 89, 96, 157

Mexico 98

Meyers, Samuel 104

Middle East (see also Israel, Palestine) 134, *158*, 159

migration, see emigration, immigration

Miller, Syd *69*, *186*

Mirboo, Vic 157

mischling 13, 16

Mitchell, Donald 88, *92*, 178

Montefiore Home, Hunters Hill, NSW 50, 123, 176

Morgan, family *84*; Freda 11, *84* *and photo*, 87, 132, *133*, 145, 173, 174, 196; Maurice *84 and photo*, 91, 132, *133*, 174; Percy *84 and photo*, 132, *133*, 196

Movement for the Care of Children from Germany, see Refugee Children's Movement

Muenz, Keith 21, *34*, 155

Murray Bridge, SA 132

Nagasaki 159

Nagel, Max (see Nagelberg) 56, *60*, 62, 64, 66, 67, 68, *69*, 151, 154, 155, 157, 159, *161*, 162, 167, 181, 190 *and photo*

Nagelberg, family *60*; Mr (see Nagel, Max, his son) 67, 68, 151, 162

name changes 103, 150

National Security Act 77

National Union of Teachers, UK 80

navy 77, 90, 115, 129, 144, 157, 159, 177-178

Nazi mistreatment and atrocities (see also Holocaust) 10-11, 13-25, 28, 33, 41, 54, 62-63, 67-68, 95-99, 106, 157-158; wartime 163-166; 182, 184-185, 187-188, 195; other matters 7, 8, *17*, 19,

Nestor (ship) 82-83, *88*, 86-93, *94*, 130, 203, 209

Netherlands 26-27, 31, 53, 71-72, 76, 78, 82, 88

New Guinea 100, *149*, *158*, 159

New South Wales (see also Sydney) 29, 31, 35-36, 38, 40, 50, 73, 131-141, 156, 160

New York 45, 88, 181

New Zealand 75, 89, 98, 100, 157

New Zealand farm, NSW 157

Newcastle, NSW 72, 144, 174

North Carlton, Vic 133

North Head Quarantine Station, Sydney 131

Northcote children's home 28

Northern Territory 131, 143

Norway 76, 78

Nuremberg Laws 13, 20

nursing 123, 167, 170

Oats, Bill 93

Orama (ship) 12, 28-29, 34, 41, 49, *53*, 103, 188, 202, 203

Orion (ship) 86

Oronsay (ship) 67

orphans and orphanages 7, 25-29, 40, 45, 50-54, 61, 71-75, 78, 86, 89, 97-98, 101, 113, 118, 122-124, 138, 141, 167, 180-184, 192, 197

INDEX

ORT (Organisation for rehabilitation through training department, part of JEAS) 61, 64-65, 185

OSE-ORT 185

Overseas Children scheme (see also CORB) 78, 129, 131

Palestine 19-21, 26, 59, 65, 99-100, 110, 125, 161, 164-169, *168*, 183, *189*

parents (see also foster families, children, reunions): Austrian and German 8, 12-13, 19-28, 35, 41-48, 51, 164, 166, 182; British 8, 29, 71, 74-77, 82-84, 94, 134-136, 144-146, 171-179, 185, 189; death of 122-123, 139, 164-168, 180, 195; emotional states related to sending away children 47-48, 65, 66, 84, 88, 101-102, 104, 131, 151, 162, 164, 183-184, 187-188, 196; from British colonies 94, 100-102, 179; letters from 11, 41, 66-68, 83, 86, 88, 109-110, 122, 131, 138, 145, 151, 162-163, 196; letters to 11, 50, 67, *90*, 103, 109-110, 123, 162-163; migration to Australia 44, 51-52, 54, 71, 144, 153, 156, 167, 183, 185; Polish 56-58, 62-68, 98, 150, 162, 165-166, 182; refugee parents in Australia 51, 109, 113, 121; separation from 109-111, 120-123, 126-128, 136-137, 143, 145, 151, 179, 187-188, 190, 192-198

Paterson, Ian 93, *94*

Patriotic Fund 133

Paxton, NSW 131, 144

Payne, Bob 106-107

Penang 101

Perl, George 56-57, 64, 67, *69*, 150-152, 155-159, 163, 181, *186*

Persia, see Iran

Perth, WA 39-40, 51-52, 73, 103, 129, 155, 159, 181

Peters, Albert Robert 52

Piccadilly, SA 154

Pinjarra, WA 29, 37

Poland 27, 33, 55-61 *and photos*, 63, 64-65, 68, 71, 78, 95-96, 99, 150-155, 162, 165, 182

police 23-26, 34, 62, 78, 113, 157, 165

Polish (see refugee children and youth): anti-semitism 55-59; boy scouts 95-96; see Carlton; Catholics *55*, *57*; see children; emigration 59-61, 64-67, 96, 98, 99, 185, 188, 191; exodus from Russia 98; see Kadimah;

language 12, 150; deportations from Germany 22, 62-63; government 22, 62, 96, 99; nationals in Germany 22, 45, 56, 61-63; peasant life 57-58, 163; pogroms 57; poverty 56-58, 61, 65-66, 155; Polish Jewish Relief Fund (see Pushett) 59, 61, 64, 65, 68, 148, 152, 153, *186*, 191, 200; Polishness 150; ships (see Batory) 82, 87

Porter, Michael 65-66, *69*, 149, 168

Portugal 95, 97

Potsdam, Germany 23

Presbyterian Church 35, 36

prisoners of war 159, *161*, 171, 173, *190*

propaganda *17*, 79, 160, 171

prostitution 13, 156, 165

Pushett, Jonas 148-149, 152-156, 168, 186

Quakers, see Society of Friends

Queensland (see also Brisbane) 96, 130, 143, 159, 161

racism (see anti-semitism) 15-16, 17, 55, 80, 150

radio 21, 117; broadcasts 137, *140*, *141*, 145

Rangitane (ship) 89

rationing 123, 174

Red Cross 109, 111, 117, 122, 162-164, 167, 180, 195; message *128*

refugee children and youth (see also Refugee Children's Movement) 8-10, 31, 36, 38, 97-98, 183-187, 196-197; allied 71-75, 78-79; Belgian 53-54, 71-74, 78; Czechoslovakian 27, 28, 74, 78; Danish 73; Dutch 33, 53-54, 71-74, 78; ; French 78, 79, 97; from Asia 100; from Pacific region 100; German and Austrian 12, 20, 21, 26-28, 32-54, 79, 103-128, 148, 155-157, 191-193, 200-202; Hungarian 99-100; in Britain 8, 20, 26-28, 35, 38, 52, 71-74, 77-79, 183; Polish 29, 61-64, 68, 74, 78, 96, 148-163, 190-191, 200-201; Norwegian 73-74; Polish in Russia and Iran 98-100; post war 169, 185

Refugee Children's Movement formerly Movement for the Care of Children from Germany 26-28, 35, 38, 41, 77, 187;

Refugee Council of Tasmania 73

Reichsvertretung der Juden (National Organisation of German Jews) 14, 18, 20, 32, 39-45

reparations 32, 45, 47, 75, 78, 90, 103, 168, 176, 179-180

reunions 12, 95, 109, 145, 163, 167, 170-176, 180, 195

Rhodesia 98

Rights of the Child 7, 183, 196-197; children's rights 196

Robinson, Philip 143-144

Roman Catholics 57, 80, 96, 160, 187

Romania 95-96

Romford, UK 86

Roosevelt, Mrs 79

Rose, Arthur S 59, 68, 148, 152

Rostock, Germany 180

Rothschild, Ellen 15, 22, 42, *50*, *53*, 112 *and photo*, 115, *116*, 117, 118, 123, 166, 167, *168*, 169, 171, 193; family 50

Russia *55*, 57, 68, 95, 98, 162-167, 182; labour camps 98; partisans *58*, 166; Russian *58*, 68, 165

Rwanda 197

Sadan, Inge 171, 180

Salvation Army 33, 35-36

Sarny, Poland 56, *58*, 64-65, *99*, 165-166

Sarpedon (ship) 101

Save the Children organisation 7, 20, 197

Schaechter, Ellen 44-45, *53*, 104, *116*, *166*, *193*

Schiff, Otto 97

Schindler, family *60*; Norman *60*, 62-64, *69*, 149-153, *186*

Schneider, Gisella 121

schools, boarding 23, 94, 98, 100, 101, 139, 142-143, 175-176, 188, 191; Catholic 20; co-educational 143; Hebrew 118; English 20; see also German (schools); Germany 15-18, *17*, *35*, 43, 44, 104; Poland *55*; private 15, 76, 78, 142; state 15, 18, 24, 44, 57, 65, 76, 104-107, 115-116, 123, 130, 143, 192; technical schools 64-65, 116, 123-124, 155, 165

Schultz: Phillip *85*, *140*, *178*; Rosalie *85*, 139, *140*, 142, 176, *178*; their family *85*, *178*;

Schultz, Jean *129*, 138, 145, 176, 177, 190

Schwartz, Jack 65, *69*, 149, *186*

Scotland 77

Scullin, James 7
Shakespeare, Geoffrey 74-82, 86, 89, 140
Shanghai 43, *46*, 50, 95, 109-110, 164-170
Sheinfeld, Max *69*
Simpson, Derek 84, 177
Singapore 93, 101, 173
Singing Ship (Batory) 91, 130, 172
Smith, Beryl 86, 90, 131, 133, 143, 175
Society of Friends (Quakers) 12, 20, 27, 33-34, 106; Friends Centre 21; see also German Emergency (Fellowship) Committee
Solomon Islands 101-102, 142, 179
South America 162
South Australia (see also Adelaide) 29, 73, 130-131, *149*, 154
Southampton, UK 48-49
Soviet, see Russia
Spanish refugees 97
Spiegel, Alwin 63-64, 67, *69*, 148, 150, 158-161, *158*, 167, *186*
SS (Schutzstaffel) 15, 21, 24, 48, 62, 165
St Kilda, Vic 118, 171
Stalin, Josef 98
Stein, Ernest 34
Steinberg, Isaac 184, 186
Stocks, Alfred *42*, 43, *53*, *106*, 113-116, 124, *126*, *166*, *193*
Strathallan (ship) 201
Stratheden (ship) 93-94
Stricker, Alfred 21; see also Isabella Lazarus Home
Sudetenland, Czeckoslavakia 22
suicide 20-22, 49, *50*, 51, 122, 156
Sumatra 100
Switzerland 27, 37, 97, 98, 126, 165, 185, 194
Sydney 32, 34, 39-52, 71-75, 89, 96, 102, 123, 130, 137-138, 142, 153-160, *163*, 169, 172, 176, *178*, 178-179, 184, *189*, 201, 203; University 179

synagogues 22, 103, 118-119, 123-124, 155, 161, 165, 192
Syria 99

Tanganyika 98
Tasmania (see also Hobart) 73, 104, 112
Taylor, Rolf *53*, 124, 150, *193*
teachers 15, 16, 18, 57, 80, 86, 107, 143, 191
Teitel, family (see also parent, letters from) *58*, *63*, 165; Isilein *58*, 62, 66, 162; Waltraut *58*, 62, 67, 165; Werner *58*, 62-68, *63*, *69*, 148-155, *149*, 158-159, *161*, 162, 165, 167, *186*;
Templeton, John 138, 144, 179
Timmins, Alan 84, 133, 140, 174, 177
Tocumwal, NSW 159
trade unions 167-168
Trainor, Charlie 23, 39, 156, *163*
trauma 10, 11, 44, 47, 57, 102, 118, 124, 126, 175, 187, 197
Turkey 95-96
Twickenham, UK 85, 86

Ukrainians 55, 57-58, 166
unemployment 45, 64, 71
United Nations: Convention on the Rights of the Child 196-197; Relief and Rehabilitation Administration (UNRRA) 164
United States of America, see army, Evian and Bermuda Conferences, Horthy Plan; American Jewry 14, 20-21; armed forces 159, 179; evacuation to 79, 81, 191; migration 167-169, 180-181; response to refugee children and youth 20-21, 28, 79
University Women's Association, Vic 78

Vichy France 97
Victoria (see also Melbourne) 31, 40, 72, 78, 131, 144, 154-155, 191
Victorian International Refugee Emergency Council (VIREC) 37
Vienna 20-27, 34, 49, 157

Vincent, Anne *85*, 86, 134, *139*, 175, 178, *196*
Volendam (ship) 88
Voluntary Aid Detachment (VAD) 130-131
vom Rath, Ernst 22

Wales, UK 84
Wangaratta, Vic 124, 155-156
Ward, Eric 84, 91, 131, 132, *135*, 175, 177; Phyllis 90, 92, 131, 132, *135*, 175, 177
Warsaw *50*, 56, 61, 66-67
Wedgwood, Camilla 34, 37, 120; Colonel Josiah 79
Weizmann, Chaim 19
Wheeler, Major (see also Australia House, Australian High Commission) 36, 49
White, Colonel Thomas 33, 61
Wilson, Alexander (Spareline) 101, 142, 179; Andrea 101-102, 142, 179
Winton, Nicholas 28, 185
Woburn House, London 32-33, 39-40, 49
Wollheim, Norbert 28
Wollongong, NSW 157
World War One, see First World War
WRNS 174
Wynn, Samuel 154, 169, 170

Yass, NSW 132, 135, 146, 175, 177
Yiddish 11, 12; 56, 103, 150, 155
YMCA 33-36, 136, 156-157, 183
youth: see refugee children and youth; migration 20, 30, 32-36, 39, 43, 98, 172; Youth Aliyah 20
Yugoslavia 95, 197

Zbonszyn, Poland 22, 60, 62, 63 and photo, 64, 66, 67, 68, 161, 201
Zentralausschuss (Central Committee for Relief and Reconstruction, Germany) 14
Zionists 19-20, 59, 67, 155, 165, 168-169, 180